The Western Australian Jurist

Volume 11

Fundamental Rights
in the Age of COVID-19

The Western Australian Jurist

Volume 11

Fundamental Rights in the Age of COVID-19

Augusto Zimmermann

(Editor-in-Chief)

&

Joshua Forrester

(Editor)

Connor Court Publishing

Connor Court Publishing Pty Ltd

PO Box 7257
Redland Bay QLD 4165
sales@connorcourt.com
www.connorcourt.com

ISBN: 9781922449375

Cover design by Maria Giordano

Front Cover Image: CC0 Public Domain, Free for personal and commercial use.

Printed in Australia

THE
WESTERN AUSTRALIAN
JURIST

Editor-in-Chief
Professor Augusto Zimmermann
Sheridan Institute of Higher Education, Australia

Editor
Joshua Forrester
Murdoch University, Australia

International Editorial Advisory Board
Distinguished Professor Emeritus William Wagner
Western Michigan University, United States of America

Emeritus Professor Jeffrey Goldsworthy
Monash University, Australia

Emeritus Professor Gabriël A. Moens
The University of Queensland, Australia

Professor Nicholas Aroney
The University of Queensland, Australia

Dr Grzegorz Jan Blicharz
Jagiellonian University, Poland

Professor Luigi Lacchè
Università di Macerata, Italy

Professor Gábor Hamza
Eötvös Loránd University, Hungary

FUNDAMENTAL RIGHTS IN THE AGE OF COVID-19

Professor James Allan
The University of Queensland, Australia

Professor Ermanno Calzolaio
Università di Macerata, Italy

Professor Paulo Emílio Vauthier Borges de Macedo
Universidade do Estado do Rio de Janeiro, Brazil

Professor Thomas Crofts
University of Sydney, Australia

Professor Neville Rochow SC
The University of Adelaide, Australia

CONTENTS

THE EDITORS

Augusto Zimmermann LLB (Hons.), LLM cum laude, PhD (Monash), DipEd, CertArb is Professor and Head of Law at Sheridan Institute of Higher Education in Perth, WA, and Professor of Law (Adjunct) at the University of Notre Dame Australia, Sydney campus. He is also President of the Western Australian Legal Theory Association (WALTA), and formerly a Law Reform Commissioner with the Law Reform Commission of Western Australia, from 2012-2017. Professor Zimmermann is also the Editor-in-Chief of *The Western Australian Jurist* law journal, an Elected Fellow at the International Academy for the Study of the Jurisprudence of the Family, and a former Vice-President of the Australasian Society of Legal Philosophy. He was also Associate Dean (Research) at Murdoch Law School from 2009 to 2013. While working at Murdoch, Professor Zimmermann was awarded the prestigious Vice-Chancellor's Award for Excellence in Research, in 2012, as well as 2 Law Dean's Research Awards, in 2010 and 2011. A leading advocate for free speech and prolific writer of numerous articles and books, he is considered by the Washington-based Heritage Foundation as one of the 12 most influential policy makers in Australia. His books include, among many others, *Christian Foundations of the Common Law* (3 Volumes, Connor Court, 2017), *No Offence Intended: Why 18c is Wrong* (Connor Court, 2016 (with Joshua Forrester and Lorraine Finlay); *Global Perspectives on Subsidiarity* (Springer, 2014) (with Michelle Evans), and *Western Legal Theory: History, Concepts and Perspectives* (LexisNexis, 2013).

Joshua Forrester graduated with First Class Honours in Politics and International Studies from Murdoch University in 1999. He then graduated with First Class Honours in Law from the University of Western Australia in 2003, with his prizes including those in corporations law and criminal law. His honours thesis explored using breach of confidence in Equity to protect corporate policy. The supervisor of his honour thesis (and an academic referee for his PhD application) was Dr James Edelman, who is now a Justice of the High Court of Australia. Joshua was awarded a Vice-Chancellor's Commendation for Teaching at the University of Notre Dame Australia. He is the Editor of *The Western Australian* law journal, and author of a number of articles in law journals. Joshua lead author of *No Offence Intended: Why 18C is Wrong*, which is listed as one of *The Spectator*'s best books of 2016. He has also appeared before various parliamentary inquiries, including the Parliamentary Joint Committee on Human Rights inquiry into s 18c, and the Joint Standing Committee on Foreign Affairs, Defence and Trade Human Rights Sub-Committee inquiry into freedom of religion and belief.

CONTRIBUTORS

Rex Ahdar LLB (Hons), LLM (Canterbury); PhD (Otago) is a Professor at the Faculty of Law, University of Otago, where he has taught since 1986, in subjects ranging from Competition Law and Contract Law to Law & Religion. He is also an Adjunct Professor at the School of Law, the University of Notre Dame Australia (Sydney), and in 2018 was a Visiting Professor at the Faculty of Law, The Hebrew University, Jerusalem. He is a former Fulbright Senior Research Scholar at the University of California at Berkeley (1991). His books include: *Law and Religion* (Ashgate 2000); *Worlds Colliding: Conservative Christians and the Law* (Ashgate 2001); *Religious Freedom in the Liberal State* (2nd ed, Oxford University Press, 2013) (with Ian Leigh); *Research Handbook on Law and Religion* (Edward Elgar, 2018); and *The Evolution of Competition Law in New Zealand* (Oxford University Press, 2020). He has published articles in journals such as the *Oxford Journal of Legal Studies*, *Cambridge Law Journal, Modern Law Review, Stanford Journal of Civil Rights & Civil Liberties*, and the *Oxford Journal of Law and Religion*. He is on the Editorial Board of the *Journal of Church and State*, the *Australian Business Law Review* and the *New Zealand Business Law Quarterly*.

James Allan is the Garrick Professor of Law at the University of Queensland. He has degrees from Queen's University, the London School of Economics and the University of Hong Kong. Before arriving in Australia in February of 2005, he spent 11 years teaching law in New Zealand at the University of Otago and before that lectured law in Hong Kong. Professor Allan has had sabbaticals at the Cornell Law School, at the Dalhousie Law School in Canada as the Bertha Wilson Visiting Professor in Human Rights, and at the University of San Diego School of Law. His main areas of interest are legal and moral philosophy, constitutional law and bills of rights. He has published widely in these areas, including in all the top English language legal philosophy journals in the U.S., the U.K., Canada and Australia, much the same being true of constitutional law journals as well. He writes regularly for *The Spectator Australia, Quadrant and The Australian*

Morgan Begg is a Research Fellow with the Institute of Public Affairs ('IPA'). He joined the IPA in 2014 to advance a major report into 'The State of Fundamental Legal Rights in Australia', which was referenced extensively in the Australian Law Reform Commission's seminal 'Freedoms Inquiry' released in March 2016. He specialises in legal and policy issues as they relate to proposals for constitutional change, freedom of speech and religion, the rule of law and the meaning of legal conservatism in the Australian context. His published articles and submissions to parliamentary inquiries have complemented significant research papers on the GST and federalism, red tape and centralisation, the unique threat to religious liberty from anti-discrimination laws.

Grzegorz Jan Blicharz PhD (Law), MA (Law, Philosophy), Assistant Professor at the Chair of Roman Law, Faculty of Law and Administration, Jagiellonian University in Kraków, recipient of the NCN Scientific Grant – Sonata 14 (2019) and the Scholarship of the Polish Ministry of Science and Higher Education for outstanding young scholars 2018–2021, Academic Visitor at University of Oxford (2020). He completed post-graduate studies in Roman law at the University of Rome La Sapienza and Program for Development of Soft Skills and Entrepreneurship at Alberta School of Business in Edmonton. Executive Manager of Utriusque Iuris Foundation and co-editor of Forum Prawnicze. He also teaches at the Faculty of Law at Lazarski University in Warsaw and Copernicus College.

Lorraine Finlay B.A (UWA), LL.B (UWA), LL.M (NUS), LL.M (NYU) is a lecturer in the School of Law at Murdoch University. She is also an adjunct senior law lecturer in the Sydney School of Law at the University of Notre Dame Australia. Her research interests include criminal law, constitutional law, international criminal law and public international law. Lorraine is also a Research Scholar with the Centre for Public, International & Comparative Law (University of Queensland) and a Fellow with the Murdoch Learning Excellence Academy (LEAD). Before moving to academia in 2010, Lorraine worked as a State Prosecutor at the Office of the Director of Public Prosecutions (WA). She has also previously worked at the High Court of Australia, initially as the Legal Research Officer and then as an Associate to The Hon. Justice Dyson Heydon. In 2009 she was selected as a Singapore Scholar with the NYU@NUS program. As part of this program she was awarded a dual LL.M in Law and the Global Economy (with a concentration in Justice and Human Rights) from New York University and in International & Comparative Law from the National University of Singapore.

David Edward Flint AM is Emeritus Professor at UTS and read law and economics at the Universities of Sydney, London and the Sorbonne, Paris. He has been Chairman of the Australian Press Council, Broadcasting Authority and Law Deans, and World Association of Press Councils. He is National Convenor of Australians for Constitutional Monarchy, which prevailed in all states in the republic referendum. Named World Outstanding Legal Scholar by the World Jurist Association at Barcelona, he is a Member of the Order of Australia and Grand Officer of the Order of the Star of Honor of Ethiopia. He comments in the media (especially *Spectator Australia, Epoch Times,* 2GB/4BC and in *Take Back Your Country* on *goodsauce.news*), has published widely on topics including the media, international economic and constitutional law, including explaining what would be the likely results in the UK referendum, and the 2016 American and 2019 Australian elections.

Anthony Gray is a Professor of Law and Associate Head – Research at the School of Law and Justice at the University of Southern Queensland. He has published more than 130 sole-authored refereed articles, and has authored numerous research monographs, including 'Evolution from Strict Liability to Fault in Law of Torts' (forthcoming, Hart, 2021), 'Freedom of Speech in Practice: Controversial Applications of Law and Theory' (Lexington, 2019), and 'Freedom of Speech in the West: Comparison and Critique' (Lexington, 2019). He specialises in constitutional law and human rights, including freedom of speech. He is a former Director at the Queensland Law Society, and former consultant with Engineering Education Australia.

Weronika Kudła PhD (Law) and MA (Law, Italian Studies) at Jagiellonian University in Kraków (Poland). She is also a participant of the Erasmus Program Studies at Tor Vergata University of Rome (Italy) and the VIII Edition of Academy of Young Diplomats in Warsaw (Poland). She is the author of an academic book called 'Hostility to Religion: Warnings from the Supreme Court of the United States'. Her research interests are freedom of religion and freedom of artistic expression.

Rocco Loiacono is a Senior Lecturer in the Curtin University Law School, where he teaches in the areas of property law and advanced legal research. In his capacity as a NAATI (National Accreditation Authority for Interpreters and Translators) Certified Translator (Italian>English), he is also a lecturer in the Masters of Translation Studies at the University of Western Australia. After graduating with a combined Law and Languages (First Class Honours) degree, he practised as a lawyer for ten years, most of that time at Clayton Utz, one of Australia's largest law firms. Dr Loiacono received the award of his PhD from the University of Western Australia in 2014. His particular research interest is the translation difficulties arising from the differences that exist between continental legal systems and the English common law, and he has published widely on this research in peer-reviewed journals of translation, linguistics and law. He has written for *Quadrant* and *The Spectator Australia*.

Gabriël A. Moens AM is Emeritus Professor of Law, The University of Queensland, and Adjunct Professor of Law at Curtin University, and at The University of Notre Dame Australia, Sydney. Professor Moens received the Australian Award for University Teaching in Law and Legal Studies in 1999. In 2003, the Prime Minister of Australia awarded him the Australian Centenary Medal for services to education. He was named the 'International Alumnus of the Year' by the Pritzker Law School of Northwestern University in 2019. In June 2019 he was appointed a Member of the Order of Australia (AM) for services to the law and higher education. Professor Moens is a *Membre Titulaire*, International Academy of Comparative Law, Paris, a Fellow of the Australian Institute of Management (WA), a Fellow of the College of Law, and a Fellow of the Australian Academy of Law. He is co-author/co-editor of numerous books, including *The Himalaya Clause* (Connor Court Publishing, 2020); *Law of International Business in Australasia* (2nd ed, The Federation Press, 2019); *The Constitution of the Commonwealth of Australia Annotated* (9th ed, LexisNexis Butterworths, 2016); and *Jurisprudence of Liberty* (2nd ed, LexisNexis, 2011).

Bill Muehlenberg BA (Hon., Chicago), MA (Highest Hon., Boston) has worked in social policy research for various organisations, including the Institute of Public Affairs and the Australian Family Association. He has authored a number of books including 'Modern Conservative Thought' and *'The Challenge of Euthanasia'*. He has also written thousands of articles – many hundreds published - on a wide range of topics, including politics, economics, theology, ethics and social issues. He has lectured part-time in theology, philosophy and ethics, and runs the website 'CultureWatch'.

Monika Nagel Cert. Ed. (Vienna), B. Psych. (Murdoch), PhD (Org. Psych.) is the author of the book *Fatal Cocktails*, a provocative and compelling exposition on the reasons of the ills in our world with a call for change. She is passionate about reminding societies that rights can only be upheld with correlating responsibility. She has engaged in public speaking. Her PhD research was about the impact of organisational culture on an organisation's performance. Her doctoral thesis also investigated how well students are prepared for work. Before undertaking her doctoral research, Monika was a successful educator in Austria and Australia, teaching mathematics, science and arts, and working at a school for children with learning disabilities. Her qualification in psychology has prompted her special interest and research in human behaviour at work, addiction, and human rights.

Steven Alan Samson is a retired Professor of Government and former Department Chairman with the Helms School of Government at Liberty University. His research and writing focus on the European and American intellectual, cultural, and constitutional traditions, giving particular attention to their ideological challengers. Dr Samson holds the B.A. and M.A. degrees in political science from the University of Colorado and the Ph.D. from the University of Oregon. A resident of Washington State, he occasionally gives guest lectures and writes for such publications as *The Market for Ideas, Townhall Finance*, and *Review of Social and Economic Issues.*

Johnny M Sakr is admitted as a lawyer of the Supreme Court of New South Wales. He is also an Adjunct Lecturer for the School of Law at the University of Notre Dame, Sydney. Johnny has completed a Bachelor of Laws, Graduate Diploma in Legal Practise, Master of Laws (Commercial Transactions) and a Master of Philosophy (Law). Johnny is currently undertaking his PhD (Law) research at the University of Southern Queensland and has written a number of academic articles on a variety of topics, including freedom of religion, philosophy and theology.

William Wagner currently serves as President and Chairman of Salt & Light Global. In academia, he holds the academic rank of Distinguished Professor Emeritus at Western Michigan University. Professor Wagner is an internationally recognized expert in constitutional law and good governance. As lead amicus counsel in many matters before the U.S. Supreme Court, he has authored briefs on behalf of various Christian organizations. He has also authored written testimony, evidence, and briefs in such forums as the Swedish Supreme Court, the U.S. Congress, and the U.K. Parliament. He has further addressed many executive, legislative, parliamentary, and judicial audiences throughout the world, and presented at various diplomatic forums including the U.N. Human Rights Council in Geneva. Professor Wagner's public service includes serving as a Federal judge in the United States Courts, legal counsel in the U.S. Senate, senior assistant United States attorney in the Department of Justice, and as an American diplomat. His writing is published in numerous journals, books, and other publications.

1

Introduction:

Protecting Fundamental Rights in the Age of Covid-19

AUGUSTO ZIMMERMANN AND JOSHUA FORRESTER

The Covid-19 pandemic is a turning point in history. Its impact will be felt for many years both domestically and internationally. Certain measures to fight Covid-19 have profoundly affected fundamental rights, particularly freedom of movement, expression, privacy and association, potentially for a very long time. Further, these measures have caused many people to endure deeply stressful and traumatic situations, including home confinement, job losses, financial ruin, drug and alcohol problems, domestic violence and family breakdown, and a host of mental and physical illnesses.

This special edition of *The Western Australian Jurist* is dedicated to the important topic of 'Protecting Fundamental Rights in the Age of Covid-19'. We are proud to have gathered an impressive list of contributors to address the dramatic impact of government measures on our fundamental rights and freedoms. We are also proud to be working in partnership with Connor Court to produce this special edition of our law journal as a book. We hope this work becomes a major reference on the subject, and help promote *The Western Australian Jurist* as a leading publication in the field of legal theory and jurisprudential thought.

As to our contributors, Professor Rex Ahdar critically reflects upon the serious cost of lockdowns. His chapter shows that the mitigation strategy, ultimately ignored by New Zealand's government was and is a preferable strategy once the indirect and long-term costs and benefits of more radical measures are considered.

Professor James Allan explains how the Australian government mishandled its response to the coronavirus, significantly infringing civil liberties and dramatically expanding the government's role with no palatable route out of this situation. After exposing the over-reaction by most governments, he goes on to predict that such measures will be seen in the future as one of the worst public policy fiascos of the century.

Morgan Begg critically analyses of Victoria's public health emergency laws. First, he explores the history of these laws in Victoria, highlighting how modern emergency powers are ahistorical and atypical. He then proceeds to an examination of the heavy costs of policy responses, indicating that Victoria's modern public health legislation gives too much scope to ministers and the Chief Health Officer. These policy responses not only expose serious structural flaws in the legislation but also have not achieved a desirable balance between protecting public health and maintaining the freedoms of Victorians.

Professor David Flint AM argues that the Australian government's response to the coronavirus was based on an overreaction that failed to pay due regard to the best available evidence. There was no guarantee of minimal restrictions on the exercise of fundamental rights. To the contrary, the response of Australia's political authorities was disastrous, proving costly to millions of Australians. Since so much of what has been done by our political authorities was unnecessary and counterproductive, Professor Flint concludes his article by recommending an in-depth review by the people of the nation's constitutional arrangements.

Professor Anthony Gray considers whether Western Australia's border restrictions in response to Covid-19 are consistent with section 92 of the *Australian Constitution*, which provides that trade, commerce and intercourse among the States shall be absolutely free. Professor Gray argues explores a number of tests that the High Court has used when applying s 92. He concludes that there is a strong chance that Western Australia's border restrictions are constitutionally invalid because they are not proportionate to a legitimate objective, and because they cannot be shown to be reasonably necessary.

Doctor Weronika Kudła and Dr Grzegorz Jan Blicharz undertake a comparative analysis of the impact of public health measures on religious freedom in Italy and Poland. They analyse the impact of safety measures by civil authorities of these two countries on religious liberty, particularly in light of the right to religious gatherings in situations of health emergency. According to them, an assessment of restrictions imposed on religious worship in these countries can offer an instructive lesson with regards to adequacy and proportionality of measures aimed at fighting and co-existing with the virus.

Doctor Rocco Loiacono provides an exposure of the 'dictatorship of the health bureaucracy' whereby Covid-19 has been used to undermine our fundamental rights and freedoms with the stroke of a pen. As he points out, recent events have revealed the potential for health officials to enact oppressive policies that exert unreasonable control over our lives. This could have, according to him, very serious implications for important principles such as the right to informed consent, which is fundamental in the administration of any medical treatment.

Professor Gabriël A Moens AM examines the disrupting effects of Covid-19 in Australia. First, he briefly describes the restrictions imposed on people to allegedly combat the virus. Professor Moens then characterises such restrictions as deeply paternalistic in nature, having an enormous and deleterious effect on the rights of people, including unintended consequences for the protection of their own health. Professor Moens also assesses the constitutionality of Covid-19 laws and regulations, highlighting the perceived weaknesses of government actions.

Bill Muehlenberg argues that government overreactions to Covid-19 has led to individual liberties being infringed far too much and governments expanding much too far. He examines various issues concerning the Covid-19 crisis, including whether just revolution is warranted should government overreach become too onerous.

Doctor Monika Nagel, who argues that globalisation may have worked well both economically and politically since the early 1980s, but now has failed to respond to health crisis. She notes the decline of moral values along with the rise of identity politics, and argues that the focus of human rights should shift towards protecting fundamental rights.

Doctor Johnny M Sakr discusses the implications of Molinism to explain how God exercises sovereign control over his world while honouring the genuine freedom he has bestowed upon his creatures. He explains how Molinism, a concept coined after Roman Catholic Jesuit Luis de Molina, not only provides a reconciliation between God's sovereignty and human freedom, but also promotes human efforts to prevent epidemics, cope with them, and change our ways of life to lower their impact.

Professor Steven Samson examines the role of interposition in protecting against tyranny. Citing historical political and religious examples, Professor Samson notes that freedoms have emerged from the contest of powerful stakeholders, including those who interpose, that is, use their power to shield others against the tyrannical exercise of power by others. He considers the role of interpositions in the age of the "administrative state" and Covid-19.

Professor William Wagner argues that certain State Governors in the United States have seen Covid-19 as an opportunity to expand powers and ignore constitutional constraints, autocratically issuing edicts that violate our liberty and undermine the rule of law. He further argues that such actions from these State Governors threaten to destroy the foundations of good governance under the rule of law. Professor Wagner concludes that the Federal Government of the United States might have to exercise its constitutional power under the Commerce Clause in order to re-establish order and enact pre-emptive legislation

Professor Augusto Zimmermann explains the legal and moral consequences of government measures to fight the coronavirus. These measures are arbitrary and ultimately constitute a gross violation of fundamental rights. There is nothing that could possibly justify the

4

use of such extreme measures. Relying on a few "experts", political authorities have used their recently acquired "emergency powers" to impose oppressive lockdowns and other ill-conceived measures that have destroyed jobs and much of the productive sector, while leaving the bloated public sector completely intact. Professor Zimmermann appeals to our classical liberal tradition of civil resistance to political tyranny, reminding the readers of their right to demand the lifting of draconian measures that infringe fundamental rights and freedoms.

Finally, Lorraine Finlay reviews Professor Moens's book *A Twisted Choice*, a novel concerning the origins of the Covid-19 pandemic. She comments that this thought-provoking book raises some critical questions about human nature, government power and individual choice. The novel investigates the origins of the pandemic, and weaves a tapestry of intrigue with the threads of many factual events happening around the globe. It follows the exploits of a Chinese virologist, studying at an American university where he meets an American lawyer, who follows him back to Wuhan in China.

There is a final point we would like to make. We have used Covid-19 in this introduction. However, we have left it the authors to refer to SARS-CoV-2 using their own terms. Hence, you will see terms like 'coronavirus' and 'Wuhan virus' used throughout this volume. Certain terms used to refer to SARS-CoV-2 are themselves controversial. However, in this volume we have adopted an approach consistent with the fundamental right to freedom of expression, that is, recognising that the authors are free to call the virus whatever they like.

To conclude, it is beyond any doubt that certain government actions in response to Covid-19 threaten fundamental rights. And since it is rightly said that the price of liberty is eternal vigilance, we call upon those who value fundamental rights to be more vigilant than ever in the Covid-19 era.

2

Reflecting upon the Costs of Lockdown

REX AHDAR*

ABSTRACT

This article endeavours to show that the indirect, downstream and long-term costs of a mandated lockdown in response to severe acute respiratory syndrome coronavirus 2 (SARS-CoV-2) producing coronavirus disease 2019 (Covid-19) are too often ignored. The New Zealand Government did not much talk about them at the time it implemented a strict lockdown based upon its elimination strategy. Yet these costs need to be taken into account and weighed against the benefits of the strict lockdown approach that New Zealand adopted. Furthermore, the costs and benefits of a milder mitigation strategy (of the kind Sweden adopted) also need to be estimated and compared to the strict lockdown approach. I argue the mitigation strategy was and is a preferable one once the indirect and long-term costs and benefits are taken into account.

I INTRODUCTION

In April this year I wrote an opinion piece on the costs of the coronavirus lockdown for New Zealand.[1] I sought to show that the indirect and longer term costs of the mandated lockdown in response to severe

* Professor, Faculty of Law, University of Otago; Adjunct Professor, School of Law, University of Notre Dame Australia, Sydney.
[1] My thanks to Tony Binns, Bruce Logan and Noel Carroll for comments on a draft of this article. Rex Ahdar, 'The Costs of Lockdown: Lives Now versus Lives Later', *Pundit.co.nz*, 16 April 2020 <https://www.pundit.co.nz/content/the-cost-of-lockdown-lives-now-vs-lives-later>.*Pundit* is a popular blog devoted to political and social issues in New Zealand.

acute respiratory syndrome coronavirus 2 (SARS-CoV-2) producing coronavirus disease 2019 (Covid-19), were being ignored. The New Zealand Government did not much talk about them at the time. It was difficult to find any media commentators doing so either.[2] Yet these costs, I argued, needed to be taken into account and weighed against the benefits of the strict lockdown approach that New Zealand adopted. This strict regime was called, in our classification,[3] a Level 4 ('L4') approach. It aimed at the elimination[4] of the virus not just "flattening the curve". It proved to be effective.

If New Zealand adopted a milder mitigation strategy that did not entail a (near) complete closing down of businesses, schools, travel, and so on (as well as the closing of borders), then it would have, in all probability, resulted in a greater number of immediate deaths from Covid-19, but saved many more lives downstream, so to speak. The gravamen of my short piece was to argue that each strategy – strict closure of all social and commercial activity versus complete abstention, as well as everything in between – has its costs. Most importantly, it was, I contended, never a stark choice between saving lives versus protecting the economy, as many were wont to erroneously characterise it. It was never a matter of "lives versus the economy", but always, I maintained, "lives v lives".[5]

[2] As I finish writing this article, criticism by New Zealand media pundits is belatedly appearing: see eg, Damien Grant, 'The Price of Our Vain Belief in Covid-19 Exceptionalism', *Stuff.co.nz*, 16 August 2020, <https://www.stuff.co.nz/opinion/300082155/coronavirus-the-price-of-our-vain-belief-in-covid19-exceptionalism> ; Ryan Bridge, 'The Team of Five Million is Splintering", *Newsroom.co.nz*, 15 August 2020 < https://www.newsroom.co.nz/ryan-bridge>.

[3] The New Zealand four-level Covid-19 alert classification is in Appendix 1.

[4] "Elimination" turns out to be a medical term of art. It does not mean eradication or 100 percent purging, but negligible cases that can be swiftly managed. 'Elimination does not mean eradicating the virus permanently from New Zealand; rather it is being confident we have eliminated chains of transmission in our community for at least 28 days and can effectively contain any future imported cases from overseas.' Ministry of Health, 'COVID-19: Elimination Strategy for New Zealand', *health.govt. nz*, 8 May 2020 <https://www.health.govt.nz/our-work/diseases-and-conditions/covid-19-novel-coronavirus/covid-19-current-situation/covid-19-elimination-strategy-aotearoa-new-zealand>.

[5] Jayanta Bhattacharya and Mikko Packalen, 'Lives vs Lives—The Global Cost of

How is this so? It is not, admittedly, immediately obvious. Here we have to place ourselves again in the fevered environment that was the early days of the Covid-19 pandemic. It was the fervent hope that many lives would be saved in the immediate and short term if strict and decisive measures were taken. The ghastly nightly pictures on TV of mass graves in New York, Italy and so on, understandably triggered fear and alarm. The need to do some *now*, and something comprehensive, became the almost complete focus of the mainstream media and governments globally. A government must, it was said, err on the side of caution: 'better safe than sorry' and 'safety-first' were the catch-cries. 'On the evidence available', observed Prof Grant Guilford, 'to the [New Zealand] Government at the time it made its decision, the lockdown was a sensible step and one that aligned with the prevailing public sentiment.'[6]

Yet, this focus, as natural as it was at the time, ignores the lives that may, indeed will, be lost in the medium to longer term from the consequences of the severe lockdown. The lives lost in the future might conceivably outweigh the lives saved now, and thus, as some put it (most infamously President Donald Trump), the cure might be worse than the disease.[7]

Lockdown', *The Spectator*, 16 May 2020, < https://www.spectator.co.uk/article/lives-vs-lives-the-global-cost-of-lockdown>. Grant (n 1), observes: 'Commentators dismiss such concerns [about the enormous costs of lockdown] as placing the economy ahead of lives but they fail to understand that the 'economy' is a word we use describe the aggregation of all our lives. It is the means by which we feed, clothe and educate ourselves.' In a similar vein, Dr Vovek Goel, a professor at the University of Toronto Dalla Lana School of Public Health, observed: 'So often the shutdown gets framed as a debate between health and the economy, but the economy is health too.' Laurie Monsebraaten, 'Ontario's COVID-19 Lockdown is Now Harming Health More Than Its Helping, Some Experts Say', *Our Windsor. Ca*, 4 June 2020 <https://www.the-star.com/news/gta/2020/06/04/ontarios-covid-19-lockdown-is-now-harming-health-more-than-its-helping-some-experts-say.html>.

[6] Grant Guilford, 'Will An Extended Lockdown Cost More Lives Than It Saves?', *Newsroom.co.nz*, 9 April 2020. <https://www.newsroom.co.nz/ideasroom/will-an-extended-lockdown-cost-more-lives-than-it-saves>

[7] Maggie Haberman and David Sanger, 'Trump Says Coronavirus Cure Cannot 'Be Worse Than the Problem Itself'', *New York Times*, 23 March 2020. <https://www.nytimes.com/2020/03/23/us/politics/trump-coronavirus-restrictions.html>. The actual words, con-

Some economists who attempted to answer this thorny question are confident that strict lockdown is, or has been, worth it.

> The overall cost of letting Covid-19 run through the entire population could add up to around 30% of GDP, or over E300 billion for the EU. On this metric, the economic cost of the great lockdown (7-8% of GDP) would seem to be much lower than that of the unchecked spread of the virus. One could of course argue that measures other than a lockdown, less damaging for economic activity, might have achieved a similar reduction in infections. But the real world question is whether choosing lockdown meant that the (imperfect) cure was worse than the disease. Our results suggest a resounding no.[8]

There are two points to note about this conclusion. First, the economist dismisses strategies other than a strict lockdown (of the L4 variety). Yet, one ought, rationally, to have endeavoured to compare the lives saved (and lost) from a strict L4 lockdown versus the lives saved (and lost) from a milder, less pervasive, mitigation approach. Sweden most famously took this approach, but that was just one version. In New Zealand, a milder approach would correspond to Level 2 ('L2').

Second, he compares lockdown to abstention. But unlike some nations, for example, the United Kingdom, that flirted initially with the notion of abstention and letting the virus run its course – so that, in time, the population would develop so-called "herd immunity" – abstention was never an option for New Zealand, or indeed, most countries. I do not recall anyone arguing for this. I did not. The hands-off, do-nothing option was never a serious contender. To compare strict lockdown to abstention is something of a straw man and simply loads the policy dice in favour of the former.

There are, broadly speaking, three main approaches—suppression (which includes as a major strand, elimination), mitigation or absten-

---

tained in a tweet, were: 'We cannot let the cure be worse than the problem itself.'
[8] Daniel Gros, *The Great Lockdown: Was It Worth it?*, (CEPS Policy Insights, No 2020-11, May 2020).

tion.[9] The only real contest in the New Zealand context, and even then it was decidedly muted, was between the suppression (or elimination) advocates and those very few proposing a milder mitigation strategy à la Sweden or, closer to home, the less stringent lockdown measures taken by the Australia states.

Sweden took a mitigation strategy from the outset. It relied upon the public's voluntary co-operation to curtail the virus in terms of practising physical-distancing, hand-washing, self-isolation at home if one was exhibiting symptoms, and so on. Public gatherings of more than 50 people were prohibited, but cafes, bars, restaurants, barbers, gyms, shops – with social distancing – and schools (for children under 16) were allowed to stay open.[10]

While each Australian state government took a slightly different approach, the general pattern was similar:

> Australia's lockdown approach substantially reduced activities which involve large number of random interactions between individuals (in bars, restaurants, entertainment and sports venues) but largely left the economy free to operate subject to compliance with guidance about workers keeping social distance. This means businesses can still function, even if in a low-level holding pattern. For example, even if

---

[9] See eg Alister Heath, 'Sweden's Success Shows The True Cost Of Our Arrogant, Failed Establishment', *Daily Telegraph*, 12 August 2020. There are, he observes, three ways politicians can react: do nothing and 'allow the disease to rip until herd immunity is reached', impose 'proportionate restrictions to facilitate social distancing' etc, and enact a 'full-on statist approach…with a legally-binding lockdown'. A more formal taxonomy is that by the NZ Ministry of Health, 'Background and Overview of Approaches to COVID-19 Pandemic Control in Aotearoa/New Zealand', *health. govt.nz*, 30 March 2020. It lists five strategies (which are not mutually exclusive): 'Elimination; Sustained stamp it out, Sequestration [which I have called 'abstention'], Mitigation and Suppression."

[10] Heba Habib, 'Has Sweden's Controversial Covid-19 Strategy Been Successful?', *British Medical Journal*, 12 June 2020: doi.org/10.1136/bmj.m2376; Maddy Savage, 'Did Sweden's Coronavirus Strategy Succeed or Fail'? *BBC News*, 24 July 2020; Kristina Flore, 'How Did Sweden Flatten Its Curve Without a Lockdown?', *MedPage Today*, 29 July 2020; Ian Birrell, 'Will Sweden Get the Last Laugh?', *Daily Mail*, 10 August 2020; Heath (n 9).

a business is closed (for example, a pub) business owners can visit the premises to maintain equipment or catch up on paperwork. Employees can go to work, unless they are able to work from home. [11]

By contrast, New Zealand's L4 lockdown was stricter. New Zealand households were confined to their own "bubble". Only "essential" businesses, narrowly defined, were allowed to continue and all non-essential business that could not be carried on from home ceased. All retailers except supermarkets, dairies (convenience stores), petrol stations and pharmacies closed.

In New Zealand, the most prominent dissenters were a cross-disciplinary group of six academics[12] who put forward an "alternative Plan B" as they called it. [13] They summarised it thus:

> The government and its advisors have articulated a strategy of ongoing lockdowns of New Zealand society for the foreseeable future in an attempt to eradicate the virus. We believe that holding out for vaccine development or pursuing an aggressive eradication policy are not realistic.
>
> We are a group of academics who are concerned that such a strategy is not proportional to the threat posed by Covid-19 to New Zealanders' health and that it is likely to substantially harm the nation's long-term health and well-being, social fabric, economy, and education. . . .

---

[11] Andreas Heuser and Alex Sundakov, 'Comparing the New Zealand and Australian States' Responses to COVID-19", *Castalia-advisors.com*, 14 April 2020.

[12] Dr Simon Thornley, Senior Lecturer of Epidemiology and Biostatistics, University of Auckland; Dr Grant Schofield, Professor of Public Health, Auckland University of Technology; Dr Gerhard Sundborn, Senior Lecturer of Population and Pacific Health, University of Auckland; Dr Grant Morris, Associate Professor of Law, Victoria University of Wellington; Dr Ananish Chaudhuri, Professor of Experimental Economics, University of Auckland and Visiting Professor of Public Policy and Decision Making, Harvard University; Dr Michael Jackson, Postdoctoral researcher with expertise in biostatistics and biodiscovery, Victoria University of Wellington.

[13] Marc Daalder, 'Contrarian Academics Oppose Lockdown', *Newsroom*, 14 April 2020; Madison Reidy, 'Coronavirus: Health Experts Feel Censored Over Alternative Lockdown Plan", *News Hub*, 19 April 2020.

> We believe that it is in the best interests of the country to rapidly transition to a situation similar to the government's alert level 2, while closely monitoring the spread of the virus and its impact on the health system. This would enable the majority of businesses to continue to operate and schools and universities to open. It would also allow essential domestic travel to resume.[14]

I also advocated this approach and I shall say more about that later.

It is now a matter of history that the strict lockdown supporters won the day and so on 25 March 2020, New Zealand began a five-week period of L4 lockdown.[15] This was relaxed to a L3 alert on 27 April which lasted for another 17 days. On 13 May, New Zealand eased into a L2 status and finally, on 8 June 2020, we moved to L1. This lowest alert phase, which prevailed for over three months, represented a return to normal, with untrammelled commercial activity, restaurants, pubs, shops, schools and universities open, churches, sports events and other mass gatherings underway, domestic travel permitted. On 9 August 2020, New Zealand marked 100 days since the last confirmed case of Covid-19 acquired locally (from an unknown source) via community transmission.[16] Ironically, two days later any lingering celebrations were to be dispelled as four cases of locally-contracted coronavirus in South Auckland were confirmed.[17] This unwelcome

---

[14] Simon Thornley et al, 'A Balanced Response to Covid-19', 12 April 2020. <https://www.covidplanb.co.nz> They reaffirmed this stance when the partial lockdown was imposed in August: Ananish Chaudiri and Simon Thornley, 'Do We Really Need Yet Another Lockdown?", *Covidplanb.co.nz*, 13 August 2020, <https://www.covidplanb.co.nz/our-posts/do-we-really-need-yet-another-lockdown/>.

[15] Appendix 2 sets out a brief chronology of the major milestones in New Zealand's response to Covid-19.

[16] Hannah Martin and Torika Tokalau, 'NZ Marks 100 Days Since Last Community Transmission Covid-19 Case', *Stuff.co.nz*, 9 August 2020 <https://www.stuff.co.nz/national/health/coronavirus/300073831/nz-marks-100-days-since-last-community-transmission-covid19-case>.

[17] Ameila Wade and Derek Cheng, 'Auckland in lockdown, rest of country in level 2: Four cases of community transmission', *NZ Herald*, 11 August 2020. The move to L3 (Auckland) and L2 (the rest of NZ) occurred at noon on 12 August, with these alert

discovery plunged greater Auckland into L3 lockdown and the rest of the country into L2.

The only difference from the pre-Covid 19 world for level L1, should New Zealand recover quickly from that latest coronavirus "hiccough", is that the borders remain closed to visitors from overseas. There are two exceptions to the border closure. First, there has been a limited number of exemptions of "significant economic value" granted by the Minister of Economic Development, most notably an exemption for a US film-making company led by James Cameron (working on a sequel to Avatar) to establish itself in New Zealand.[18] Second, and far more significantly in terms of scale, New Zealand citizens and permanent residents are allowed to return subject to a testing and a mandatory 14-day quarantine-like period.[19]

II THE DARK-SIDE OF STRICT LOCKDOWN

There is no doubt that strict lockdown curtailed the spread of the virus and saved lives along with reducing Covid-19's various non-fatal disease effects (eg, time spent sick, ongoing residual pernicious symptoms) in New Zealand. The total number of fatalities was mercifully low, just 22 deaths at the time of writing.[20] This is one of the lowest

---

levels initially scheduled to stay in place for 3 days until midnight 14 August. On 14 August 2020, the government extended the respective alert levels (in the same areas) for another 12 days, with the expiry set for midnight on 26 August (albeit Cabinet will review the developments on 21 August).

[18] Amelia Wade, 'Access Hollywood: Hundreds of foreigners slip through border as Avatar production resumes', *NZ Herald*, 26 May 2020; Collette Devlin and Tom Hunt, 'Coronavirus: Film workers among 150 exemptions to enter NZ amid border lockdown', *Stuff.co.nz*, 27 May 2020 < https://www.stuff.co.nz/entertainment/film/121643649/coronavirus-film-workers-among-150-given-exemptions-to-enter-nz-amid-border-lockdown>.

[19] NZ Ministry of Health, 'Covid-19: Border Controls', 29 July 2020. According to the Ministry: 'Only New Zealand residents and citizens (and their children and partners) are permitted to enter New Zealand.' Thereafter they 'must stay in managed isolation or quarantine for at least 14 days and complete a health assessment and return a negative COVID-19 test before they can go into the community.'

[20] NZ Ministry of Health, 'Covid-19: Current Cases', *health.govt.nz* (6 August 2020).

totals globally, albeit not quite the lowest.[21] Precisely how many lives were saved by the stringent approach is unknown and unknowable, but some estimates put it in the thousands. Modelling provided to the government put the figure at 14,400 fatalities if the coronavirus spiralled out of control under an abstention approach.[22]

There were sufficiently few deaths that the government concluded that its elimination strategy had worked and thus it moved from L4 after 5 weeks and to L1 after 11 weeks. The elimination strategy has been met with continuing overwhelming public approval.[23] It has also earned New Zealand many plaudits overseas.[24] The WHO's Director

---

[21] See 'WHO Coronavirus Disease (COVID-19) Situation Report 190, *World Health Organization*, 28 July 2020. Singapore, at the same date, had 27 deaths; Sri Lanka 23, Australia 161. Taiwan is not included in the WHO data. As at 29 June 2020, Taiwan (population 23.8 m) had just 7 deaths from Covid-19 and, at the same date, Iceland had 10 deaths: 'What Coronavirus Success of Taiwan and Iceland Has in Common', *The Conversation*, 29 June 2020 <https://theconversation.com/what-coronavirus-success-of-taiwan-and-iceland-has-in-common-140455>.

[22] Jamie Morton, 'Covid-19: Uncontrolled Spread Could Kill 14,000 in NZ', *NZ Herald,* 5 April 2020. The modelling was provided by University of Otago researchers whose work predicted that 'uncontrolled spread in the country could see up to 64 per cent of the population infected, 32,000 people hospitalised, and up to 14,400 deaths.' An alternative model by the same team predicted an even more grim scenario: 'A total of 3.32 million New Zealanders would be expected to get symptomatic illness; 146,000 would be sick enough to require hospital admission; 36,600 would be sick enough to require critical care (in an ICU); and 27,600 would be expected to die.' See further Ministry of Health, 'COVID19 Modelling and Other Commissioned Reports', *health.govt.nz*, 31 March 2020.

[23] ThomasCoughlan,'Coronavirus:TheGovernment'sCovid-19lockdownmeasureshave overwhelmingpublicsupport,accordingtoapoll',*Stuff.co.nz*,23April2020<https://www.stuff.co.nz/national/121231591/coronavirus-the-governments-covid19-lockdown-measures-have-overwhelming-public-support-according-to-a-poll (87 percent of New Zealanders approve the Government strict lockdown measures).

[24] See eg 'Coronavirus: How New Zealand Relied on Science and Empathy', *BBC News*, 20 April 2020. For a contrary view, see eg Australian economics journalist, Adam Creighton: 'New Zealand is held out as a role model, but it's a small, remote country. Its biggest industry, tourism, has been ruined, and at some point its citizens may want to come and go. . . Observing a decline in death or case number after a government took a sledgehammer to its economy says nothing about the effectiveness. Pointing to New Zealand in rapture proves nothing.' Lane Andelane, 'Coronavirus: New Zealand's COVID-19 Response Criticised by Australian Economics Journalist', *Newshub*, 6 August 2020.

General Dr Tedros Adhanom Ghebreyesus enthused that, by following the WHO's advice, 'the people and government of New Zealand, led by Jacinda Ardern, have shown Covid-19 can be overcome through commitment, action and vigilance.'[25]

The L4 approach, however, is not without its costs. Aside from the immediate economic expenditure by the government (the massive NZ$12.1 billion rescue package)[26] and the drop in economic activity and GDP, it will cost lives in the future.

A useful overseas instance of this argument occurred in the United States where 600 doctors wrote a much-publicised letter to President Trump on 19 May, 2020 to 'express our alarm over the exponentially growing negative health consequences of the national shutdown.'[27] The physicians likened the pandemic shutdown to a "mass casualty incident" in which standard triage techniques ought to be applied. The first group, triage level black, require too many resources to be saved in a crisis. The next in priority, the red group, has injuries that are survivable if treated. Thereafter, the yellow group (sustaining serious injuries that are not life-threatening) and green group (minor injuries) are attended to. The red band merits top priority and then the next step is to ensure the other two groups do not deteriorate. Extensive experience has, continued the letter, 'shown that by strictly following this algorithm, we save the maximum number of lives.'[28] It continued:

---

[25] 'Coronavirus: World Health Organisation Praises NZ's Covid-19 Response', *Stuff. co.nz*, 8 July 2020 <https://www.stuff.co.nz/national/health/coronavirus/122074593/ coronavirus-world-health-organisation-praises-nzs-covid19-response>.

[26] Grant Robertson [Minister of Finance], '$12.1 Billion Support for New Zealanders and Business', *Beehive.govt.nz*, 17 March 2020 <https://www.beehive.govt.nz/ release/121-billion-support-new-zealanders-and-business>. According to the Minister of Finance, the package was 'one of the largest in the world on a per capita basis [and] it represents 4.0% of GDP'''.

[27] See eg Grace-Marie Turner, '600 physicians say lockdown are a "mass casualty incident"', *Forbes*, 22 May 2020; Matthew Wright, 'More Than 500 Trump-backing Doctors Sign Letter Asking Him to End Shutdown', *Daily Mail*, 21 May 2020 <https://www. dailymail.co.uk/news/article-8342497/More-500-doctors-sign-letter-Trump-pushing-end-shutdown.html>. The link to full letter, whose lead signer was Dr Simone Gold, an emergency medicine specialist in Los Angeles, is set out in both these articles.

[28] Letter by Simone Gold et al, ibid.

Millions of Americans are already at triage level red. These include 150,000 Americans per month who would have had a new cancer detected through routine screening that hasn't happened, millions who have missed routine dental care to fix problems strongly linked to heart disease/death, and preventable cases of stroke, heart attack, and child abuse. Suicide hotline phone calls have increased 600%.[29]

The letter concluded:

The millions of casualties of a continued shutdown will be hiding in plain sight, but they will be called alcoholism, homelessness, suicide, heart attack, stroke, or kidney failure. In youths it will be called financial instability, unemployment, despair, drug addiction, unplanned pregnancies, poverty, and abuse. Because the harm is diffuse, there are those who hold that it does not exist. We, the undersigned, know otherwise.[30]

The following are, as I see it, the major causes of likely future fatalities attributable (in whole or in part) to the strict lockdown:

- **Suicides**

Social isolation, loneliness, bankrupt businesses, ruined livelihoods and mass unemployment, induce depression, despair and other psychosocial malaises and thereafter may lead to suicide.[31] For example, some studies point to an increase in suicides for every one percentage point in unemployment.[32]

---

[29] Ibid.

[30] Ibid.

[31] Malcom Kendrick, 'As a GP, I Fear Our Covid-19 Lockdown Will Result In Significantly More Deaths Than We Are Trying To Prevent', *RT.com*, 6 April 2020 <https://www.rt.com/op-ed/485110-covid-19-lockdown-deaths/>.

[32] Gigi Foster, 'Covid Lockdowns Have Human Costs As Well As Benefits', *The Conversation*, 30 April 2020 <https://theconversation.com/covid-lockdowns-have-human-costs-as-well-as-benefits-its-time-to-consider-both-137233>. Aside from suicide per se, Monsebraaten(n 4), quotes Dr Goel who explained that studies on past economic downturns had shown that unemployment increased a person's risk of death by about 1.7 per cent.

- **Deaths due to domestic violence**

With confinement indoors for long periods in often cramped houses or flats, exacerbated by the loss of recreational activities, social mingling at pubs and clubs and so on, domestic violence is likely to increase. In the UK it appears deaths from domestic violence more than doubled during Covid-19 restrictions.[33]

- **Deaths through delayed treatment or non-treatment**

Non-urgent or non-essential operations, treatments and tests were postponed and the importune candidates deteriorated, and some died. 'Thousands of elective procedures have been cancelled, jeopardising the health of many patients.'[34] 'Cancer Research UK has warned that the [Covid-19] crisis could mean an extra 18,000 deaths from cancer this year alone as urgent referrals across England dropped by 62 per cent, while chemotherapy treatments have been running at just 70 per cent of normal levels.'[35] Turning to the initial hotspot in the United States, New York City, a *New England Journal of Medicine* study reported that

> we investigated the striking *X-curve* of ICU utilization: a surge in Covid-19 patients accompanied with dramatic drop in non-Covid-19 patients. We found there was an 88% drop in non–Covid-19 ICU volume within the period from February 15 to April 15, 2020. The changing distribution of ICU patients' diagnoses across the study period raises the spectre of illness hidden and illness deferred.
>
> A more tragic dimension of illness hidden to our hospitals is the possibility that patients who would have otherwise been hospitalized in an ICU were instead dying at home. There was some evidence that this was happening. A preliminary estimate of excess deaths (number of deaths above expected seasonal baseline levels) in New York City during March 11–

---

[33] Foster, ibid.
[34] Guilford, (n 6).
[35] Sarah Knapton, 'Why Lockdown Could Cost More Lives Than It Saves", *Daily Telegraph*, 7 June 2020.

May 2, 2020 found 5,293 deaths that were not identified as either laboratory-confirmed or probable Covid-19–associated deaths.[36]

They concluded that there was a need to 'pay attention to the pandemic's reverberating effects, including illness hidden and illness deferred, which are more likely to cause suffering among low incomes and marginalized patient populations.'[37]

- **Deaths due to decreased funding of health services**

Economic decline reduces the wealth of the nation and reduces the tax revenue to fund hospitals, medicines, medical research and so on. The diminished economic prosperity leads to reduced governmental (and private sector) ability to sustain life.

> The tax dollars needed to invest in highly trained professionals, pharmaceuticals and facilities required by a high performing health sector are rapidly evaporating. The resulting impoverishment will compromise our progress in reducing deaths from cancer, heart disease and the other major diseases that afflict our population.[38]

Some of the gloomier predictions are that any lives saved by the lockdown will be wiped out by those lost from the impact of the recession. British economist Prof Philip Thomas of Bristol University estimated that more people (675,000) could die from the "collateral damage" from the lockdown measures 'than the 577,000 [sic: 510,000] deaths predicted by Imperial College if corona virus had been allowed to run through the population unchecked.'[39] Interestingly, it should be noted that the Imperial College modelling, led by Prof Neil Ferguson[40] –

---

[36] Spriha Gogia et al, 'Covid-19 X-Curves: Illness Hidden, Illness Deferred', *New England Journal of Medicine*, 26 May 2020.

[37] Ibid.

[38] Guilford (n 6).

[39] Knapton, (n 35).

[40] Neil M Ferguson et al, 'Impact of Non-Pharmaceutical Interventions (NPIs) to Reduce COVID-19 Mortality and Healthcare Demand', *Imperial College Covid-19 Response Team*, 16 March 2020 <https://doi.org/10.25561/77482>. In their report, at

which appears to have been the primary basis for the UK and US Governments' decisions to jettison their then rather laissez-faire stance and instead adopt, at least in Britain's case, a strict lockdown[41] – itself received trenchant criticism.[42] Other researchers maintained that the Imperial College findings were unreliable and inaccurate having yielded estimated fatalities that were greatly overstated.[43]

III THE MITIGATION STRATEGY

We may grant, on the one hand, that a mitigation strategy (say L2 in the New Zealand schema) would result in immediate deaths and these would be a greater number, one presumes, than for the L4 approach. How many more people would have died under a less strict regime is again unknowable. It would depend, of course, on the details of the mitigation strategy, for there are many variants besides the Swedish one.

While the present deaths total would be higher, on the other hand we may speculate that there would be a much lower number of future deaths than under the elimination approach, due to the less restrictive effects upon the economy and the improved mental health of society. So, the future lives lost under the mitigation approach would be less than the future lives lost under the strict lockdown. I have set out the

7, they state: 'In total, in an unmitigated epidemic, we would predict approximately 510,000 deaths in GB and 2.2 million in the US, not accounting for the potential negative effects of health systems being overwhelmed on mortality.'

[41] Katherine Rushton and Daniel Foggo, 'Neil Ferguson, The Scientist Who Convinced Boris Johnson of UK coronavirus Lockdown, Criticised in Past for Flawed Research', *Daily Telegraph*, 28 March 2020; Mark Landler and Stephen Castle, 'Behind the Virus Report That Jarred the U.S. and the U.K. to Action', *New York Times*, 2 April 2020.

[42] See eg Tom Morgan, 'Lockdown Saved No Lives And May Have Cost Them, Nobel Prize Winner Believes', *Daily Telegraph*, 23 May 2020 (criticism by Prof Michael Levitt of Stanford University that Prof Ferguson's predictions of the trajectory of the pandemic were over-estimated by 10 to 12 times).

[43] See, most notably, David Richards and Konstantin Boudnik, 'Neil Ferguson's Imperial model could be the most devastating software mistake of all time', *Daily Telegraph*, 16 May 2020. For a similar critique, see 'Questions Over Virus Models That Prompted Lockdowns', *Medical Press*, 12 June 2020.

broad outcomes of the alternative approaches in the table below and, for the sake of completeness, I have included the abstention strategy (herd immunity):

	Elimination approach	Mitigation approach	Abstention approach
Lives saved (present)	very high; maximised	medium	minimal
Deaths (present)	very low	medium	very high; maximised
Deaths (future)	high	medium	low

These are estimates expressed as generalities. All this is very difficult, if not impossible, to assess with any accuracy since the variables are unknown and can only be estimated.[44]

The only figure that is quantified is the number of deaths from Covid-19. Even there, however, at least in some countries (not New Zealand), controversy surrounds whether this is an accurate total and has not been inflated. There is a suspicion (not unaccompanied by evidence) that the cause of death was being consistently attributed to the coronavirus despite the presence of operative co-morbidities.[45] Take the United Kingdom. In July 2020, the Health Secretary, Matt Hancock, asked for a review of the collation of Covid-19 death figures:

---

[44] For one attempt, see eg Dr Martin Lally who estimated some 1500 deaths if New Zealand had followed under a Swedish style mitigation approach: Martin Lally, 'The Costs and Benefits of a Covid-19 Lockdown', original version: 20 March 2020, revised version: 11 August 2020 <https://croakingcassandra.files.wordpress.com/2020/08/martin-lally-cost-benefit-assessment-of-covid-lockdown-august-2020.pdf>.

[45] Jessica Priest, 'One In 3 Death Certificates Were Wrong Before Coronavirus. It's About To Get Even Worse', *USA Today*, 25 April 2020. David Adam, 'It's So Hard To Know Who's Dying of Covid-19—And When', *The Scientist*, 18 May 2020.

> The Secretary of State has asked PHE [Public Health England] to urgently review their estimation of daily health statistics. . . . Currently the daily measure counts all people who have tested positive for coronavirus and since died, with no cut-off between time of testing and date of death.[46]

It appears that in England the fatalities include anyone who has ever tested positive for Covid-19 regardless of whether they died for another reason – say 'they had a heart attack or were run over by a bus three months later'[47] – thus leading some to question whether the (then) total of 45,000 coronavirus deaths may be exaggerated. Profs Carl Heneghan of Oxford University and Yoon Loke of the University of East Anglia observed: 'By this PHE definition, no one with Covid in England is allowed to ever recover from their illness.'[48] Hence, in August, 5,377 deaths were deducted from the official Covid-19 death toll after it was revealed that thousands of people may have recovered from the virus before they died.[49]

Answers to key questions remain elusive. Just how deadly is the coronavirus and what is the death rate or Case Fatality Rate ('CFR'), the proportion of deaths from those who have tested-positive for Covid-19?[50] At the early stage of the pandemic, the WHO speculated that

---

[46] 'UK Reviews Covid-19 Death Toll Figure Amid Fear of Inaccuracy', *Times of India*, 18 July 2020 (quoting the Government website). See also Matta Busby and Heather Stewart, 'Daily Updates on English Covid-19 Deaths Paused Amid Accuracy Concerns', *Guardian*, 18 July 2020.

[47] The examples given by Profs Heneghan and Loke in their paper, 'Why No One Can Ever Recover From Covid-19 in England–A Statistical Anomaly', *Centre for Evidence-Based Medicine*, 16 July 2020.

[48] 'UK Reviews Covid-19 Death Toll' (n 46). See similarly Sarah Knapton, 'No Reliable Way to Track Covid Pandemic in UK After PHE Data Row, Says Expert', *Daily Telegraph*, 19 July 2020 (quoting Prof Carl Heneghan and Prof Yoon K Loke of the University of East Anglia who jointly discovered the "statistical anomaly").

[49] Pamela Duncan et al, 'Coronavirus Death Toll in England Revised Down by More Than 5,000', *Guardian*, 12 August 2020. The official UK total from Public Health England, was decreased from 46,706 to 41,329—a reduction of 11.5%. From now on the official government death toll will only include people who died within 28 days of testing positive for the virus.

[50] See eg Smriti Mallapty 'How Deadly Is The Coronavirus? Scientists Are Close To An Answer', *Nature*, 16 June 2020.

it was above 3%,[51] but this was a rather high estimate and ignored undetected infections in asymptomatic people.[52] It appears that the Infection Fatality Rate ('IFR'), yet another measure of the death rate,[53] is in the vicinity of half of one per cent.[54]

> When deaths from COVID-19 are divided by the total number of cases – not just reported cases [ie, CFR] – you get a statistic called the infection fatality rate (IFR), or colloquially, the death rate. The [United States] Centers for Disease Control and Prevention currently has a best guess of 0.65 % for the IFR. But current estimates fall anywhere between 0.2% and 1%, a surprisingly large range when calculating the infection fatality rate should be as simple as dividing the number of deaths by total infections. And these estimates are changing all the time. In fact, in the time it took to write this article, the CDC changed its best estimate of the fatality rate from 0.26% to 0.65%.[55]

What is the R number, the reproduction rate or average number of secondary cases generated by primary cases?[56] Is it below the critical

---

[51] Report of the WHO-China Joint Mission on Coronavirus Disease 2019 (COVID-19) (16-24 February 2020) 12 (as at 20 February the crude fatality rate was 3.8 %, viz, 2114 of 55,924 laboratory confirmed cases had died in China). On 3 March 2020, WHO reported that 'Globally, about 3.4% of reported cases have died.': WHO Director-General's opening remarks at the media briefing on COVID-19 — 3 March 2020 <https://www.who.int/dg/speeches/detail/who-director-general-s-opening-remarks-at-the-media-briefing-on-covid-19-3-march-2020>.

[52] Thornley et al (n 14).

[53] See 'Estimating mortality from COVID-19: Scientific Brief', WHO, 4 August 2020. <https://www.who.int/news-room/commentaries/detail/estimating-mortality-from-covid-19>.

[54] See eg John Ioannidis, 'The Infection Fatality Rate of COVID-19 Inferred From Seroprevalence Data' *Medrxiv.org*, 14 July 2020. <https://doi.org/10.1101/2020.05.13.20101253>

[55] Justin Silverman and Alex Washburne, 'How Deadly Is The Coronavirus? The True Fatality Rate Is Tricky To Find, But Researchers Are Getting Closer', *The Conversation*, 15 July 2020.

[56] See Roy Anderson et al,'COVID-19 Spread in the UK: The End of the Beginning?', *The Lancet*, 3 August 2020: doi.org/10.1016/ S0140-6736(20)31689-5.

figure of 1.0?[57] How many "excess deaths" (the number of deaths in a given period and region less the usual average number for that period and region) have resulted?[58] Putting aside the deaths from Covid-19 for a moment, what are the non-fatal disease effects and how serious are they?[59] There is disquieting emerging evidence that the legacy of a bout of Covid-19 for those (the vast majority) who survive may be severe, ranging from chronic fatigue to micro-structural changes to the brain.[60]

The kinds of technical questions that are staple fare for epidemiologists, immunologists and virologists became part of the public discourse in the way that the language of economics has done over the years. Suddenly many people became, at least by their own lights, amateur epidemiologists. Perhaps the author can be accused of being one.

More testing is needed. Even some eight or so months out from the initial outbreak and extensive testing we do not have sufficient data yet, although, obviously, the picture is becoming somewhat clearer.

---

[57] Ibid: "R<1 is the goal for stopping transmission over a long decay period".

[58] See Charles Tallack, 'Understanding Excess Mortality: Comparing COVID-19's Impact in the UK to Other European Countries", *The Health Foundation*, 30 June 2020. Excess deaths are "a more comparable measure across countries than deaths from COVID-19, because different countries count COVID-19 deaths in different ways." From this article we learn that the UK had 64, 451 excess deaths in the 11-week worst pandemic period chosen for investigation. The risk of death in the UK increased by 52%. This equated to an additional 965 deaths per million of the population (or just under one in a thousand).

[59] See Megan McArdle, 'Don't Just Look at Covid-19 Fatality Rates. Look at People Who Survive—But Don't Entirely Recover', *Washington Post*, 17 August 2020; Margot Witvliet, 'I'm a COVID-19 Long-Hauler and an Epidemiologist—Here's How It Feels When Symptoms Last For Months', *The Conversation*, 11 August 2020 <https://theconversation.com/im-a-covid-19-long-hauler-and-an-epidemiologist-heres-how-it-feels-when-symptoms-last-for-months-143676>.

[60] See Ryan Prior, 'Chronic fatigue syndrome a possible long-term effect of Covid-19, experts say', *CNN*, 7 August 2020; Jennifer Couzin-Frankel, 'From "Brain Fog" to Heart Damage, COVID-19's Lingering Problems Alarm Scientists', *Science*, 31 July 2020; Nicole Lyn Pesce, '55% of Coronavirus Patients Still Have Neurological Problems Three Months Later: Study', *Marketwatch.com*, 9 August 2020 <https://www.marketwatch.com/story/55-of-coronavirus-patients-still-have-neurological-problems-three-months-later-study-2020-08-07>; Yiping Lu et al, 'Cerebral Micro-Structural Changes in COVD-19 Patients', *The Lancet*, 3 August 2020 <https://doi.org/10.1016/j.eclinm.2020.100484>.

The broad point is that the L4 lockdown cost in the future needs to be weighed against the benefits of this strict lockdown.[61] Secondly, the L4 lockdown cost-benefit calculus needs to be compared to the costs and benefits of a more focused L2-type mitigation strategy, a path which, to reiterate, New Zealand did not take.

It is hard (especially for politicians) to pause and momentarily ignore the present deaths to consider the need to prevent an unknown number of future deaths, or to consider an alternative approach. Perhaps, mused Prof Michael Levitt, 'the real virus was the panic virus.'[62] Perhaps. Every instinct at the time cried out to take an immediate hard-line strategy. But rational public policy required us to consider the alternatives.

Epidemiologists gave their prognoses about the rate of spread of the disease and the measures necessary to curtail it. But, as one critic put it, they 'remained firmly enclosed in their own silos of expertise, unable or unwilling to see the broader picture.'[63] That is perhaps a little unfair. It is, after-all, the job of the politicians to see the bigger picture and make the sorts of difficult trade-offs called for. 'Trade-offs between alternatives have always been central to our economic policy and political debate. Lockdown is no different to any other policy. It has both benefits and costs.'[64]

IV ANALYTICAL ATTEMPTS: QALYS AND ALL THAT

For decades governments in the West have been making calculations about the rational use of the public purse to maximise the provision of health services. They most commonly use something called a cost per QALY (Quality Adjusted Life Year) approach.

The Quality Adjusted Life Year (QALY) is a recognised metric used by health economists, governments and healthcare

---

[61] Foster (n 32).
[62] Quoted in Morgan (n 42).
[63] Paul Ormerod, 'The Costs of Lockdown Could Far Outweigh the Benefits', *Cityam. com*, 8 July 2021 <https://www.cityam.com/the-costs-of-lockdown-could-far-out-weigh-the-benefits/>.
[64] Ibid.

specialists, amongst others, to evaluate new and innovative healthcare treatments. It enables optimisation of resource allocation via rational and explicit methodologies. The QALY, which was popularised in the 1970s in response to a need for improved decision-making around healthcare expenditure. . . Globally, governments are employing QALY calculations to rationalise multi-billion dollar healthcare investments...[65]

How much should we spend to gain one year of completely healthy life, namely, one QALY?[66] For spending $1b dollars how any QALYs could we gain?

For some, this kind of analysis is a cold-hearted, callous, almost inhumane approach. Paul Nuki blasted:

Was it worth it? If you take a very narrow view and weigh human life only in terms of economic value, then the answer is probably not. Lockdown has saved hundreds of thousands of British lives but you could argue that most are old, unwell or otherwise unproductive in economic terms. It's also true that lockdown will, for decades to come, cause many thousands of indirect deaths as a result of the economic storm to come. Deaths caused by unemployment, crime, mental health issues and a withered NHS.

But such arguments are as unworkable as they are contemptible. They are the arguments of First World War generals and nineteenth-century colonialists – people who regarded others as little more than a herdable commodity. They are not fit for a modern democracy.[67]

---

[65] D A Pettit et al, 'The Limitations of QALY: A Literature Review' (2016) 6(4) *Journal of Stem Cell Research & Therapy* 334.

[66] Under this model, 1 represents ideal health and 0 equals death and thus, for example, patients having to undergo regular kidney dialysis might have a QALY of 0.75, signifying a 25 percent reduction in the value of life relative to being in optimal health: Chris Conover, 'How economists calculate the costs and befits of Covid-19 lockdowns', *The Apothecary*, 27 March 2020.

[67] Global Health Security Editor of the *Daily Telegraph* (UK) in Russell Lynch, 'Was lockdown really worth it? Telegraph writers and experts give their verdict', *Daily Telegraph*, 5 July 2020.

I suggest such charges are misplaced. First, economic analysis is being used all the time to determine the most rational deployment of scarce resources when it comes to spending on medical treatments, hospital care, pharmaceuticals and so on. Ethical objections to the QALY approach have been levelled from the very start,[68] but this has not led to the QALY method being jettisoned. Second, a hard-nosed assessment involving difficult trade-offs (economic, moral, political) is what government is about. As the Economics Editor of the Daily Telegraph explained:

> Weighing human lives in cash terms is an unpalatable task when families are losing loved ones, but it is the responsibility of being in government. Judged by standards that the National Institute of Clinical Excellence applies to other health treatments, which put a £30,000 limit on the price of extending life by a year, the lockdown has been massively expensive compared to the benefits gained.[69]

A cost-benefit study of the our Covid-19 L4 strategy by a NZ economist, Dr Martin Lally, utilizes this concept.[70] Lally noted that in New Zealand the cost per QALY is put at approximately NZ$45,000.[71] This compares, for example, as we just saw above, with £30,000 per QALY in the UK or between US$50,000 to $150,000 in the United States.[72] Lally concluded:

---

[68] The standard ethical objections – the appropriateness of valuing one individual's life over another's, the adoption of an overly utilitarian method, and so on— are discussed in Pettit et al (n 65). There are also, needless to say, numerous methodological limitations that critics have levelled against the QALY approach (eg, diverse populations may have difference preferences and evaluate medical conditions differently): again, see Pettit et al.

[69] Lynch (n 66).

[70] Lally (n 43) .

[71] Ibid. See also Bryce Wilkinson, 'Research Note: Quantifying the Wellbeing Costs of COVID-19', *The New Zealand Initiative*, 9 April 2020 <https://nzinitiative.org.nz/reports-and-media/reports/research-note-quantifying-the-wellbeing-costs-of-covid-19/>.

[72] Conover (n 66). Stephen Archer, 'Providing Care for the 99.9% During the COVID-19 Pandemic: How Ethics, Equity, Epidemiology, and Cost Per QALY Inform Healthcare Policy', *Health Management Forum*, 8 July 2020, states it is US$50,000 for the United States.

World-wide, many governments have implemented substantial curtailments of normal economic activity in order to reduce the expected death toll from Covid-19. This paper considers the effect of the New Zealand government adopting
a suppression policy versus a milder mitigation policy, with
the actions of other governments taken as given. The cost
per QALY saved from doing so would seem to have been
vastly in excess of the currently used value for a QALY of
$45,000. Consideration of alternative parameter values and
recognition of factors omitted from the analysis would not
likely reverse this imbalance in cost per QALY saved versus
currently accepted figures for the value of a QALY. The suppression policy was therefore dramatically inconsistent with
long-established views about the value of a QALY.[73]

Let us delve into his reasoning. New Zealand's GDP in 2019 was
approximately NZ$331b. The loss in GDP from the pandemic is esti-
mated by Lally to be 28 percent or $87b. Next, one needs to estimate
the GDP losses from adopting a strict L4 lockdown approach instead
of a mitigation strategy. Lally put this difference at about 25 percent;
thus, 25 percent of $87b is $21.75b. The QALYs saved by a strict
lockdown rather than a mitigation approach were calculated by him to
be 2,500. Put this all together and the cost per QALY saved would be
$21b divided by 2,500 which equals $8.5m per QALY saved. Recall,
that the pre-Covid-19 value of a QALY in New Zealand was about
$45,000. Thus, 'with Covid-19, the costs of adopting a suppression
rather than a mitigation policy per additional QALY saved would be at
least 190 times the pre-Covid-19 values for a QALY [190 x $45,000
= $8.55m]. This is an extraordinary difference.' Lally admits, quite
rightly, that 'the parameters used in [his] analysis are debateable.'[74]
He went on then to vary the estimates lest his initial calculations be
extreme. If the death rate under a mitigation strategy were larger, say
double, then the cost per QALY saved would halve to $4.25m, but
that would, he calculated, still be 94 times the usually accepted figure

[73] Lally (n 44).
[74] Ibid.

($4.25m divided by 94 equals $45,000). Next, if the GDP loss from the pandemic was smaller and one halved it (in addition to the death rate being doubled as before), then the cost per QALY saved would fall further to $2.12m, but this would still represent about 47 times the usual figure accepted ($2.12m /47 = $45,000).

All this number crunching is perhaps headache inducing, but the broad point is, I trust, clear. New Zealand would be spending many times what we would spend for health improvements for other long-standing diseases to cure this disease (and thus give the Covid-19 patients additional QALYs). Is this too much?[75] Dr Malcolm Kendrick, an English GP, put it this way in the context of the UK's response to the pandemic:

> Are we paying too much to lock-down Covid? The answer from most people may well be that 'I don't care, we need to spend as much as it takes.' My fear is that, if we are not very careful, the actions we are taking will result in significantly more deaths than we are trying to prevent. Even if we restrict the analysis purely to the cost per QALY and narrow the 'health' analysis purely to Covid, and deaths from Covid, it remains difficult to justify spending £350 billion [the sum set aside by the UK Government to deal with the crisis] to control a single disease.[76]

There was a need, he contended, to 'normalise'[77] how COVID-19 is viewed and assess its costs and risks alongside the more familiar health problems such as cancer, cardiac disease, diabetes and so on.

Dr Stephen Archer, Head of the Department of Medicine at Queen's University, Ontario, makes a similar point: 'policy focused on [Covid-19] pandemic management can inadvertently lead to excess morbidity and mortality from other diseases' and that '4 months into the epidemic, the consequences of an initial laser focus on Covid-19 at

---

[75] In the words of one critic (Grant (n 1): 'We have built our political and economic infrastructure around a single metric: Covid. Nothing else matters.'

[76] Kendrick (n 31) (italics in original).

[77] Ormerod (n 63).

the expense of all other care are emerging.'[78] He noted that cancer and cardiovascular disease accounted for more than 54 percent of all Canadian deaths and it was likely that the 'excessive focus on Covid-19' would engender delayed care for those endemic conditions would lead to a significant increase in excess deaths in the near future.[79]

The NZ Prime Minister repeatedly urged: eliminate Covid-19 for that is the best economic strategy; ensure the coronavirus is squashed and we can then revive the economy.[80] But, as I have endeavoured to explain, it is not that simple. 'Locking down hard, while costly initially, is – these champions [of the government] conveniently claim—its own reward; initial losses [are] more than outweighed by the subsequent gains (faster sustained recovery etc).'[81] That is the theory, 'but there is no actual evidence for these claims – at best such an outcome could be considered as one scenario.'[82] Furthermore, there is little evidence of serious analysis having been given to a credible exit strategy.[83] If the virus does not die out or it mutates or an effective vaccine is many years away, then the worth of an elimination strategy, with repeated lockdowns, becomes highly suspect, if not untenable.

V CONCLUDING THOUGHTS

There are few certainties in this whole vexed subject. Nonetheless, one is that all assessments are premature and we need to wait considerably longer, perhaps years,[84] to make a sound judgment on what was

---

[78] Archer (n 72).

[79] Ibid.

[80] A repeated refrain at the daily afternoon live media conferences broadcasting on radio and television. These were usually headed by the Prime Minister (or at least a senior Cabinet minister) and the Director General of Health, Dr Ashley Bloomfield. See eg Derek Cheng, 'NZ not "Out of the woods"—Prime Minister Jacinda Ardern', *NZ Herald*, 28 April 2020 (PM maintains continuing to stamp out Covid-19 was the best economic response)

[81] Michael Reddell, 'Evaluating Choices', *Croaking Cassandra*, 14 August 2020<https://croakingcassandra.com/2020/08/14/evaluating-choices/>.

[82] Ibid.

[83] Ibid.

[84] Telegraph Editors, above (n 67).

the preferable approach to have taken. As Dr Anders Tegnell, the chief epidemiologist for Sweden put it, we are, "shooting in the dark" when confronting this new virulent disease.[85] The Swedes also emphasized that the pandemic was better described as "a marathon rather than a sprint".[86]. Dr Tegnell admitted that Sweden could have done some things much better (for example, taken stricter measures to protect the elderly in retirement homes) but, overall, at this relatively early point, he was satisfied with the approach Sweden did take.[87]

I have ruminated upon about the cost of a L4 lockdown in terms of lives lost. We needed, I argued, to consider the future costs of the L4 approach in terms of lives lost in the months and years to come.[88] Moreover, it was also, I submit, salutary and necessary to consider whether a mitigation L2-type approach would have been preferable. It appears that the policy-makers in the New Zealand government were remiss in that respect.[89]

In this article, I did not consider a raft of losses outside of fatalities, such as people whose health deteriorated due to delayed or non-treatment, the lost educational opportunities for children who missed

---

[85] Birrell (n 10).

[86] Savage (n 10).

[87] See Savage, (n 10). See also 'Swedish Epidemiology Boss Says Questioned COVID-19 Strategy Seems To Be Working', *Reuters*, 22 July 2020. Sweden's fatality rate (5,770 deaths at a rate of 571 deaths per million is much higher than its Scandinavian neighbours (Norway, 47/m [deaths per million]; Finland, 60/m]; Denmark, 107/m) but lower than several European nations such as Italy, Spain, Britain and Belgium (583 p/m; 611/m; 686/m; and 852/m, respectively) which pursued strict lockdown strategies. The figures quoted are from *Worldometer Covid-19 Coronavirus Pandemic*, 12 August 2020.

[88] I am cognisant that one would also need to take into account the nascent non-fatal disease effects in any overall calculus.

[89] One economist, Reddell, (n 81), castigates: 'What was striking, even at the time, was that there was no sign that the [NZ] government had commissioned from officials, or officials had undertaken anyway, any sort of serious cost-benefit analysis of the sorts of intervention they were looking at and imposed. . . when the government finally got round to publishing the relevant documents, sure enough there was no serious structured attempt to cost and evaluate alternative policy options. (It is not, I hasten to add, that any cost-benefit analysis can give one "the" answers, but it provides a disciplined framework to analyse the options, assumptions and sensitivities.)'

out on school, and so on. I have not talked about the severe restriction upon our civil liberties and fundamental freedoms, nor the effective abdication of political decision-making to scientists, especially, medical experts, epidemiologists, virologists, and so on. As for the former, emergency restrictions have a habit of stubbornly remaining and the level of civic freedoms often does not return to what it was.[90] As for government by unelected medical experts and bureaucrats, this is a myopic and anti-democratic way of governing. These concerns have been traversed by others.

Yet another issue of significance, worthy of separate article, was whether the NZ Government's initial imposition of strict lockdown measures in late March was lawful. In April, two citizens argued that the lockdown was unlawful and thus their 'detention', or at least, the manifold restrictions upon their movement, was illegal. They failed in their action to be granted the remedy of habeas corpus in both the High Court and Court of Appeal.[91] Next, an action for judicial review in the High Court was brought in July to further evaluate the legality of the lockdown.[92] The result of this high-powered suit, brought by a former Parliamentary Counsel and law lecturer, Dr Andrew Borrowdale, has yet to be handed down at the time of writing.

I have spoken of New Zealand's *initial* lockdown. The Government sought to counter any lingering doubts about the legal basis for

---

[90] See eg Kenan Malik, 'Yes, Expect More Surveillance During A Crisis, But Beware It Once The Danger Has Passed', *Guardian*, 12 April 2020.

[91] *Nottingham v Arden* [2020] NZHC 796 (HC)(writ of habeas corpus declined); [2020] NZCA 144 (CA)(appeal by applicants seeking the writ denied).

[92] Hamish Cardwell, 'High Court Case Begins To Determine Whether Level 4 Lockdown Was Lawful', *RNZ*, 27 July 2020; Prof Andrew Geddis, 'Today The Legality Of The Lockdown Will Be Sternly Challenged. And So It Should Be', *The Spinoff*, 27 July 2020; Dean Knight, 'Lockdown's Legality and The Rule of Law", *Newsroom*, 4 August 2020. The judicial review proceedings were brought by Dr Borrowdale against the Director-General of Health, Dr Ashley Bloomfield. *Borrowdale v Director-General of Health* was heard in the Wellington High Court, unusually before a bench of three judges (not the usual single High Court justice). Following an invitation by the High Court, the New Zealand Law Society was granted leave to intervene: *Borrowdale v Director-General of Health* [2020] NZHC 1379 (NZ Law Society granted leave).

its comprehensive anti-Covid-19 public restrictions and, accordingly, on the same day New Zealand went into L2, 13 May 2020, it passed the *COVID-19 Public Health Response Act 2020.*[93] The Act came into force that same day. The passage of the Bill was rushed to say the least. It was introduced on the 12 May and the Opposition had received less than three days to study it.[94] Furthermore, the Bill did not go through a Select Committee vetting, the usual mandatory step. This was, instead, to occur ex post facto. Parliament required the Select Committee to review it before the end of July, in time for the House to decide whether to renew the Act in accordance with the 90-day review specified in the Act.[95] In brief, the key provision is s 11 which gives the Minister or Director-General of Health sweeping powers to make orders 'to require persons to refrain from taking any specified actions that contribute or are likely to contribute to the risk of the outbreak or spread of COVID-19'.[96] Intentional non-compliance with a s 11 order renders the transgressor liable to a fine not exceeding $4,000 or imprisonment of up to 6 months.[97]

---

[93] See Collette Devlin, 'Parliament Sends Controversial New Covid-19 Level 2 Law to be Reviewed at Select Committee', 15 May 2020; Amelia Wade, 'Controversial Bill Passed to Enforce Alert Level 2 Powers', *NZ Herald*, 13 May 2020. The Chief Human Rights Commissioner, Paul Hunt, stated the Commission was 'deeply concerned' about the lack of scrutiny and rushed process for the Covid-19 Public Health Response Bill despite the Government knowing for weeks that New Zealand would be moving to Alert Level 2: Kurt Bayer, 'Human Rights Commission "Deeply concerned" About Public Health Response Bill', *NZ Herald*, 13 May 2020.

[94] My colleague at Otago Law Faculty, Professor Andrew Geddis, noted that he was given (along with others) an advance copy of the bill on late Monday afternoon at 5.30pm (11 May), with the Bill being introduced the next afternoon (Tuesday) and passed under urgency the day after (Wednesday): Geddis, 'The Level Two Law Is Necessary—And Full of Flaws', *The Spinoff*, 14 May 2020 <https://thespinoff.co.nz/politics/14-05-2020/andrew-geddis-the-level-two-law-is-necessary-and-full-of-flaws/>.

[95] The Act is repealed at the end of the period of 90 days after its commencement if no resolution by the House is passed to continue its operation: *COVID-19 Public Health Response Act 2020* s 3(1)(2).

[96] The section goes on to list 9 non-exhaustive instances of the types of order that might be made. Additionally, s 12 provides that different kinds of orders may be made, that may, for example, differentiate between classes of persons upon whom the orders are to be imposed or between regions of New Zealand to which they may apply.

[97] *COVID-19 Public Health Response Act* 2020 s 26.

In conclusion, there are costs in every path we take, whether as an individual, community or as a nation. We look through a glass darkly[98], and in the case of a new widespread fatal disease we work under conditions of urgency and incomplete information. As we gain greater experience with a novel disease and accumulate more scientific data on the nitty-gritty of the origins, transmission, long-term effects, recovery and fatality rates of Covid-19 we see where we may have done better. With the wondrous clarity of hindsight, we may learn that some of the earliest steps were unwise, or at least in need of greater refinement. As New Zealand, and the world, continue to learn more about this infernal disease, let us hope that the costs of the strict lockdown experiment prove to be ones that we can bear.

APPENDIX 1: THE NEW ZEALAND COVID-19 ALERT FRAMEWORK

Level	Risk assessment	Range of measures that can be applied locally or nationally
Level 4: Lockdown Likely that disease is not contained.	Sustained and intensive transmission is occurring. Widespread outbreaks	People instructed to stay at home in their bubble other than for essential personal movement. Educational facilities closed. Safe recreational activity is allowed in the local area. All gatherings cancelled and all public venues closed. Rationing of supplies and requisitioning of facilities possible. Businesses closed except for essential services (e.g. supermarkets, pharmacies, clinics, petrol stations) and lifeline utilities. Travel is severely limited. Reprioritisation of healthcare services.
Level 3: Restrict High risk the disease is not contained.	Multiple cases of community transmission occurring.	People instructed to stay home in their bubble other than for essential personal movement— including to shop, go to work or school if they have to, local recreation, or to seek medical care.

---

[98] 1 Corinthians 13:12 (KJV).

	Multiple active clusters in multiple regions	Physical distancing of 2 metres outside home, or 1 metre in controlled environments like schools and workplaces. Wearing a face covering is strongly encouraged when outside of the home for people 7 years of age and older. People must stay within their immediate household bubble, but can expand this to reconnect with close family/whānau, or bring in caregivers or support isolated people. This extended bubble must remain exclusive. Early learning centres and schools are open for children whose parents have to go to work and have no care giver arrangements, particularly essential workers. People must work from home unless that is not possible. Businesses can open premises, but cannot physically interact with customers. Workers should be kept at least 1 metre apart where possible, and face coverings are strongly recommended. All businesses must display a government issued QR code for use with the NZ COVID Tracer App by 19 August 2020 Low-risk local recreation activities are allowed. Public venues are closed (e.g. libraries, museums, cinemas, food courts, gyms, pools, playgrounds, markets). Gatherings of up to 10 people are allowed but only for wedding services, funerals and tangihanga. Physical distancing and public health measures must be maintained. Inter-regional travel is highly limited (e.g. essential workers, people returning to their primary residence, with limited exemptions for others). People at high risk of severe illness (older people and those with existing medical conditions) are encouraged to stay at home where possible, and take additional precautions when leaving home. They may choose to work.

Level 2: Reduce The disease is contained, but the risk of community transmission remains.	Limited community transmission could be occurring. Active clusters in more than one region.	People can connect with friends and family, and socialise in groups of up to 100, go shopping or travel domestically if following public health guidance. Keep physical distancing of 2 metres from people you don't know when out in public or in retail stores. Keep 1 metre physical distancing in controlled environments like workplaces, where practicable. No more than 100 people at gatherings, including weddings, birthdays and funerals and tangihanga. Businesses can open to the public if following public health guidance including physical distancing and record keeping. Alternative ways of working encouraged where possible. Hospitality businesses must keep groups of customers separated, seated and served by a single person. Maximum of 100 people at a time. Sport and recreation activities are allowed, subject to conditions on gatherings, record keeping, and—where practicable—physical distancing. Public venues such as museums, libraries and pools can open if they comply with public health measures and ensure 1 metre physical distancing and record keeping. Event facilities, including cinemas, stadiums, concert venues and casinos can have more than 100 people at a time, provided there are no more than 100 in a defined space, and the groups do not mix. It is safe to send your children to schools, early learning services and tertiary education. There will be appropriate measures in place. People at higher risk of severe illness from COVID-19 (e.g. those with underlying medical conditions, especially if not well-controlled, and seniors), are encouraged to take additional precautions when leaving home. They may work if they agree with their employer that they can do so safely.

Level 1: **Prepare** The disease is contained in New Zealand	COVID-19 is uncontrolled overseas. Sporadic imported cases. Isolated local transmission could be occurring in New Zealand.	Border entry measures to minimise risk of importing COVID-19 cases. Intensive testing for COVID-19. Rapid contact tracing of any positive case. Self-isolation and quarantine required. Schools and workplaces open, and must operate safely. No restrictions on personal movement but people are encouraged to maintain a record of where they have been. No restrictions on gatherings but organisers encouraged to maintain records to enable contact tracing. Stay home if you're sick, report flu-like symptoms. Wash and dry your hands, cough into your elbow, don't touch your face. No restrictions on domestic transport — avoid public transport or travel if you're sick. No restrictions on workplaces or services but they are encouraged to maintain records to enable contact tracing.

Source: New Zealand Government, Unite Against Covid-19: Alert System Overview (as at 15 August 2020) < https://covid19.govt.nz/covid-19/alert-system/alert-system-overview/>

APPENDIX 2: A CHRONOLOGY OF NEW ZEALAND'S COVID-19 PANDEMIC RESPONSE

28 January — National Health Coordination Centre activated to coordinate and manage the response to Covid-19

30 January — Covid-19 becomes a notifiable disease.

3 February — Entry restrictions for foreign nationals entering from, or transiting through mainland China. Those who enter must self-isolate for 14 days.

5 February — Evacuation of 190 New Zealanders from Wuhan and managed isolation in Whanagaparoa Reception Centre.

7 February — Ministry of Health advice: people who have travelled from or via China should self-isolate for 14 days on arrival in New Zealand.

28 February — First case of Covid-19 in New Zealand (recent returnee from Iran). Contact tracing initiated, close contracts in monitored self-isolation.

4 March — Second case of Covid-19 confirmed.

14 March — Border restrictions start, anyone entering New Zealand must self isolate for 14 days.

19 March — Indoor gatherings of more than 100 people banned. Border closed to all but New Zealand citizens and permanent residents.

21 March — First community transmission suspected. Government announces a four-level alert system. New Zealand is at Alert Level 2.

23 March — New Zealand moves to Alert Level 3.

24 March	Epidemic notice issued and National notice to activate s 70 of the Health Act 1956. Schools and educational facilities closed.
25 March	State of Emergency declared. At 11.59pm, New Zealand moves to Alert Level 4.
29 March	First Covid-19 death recorded.
2 April	Biggest increase of cases diagnosed in one day recorded: 89 cases.
17 April	New cases are all linked to confirmed cases—no evidence of community transmission.
27 April	11.59 pm New Zealand moves to Alert Level 3.
4 May	No new cases of Covid-19 reported. Over the next 10 days, 0-3 cases per day are confirmed.
13 May	11.59 pm New Zealand moves to Alert Level 2. Covid-19 Public Health Response Act 2020 enacted and immediately comes into force.
27 May	Last death (to date) due to Covid-19. Total of 22 deaths.
8 June	No active cases of Covid-19 in the country. New Zealand moves to Alert Level 1. Border controls, with restricted entry to non-residents remain in place. All arrivals subject to mandatory 14 days of managed isolation /quarantine.
16 June	First case of Covid-19 reported in returning citizen (held in managed isolation or quarantine). Since then there have been more cases diagnosed in returning citizens whilst they are held in managed isolation.

27 July   High Court hears judicial review on the legality of the March L4 lockdown.

9 August   100 days since last community transmission Covid-19 case (that date being 1 May 2020).

11 August   First new cases of community transmission detected in Auckland (102 days after the last one).

12 August   Greater Auckland placed in L3 lockdown and the rest of NZ moved to L2 for 14 days.

3

Politicians, the Press and 'Skin in the Game'

JAMES ALLAN*

ABSTRACT

In this article the author argues that the Australian government (and indeed most other democratic governments) has badly mishandled its response to the corona virus. It has significantly infringed on civil liberties; mistrusted the public to act sensibly; noticeably expanded debt and deficits, and hence Big Government, with no palatable route out of that situation; failed to follow the better Swedish model; and is in danger of being seen, not too far in the future, as having indulged in one of the worst public policy fiascos of the century.

I INTRODUCTORY CLAIMS

The essayist Nassim Taleb, who made his name with the wider public with his 2007 book *The Black Swan*[1] (a book with some very powerful insights but a miserable prose style), has long had a fascination with uncertainty and events that fall at the far ends of statistical distributions. He is also a firm believer in only being guided by those who have 'skin in the game' – this catchphrase also being the title of his most recent 2018 book.[2] The idea is that those who will bear the costs and benefits of any decisions they make will tend, in the face of uncertainty, to make better calls. Remember that claim, that insight, because I will come back to it later in this article.

    Meantime, let me turn to the Wuhan virus, in politer, more po-

---

[1] Nassim Taleb, *The Black Swan* (Random House, 2007).
[2] Nassim Taleb, *Skin in the Game* (Penguin Random House, 2018).
* Garrick Professor of Law, The University of Queensland.

litically correct circles (so all of media and government) also known as the corona virus giving rise to 'Covid-19'. As I have made clear elsewhere,[3] were it up to me I would not have abandoned the original label of 'Wuhan virus' even if that amounts to little more than an idiosyncratic protest against some of the more tangential idiocies of political correctness with their willingness to stop speaking the truth if such talk might, just might, offend others. I, overwhelmingly, am on the side of free speech[4] and the J.S. Mill notion that blunt speaking in the back-and-forth cauldron of competing views is the least-bad and most effective method of discovering truth – feelings of offence or psychic harm be damned. But whatever you choose to call this virus, the Australian government's response to it is at the core of this law review's special issue. Indeed, it was to write on some aspect of the government's handling of this Wuhan or corona virus that the editor of this law journal invited me to contribute – a very kind invitation that I gladly accepted. What follows is my short article on that general theme.

Let me begin by laying my cards on the table. I have been a sceptic of the Australian, and most other, government's reactions to this virus virtually from day one. In fact, I started expressing my scepticism about the heavy-handed, lockdown-driven road the Morrison

---

[3] As it happens, at the same time I was approached and asked to write an article by this law review for a special issue on the theme of the coronavirus, I was also approached by another Australian law review for a piece on the same general theme. In that other law review I wrote on how the government's response was differentially affecting the young and the old – that the costs were overwhelmingly falling on the young while the benefits of the government response went to the old. That other article should appear more or less when this issue appears and I make the same point about being a strong supporter of free speech there as I do here. See James Allan, 'The Corona Virus: Old vs Young' *Griffith Journal of Law & Human Dignity* (forthcoming).

[4] See, for example, academic pieces of mine such as James Allan, 'Hate Speech Law and Disagreement' (2013) 29 *Constitutional Commentary* 59; James Allan, 'Free Speech is Far too Important to be Left to Unelected Judges' (2013) 4 *The Western Australian Jurist* 5; and James Allan, 'The Administration of Australian Universities: A National Scandal? Or Amiss in Funderland?' in W Coleman (ed) *Campus Meltdown: The Deepening Crisis in Australian Universities* (Connor Court, 2019) 23 together with many of my weekly columns in the *Spectator Australia*.

government was travelling on way back at the start of April in the pages of the Spectator Australia.[5] Nothing I have read about the virus since then has changed my mind that in big picture terms the Swedish government got this right (as did Taiwan's) and virtually the whole of the rest of the democratic world's political class made a big time mess of things. What I said back then I'll repeat now: in a decade this will be looked back on as one of the most colossal public policy fiascos of the century.

And the general recipe followed by Australia's, Britain's, Canada's and virtually all Western governments involved some combination of the following: shut down or lockdown businesses the bureaucratic-political complex deems 'inessential' as well as whole swathes of civil society including churches, gyms, clubs and more; indulge in extraordinary inroads into people's civil liberties; do not trust average citizens to make sensible decisions as regards how to deal with the virus but rather churn out regulations, one of whose effects is to turn the police into an arm of the nanny state; in this way lockdown huge chunks of the productive economy; pay – make that over-pay – all sorts of people to do nothing at all while having no plausible politically palatable route out of that situation; and in doing all that become the biggest government spenders possibly in the country's history, saddling the next generation with untold debts and much poorer employment and life prospects.[6]

Now those unprecedented steps make up the sort of package of policies you might unleash when faced with the 14th century's Black Death, which is estimated to have killed from a third to a half of Eu-

---

[5] See, for a few instances, James Allan, 'End of the World? Call me Sceptical' *Spectator Australia*, 4 April 2020; James Allan, '"We're all in this Together?" and other Myths of the Corona Crisis', *Spectator Australia Flat White*, 8 April 2020 <https://www.spectator.com.au/2020/04/were-all-in-this-together-and-other-myths-of-the-corona-crisis/>; James Allan, 'Corona Notes', *Spectator Australia*, 18 April 2020; James Allan, 'Churchill in Reverse' *Spectator Australia*, 9 May 2020; and James Allan, 'Fear Porn Panic' *Spectator Australia*, 23 May 2020.

[6] These effects on the young are more fully set out in James Allan, 'The Corona Virus: Old vs Young' *Griffith Journal of Law & Human Dignity* (forthcoming). See also (n 3). For the financial carnage looming, see below.

rope's population.[7] By contrast, Professor John Ioannadis (a Professor of Medicine, of Health Research and Policy and of Biomedical Data Science, at the Stanford University School of Medicine), using data up to July 11th, 2020 and in a paper yet to be peer-reviewed, concluded of the corona virus that:

Across 32 different locations, the median infection fatality rate [meaning if you get it this is your odds of dying] was 0.27 % (corrected 0.24%).... [Concluding that] the infection fatality rate of COVID-19 can vary substantially across different locations and this may reflect differences in population age structure and case-mix of infected and deceased patients as well as multiple other factors. Estimates of infection fatality rates inferred from seroprevalence studies tend to be much lower than original speculations made in the early days of the pandemic.[8]

Likewise, in June 2020, Aynsley Kellow claimed that '[t]here are at the time of writing fifty-one studies based upon the polymerase chain reaction or seriological studies that give a mean IFR [Infection Fatality Rate] of 0.27 per cent'.[9] Now clearly there is much uncertainty surrounding this corona virus – much that is contested about its prevalence and its lethality and more. Still, it has been plain for some time that we are not dealing with the Black Death or anything remotely in that league; in fact, the corona virus does not even come near to approaching the lethality and seriousness of the Spanish Flu. Here is how *The Wall Street Journal* sums it up:

About 80% of Americans who have died of Covid-19 are older than 65, and the median age is 80. A review by Stanford medical pro-

---

[7] See Sharon N DeWitte, 'Mortality Risk and Survival in the Aftermath of the Medieval Black Death' (2014) 9(5) *PLos One* 1.

[8] John Ionnadis, 'The Infection fatality rate of COVID-19 inferred from Seroprevalence Data', *medRxiv*, 13 July 2020 <https://www.medrxiv.org/content/10.1101/2020.05.13.20101253v3>.

[9] See Aynsley Kellow, 'COVID-19 and the Problem with Official Science' 2020 (June) *Quadrant* 14. See too at 19: 'All the evidence on the IFR of COVID-19 suggests it is about as lethal as seasonal flu, and we would do well to recall that the 1968-69 Hong Kong flu killed an estimated one million worldwide and about 100,000 in the US, but did not even lead to the cancellation of the Woodstock festival.'

fessor John Ioannidis last month found that individuals under 65 accounted for 4.8% of all Covid-19 deaths in 10 European countries and 7.8% to 23.9% in 12 US locations. For most people under the age of 65, the study found, the risk of dying from Covid-19 isn't much higher than from getting in a car accident driving to work.... Fatality rate comparisons between Covid-19 and the flu are inapt because they affect populations differently. Children under age 14 are between 6.8 and 17 times less likely to die of Covid-19 than the seasonal flu or pneumonia, assuming 150,000 coronavirus deaths this year....[T]hose over 75 make up about two-thirds of deaths while those younger than 45 make up less than 2%....[Nonetheless], the good news is that most people over age 65 who are in generally good health are unlikely to die or get severely ill from Covid-19.[10]

Or, to take just one representative US State, the State of Pennsylvania, more people over 100 years of age have died of the corona virus than under 45, more over 95 years of age than under 65, and more over 85 than under 80.[11] For those under 15 in Britain there is a greater chance of dying from being hit by lightning.[12]

My point is that all the extraordinary steps taken by Australia's government, and to be fair by those of almost all other democracies, were taken to combat a virus that looks not much worse than a bad flu season that kills about 0.2 percent of people who catch it.[13] For that, the political class, on the advice of its medical experts, ordered businesses to shut; indulged in extraordinary inroads into people's civil liberties; went a good way towards annihilating the economy; and ru-

---

[10] See The Wall Street Journal Editorial Board, 'The Covid Age Penalty', *The Wall Street Journal*, 12 June 2020.

[11] See Pennsylvania Department of Heath Bureau of Health, 'Weekly Report for Deaths Attributed to Covid-19', Statistics and Registries, 17 May 2020.

[12] Or so says Professor David Spiegelhalter of the University of Cambridge's Winton Centre for Risk. This was widely reported including in 'School Age Children more likely to be hit by lightning than die of the coronavirus' *London Telegraph*, 9 June 2020 <https://www.telegraph.co.uk/politics/2020/06/09/school-age-children-likely-hit-lightning-die-coronavirus-oxbridge/>.

[13] Full Fact, 'How does the new coronavirus compare to influenza?', 11 March 2020, <https://fullfact.org/health/coronavirus-compare-influenza/>.

ined the businesses and lives of many in the private sector. And they did all this – to put the point in further contrast – when it is the case that 161,000 or so people die every year in this country;[14] when it is the case that between 1,500 and 3,000 Australians die every year of the flu;[15] and when about 1,200 Australians die yearly in car accidents.[16] Meanwhile the Wuhan/corona virus has not even made it into the top 50 causes of death in Australia.[17]

II SWEDEN, CIVIL LIBERTIES AND 'NO SKIN IN THE GAME' PRESS & POLITICIANS

In the remainder of this short article I want to consider, or speculate on, why this has happened and dole out some blame. However, I will first digress briefly to Sweden. Then remind readers of the economic costs of these governmental decisions to lockdown, as well as the civil liberties' costs. Then I will turn to consider the press and the politicians, and the fact that many have no skin in the game. I will finish with thoughts on the voters more widely.

First, then, comes my digression to Sweden. You see Sweden did not impose a government lockdown or shut down on businesses or drive a

---

[14] See, for example, Australian Bureau of Statistics, 'Causes of Death, Australia, 2018' (September 25, 2019). <https://www.abs.gov.au/ausstats/abs@.nsf/0/47E19 CA15036B04BCA2577570014668B?Opendocument>; Australian Bureau of Statistics, 'Causes of Death, Australia, 2017', 26 September 2018, <https://www.abs.gov.au/ausstats/abs@.nsf/Lookup/by%20Subject/3303.0~2017~Main%20 Features~Summary%20of%20findings~1>.

[15] See table titled 'Leading causes of death, Australia, selected years – 2009, 2013, 2018' at Australian Bureau of Statistics, 'Causes of Death, Australia, 2018', 25 September 2019, <https://www.abs.gov.au/ausstats/abs @.nsf/0/47E19CA15036B04BC A2577570014668B?Opendocument>

[16] Australian Government, Department of Infrastructure, Transport, Regional Development and Communications, 'Road deaths: 12 month total Australia', June 2020, <https://app.powerbi.com/view?r=eyJrIjoiMTU1MjFmMWEtNWI2Yy00Mjc2LTg1N-zQtZmUwOGE0MTE0MTVhIiwidCI6ImFhMjFiNjQwLWJhYzItNDU2ZC04NTA1L-WYyY2MwN2Y1MTc4NCNCJ9>.

[17] Ramesh Thakur, 'Let's learn from this pandemic to be better prepared for the really big one', May 30, 2020, <https://johnmenadue.com/ramesh-thakur-lets-learn-from-this-pandemic-to-be-better-prepared-for-the-really-big-one/>.

truck through civil liberties. It gave its citizens advice, trusted them – which, yes, did mean that businesses suffered from the choices some citizens voluntarily made to be cautious and stay home, though the economic suffering was nothing like what happened to similar businesses elsewhere under government-mandated lockdowns – and then tried to protect the elderly and frail (though they were far from perfect on that latter front).[18] And yet so far, and including the fact authorities almost everywhere count deaths with corona as part of deaths *because* of corona, there have been all up 5,697 deaths in Sweden from the virus. (Translated to Australia's population that would be about 14,000.) In terms of deaths per million Sweden's deaths have been fewer than in Belgium, the UK, Spain and Italy, not all that much above France, and within sight of the US – all the others being keen lockdowners.[19] Or put differently and less sensationally, 99.95 percent of Swedes have not died of the corona virus, so some way short of the Black Death. For those Swedes under 60 years of age, 99.998 percent have not died from it.[20]

And Sweden matters because it goes some way to giving us a real-life counter-factual instance of what would happen if a country had opted not to impose a heavy-handed, civil liberties-curtailing lockdown. On top of that Sweden matters because the temptation for many is to treat correlation as causation – reasoning that as Australia's death toll is low, and as this country did experience lockdowns, therefore the

---

[18] As the Swedish epidemiologist advising his government, Anders Tegnell, admits. See Mark Corcoran and Bronwen Reed, 'Anders Tegnell, the man behind Sweden's contentious coronavirus plan, has a legion of fans – and critics', *ABC News*, 30 June 2020 <https://www.abc.net.au/news/2020-06-30/anders-tegnell-architect-of-the-swedish-model-coronavirus/12384966>.

[19] On 27 July 2020 at 1pm the numbers of deaths per million of population were: Belgium 847; the UK 674; Spain 608; Italy 581; Sweden 564; France 462; and the US 453. And total Swedish corona deaths were as stated, 5,697: <https://www.worldometers.info/coronavirus/#countries>.

[20] This plainly makes it a negligible cause of death for Swedes under 60, see Ramesh Thakur, 'The Rise and Fall of Coronavirus Modelling', 27 May 2020 <https://johnmenadue.com/ramesh-thakur-the-rise-and-fall-of-the-coronavirus-models/>: 'The best-known example of a country bucking the model is Sweden. Without compulsory lockdowns and with much of activity as normal, 99.998% of Swedes under 60 have survived.'

latter must have caused the former.[21] Yet as Sweden's top infectious disease expert, Anders Tegnell, early on stated, there is little to no scientific evidence that lockdowns work[22] – the implication being that Australia's very low death count was a function of causes other than the lockdowns. Indeed, even the establishment British medical journal *The Lancet* is now running articles that come to the same conclusion about lockdowns not being associated with lower coronavirus death counts.[23] And even if that is incorrect, and lockdowns are a net positive on the purely 'do they end up lowering immediate deaths from the corona virus' side of the ledger,[24] it is still true that lockdowns have staggeringly huge economic impacts, which themselves, in turn, have big health impacts. As the American writer Heather MacDonald has noted:

---

[21] All of the above explains why the press (which in large part has been an enthusiastic supporter of lockdowns) and the medical bureaucracies seem at times to be hoping for the worst for Sweden, in order to show that they were right and Sweden's bucking of the received orthodoxy was wrong.

[22] In Jon Miltmore, 'Why Sweden Succeeded in "Flattening the Curve" and New York Failed' *Foundation for Economic Education* (15 July 2020). Note, too, that in the United States per capita Covid fatalities were 75% lower in non-lockdown states than in lockdown states. See 'News From the Non-Lockdown States' *The Wall Street Journal*, 23 June 2020 <https://www.wsj.com/articles/news-from-the-non-lockdown-states-11592954700>.

[23] See Chaudry, Dranitsaris, Mubashir, Bartoszko and Riazi, 'A country level analysis measuring the impact of government actions, country preparedness and socioeconomic factors on COVID-19 mortality and related health outcomes' *The Lancet*, 21 July 2020) <https://www.thelancet.com/journals/eclinm/article/PIIS2589-5370(20)30208-X/fulltext>. In the 'Findings' section the authors state: 'Rapid border closures, full lockdowns, and wide-spread testing were not associated with COVID-19 mortality per million people'.

[24] Whether that be the case or not, there are non-corona virus deaths to be considered too – namely, other sorts of deaths caused by lockdowns. In the context of Britain, see for example Laura Donnelly and Sarah Knapton, '"Lockdown has killed 21,000 people", say experts' *London Telegraph*, 29 July 2020. The research referred to in that article also claims that there could be up to 35,000 extra cancer deaths from missed screening. The general point here is about the possibility that the lockdowns themselves may cause other sorts of deaths in the medium to longer term – such as suicides from loneliness, deaths that flow from missing cancer (or other medical) screenings, later deaths from the economic carnage these things cause, and so on.

Anyone who warned that the effects of the lockdowns would be more devastating than anything the coronavirus could inflict was accused of being a heartless capitalist who only cared about profits. But to care about the economy is to care about human life, since the economy is how life is sustained. It is a source of meaning, as well as sustenance, binding humans to each other in a web of voluntary exchange. To its workers, every business is essential, and to many of its customers as well. Even judged by the narrowest possible definition of public health – lives lost – the toll from the lockdowns will exceed that of the virus, due to the cancellation of elective medical procedures, patients' unnecessary fear of seeking treatment, and the psychological effects of unemployment.[25]

So let me say just a few brief words as regards the economic costs of these lockdowns with their extraordinary inroads into people's civil liberties and their concomitant economic effects – not least the politicians' felt need, as the instigators of the economic hibernation, to over-pay all sorts of people to do next to nothing at all. And to do so with no plausible, politically palatable route out of that situation, to such an extent that the government that imposed the lockdowns, shut down much of commerce, and then paid the affected workers becomes quite likely the biggest spender in the country's history, saddling the next generation with untold debts and much poorer employment and life prospects.[26] In brief, and admitting that there is huge uncertainty in any predictions, what is clear is that the economy is in for a giant

---

[25] Heather MacDonald, 'Four Months of Unprecedented Government Malfeasance' (2020) 49(5) *Imprimis* 7 (emphasis in original).

[26] See, eg, Alan Collins and Adam Cox, 'Coronavirus: why lockdown may cost young lives over time', *The Conversation*, 26 March 2020 <https://theconversation.com/coronavirus-why-lockdown-may-cost-young-lives-over-time-134580>; Jeff Borland, 'The next employment challenge from coronavirus: how to help the young', *The Conversation*, 15 April 2020 <https://theconversation.com/the-next-employment-challenge-from-coronavirus-how-to-help-the-young-135676>; Gigi Foster, 'Correctly counting the cost shows Australia's lockdown was a mistake', *Financial Review*, 25 May 2020 <https://www.afr.com/policy/economy/correctly-counting-the-cost-shows-australia-s-lockdown-was-a-mistake-20200525-p54w1o>; See also (n 3).

hit because of the steps governments have taken – from locking down the economy to be blunt. Global growth will be down 4 or 5 percent, at least. Unemployment rates will skyrocket. Government debt and deficits will balloon out. The economic numbers will be horrific.[27] And the costs will fall on the young and on future generations.

If that is a rough sketch of the likely economic costs of these lockdowns, the costs in terms of civil liberties have arguably been even greater. Recently retired UK Supreme Court Justice Jonathan Sumption describes the lockdown rules being imposed in Britain as 'the greatest interference with personal liberty in our history'.[28] Take a moment and allow that to sink in – a recently retired top British judge describes his and other governments' lockdown responses as being so heavy-handed that they constitute (it bears repeating) the greatest interference with personal liberty in our history. Indeed Lord Sumption goes so far as to say the lockdown laws are so morally egregious that he admits to having broken them.[29] And then

---

[27] See, for example, the IMF's 'World Economic Outlook Update: A Crisis Like No Other, An Uncertain Recovery', June 2020 <https://www.imf.org/en/Publications/WEO. And two University of Chicago Studies at: https://review.chicagobooth.edu/economics/2020/article/how-much-exactly-have-covid-19-lockdowns-affected-economy> and <https://review.chicagobooth.edu/economics/2020/article/why-us-unemployment-even-worse-official-numbers-say>. And remember that many economists believe that the economic costs of a lockdown increase exponentially with the length of time of the lockdown. The fear of future lockdowns decreases consumption and investment as people become more cautious. And possibly the worst economic scenario is where there are threats of repeated lockdowns. Note, as well, that the impact will likely be very uneven with some sectors badly impacted (airlines, hotels) and others suffering very little (IT, govt employees). And it will hurt the poor worse than the well-off. See Harry Yorke and Russell Lynch, 'UK facing "K-shaped" economic recovery as the gulf between the "haves" and "have nots" widens' *London Telegraph*, 28 July 2020.

[28] See Edward Stringham, 'The Lockdown Is Without Doubt the Greatest Interference with Personal Liberty in our History' *American Institute for Economic Research*, 9 May 2020 <https://www.aier.org/article/lord-sumption-the-lockdown-is-without-doubt-the-greatest-interference-with-personal-liberty-in-our-history/>.

[29] See Thomas Connelly, 'Lord Sumption admits breaking 'absurd' lockdown laws' *Legal Cheek*, 22 July 2020 <https://www.legalcheek.com/2020/07/lord-sumption-admits-breaking-absurd-lockdown-laws/>.

realise that the lockdowns in the State of Victoria are every bit as harsh as in Britain, harsher in fact. And this in the State that brought us the first statutory bill of rights at the State level[30] and where so many law professors and lawyers and Labor State politicians profess a strong commitment to rights-respectingness. Yet, or so it seems to me, at the first sign of a health scare that comes nowhere near Spanish Flu or even 1969 Hong Kong flu levels, many abandon nearly all concern for civil liberties. Indeed, many seem to applaud the police as they enforce – on any view of the virulence of the virus – what amounts to the ridiculous over-regulation of citizens' lives (on pain of big fines).[31]

So why has this happened? For one explanation go back to Nassim Taleb and the quote with which I began this article. You see throughout this crisis in Australia the politicians have carried on with their same pay. So have those in the public service, perhaps at worst putting

---

[30] To lay my cards on the table I am a long-time sceptic of bills of rights, including statutory versions of them. For only a small sample of my writings on this topic see James Allan, 'Bills of Rights and Judicial Power – A Liberal's Quandary?' (1996) 16 *Oxford Journal of Legal Studies* 337; James Allan and Grant Huscroft, 'Rights Internationalism Coming Home to Roost?'(2006) 42 *San Diego Law Review* 1; James Allan, 'Portia, Bassanio or Dick the Butcher? Constraining Judges in the Twenty-First Century' (2006) 17 *King's College Law Journal* 1; James Allan and Michael Kirby, 'A Public Conversation on Constitutionalism and the Judiciary between Professor James Allan and the Honourable Michael Kirby' (2009) 33 *Melbourne University Law Review* 1032; James Allan, 'Why Politics Matters – A Review of Why Law Matters' (2018) 9 *Jurisprudence* 132; James Allan, 'Statutory Bills of Rights: You Read Words In, You Read Words Out, You Take Parliament's Clear Intention and You Shake It All About', in *The Legal Protection of Human Rights: Sceptical Essays* edited by Tom Campbell, K D Ewing and Adam Tomkins (Oxford University Press, 2011) 108; and James Allan, *Democracy in Decline: Steps in the Wrong Direction* (McGill-Queen's University Press, 2014).. On the Victorian statutory bill of rights itself, giving my criticisms, see James Allan, 'The Victorian Charter of Human Rights and Responsibilities: Exegesis and Criticisms' (2006) 30(3) *Melbourne University Law Review* 906.

[31] It is not just the turning of the police into a branch of the nanny state, it is doing this to stop people from playing golf, fishing, going for isolated walks – all of which are less dangerous than being confined in one's small apartment for weeks on end. See, for example, *ABC News*, 'Coronavirus restrictions around gatherings in each state and territory, and who has been fined', 6 April 2020. <https://www.abc.net.au/news/2020-04-06/coronavirus-enforcement-covid-19-gathering-laws-state-territory/12124334>.

off for a few months a foreshadowed pay rise. Ditto the journalists at the public broadcaster, the ABC. Likewise most (not all) of those in the universities and medical establishment. All this while many in the private sector lose their businesses, and those with personal guarantees on them lose their homes too. And they do so because politicians and bureaucrats got to decide what was 'essential' – unlike in Sweden let me repeat. On any understanding other than one couched in terms of sloganeering, or politicking, it is simply a lie to say as the Prime Minister does that 'we are all in this together'.[32] Put differently, the politicians have not had any skin in the game. They have not borne any (or not many) of the costs of their decisions. And the decisions they have made, as Taleb predicted, have been the worse for it.

The same, as I said, is largely true of the national broadcaster, the ABC. With no skin in the game it is far easier to choose the most alarming way to report facts about the virus – so 'deaths' not 'deaths per million'; percentage increase or absolute numbers, whichever is worse; saying new cases going up but ignoring death rate is going down; no reporting of normal yearly flu deaths, or car deaths, or that corona has not cracked the top 50 causes of death, or that for those under 45 corona is less lethal (and I mean everywhere in the world) than getting in a car and going for a Sunday drive.[33] The science writer Tom Chivers notes that 'the media is uniquely bad at telling us about [ ] risks'.[34] The ways in which media misreport risk include: 1) selecting and reporting on the dependent variable, rather

---

[32] Scott Morrison, 'Ministerial Statement', 8 April 8 2020 <https://www.pm.gov.au/media/ministerial-statement-australian-parliament-house-act-080420> (repeated various times thereafter).

[33] See, for example, David C Roberts, 'Putting the Risk of Covid-19 in Perspective', *The New York Times*, 22 May 2020 <https://www.nytimes.com/2020/05/22/well/live/putting-the-risk-of-covid-19-in-perspective.html>. And in Florida, to give this more context, those over 85 years of age have faced a 1 in 300 chance of dying while those under 55 years of age have faced a 1 in 33,000 chance.

[34] Tom Chivers, 'From Covid to Crime: How Media Hype Distorts Risk' *Unherd*, 28 July 2020 <https://unherd.com/2020/07/from-covid-to-crime-how-media-hype-distorts-risk/>.

than the independent variable;[35] 2) giving numbers without context; 3) talking in percentage terms (e.g., 18% more likely to die) that ignores absolute risk (on the same example, your risk has gone up from 0.024% to 0.028%, a relative increase of 18%, true, but one not worth worrying about); 4) cherry-picking numbers; 5) suggesting there is a causal link where there is not, which is to say treating correlation as causation.

No skin in the game readers. So the politicians and public broadcaster can focus on the deaths from the corona virus (here and now) while virtually ignoring deaths caused by the lockdown itself (in the near, medium and more distant future) – say, suicides, cancer and other deaths due to missed screening, all the devastation in the Third World from the ruined World economy,[36] deaths from the less well-funded future health care sector that will come with a ruined economy. This sort of reporting is effectively cost-benefit analysis that looks only at one side of the ledger. To return to Heather MacDonald mentioned above, she put it in these terms:

The politicians' ignorance about the complexity of economic life was stunning, as was their hypocrisy. To a person, every elected official, every public health expert, and every media pundit who lectured Americans about the need to stay in indefinite lockdown had a secure ('essential') job. Not one of them feared his employer would go bankrupt.[37]

Yet that is just a more detailed, more damning way of saying 'no skin in the game'.

---

[35] 'The dependent variable is the thing you're trying to measure; the independent variable is the thing you change.': Ibid. In a drug trial, say, the independent variable might be the drug dose while the dependent variable is whether the patient survives. Chivers argues that for the media 'the dependent variable is whether [something] is interesting' – four new corona deaths, say, or 183 new cases, or a grisly murder: ibid. But these are chosen without any eye on how likely they are to occur or to kill you.

[36] See (n 3) and (n 24). And see Jayanta Bhattacharya and Mikko Packalen, 'Lives vs Lives', *The Spectator*, 16 May 2020, 10.

[37] Heather MacDonald, 'Four Months of Unprecedented Government Malfeasance' (2020) 49(5) *Imprimis* 7.

III FINAL CONSIDERATIONS

I will finish this article by spreading the blame for this disastrous re-action to the corona virus beyond the confines of the political class and much of the media (who, in my view, certainly deserve a hefty share of it). At the end of the day, in a functioning democracy, bad decisions are the ultimate fault of the voters, of citizens. If the vast preponderance of voters allow themselves, meekly or even willingly, to have their civil liberties taken from them due to some distorted fear of death[38] (and opinion polls of democratic leaders who have led these lockdowns certainly appear to give those leaders good polling results in New Zealand, Australia, Canada and Britain),[39] then the fault, in the final analysis, is theirs – the voters'. Likewise, if voters become over-committed to a 'health and safety' worldview, they will deservedly suffer the consequences. What is not a function of desert, of course, is that much of these consequences will fall on the young.[40] Here is how the author Lionel Shriver puts this point:

> We've prioritised the preservation of life in a literal, short-term sense – possibly losing more lives than we've saved,

---

[38] Recent polling from *Kekst CNC* has revealed that on average the British public believes a rather massive 7% of the United Kingdom population has died from co-rona virus. That number is actually 100 times higher than the recorded-death reality. See 'Research Report: COVID-19 Opinion Tracker – Edition 4', 10-15 July 2020 10-15) 6 <https://www.kekstcnc.com/media/2793/kekstcnc_research_covid-19_opin-ion_tracker_wave-4.pdf>.

[39] For example, the recent '1 News Colmar Brunton Poll' (25-29 July 2020) has the NZ Prime Minister's party up over 20 points in the polls with an election only six weeks away <https://www.colmarbrunton.co.nz/what-we-do/1-news-poll/>. In Aus-tralia the August 4th 'Newspoll' has Prime Minister Morrison's Coalition government up 53-47 in two-party preferred terms, and the PM far ahead in terms of preferred PM. <https://www.theaustralian.com.au/nation/newspoll>. In Canada the 'CBC News Canada Tracker Poll' (updated to 30 July 2020) has Prime Minister Trudeau's Liberal Party up 37.5% to 28.6% against the Opposition Conservatives <https://newsinterac-tives.cbc.ca/elections/poll-tracker/canada/>. And lastly, in Britain the 'Politico Poll of Polls' (31 July 2020) has the Prime Minister's Conservative Party up 43% to 37% over the Opposition Labour Party (albeit with some four years left before the next needed election) <https://www.politico.eu/europe-poll-of-polls/united-kingdom/>.

[40] See (n 3).

once the collateral damage totals are in – while giving no priority to everything that makes life worth living, like the experience of bravery that young man leaping a gap in the wall relished last week. Worse, we've thrown the future of a generation under the bus. Safety is fine as far as it goes, but it's not the driver of a vibrant culture. Safety is about stasis. If all you care about is safety, you never leave the house, lockdown or no lockdown. Obsession with safety is the very opposite of ambition.[41]

Life involves risk. In a democracy, the prima facie, default assumption ought to be that each citizen be left to decide how to act for him or herself. Governments can give advice, make suggestions, take special measures for the vulnerable and frail, but the presumption ought to be against any heavy-handed, economy-ruining state edicts. At the very least the onus ought heavily to be on those in favour of such lockdown edicts to make a convincing case that Spanish Flu-like results will otherwise eventuate. Yet the facts were never close to showing that in the case of the Wuhan virus. What we have seen is an epic over-reaction by most governments – not Sweden's and Taiwan's I note again – one that has largely been embraced by many citizens. That fact is certainly depressing, at least I find it so.

---

[41] Lionel Shriver, 'Is Living without Risk really Living at all?', *The Spectator*, 30 May 2020 19.

4

An Analysis of Victoria's
Public Health Emergency Laws: 1865-2020

MORGAN BEGG*

ABSTRACT

In response to the COVID-19 pandemic, the state government of Victoria in Australia has under the Public Health and Well-being Act 2008 declared a prolonged State of Emergency and given to the Chief Health Officer emergency powers to impose a draconian social and economic lockdown. While times of emergency will necessitate greater government action, there has been little scepticism to the assumption that the measures adopted are a normal exercise of government emergency powers, and the claim that the response has been proportionate to the threat has been in many cases been accepted at face value. The purpose of this article is to explore the history of public health emergency laws in Victoria since the Public Health Statute of 1865, to highlight how the modern emergency powers are ahistorical and atypical, while the costs of the policy response indicates that Victoria's modern public health legislation gives too much scope to ministers and the Chief Health Officer to exercise its powers without oversight and accountability. COVID-19 has exposed serious structural flaws in the legislation that require genuine reform and a reassessment of whether historical public health legislation achieved a more desirable balance of protecting public health and protecting the freedoms of Victorians.

* Morgan Begg is a Research Fellow at the Institute of Public Affairs in Melbourne.

I INTRODUCTION

On 24 August 2020 the Premier of Victoria, the Hon Daniel Andrews MLA, announced that the state government would seek to extend the declared State of Emergency beyond the statutory limit of six months.[1] The State of Emergency was initially declared on 16 March 2020 by the Victorian premier to confer on the Chief Health Officer the power to 'do whatever is necessary to contain the spread of the [coronavirus] and reduce the risk to the health of Victorians.' These extraordinary powers have been used to impose the most severe regime of social and economic restrictions restriction in Australian history, while democratic government and the rule of law have been effectively suspended in favour of ministerial declarations announced in press conferences and rule by decree of the unelected Chief Health Officer.

The power to declare a State of Emergency is allowed under section 198 of the *Public Health and Wellbeing Act 2008* (Vic) ('PHWA') and such a declaration 'continues in force for a period not exceeding four weeks specified in the declaration'. The declaration may however be 'extended by another declaration for further periods not exceeding four weeks but the total period that the declaration continues in force cannot exceed six months.' However by August 2020 the state government asserted that it was not willing to allow the State of Emergency to lapse, and announced that it would seek to extend it effectively indefinitely. In a press conference, Premier Andrews said the government was not seeking an "unlimited extension," instead seeking to extend the time limit of State of Emergency's by an additional 12 months. However, the Premier conceded that it could be extended again if for instance a vaccine was not available.[2] While it had been speculated that the state government might use the powers under the

---

[1] Daniel Andrews, 'Keeping the tools we need to continue Coronavirus fight' (Press Release, Premier of Victoria, 24 August 2020) (accessed 27 August 2020) <https://www.premier.vic.gov.au/keeping-tools-we-need-continue-coronavirus-fight>.

[2] Calla Wahlquist, 'Victorian plan to extend state of emergency by 12 months prompts human rights concerns,' *The Guardian*, 24 August 2020 (accessed 3 October 2020) <https://www.theguardian.com/australia-news/2020/aug/24/victorian-plan-to-extend-state-of-emergency-by-12-months-prompts-human-rights-concerns>.

declared State of Disaster to override legislation that is currently in force to negate the six month limit under the PHWA,[3] this step was ultimately not required to be taken. Parliament quickly accepted the *Public Health and Wellbeing Amendment (State of Emergency Extension and Other Matters) Bill 2020* which temporarily amended the PHWA so that the State of Emergency as it related to COVID-19 could stay in force for a total of 12 months. Each of the options explored by the government represented a unique threat to Australia's democratic norms of constitutional parliamentary government that that has not been seen since the constitutional crises in the Commonwealth in 1975 and New South Wales in 1932, both of which resulted in the vice-regal representative dismissing the governments led by Gough Whitlam and Jack Lang, respectively.

While times of emergency will often necessitate a more active government in the affairs of its citizens, there has been relatively little scepticism of the claim that the measures adopted, including business closures, stay at home orders to all Victorian residents, and restrictions on any small, private gatherings, are a proportional response to a public health crisis. The ongoing claim for the need to exercise these powers is reminiscent of the claim made by the Austrian economist, philosopher, and the 1974 recipient of the Nobel Prize in Economics, Friedrich Hayek in 1981. In his seminal work, *Law, Legislation and Liberty*, Hayek noted that nothing is so permanent as the "temporary" measures introduced to respond to an emergency:

> The conditions under which such emergency powers may be granted without creating the danger that they will be retained when the absolute necessity has passed are among the most difficult and important points a constitution must decide on. 'Emergencies' have always been the pretext on which the safeguards of individual liberty have been eroded – and once

---

[3] See for instance Chip Le Grand and Sumeyya Ilanbey, "We can't keep living like this': COVID-19 state of emergency opens political divide,' *The Age*, 23 August 2020 (accessed 27 August 2020) <https://www.theage.com.au/politics/victoria/we-can-t-keep-living-like-this-covid-19-state-of-emergency-opens-political-divide-20200823-p55oi7.html>.

they are suspended it is not difficult for anyone who has assumed such emergency powers to see to it that the emergency will persist.[4]

This article will explore the background and evolution of the public health emergency powers in Victoria. For these purposes, public health emergency laws refer to the provisions in state legislation which purport to give to ministers or senior government officials the power to make declarations to respond to a perceived threat to the general health of the public.

As this article will show, the concept of public health legislation in Victoria has dramatically evolved, at first slowly during the 20th Century and more rapidly during the 21st Century. Also explored is the accelerated legislative change that took place in the 21st century and how the World Health Organization's *International Health Regulations (2005)* influenced that reform, raising questions about how international law is influencing domestic legislative change and the repercussions that has for individual liberties. Finally, the question of whether the illiberal response has been proportional to the threat will be considered.

II THE EVOLUTION OF VICTORIAN PUBLIC HEALTH EMERGENCY LAWS PRE-2000

Victorian health legislation has long made provision for authorities to deal specifically with persons infected with contagious diseases and for disinfecting property. Section 14 of *The Public Health Statute 1865* provides an early example of giving to central board of health the power to issue orders for the 'prevention as far as possible or mitigation of such epidemic endemic or contagious diseases' followed by a discrete list of responsibilities including the power to order the cleansing, purifying, ventilating and disinfecting of buildings, the speedy interment of the dead, and to treat infected persons. Part VI of the Statute is targeted to quarantining vessels, goods and passengers

---

[4] Friedrich A Hayek, *Law, Legislation and Liberty* (University of Chicago Press, 1981) vol 3, ch 17.

arriving from a place declared to be infected with an infectious or contagious disease that may be likely to be transmitted to Victoria, including under s 90 the right of the Governor-in-Council to make orders 'as shall be deemed expedient upon any unforeseen emergency' to 'cut off all communication between any persons infected with any such disease and the rest of Her Majesty's subjects'. A read of the Statute reflected the appropriate role of the state in mitigating a public health crisis, but was appropriately limited to a specific list of activities and responsibilities.

Section 14 was rewritten under section 15 of the *Health Act 1890* (Vic) ('1890 Act') to clarify that the powers were to be exercised in 'any emergency or sudden necessity' as determined by the Board of Public Health. Additionally the powers were defined to extend to do exercise any or all powers and duties vested in local councils by any Act of Parliament relating to the public health. Part VIII of the 1890 Act covers 'Infectious Diseases and Quarantine' which gave the Board of Public Health the powers to order sanitisation of property or detail or control the movement of infected persons, and imposed criminal penalties for failing to disinfect property when required to do so or infecting others or failing to notify the authorities of an infection.

By 1915 declaratory public health emergency powers were beginning to take a more concrete form. Section 5 of the *Health Act 1915 (No. 2)* (Vic) ('1915 Act'), the Board was permitted to, if authorised in writing by the Minister, exercise a range of 'special powers' in any case of emergency or sudden necessity. This included the power to declare land and buildings insanitary and forbid their use, order the destruction of insanitary property, isolate or disinfect persons or things as he saw fit and the inspection and examination of houses and buildings. In 1918 the 1915 Act was amended so that the Board could declare any specified area to be an infected area, from which no person was permitted to leave without the satisfaction of the chairman that the person was not liable to convey a contagious disease. Section 5 of the 1915 Act eventually became section 123 of the *Health Act 1919* (Vic).

The Health Acts were reconsolidated in 1928 and 1958, in both cases providing an extensive list of responsibilities and permitted actions for the government to take to respond to infectious diseases. The last major revision to the public health emergency powers under the consolidated *Health Act 1958* (Vic) ('1958 Act') in the 20ᵗʰ Century took place in 1988 with the passage of the *Health (General Amendment) Act* (Vic). The Part dealing with infectious diseases was substituted and the power of the Governor in Council to proclaim emergency for the purposes of stopping, limiting or preventing the spread of an infectious disease was included in s 123. Notably the last iteration of emergency powers was quite narrow: when an emergency was proclaimed the Chief General Manager was empowered to make an order to prevent people from entering or leaving a proclaimed area, that persons of a specified class may be arrested without warrant and detained in the proclaimed area; that land, buildings or things in the proclaimed area may be seized to be used, disinfected or destroyed to stop the spread of infection, and any other provision required to ensure that the order is carried into effect. Importantly, s 123 provided for some democratic control of the emergency proclamation process. Subsection 123(3)(b) and (4) provided that a proclamation may be revoked by a resolution of either house of the state parliament, and that if the parliament was not sitting at the time the emergency was proclaimed that a petition of 20 members of the Legislative Assembly or 30 members of the whole parliament requesting parliament be summoned must meet as soon as possible.

III THE *INTERNATIONAL HEALTH REGULATIONS* (2005) AND THE *PUBLIC HEALTH AND WELLBEING ACT 2008* (VIC)

In the 21ˢᵗ century international law had begun to take a more prominent role in the domestic policy settings in relation to public health and the control of infectious diseases. In 2001 the federal Minister for Foreign Affairs and Trade gave approval for the Department of Health and Ageing to lead consultations relating to the revisions of the *International Health Regulations 1969* ('IHR69'). In October 2004 an

International Health Regulations (2005) Interdepartmental Committee comprising representatives from various Commonwealth departments was convened to develop Australia's position for negotiating at the World Health Organization's Intergovernmental Working Group on the IHRs in Geneva in November of that same year.[5]

The scope of IHR69, which the Commonwealth was not a signatory to, was limited to obliging member states to develop a reporting framework in relation to the occurrence in their territories of cholera, plague, and yellow fever. As a part of the Intergovernmental Working Group, Australia supported the extension of the scope of the IHRs. At a meeting of the Standing Committee on Treaties ('SCOT') on 25 November 2004 the Commonwealth government advised the States and Territories of its intention to adopt the IHRs.[6]

Australia was present at the 58th meeting of the World Health Assembly (the main constituent body of the World Health Organization) on 23 May 2005, which unanimously adopted Resolution WHA58.3 approving the revised International Health Regulations 2005 ('IHR05'). Although the justification for the revisions were said to be made on the basis that the focus on a small number of listed diseases meant the IHR69 did not address the multiple and varied public health challenges facing the world,[7] the World Health Organization nonetheless took the opportunity to call on states to expand their domestic capacity for dealing with public health issues. As provided under Article 13.1 of the IHR05:

> Each state party shall develop, strengthen and maintain, as soon as possible but no later than five years from the entry into force of these Regulations for that State Party, the capacity to respond promptly and effectively to public health risks and public health emergencies of international concern as set out in Annex 1.

---

[5] *National Interest Analysis* [2006] ATNIA 27, Attachment on Consultation [1]-[2].
[6] Ibid [5].
[7] World Health Organization, "Why were the IHR revised?" <www.who.int/csr/ihr/howtheywork/faq/en/index.html.>.

On 2 March 2006 the Australian Health Ministers' Advisory Council tasked the new Australian Health Protection Committee to analyse the scope of necessary action required by States and Territories to enable Australia to comply with the obligations contained in the IHRs. A National Interest Analysis of the IHR05 notes that necessary changes to current legislation and administrative practices had been discussed during consultations and the AHPC had confirmed that jurisdictions expressed willingness to comply with the IHR05. An Interdepartmental Committee was convened to progress consultations with other Australian Government agencies on specific policy issues to develop a whole-of-government position on the implementation of the treaty including areas such as border protection and quarantine.[8]

In 2008 the Council of Australian Governments ('COAG') adopted the *Model Arrangements for Leadership During Emergencies of National Consequence* to facilitate a coordinated approach to emergency management. The Australian Health Protection Committee was established by the Australian Health Ministers' Advisory Council in 2006, representing each of the states and territories. The responsibilities of AHPC include *inter alia* reviewing and refining the framework for coordination of the health sector in responding to public health events of national significance. Additionally a National Incident Room has been established 'to ensure a nationally consistent and coordinated response to a national health emergency' and national capability audits have been undertaken to identify strengths and gaps in Australia's ability to manage and respond to health disasters.[9]

The consequence of these developments was to add significant pressure on the political system and reform environment to expand the legal measures for the prevention and control of infectious diseases, whereas there has been no corresponding pressure ensuring that legal reform retains individual liberties and ensuring that the role of government in re-

---

[8] National Interest Analysis [2006] ATNIA 27, Attachment on Consultation [6]-[7].

[9] Belinda Bennett, Terry Carney, and Richard Bailey, 'Emergency powers & pandemics: Federalism and the Management of Public Health Emergencies in Australia,' (2012) 31(1) *University of Tasmania Law Review* 37, 47.

sponding to public health threats is appropriately limited. The outcome for this pressure is that, between 1997 and 2016, each State and Territory has revised their respective public health legislation..[10]

In Victoria, the legislative reform effort was led by Daniel Andrews, who was at the time the Health Minister in the Labor Government. Andrews introduced into the Victorian Legislative Assembly the *Public Health and Wellbeing Bill 2008* ('2008 Act'), which represents a significant expansion of the state's ability to control the movement and actions of its citizens in the event of a declared state of emergency. Under s 198 of the 2008 Act, the Minister for Health may, on the advice of the Chief Health Officer and after consultation with the Emergency Management Commissioner, declare a state of emergency 'arising out of any circumstances causing a serious risk to public health.' A declaration made under this provision 'continues in force for a period not exceeding 4 weeks but the total period that the declaration continues in force cannot exceed 6 months.'

Under the terms of the new laws, a state of emergency gives to the Chief Health Officer or authorised officer emergency powers under s 200(1) of the 2008 Act, including the power to

- … detain any person or group of persons in the emergency area for the period reasonably necessary to eliminate or reduce a serious risk for public health;
- restrict the movement of any person or group of persons within the emergency area;
- prevent any person or group of persons from entering the emergency area;
- give any other direction that the authorised officer considers is reasonably necessary to protect public health.

---

[10] *Public Health Act 1997* (Tasmania); *Public Health Act 1997* (Australian Capital Territory); *Emergency Management Act 2004* (South Australia); *Emergency Management Act 2005* (Western Australia); *Public Health Act 2005* (Queensland); *Emergency Management Act 2006* (Tasmania); *Public Health and Wellbeing Act 2008* (Victoria); *Public Health Act 2010* (New South Wales); *Public Health Act 2011* (South Australia); *Public and Environmental Health Act 2011* (Northern Territory); *Public Health Act 2016* (Western Australia).

As can be observed, the powers in the 2008 Act to limit and restrict the movement of people from entering or leaving a public health emergency area was expanded to include the power to restrict the movement of people of within the emergency area. The importance of this should not be understated. Since it was not possible to control the movement of non-infected people within an emergency area under the 1958 Act, it would have been necessary for the government to declare a specific area if it intended to control the movement of people in a meaningful way. But having now the power to control the movement of people within an emergency area, there is no reason not to extend the definition of the emergency area to the entirety of the state. And this is exactly what occurred under the first declared State of Emergency of 16 March 2020.

A further substantive change that prepared the state for its departure from Victoria's democratic norms. Section 123(3) and (4), which gave the parliament the right to overrule the declaration of a state of emergency, was not included in the new public health legislation, and there is nothing comparable in the present law to restrain the government's exercise of its emergency powers.

IV WAS THE EXERCISE OF VICTORIA'S PUBLIC HEALTH EMERGENCY POWERS DISPROPORTIONATE TO THE PUBLIC HEALTH THREAT?

The test of whether a policy response is proportionate or disproportionate will turn on whether a policy response achieves a reasonable balance between its costs and the benefits that are derived from the policy, as well as a consideration of the means that were used to achieve the ends of the policy. In other words, in the context of a pandemic, proportionality should consider the type and rationale of the response, the means used to implement the response, whether the lockdown strategy was successful in Victoria or elsewhere, and a consideration of the economic and social costs of prolonged lockdown and isolation.

There can be no doubt that the Victorian state government has made full use of the powers available s 200 of the 2008 Act. The declaration was made under s 198 on 16 March 2020, initially to implement and enforce the recommendations of the National Cabinet to prohibit large mass gatherings and to enforce quarantine measures for persons returning from overseas travel, both of which were implemented on 18 March 2020.[11] The strategy initially adopted by Australian governments was to flatten the curve, meaning to reduce the spread of the virus so that, rather than allowing the health system to overwhelmed at one, it would have time to prepare capacity to treat the patients who would inevitably be infected with the virus. Over time the strategy evolved to a strategy of suppression and de facto elimination of the virus. In August the Deputy Chief Health Officer said cases must be 'substantially lower' than they were at the time, meaning cases would need to be in the range of 'single digits or even low double digits' before restrictions could be eased.[12] Moving to a strategy that makes the timeline for relaxing restrictions uncertain and indefinite is not consistent with proportionality.

On 25 March 2020 *Prohibited Gatherings Directions* were issued limiting the number of people who could attend weddings, funerals, social sports gatherings. These directions were ultimately replaced with *Stay at Home Directions*. On 30 March 2020 the stay at home directions required every person in Victoria to limit their interactions with others by 'restricting the circumstances in which they may leave the premises where they ordinarily reside... and placing restrictions on gatherings.'[13] By 31 May 2020 the *Stay at Home Directions* were replaced by the *Stay Safe Directions*, loosening restrictions and permitting gatherings of 20 people in homes. However by 22 July Mel-

---

[11] 18 March 2020 – first mass gatherings direction was issued, limiting gatherings of 500 or more in a single outdoor space, and 100 or more in an undivided indoor space. These directions were "firmed" on 21 March.

[12] Lucy Mae Beers, 'Victoria coronavirus cases should be single digits to leave Stage 4, deputy chief medical officer says', *7news.com.au*, 20 August 2020 <https://7news.com.au/lifestyle/health-wellbeing/victoria-coronavirus-cases-need-to-be-single-digits-to-leave-stage-4-c-1253300>.

[13] *Stay at Home Directions*, 30 March 2020.

bourne and Mitchell Shire were placed on tighter restrictions again and a person was only permitted to leave their home if they 'wear a face mask at all times', unless an exception applies.[14] At 6pm on 2 August 2020, Victoria entered a State of Disaster and moved to the harshest round of restrictions to date, known as "Stage 4" lockdown which would go into force on 5 August 2020. Stage 4 includes imposing a curfew from 8pm to 5am, subject to exceptions for work, medical care and caregiving, limiting exercise to a maximum of one hour per day and no more than five kilometres from home; no weddings in Melbourne; and closure of early childhood services. The following day the Premier announced new restrictions for businesses and workers, listing which businesses were permitted to operate and which were to cease operations, and those which were required to operate under significantly different conditions.[15]

During the course of the pandemic, the State of Emergency has been extended on eight occasions and the emergency powers have been used to limit the movement of people in Victoria for extended periods of time. For instance, at one point in August, over five months after the initial declaration of a State of Emergency, people in Melbourne were directed to:

- observe a curfew which prohibited Melburnians from being in the public between 5am and 8pm;[16]
- stay at home subject to strictly limited exceptions for essential shopping and exercise for one hour each day within five kilometres of the persons home;[17]
- perform their work at home unless it was permitted to be done outside the home and the person is permitted to leave home for work;[18]

---

[14] *Restricted Activity Directions (Restricted Areas) (No 3)* and *Stay at Home Directions (Restricted Areas) (No 4)* and *Stay Safe Directions (No 7)*, 22 July 2020.

[15] Premier of Victoria, Statement from the Premier, media release, 3 August 2020.

[16] *Stay at Home (Restricted Areas) (No 13)*, 20 August 2020, cl 5 (1AF).

[17] *Stay at Home (Restricted Areas) (No 13)*, 20 August 2020, cls 5 (1AB), (1AD), (1AG), 6, 9.

[18] *Stay at Home (Restricted Areas) (No 13)*, 20 August 2020, cls 5(1), (1AF), 7, 8; *Restricted Activity (Restricted Areas) (No 8)*, 16 August 2020; *Workplace Directions*

- wear a face covering when leaving the house;[19]
- not open certain businesses to the public and observe strict limitations on other economic and social activities;[20]
- not visit hospitals and aged and other care facilities;[21]
- be detained when arriveing in Australia from overseas in a hotel for 14 days;[22] and
- limit the movement of any person diagnosed with COVID-19 and their close contacts.[23]

At the same time, non-metropolitan Victoria was under stage 3 restrictions which meant that persons in those areas were required to stay at home subject to similar restrictions explained above, wear a face covering when they left their home for a permitted reason, limit gatherings and restrict certain activities and businesses from being open to the public.[24]

Many of the isolation and social distancing rules have gone beyond what should be required under social distancing guidelines.[25] The Commonwealth Department of Health explain for instance that keeping 1.5 metres away from other people and practising good hygiene are essential to the social distancing which is necessary to meet the public health regulatory objectives. However many of the rules imposed by the Victorian government, such as prohibitions on outdoor recreational activities and mandatory face covering rules, have

---

(No 3), 16 August 2020; *Workplace (Additional Industry Obligations) Directions (No 4)*, 16 August 2020; *Permitted Worker and Childcare Permit Scheme Directions (No 4)*, 16 August 2020.

[19] *Stay at Home (Restricted Areas) (No 13)*, 20 August 2020, cl 5(6).

[20] *Restricted Activity (Restricted Areas) (No 8)*, 16 August 2020.

[21] *Hospital Visitor Directions (No 10)*, 16 August 2020; *Care Facilities Direction (No 9)*, 16 August 2020.

[22] *Detention – Detention Notice (No 7)*, 19 July 2020.

[23] *Diagnosed Persons and Close Contacts Directions (No 10)*, 16 August 2020.

[24] *Stay at Home Direction (Non-Melbourne) (No 3)*, 16 August 2020; *Restricted Activity Directions (Non-Melbourne) (No 3)*, 16 August 2020.

[25] Morgan Begg, *States of Emergency: An Analysis of COVID-19 Petty Restrictions* (Research Paper, Institute of Public Affairs, April 2020).

failed to take into account whether activities can be undertaken while maintaining 1.5 metre distancing. The night-time curfew is especially representative of the failure to be proportionate.

Meanwhile the provisions in the 1958 Act which gave the parliament some control over the state of emergency declaration but which were not carried over to the 2008 Act, has had grave consequences for the role of parliament during the COVID-19 pandemic. Aside from a brief resumption in June, the Victorian parliament has been mostly absent between 20 March and 30 August. When the parliament was to sit finally in August, the Legislative Assembly – the chamber which is based on the United Kingdom's House of Commons and is ostensibly meant to be the people's house and the chamber in which the government of the day is formed – was delayed again from sitting on the advice of the Chief Medical Officer. Although the Legislative Council did briefly sit on 5 August 2020 but the Minister for Health refused to answer any questions for her role in the pandemic response.

The Victorian restrictions were deeper and enforced longer than in any other state. In just over 10 years since 2008 Act commenced,[26] the emergency powers have arguably been used to their fullest extent with minimal oversight and accountability during the exercise of those powers. If the exercise of these powers has been disproportionate or if the damage exceeds the benefits then this is a challenge not to the exercise of the powers, but to the scope of the powers that has allowed them to be exercised in this way.

It will be some time before there is enough research to make conclusions about relative costs of lockdowns and social distancing restrictions, and whether the costs paid contributed meaningfully to managing the spread of COVID-19. There is already some conflicting evidence being published on the efficacy of the lockdown strategy. An analysis of Sweden in July 2020 produced a counterfactual to estimate that if the Scandinavian country had imposed a lockdown COVID-19 infections and deaths would have reduced by one third and one half

---

[26] *Public Health and Wellbeing Act 2008* (Vic) s 2(2) provided that the Act came fully into force by 1 January 2010.

respectively.[27] In contrast early research is indicating that there is no statistically meaningful relationship between coercive measures and lower COVID-19 related mortality. In one exploratory analysis of data on COVID-19 related deaths across 50 countries, the researchers found no association between the degree of lockdown and death rates.[28] On 6 August 2020, Christian Bjornskov, a professor of economics at Aarhus University in Denmark and the Research Institute of Industrial Economics in Stockholm published an early draft of a research paper which conducted a cross-country comparison asking whether lockdowns have been successful. Approaching the question using a standard approach and standard econometric tools used in economics and political science instead of epidemiological modelling or single-case studies, Bjornskov compared weekly general mortality rates in the first half of the year in 2017, 2018, 2019 and 2020 in 24 European countries that took markedly different policy measures against the virus at different points in time. 'Estimating the effects of these policy measures as captured by the Blavatnik Centre's Covid 19 policy indices and taking the endogeneity of policy responses into account, the results suggest that stricter lockdown policies have not been associated with lower mortality.'[29] On 27 July 2020 Jeffrey A Tucker, the editorial director from the American Institute for Economic Research, compiled statistics from 54 countries, measuring COVID-19 death per million around the world against the Oxford University's government stringency index. As Tucker posited at the time:

> If lockdowns achieved anything you could expect there to be some predictive power here. The more you lock down, the more lives you save. The lockdown countries could at least claim to have bolstered the lives of their citizens. What you

---

[27] Benjamin Born, Alexander Dietrich and Gernot Müller, 'The Lockdown Effect: A Counterfactual for Sweden,' (CEPR Discussion Paper No 14744, Centre for Economic Policy Research, May 2020).

[28] Rabail Chaudhry et al, 'A Country Level Analysis Measuring the Impact of Government Actions, Country Preparedness and Socioeconomic Factors on COVID-19 Mortality and Related Health Outcomes' *EClinicalMedicine*, 21 July 2020.

[29] Christian Bjornskov, 'Did Lockdown Work? An Economist's Cross-Country Comparison', 6 August 2020 <https://papers.ssrn.com/sol3/papers.cfm?abstract_id=3665588>.

see instead is: nothing. There is no relationship. There is the virus. There are lockdowns. The two operate as seemingly independent variables.[30]

The efficacy of the lockdown measures will become clearer over time, but what is clear now are the direct economic and social costs of locking down the economy. On 3 August 2020 the Institute of Public Affairs released calculations that the cost of Stage 4 restrictions would reduce the Gross State Product of Victoria by $3.17 billion per week.[31] This would result in an additional 300,000 jobs being lost in the state, in addition to the 168,600 that had already been lost to that date.[32] According to the Australian Bureau of Statistics, between 14 March 2020 (the week Australia recorded its 100th confirmed COVID-19 case) and the week ending 8 August 2020, payroll jobs in businesses that are Single Touch Payroll enabled had decreased by 4.9 per cent and total wages decreased by 6.2 per cent. For Victoria the change in payroll jobs was -7.8 per cent and the change in total wages was -6.7 per cent.[33]

The economic costs are only one direct cost of the lockdown. Another cost is the severe social costs and harm to mental health caused by prolonged isolation, reduced community connectedness, and extended joblessness. A report by the University of Sydney's Brain and Mind Centre claimed that in a best-case scenario of 11.7 per cent unemployment, 19 per cent youth unemployment, and a 10 per cent reduction in community connectedness, Australia is expected to see mental health-related emergency department presentations, self-harm

---

[30] Jeffrey A Tucker, 'The Bloodless Political Class and its Lack of Empathy,' *American Institute for Economic Research*, 27 July 2020 <https://www.aier.org/article/the-bloodless-political-class-and-its-lack-of-empathy/>.

[31] John Roskam, 'Stage 4 a $3.17 Billion hit per week to the Victorian economy' (Media Release, Institute of Public Affairs, 3 August 2020).

[32] Ibid. The calculation of 300,000 job lost is based on the peak 9 per cent drop to payroll jobs experienced during Stage 3 lockdown, as measured by the Australian Bureau of Statistics. Presuming Stage 4 has a similar impact, then at least 300,000 jobs will be lost.

[33] Australian Bureau of Statistics, *Weekly Payroll Jobs and Wages in Australia, Week ending 8 August 2020* (Catalogue No 6160.0.55.001, 25 August 2020).

hospitalisations, and suicide deaths to each increase by between 11.4 and 13.7 per cent.[34] In Victoria in August the Minister for Mental Health announced that in the six weeks prior, there had already been a 33 per cent increase in people under the age of 17 presenting at emergency departments for self-harming, and a 9.5 per cent increase across all age groups when compared to the same time period in 2019.[35] This is a difficult and sensitive topic and while it cannot simply be converted into an economic measure in the way that unemployment rates or the gross state product is, but it must be assessed as an important and direct cost of the lockdown. However, the ministers comments had dropped off the news cycle nearly as soon as it appeared, drowned out by rolling coverage of infection numbers – the overwhelming majority of which will not result in hospitalisation, stays in ICU, or deaths.

In Victoria the evidence is building that the lockdown is objectively a disproportionate response to the COVID-19 pandemic. Strict lockdowns have not been proven to be especially effective in managing the spread of the virus, the specific policies have gone beyond what would be required to ensure 1.5 metre social distancing; parliamentary processes of accountability, scrutiny and review have been set aside for several months; and there has been a failure to consider the steep costs of lockdown. A failure to even consider the costs of a policy is an indicator that the policy is disproportionate.

The policy response in Victoria has been disproportionate to the threat, but the question of whether the law has been exercised in a proportionate way should not ignore the question of whether the law gives too much scope to the government to misuse it in this way. Emergency powers in Victoria are not new but the powers under the 2008 Act are a modern expression of emergency powers which allow for uniquely draconian rule making.

---

[34] Jo-An Atkinson et al, *Road to Recovery: Restoring Australia's Mental Wealth: Uncovering the Road to Recovery of our Mental Health and Wellbeing using Systems Modelling and Simulation* (The University of Sydney, Brain and Mind Centre, 27 July 2020).
[35] See Sumeyya Ilanbey, '"Your life is important": $60 million coronavirus support package for mental health,' *The Age*, 9 August 2020.

It is in this context that Victoria has been likened to a 'police state'[36] and which by September become even an more apt description. On 17 September 2020 the government introduced into the Legislative Assembly the COVID-19 Omnibus (Emergency Measures) and Other Acts Amendment Bill 2020, which passed the same chamber a day later. The purpose of the bill is to amend the PHWA give the government the power to appoint any person the Secretary of the Department of Health and Human Services deems to have the right 'attributes' to exercise emergency powers and to effectively detain any person indefinitely based on subjective criteria. It has been widely criticised and was described by the Institute of Public Affairs as the 'most significant violation of human rights in Australian history.'[37] As of writing the Legislative Council has not yet voted on the proposed legislation, but a central part of the debate must be not whether an expansion of the public health legislation can be justified, but what the limits of public health laws more generally should be.

An honest appraisal of the 2020 COVID-19 pandemic will show that the PHWA has had a deleterious impact on Victorian society, democracy, and economy. Currently the law, by giving to the Chief Health Officer and government ministers the power to rule by decree for an extended period of time, the legislation has failed to balance the legal rights and individual freedoms of Victorians in the process. The provisions under ss 198 and 200 of the PHWA are simply expressed too broadly. The specific power to control the movement of people within an emergency and the open ended power to declare any direction to respond to a public health threat has empowered the Chief Health Officer to only manage the public health threat but imposes no obligation to consider the costs of the directions.

These are serious structural flaws in the legislation that are in need of genuine reform and a reassessment of whether the emergency powers in historical legislation achieved a more desirable balance between the protection of public health and maintaining Victoria's freedoms.

---

[36] See for instance, John Roskam, 'Beautiful one day, police state the next,' *The Australian Financial Review*, 3 April 2020.

[37] Morgan Begg, 'Letter to Members of the Legislative Council of Victoria,' (Institute of Public Affairs, forthcoming, 2020).

5

Only the Australian People
Can Clean up the Mess:
Call for People's Constitutional Review

DAVID FLINT AM*

ABSTRACT

The Australian government's response to COVID-19 virus should involve the exercise of sound and mature judgement, based on the best available evidence and ensuring there would be most minimal restrictions on the exercise by the people of their fundamental rights. Sadly, that response has been well below standard and indeed, it has been a disaster. This has been at the enormous cost, not only financial and economic, to millions of Australians and those yet to be born. Most of this has been unnecessary and it is clear then that there is need for an urgent and in-depth review by the people of the constitutional arrangements of Australia. This could best be achieved under a new version of the path along which we successfully come together as a nation, that is, a Second Corowa Plan.

I FIRST CONSIDERATIONS

Australia, the first country in the world where the people voted on the approval of their constitution, is one of the world's oldest continuing democracies – democracies which have long functioned not only in

---

* Emeritus Professor of Law, former Chairman of the Australian Broadcasting Authority, and Associate Member Australian Competition and Consumer Commission from 1997 to 2004. He is also the National Convenor of Australians for Constitutional Monarchy.

the good times, but also under the stress of world war and economic depression.

Accordingly, it was reasonable to expect that government response to the COVID-19 virus would involve the exercise of sound and mature judgement, calmly based on the best available evidence and especially guided by world's best practice, but at the same time ensuring there are the most minimal restrictions on the exercise by the people of their fundamental rights.

Sadly, that response has been well below standard and indeed, it has been a disaster. It is of great importance that this be examined so that Australians can ensure that this failure is never repeated.

It is normal and proper in any constitutional state for governments to exercise exceptional powers during an emergency such as war, natural disasters and of course, plagues, or as they are called today, pandemics. At the same time, it is important that there always be rigorous controls and close surveillance and scrutiny concerning any exercise by government of emergency powers. This should be by the legislature, executive councils, the courts and a free and responsible media. Most of these controls were absent during the long government response to COVID-19.

Two self-evident considerations are crucial in a democracy. First, that the emergency powers and their exercise in curtailing rights, including those under the common law, be no greater than is absolutely necessary. Second, that they be withdrawn as soon as the emergency is over.

As is the nature of a pandemic, COVID-19 came without notice but surely not as a surprise. In this instance, the lack of notice was exacerbated by the extraordinarily deceitful behaviour of the government of the People's Republic of China ('PRC'), where the virus emerged. As is well known, the PRC is a one-party state under the control of the Chinese Communist Party (CCP). The CCP regime failed to inform the world immediately and fully about the virus, while imposing an internal lockdown and allowing its citizens and residents to travel to other countries.

Nevertheless, pandemics are neither rare nor unusual. Each has its own characteristics in relation to contagion, vulnerability and the damaging effects they can impose on victims. This means that government response must always be tailored to the particular virus; there is no 'one size fits all solution'.

Pandemics will continue to emerge and to spread. Some say they will increase because of massive increases in urbanisation, international travel and chicken and pig consumption as well as those sickening 'wet markets'. This is of course conjecture, but this should act as a warning.

Accordingly, it is important that countries plan to deal with them properly, allowing for sufficient flexibility having regard to the nature of the virus and with minimal restrictions on the exercise of fundamental rights.

Given that pandemics are not at all unusual, it is curious that Australian governments were not better prepared . Why then was the one political leader most acclaimed for his work in this area not invited to join the National Cabinet?[1]

In 2009, the Swine Flu pandemic resulted in 37,537 confirmed cases in Australia and, according to some estimates, around 1600 deaths. Flu pandemics come regularly, varying in intensity. Thus in 2019, there were 312,978 cases of influenza with 902 deaths. Neither of these pandemics produced a reaction by government similar to COVID-19. In this Australia was not alone, but there were notable exceptions.

At the time of writing, there have been 24,812 cases relating to COVID-19 in Australia, with 502 deaths. 362 over these were aged over 70, 286 over 80, and 255 or 68% in aged care. 289 or 77% of the deaths were in Victoria.[2]

Governments have not explained adequately why COVID -19 has

---

[1] David Flint, 'Missing from the National Cabinet – Tony Abbott', *Spectator Australia*, 8 May 2020 <https://www.spectator.com.au/2020/05/missing-from-the-national-cabinet-tony-abbott/>.

[2] The time of writing is 24 August 2020.

been treated differently from others. Is it that the American mainstream media used this in a blatant political campaign against the President with the Australian mainstream media following them, thus raising greater interest here?[3]

It is crucial to democracy that the rights of the people should only be limited as is absolutely necessary in any emergency, including a pandemic. It will be argued here that the Australian response has gone far too far in restricting fundamental human rights.

In failing to properly exercise their emergency powers, we have seen Australian governments panicking, abdicating the judgement for which they are elected to bureaucratic experts and questionable computer modelling, neutralising or 'duchessing' the media and behaving capriciously, applying double standards.[4]

The most glaring example of the latter was the complete exclusion of the non-essential public sector, including themselves, from the economic sacrifice they so easily imposed on others. Indeed if the politicians' frequently mantra "We're all in this together" means anything, the non-essential public sector would have been locked down first and public sector wages, including politicians', would be capped near average earnings, $80,000 pa.

There was little apparent concern demonstrated about the increasing economic burden the politicians were imposing on the nation, and thus future generations. Nor was there sufficient concern about the burden imposed on business, and especially small business and those employed in this area. Indeed, there seemed to be an assumption that a business can be easily turned off and on as if it were an electric light switch.

Notwithstanding major restrictions on fundamental rights, government failed significantly in maintaining adequate entry controls, on adequate quarantine arrangements and in protecting the vulnerable

---

[3] David Flint, 'Anyone Remember the Obama Pandemic?', *Spectator Australia*, 12 March 2020. <https://www.spectator.com.au/2020/03/anyone-remember-the-obama-pandemic/>.

[4] In colonial times, when Australian politicians were well received in official circles in London, they were said to have been 'duchessed' and more susceptible to British influence.

especially those in aged care, as well as those who were otherwise ill but whose medical attention was removed. This was done either by the completely superfluous ban on elective surgery and the way both medical professionals and patients were frightened away from medical attention.

The most significant and fundamental lapse by government in Australia was to ignore world's best practice, that of Taiwan, which was available at the time when relevant decisions were being taken.[5] It is difficult to understand how this occurred. All ministers have access to public service advice, much of which is increasingly outsourced to consultants. All ministers and especially the prime minister and premiers have for many years enjoyed the support of large corps of politically appointed but taxpayer funded advisors, too many of whom are apprentices whose ambition is a political career. (Such advisory corps were not thought necessary in either World War.)

In addition, all ministers have access to consultants, often early retired politicians and lobbyists most of whom are associated with and are influential within their party, sometimes to controlling candidate pre-selections and who are often former politicians. It is surprising that from this vast network, government ministers were not aware of Taiwan's experience and achievements which were not as apparent as they were to this author not only before governments not only decided on the lockdown, but when they were determining entry standards including the quarantine.

The disastrous ignoring of world's best practice has been hidden by playing down, with considerable mainstream media support, our considerable natural advantage in being a remote island nation. As such, it is far easier to control entry which of course is crucial — at the time of writing, Fiji has had 28 cases and one death.

---

[5] David Flint, 'The Ruby Princess Fiasco: Our Leaders' Latest Great Failure Not Only Over Coronavirus, but China as a Whole', *Spectator Australia*, 2 April 2020 <https://www.spectator.com.au/2020/04/the-ruby-princess-fiasco-our-leaders-latest-great-failure-not-only-over-coronavirus-but-china-as-a-whole/>.

Taiwan has achieved her record, one which Australia, with sound leadership, could have at least equalled or with our isolation as an island nation, surpassed. And this, without the economy being seriously damaged, lives ruined, jobs lost, a massive debt imposed and with a once free people too long effectively under house arrest. In addition, government has adopted the hallmark of a dictatorial government like that of the USSR and the German Democratic Republic, the need for rarely granted official approval to leave the country.

So why did Australia's governments ignore the lessons offered by Taiwan, a democracy which had learned from previous pandemic coming from the People's Republic of Taiwan?

From 2008 Taiwan was invited each year to attend the WHO as an observer under the name "Chinese Taipei". This ended in 2016 when the Democratic Progressive Party candidate won the presidential election. Beijing then discouraged contact with the Taiwan government. Indeed, the CCP regime has long made it clear to other governments, including Australia's. that Taiwan is to be treated a pariah. In any event, Australian governments made a serious error in ignoring the Taiwanese model which is clearly world's best practice. A question which must be asked is whether Taiwan was ignored because of the influence of the PRC within political circles.

Our political class have for long been too beholden to the CCP government, some influenced by the prospect of the fortunes they could make from this – and not only in curiously early retirement. Obsessed with a utopian version of free trade, they too readily handed over not only manufacturing to Communist China but also premium and strategic assets, including our farms.

Before briefly examining particular aspects of the government response to COVID-19, the response to any pandemic should be fourfold:

- to control its entry including any requisite quarantine;
- as far as reasonably possible to slow its spread;
- to protect the vulnerable and where appropriate;
- to recover reparations for any damage suffered by Australia through a significant breach of international obligations.

II ENTRY

Given the fact that Australia is one of the world's most remote island nations, it is easier to limit the entry of disease than for most other nations. For some years, governments have not been as insistent as in the past on the level of control and quarantine both in relation to persons and goods.

Australia was not, as has been claimed, the pioneer in imposing a travel ban on non-residents from China.[6] As late as 31 January, 2020 at a press conference with Minister Hunt, Chief Medical Officer Murphy spoke against a travel ban which he said was opposed by the WHO; hardly a surprise. If the situation worsened, he said somewhat naively, Beijing would 'stop exits from China, which is a more effective way (than a ban)'.

But later that day, against advice and with the outrage of the Democrats and mainstream media, President Donald Trump announced a travel ban on foreign nationals who were in China in the preceding 14 days. The next day, Australia turned tail and imposed its own ban.

Nevertheless, entry and quarantine controls were shown to be seriously inadequate during the first crucial two months and not only in relation to the Ruby Princess.[7] Nor were the most vulnerable properly protected, as has been sadly seen in NSW and especially Victoria.

It is clear that had the leaders properly controlled entry, we would not have the serious problem we have today. Our political leaders have significantly failed to protect Australians from COVID-19. Sitting in the National Cabinet (yet another name change for the time-honoured meetings between the Prime Minister and Premiers), they ignored widespread public concern at the absence of proper entry controls on the wharves and airports.

Had our leaders acted with elementary common sense and prudence as had the Taiwanese government, there would have been very

---

[6] David Flint, 'The Virus Is in the Political Ranks', *Spectator Australia*, 15 August 2020 <https://www.spectator.com.au/2020/08/the-virus-is-in-the-political-ranks/>.
[7] Flint, above n 5.

few cases of returning travellers innocently going home and finding out that later they in fact had the virus, having unintentionally infected many others and spread the disease. There would have been no need to impose such damage the private sector and the many workers there.

The *Ruby Princess* cruise liner debacle is but the best known; there have been many similar arrivals involving thousands of travellers, including the author of this chapter. This loophole continued until the politicians belatedly announced tighter entry controls on 26 March 2020. But, according to one source in the Daily Telegraph on the very day of the announcement a United Airlines from New York flew into Sydney 'with zero testing in place', while on the following evening 33 doctors were left to self-quarantine.

III LOCKDOWN

The decision to put Australia into serious lockdown followed the politicians' condemnation of the young for being Australian and going to the beach on a warm day in Sydney's typical Indian Summer.[8] If the virus had not been around, the weather would probably have been used as proof of global warming. Instead, the pandemic was cynically misused to justify the massive shut-down of private-sector Australia, leaving the vast non-essential parts of the taxpayer-funded public sector unscathed.

The politicians seriously blundered. Those young Australians were innocent of the alleged mass breach of the social distancing protocols. The press photographs were taken at ground level. With the well-known phenomenon in photography known as *perspective illusion*, this created the impression that people who were standing and walking were closer to one another than they actually were.

After all, this is in a city with well over one hundred beaches. And this was Bondi Beach, not a beach in China or indeed, the French Riviera in August. Australians just do not cram together, especially on a large beach like Bondi. That didn't stop the political class, includ-

---

[8] Ibid.

ing former politician Amanda Vanstone, from dismissing these young Australians to be 'selfish idiots'.[9]

This event seemed to trigger action which closed much of the nation's small business, including those in regions wholly unaffected by the virus, destroying many of them leading to serious unemployment and bringing on at least a recession.

A foreign dictatorship had given the nation the virus; our politicians used this to take exorbitant control over our lives without admitting that most of the problem comes from their gross negligence. Some were even talking about this going on for six months.

Realising the large unemployment they had created, the federal government announced a hastily concocted 'JobKeeper' allowance which was later alleged to encourage recipients not to take up work when it became available. The lock-down was completely unnecessary, yet another result of abdicating governing to computer modelling.

Unlike Donald Trump's daily White House briefing, Australian modelling was kept a closely-guarded state secret, tolerated by a media too easily dazzled by the exercise of raw power.[10] Based on the principle, *purgamentum init exit purgamentum* – garbage in garbage out – experts agree, modelling is hardly reliable. Computer modelling has been widely relied on to justify the responses adopted concerning global warming (now referred to as climate change).

In any event, the most celebrated modeller at Imperial College London, Professor Neil Ferguson was soon shown to be breaching the very distancing rules he had advised, through secret assignations

---

[9] Amanda Vanstone, 'People on Bondi Beach Win the Selfish and Stupid Award', *The Sydney Morning Herald*, 22 March 2020 <https://www.smh.com.au/national/people-on-bondi-beach-win-the-selfish-and-stupid-award-20200321-p54chx.html>.

[10] David Flint, 'Recover Reparations, Restore Independence', *Spectator Australia*, 11 April 2020. <https://www.spectator.com.au/2020/04/recover-reparations-restore-independence/>. The modelling contained a monumental error which should have been noticed: David Flint, 'National Cabinet – Our Very Own Junta. Lockdowns are Based on a Monumental Error', *Spectator Australia,* 19 September 2020 <https://spectator.com.au/2020/09/national-cabinet-our-very-own-junta/>.

with his mistress.[11] When this was exposed, he resigned as a principal government adviser, but not before the British government had acted on his warning of half a million deaths from the Wuhan virus as did the US on his warning of 2.2 million deaths there.

Professor Ferguson was probably the direct or indirect source for the similar warning of 150,000 Australian deaths, a warning which no doubt put the National Cabinet into a state of panic. What is surprising about what was referred to as the 'Professor Lockdown' affair is not so much the fact that most politicians and journalists do not seem to realise that computer modelling, while a useful tool, must always be wrong.

What is truly surprising is that anyone at the time in government took note of previous modelling from the same source which could hardly have encouraged confidence. These include 150,000 UK deaths from mad cow disease (there were 177); 200 million world-wide deaths from the bird flu pandemic (281 died) and 6,500 UK deaths from the swine flu pandemic (457 died).

Surely that record would have encouraged some reservations about his modelling concerning COVID-19. But curiously, there seemed to be no one among either the politicians, their anointed experts or, as far as we know, their vast armies of advisers who counselled against abdicating decision making to modelling.

As to the lockdown, a number of highly respected international scientists have published research concluding that lockdowns are pointless.[12] Unfortunately, the resort to such unnecessary and costly lockdowns is being greatly helped by the mainstream media's shock reporting of each and every new virus case, without balancing this by the far more important constantly decreasing death rate.

---

[11] David Flint, 'Professor Lockdown and the Hypocrisy of the Elites', *Spectator Australia*, 18 May 2020 <https://www.spectator.com.au/2020/05/professor-lockdown-and-the-hypocrisy-of-the-elites/>.

[12] Stephanie M Lee, 'An Elite Group Of Scientists Tried To Warn Trump Against Lockdowns In March', *BuzzFeed.News*, 24 July 2020 <https://www.buzzfeednews.com/article/stephaniemlee/ioannidis-trump-white-house-coronavirus-lockdowns>.

The purpose of the lockdown when first announced was not to wipe out the virus. It was to 'flatten the curve', that is, make the hospitalisation of the predicted 150,000 cases more manageable.

The sheer panic and incompetence with which the National Cabinet had imposed the mainly small business lockdown, while exempting themselves and the non-essential bureaucracy, has once more been demonstrated. This was in the recent news that they made the dole so attractive that many prefer to stay on it rather than take available jobs.

In addition, as the backpackers depart, they are not being replaced for the collection of the harvest by the long-term, able-bodied unemployed who, as a class, were undeservingly rewarded by a substantial increase in their dole.

At least we still have some backpackers here, thanks to the Senate blocking the government's plan to impose a flat 30 per cent tax on them. This would have ensured that most would have gone to other countries.

In the meantime, the politicians subtly and without explanation changed the raison d'être for the lockdown from 'flattening the curve', that is, spreading the incidence of infection over time. This was to allow the hospitals to cope with the massive number of seriously ill predicted by the modelling the politicians had accepted, so large they banned elective surgery.

'Flattening the curve' has been inexplicably turned into 'eradication', with the politicians hoping nobody noticed, especially the mainstream media who have been distracted into making panic and irrelevant announcements about someone visiting a small restaurant or similar outlet and subsequently testing positive.[13] They seem little concerned that this comes at enormous cost to that small restaurant, perhaps sufficient to destroy them.

---

[13] David Flint, 'The virus is in the political ranks', *Spectator Australia*, 15 August 2020 <https://www.spectator.com.au/2020/08/the-virus-is-in-the-political-ranks/>.

IV THE VULNERABLE

At the time of writing, there are 39 COVID-19 cases in intensive care in Australia, 32 of whom are in Victoria.

It has been in protecting the vulnerable that Australia's response has been particularly poor, especially in New South Wales and Victoria. In addition, because the Federal government has assumed responsibility with respect to aged care, they must share responsibility for some significant failures there. Indeed, the greater part of the deaths in Australia have been in aged care.

A significant outbreak in Victoria was traced to the state government's decision to leave quarantining to a security firm with alleged political connections.[14] This was notwithstanding that a request had been put in for Army assistance which was then inexplicably revoked. The Victorian government, with Federal approval then put the state into an extreme and authoritarian second lockdown.

V SCRUTINY

The response by State and Federal Governments has been subject to little parliamentary scrutiny. Legislatures have not been sitting for an exaggerated fear of infection. In any event, some Acts of Parliament deny the ability of any parliamentary chamber to disallow subordinate legislation. In similar emergencies, subordinate legislation should only be made in the executive council where the viceroy could and should insist on advice on the question of power to act.

Except challenges to border closures, litigation is not at all common and too expensive for most of those damaged. The mainstream media have been over-supportive of government, too often doing little more than rearranging press releases and using the language of government, especially in repeating and enforcing calls for obedience under the cover of calls do the "right thing".

---

[14] Remy Varga, 'Coronavirus Australia: Three sources to blame for 99pc of cases in Victoria's second wave', *The Australian*, 18 August 2020 <https://www.theaustralian. com.au/nation/coronavirus-australia-hotel-quarantine-command-unclear-inquiry-hears/news-story/569837e46a4590b759ee369f27aa1517>.

The Andrews government in Victoria could themselves do the "right thing", arrange an early election to seek a democratic endorsement for their draconian policies for the second lockdown. It is unacceptable that the only way they can be forced to an election is a vote of no confidence in the Legislative Assembly, unlikely without an ALP split and last seen in 1955. Until 2003, the Legislative Council could have forced an election. But having seen how effective this was with Whitlam, the major parties colluded to get rid of the power to reject supply.

While subordinate legislation and decisions under the relevant legislation,[15] may well, when more facts are available, constitute misfeasance in public office, the Governor is most unlikely to do what Sir Philip Game did in 1932 to Premier Jack Lang – dismiss the Premier and obtain advice for an early election.

This demonstrates an urgent need to empower the people with the right to recall politicians. Recall elections are usually triggered by a petition signed by between 10 and 40 per cent of electors. From opposition, NSW Premier Barry O'Farrell campaigned on appointing an expert panel to advise on such elections. But a subsequent favourable report was shelved, the attorney-general candidly explaining circumstances had changed – the LNP was now in government.

After well over a century, there needs to be a serious review of our constitutions, state and federal, to restore good government across our land.

VI 'UNDER THE COVER OF COVID'

In the meantime, we are seeing the signs of emerging authoritarianism and significant damage to fundamental rights. In giving legal effect to decisions of the National Cabinet, ministers have resorted to subordinate legislation which, as we indicate above, has been subject to little scrutiny.

Take for example the decision to refuse to allow most citizens and permanent residents to leave their country, once the hallmark of totali-

---

[15] *Public Health and Wellbeing Act 2008* (Vic).

tarian regimes. The Minister exercised a power under section 477 of the *Biosecurity Act 2015* (Cth), to prevent or control the spread of the virus to another country.

The subordinate legislation he made on 25 March 2020, a Determination, provides that 'an Australian citizen or permanent resident must not leave Australian territory as a passenger on an outgoing aircraft or vessel' unless he or she has an exemption for 'exceptional reasons'.[16] There are six categories listed on the official website, mainly those for official and business purposes. The only way the rank-and-file could get an exemption is by satisfying a bureaucrat that their travel overseas is to receive urgent medical treatment not available in Australia or compassionate or humanitarian grounds. According to reports few of these are approved.

The Minister's determination is clearly beyond the power granted him in the legislation. It is to control the spread of the virus to another country. This is in effect a filter, one which stops the Minister going beyond that. Parliament's intention to protect other countries could have been achieved done by requiring testing and requiring a quarantine in the welcoming country. Instead there is an almost total ban on overseas, except in those rare cases where a citizen or permanent resident is able to satisfy a faceless bureaucrat that he or she has a compelling reason to travel.

This subordinate legislation is likely to be as much an actionable misfeasance in public office as was the Gillard government's total ban on the export of live cattle to Indonesia whether or not the abattoir was up-to-standard. This is but one example of ministers wielding powers unnecessarily and capriciously restricting Australians in the exercise of their fundamental rights.

It would seem that power is going to our politicians' heads as they almost daily assail the population, like Mussolini from the balcony of the Palazzo Venezia, through the now ubiquitous TV's, radios and

---

[16] *Biosecurity (Human Biosecurity Emergency) (Human Coronavirus with Pandemic Potential) (Overseas Travel Ban Emergency Requirements) Determination 2020* (Cth).

mobile telephones. This is always with constant message of fear and panic, calls to do the "right thing" and that "we are all in this together". Reinforced by a compliant mainstream media which relishes the panic of pointless news about new cases and visitors who test positive, thus seriously damaging the business concerned.

It is difficult not to conclude that this torrent of fear and panic is designed to control the population as if Australia were a dictatorship.[17] Other undemocratic and unrelated measures also seem to be under consideration, as Sky's Paul Murray eloquently put it, all 'under the cover of Covid'. The most glaring example so far has been when, with surprising Coalition support, Western Australia's McGowan government put through what is a sinister Bill of Attainder against Clive Palmer. Under Bills of Attainder, parliament declared, without the benefit of evidence or a trial, that the target, usually prominent, was guilty of a crime for which he would be punished, often executed, with his property confiscated.

Palmer is entitled, as we all are, to the rule of law even if he is, as claimed, 'unpopular'. In arbitrations before a former High Court judge, he established that the Western Australian government was legally at fault concerning a mining investment and that he was entitled to damages, the amount still to be determined. Yet under a veritable Bill of Attainder, forbidden under the *US Constitution*, Palmer has been stripped of his rights under the arbitral awards. This was on the spurious ground that the state could not afford to pay damages, they claim, of $30 billion. Mr Palmer has ridiculed this amount. In any event there can be a vast difference between what is claimed and what would be awarded by an experienced judge.

This legislation, which was retrospective, was given Royal Assent just before midnight on 13 August.[18] But that day, Palmer registered the awards for enforcement in the Queensland Supreme Court, referred to in constitutional usage as a 'Chapter III' court —that is, Chapter III of

---

[17] David Flint, 'Under the cover of Covid', *Spectator Australia*, 22 August 2020 <https://www.spectator.com.au/2020/08/under-the-cover-of-covid/>.

[18] *Iron Ore Processing (Mineralogy Pty Ltd) Agreement Amendment Act* 2020 (WA).

the *Australian Constitution*. This would allow Palmer to challenge the validity of the legislation claiming it breached the federal separation of legislative from judicial powers.

The McGowan government says it had effectively headed this off because the legislation provides that it comes into operation on the day on which it receives Royal Assent, ie, before the sun rose on the day of registration. Either the government sensibly settles this case, or it will end up in the High Court. There Palmer could also argue that the legislation breaches the constitutional guarantee that trade, commerce and intercourse be absolutely free, as well as outlawing discrimination against residents of other states. His foreign shareholders could take action under various treaties and he could argue the untested proposition that federation was only entered into on the understanding or implication that the rule of law would forever apply.

Meanwhile in Queensland, again under the cover of fighting the virus, the Palaszczuk government introduced legislation, to make it an offence, under threat of six months' imprisonment, to report corruption complaints to the official watchdog during an election campaign.[19] This extraordinary attack on the press was far too much for the normally supportive media. The protests, and not only from the media, were such the Bill was almost immediately withdrawn.

This does not mean Australians should not be on their guard. The politicians have already gone too far, setting us back for years. We must not accept their nascent dictatorship.

VII REPARATIONS

Australia has suffered significant losses as a result of COVID-19. For reasons explained below, an inquiry by the World Health Organization ('WHO') will not result in the recovery of our losses.

It is clear that the Chinese government failed significantly both in not advising the world immediately as to its knowledge about the virus and that it was allowing the potentially infected to travel to other

---

[19] *Crime and Corruption Amendment Bill 2020* (Qld).

countries from China.[20] This has imposed an enormous cost to Australia and other countries.

In April 2020, the London-based Henry Jackson Society released a report on this question.[21] It contained valuable information on the damage sustained and the complicity of Beijing in failing in its duty to inform the world about the virus. However, there may well be a better method than they propose to obtain just reparations.

According to this and many other reports, the CCP regime behaved irresponsibly when the virus emerged, suppressing information, harassing those medical practitioners who tried to warn about what was happening and, in particular, that the virus was being transmitted between humans.[22] The WHO supported Beijing in the suppression of information concerning the virus. Clearly, the WHO leadership is captured.

The irresponsibility of the authorities is graphically illustrated by the arrest of the principal whistleblower, Dr Li Wenliang, who was required to sign a confession that he had made 'false comments' and had disturbed 'the social order.' This was consistent with the regime's position then that there was 'no clear evidence of human-to-human transmission'. Tragically, Li died in February, reportedly from the virus.[23]

There is a widespread view that Beijing's attempts to suppress the facts and failure to warn the world led directly to the spread of the virus without the authorities in other countries being aware of the danger. Had Beijing warned the world, the virus could have been contained much earlier than it has been.

---

[20] David Flint, 'CCP Virus: Just Reparations', *The Epoch Times*, 6 April 2020 <https://www.theepochtimes.com/ccp-virus-just-reparations_3300124.html>.
[21] Matthew Henderson, Alan Mendoza, Andrew Foxall, James Rogers, and Sam Armstrong, 'Coronavirus Compensation? Assessing China's Potential Culpability and Avenues of Legal Response', *Henry Jackson Society*, 5 April 2020 <https://henryjacksonsociety.org/publications/coronaviruscompensation/>.
[22] Flint (n 20).
[23] 'Li Wenliang: Coronavirus Kills Chinese Whistleblower Doctor', *BBC News*, 7 February 2020 <https://www.bbc.com/news/world-asia-china-51403795>.

It is widely believed that the virus escaped from a bat in a "wet market" where, in particularly unhygienic conditions, bats, rats, dogs, cats, scorpions, and other "exotic" animals are stored in cages stacked on top of one another, sharing fluids, discharge, and excrement with the carcasses of pythons and other animals on slabs. Although closed, the markets were soon operating again.[24]

Further, Communist Party officials subsequently promoted the myth that the US Army had introduced the virus into Wuhan. Given that the communist system strongly discourages autonomous and independent activity in government, it is highly unlikely that this was done without high-level approval.

According to other reports, the virus escaped from a laboratory in the Wuhan area, one possibly involved in weaponising viruses. A variation of this is that the remains of bats used in experiments were sold at a wet market.

Proponents of these alternative origins of the virus point to the rejection by the leader of the PRC of President Donald Trump's offer to send US scientists to Wuhan to help. They say this indicates a wish to keep its laboratory activities confidential. In addition, it has been reported that Beijing required the destruction of samples that Li and others had taken of the virus.

Accordingly, there are widespread demands, indeed, an expectation, that the CCP regime should pay reparations to those countries that have suffered, with people dying or seriously ill, and economies significantly damaged.

The question is, how could this be done if, as can be expected, Beijing refuses to take responsibility?

Unfortunately, without Beijing's cooperation, most of the methods suggested for legal action may fail. Legal proceedings have, in fact, already begun against Beijing with a class action in the US federal court system.

---

[24] George Knowles, 'Will They Ever Learn? Chinese Markets Are Still Selling Bats And Slaughtering Rabbits On Blood-soaked Floors As Beijing Celebrates 'Victory' Over The Coronavirus', *Daily Mail*, 28 March 2020 <https://www.dailymail.co.uk/news/article-8163761/Chinese-markets-selling-bats.html>.

However justified this class action is, it has no chance of success. This is because of the doctrine of sovereign immunity in public international law that is incorporated into most legal systems. It was consolidated in the United States in 1976 in the *Foreign Sovereign Immunities Act*, with the Supreme Court confirming that a foreign government in cases such as the one brought against Beijing is immune from the jurisdiction of US courts.

An amendment, the *Justice Against Sponsors of Terrorism Act* 2016, does not offer a wide enough window to encompass a claim for damages over the Wuhan virus. Nor would a similar chipping away of sovereign immunity in the UK in House of Lords cases involving a former head of state, the late Augusto Pinochet. An action brought in other domestic courts, including Hong Kong's, would probably meet the same hurdle.

The second suggestion is for a government to bring an action against Beijing in the World Court – the International Court of Justice – and obtain a judgment, which normally takes years, and then, seek an order for reparations.

Although a judge nominated by Beijing sits on the court and is its vice president, the Chinese government has refrained from lodging a declaration accepting the court's jurisdiction and would be most unlikely to accept it in such a case. Similar difficulties would apply to the International Court of Arbitration.

The third avenue would be for the UN Security Council or the General Assembly to seek an advisory opinion from the World Court. The problem is that Beijing would veto any Security Council action and probably be able to discourage a necessary majority to agree to General Assembly moves.

The WHO could also seek an opinion in the unlikely event that a majority of its 194-member assembly or of its 34-member board agreed. But then the court could be persuaded to find that an opinion about the economic consequences of a health issue were beyond the powers of the WHO. In fact, in 1993 the court actually rejected, for a similar reason, a request from the WHO for an opinion on the use of nuclear weapons.

Although the Australian government has been praised for its role in persuading the WHO to undertake an inquiry into the origins of the virus, it is extremely naïve to believe that anything will come of this. This will never result in an award of reparations. Indeed, it is hard to resist the conclusion that this is a pointless distraction, with some supporting this so as not to annoy the CCP regime who is feared because of its power and record in punishing those who dare offend it. In the unlikely event that an application were successful, the further problem would be that the advisory opinion, delivered many years hence, would be just that, an advisory opinion.

A fourth avenue would be for activists to establish an informal people's tribunal. These have been used to investigate mass human rights abuses in Iran, Vietnam, Indonesia and, more recently, the China Tribunal in relation to forced organ harvesting in the PRC. Decisions of such informal tribunals can provide some resolution for survivors and those close to victims. Moreover, what they discover and what they establish inform the public and the media and can encourage subsequent official action.

The London-based China Tribunal judgment was handed down in 2019.[25] It found, on the basis of strong evidence, that the Chinese state was engaging in the forced harvesting of organs for sale on demand. This trade was found to involve the killing of political dissidents, those who belong to religions or sections of religions outside of party control – Muslim, Protestant, and Catholic – and above all, Falun Gong practitioners. Chaired by a respected international lawyer, Sir Geoffrey Nice QC, who had led the prosecution of former Serbian President Slobodan Milosevic at the UN's International Criminal Tribunal for the Former Yugoslavia, the Tribunal consisted of several outstanding members.[26]

---

[25] China Tribunal Judgement, March 2020 <https://chinatribunal.com/>.

[26] These included a prominent thoracic transplant specialist and professor of cardiothoracic surgery at University College London, prominent Malaysian, Iranian, and

Obviously, Beijing would neither take part in a private tribunal over the CCP virus nor observe any ruling. As with the China Tribunal on organ harvesting, the CCP regime would be likely to use its influence to try to ensure that governments and the mainstream media would pay only nominal attention to it. This was surprisingly successful in relation to organ harvesting but would probably be less successful in relation to the CCP virus.

There is a solution in a fifth process, one that would allow the recovery of substantial damages. It would require courage on the part of the governments taking this action. This is what I would call the Nuremberg solution, based as it is on the tribunal of that name. This was established in response to the Moscow Declaration by Churchill, Roosevelt, and Stalin to pursue World War II Nazi criminals 'to the utmost ends of the earth and will deliver them to their accusers in order that justice may be done'. It would be open to selected powers, for example, the United States and similar countries, to enter into a treaty to establish a similar tribunal to hear the claim.

This need not be a treaty as defined in US constitutional law, that is, one by the president requiring the "advice and consent" of two-thirds of the Senate. It could be an executive agreement by the president, which in international law, would constitute a treaty. Now in both US law and that of the UK and Commonwealth realms such as Canada, Australia, and New Zealand, where the Crown enters into and ratifies treaties, legislation would be necessary to give effect to decisions taken by the tribunal.

The initial number of countries would not affect the enforceability of the tribunal decisions, which could be affected in each country against assets available. It would be important to provide for other countries to accede subsequently to the treaty but out of caution, only with the unanimous approval of the original signatories.

Beijing has a poor record in respecting international tribunals, even those rare ones to which it is legally subject, such as one that heard a

U.S. human rights lawyers, a businessman engaged in a range of NGOs in the fields of human rights, and a respected academic on Chinese history.

95

case brought by the Philippines concerning the South China Sea and was handed down in 2016. While Beijing would be under no obligation to appear before this tribunal and can be expected to refuse to take part, every opportunity for Beijing to appear and to give evidence at every stage should always be given.

Provision should be made in the treaty that where a government refuses to appear, one of the parties may apply for the tribunal to appoint an *amicus curiae*, a friend of the court, to appear and to present a case for Beijing. An invitation could go, for example, to the Chinese Society of International Law to fill that role.

The treaty should clearly state the questions, which should be determined by the tribunal and would include such questions as how the virus started, the obligation of Beijing to warn, whether that obligation was fulfilled, how the virus spread to the parties and other countries, and the amount of both interim and final damages.

The treaty should rule on evidentiary questions and make broad provisions for the hearing of evidence, including hearsay and in any form. The tribunal should have power to declare that the property of the Chinese state will be available to satisfy any award, a power to freeze that at any time and that such property extend to that of high-level functionaries within the Politburo, the CCP, its associates and partners, as well as all corporations and other entities formed in, domiciled in, or under the control of Beijing, the CCP, its associates and partners, wherever located and whether or not vested in nominees, trustees, or similar cover.

The process would be that once interim orders are handed down, these could be given legislative effect by the parties, for example by the US Congress and say, the Australian Parliament. In the Australian case, Beijing-owned and -controlled property could then be taken to satisfy the outstanding interim and final judgments.

The tribunal should stay in place for five years in the event of further possible accessions or the need, for any reason, to hear requests from any party or the *amicus* (appointed to represent the interests of Beijing). There should be a power to make further orders with a continuing power in the court to make or refuse those orders or to take such decisions as it deems necessary or expedient.

Such a tribunal would allow the recovery of full and fair compensation for damages incurred by Beijing's role in the crisis relating to the CCP virus.

VIII CONCLUSION

Government response to COVID-19 has fallen at each stage from preventing entry of Wuhan to Australia to protecting the vulnerable. It was well below world's best practice, the lessons from which have been ignored. This has been at the enormous cost, not only financial and economic, to millions of Australians and those yet to be born. Most of this has been unnecessary. There have been and still are serious incursions into those rights described so memorably by the American Founders when they declared,

> We hold these truths to be self-evident, that all men are created equal, that they are endowed by their creator with certain unalienable rights, that among these are life, liberty and the pursuit of happiness.

When the Australian people 'humbly relying on the blessing of Almighty God have agreed to unite in one indissoluble Federal Commonwealth under the Crown... under the Constitution' thereby established, it was assumed that those rights referred to by the American Founders would prevail in the new Commonwealth and that the elected representatives would not only never so casually remove them even when, as with the travel ban, there can be no justification. They would not be empowered so to do.

It is clear then that there is need for an urgent and in-depth review by the people of the constitutional arrangements of Australia. This could best be achieved under a new version of the path along which we successfully come together as a nation, that is, a Second Corowa Plan. That plan, by taking the issue of federation away from the politicians and handing it to the people, ensured its achievement in a remarkably short period of time, less than four years.

The greatest thing the politicians as elected public servants can do now to make up for the terrible burden they have so unnecessarily imposed on the people including the lives they have ruined is to return the Constitution to their masters, the people.

The way this can be done is to follow what our wise predecessors did: invite the people to elect a convention of delegates, not paid but whose only return will be their work for the nation, to conduct the first review by the people of their Constitution in over a century since its adoption. There, after careful and considered study and discussion, the convention would propose amendments which, after wide consultation, would in their final form be put directly to the people as was done under the First Corowa Plan.

This may well be the only way to restore this exceptional nation to its true destiny.

6

Covid-19 Border Restrictions and Section 92 of the Australian Constitution

ANTHONY GRAY*

ABSTRACT

This article considers whether the current Western Australian border restrictions implemented in response to the COVID-19 pandemic are consistent with section 92 of the Australian Constitution, and its promise that trade, commerce and intercourse among the states will be absolutely free. After charting developments in the jurisprudence of s 92, in particular the intercourse aspect, it concludes that there is a strong chance that the Western Australian laws will be declared invalid, because they are arguably not proportionate to their legitimate objective, and arguably cannot be shown to be reasonably necessary, at least in relation to intercourse with all jurisdictions other than Victoria. The article also suggests that the current factual scenario might cause the High Court to revisit its approach to s 92 questions. The current approach, where different tests are applied to the 'trade and commerce' and the 'intercourse' aspects of the section, is not desirable. This article suggests a new streamlined approach that applies consistent principles to both limbs of the section, focussed on discrimination and proportionality.

I INTRODUCTION

In March 2020, in response to the then nascent threat of the spread of coronavirus, some Australian states enacted border restrictions,

---

* Professor of Law, University of Southern Queensland. The author wishes to thank the anonymous reviewer for helpful comments on an earlier draft.

greatly inhibiting movement across state borders. In the case of Western Australia, restrictions on movement within the state were also enacted. States that implemented such restrictions claimed that they were necessary measures in order to seek to curtail the spread of the virus. Certainly, those states which implemented such restrictions, such as Western Australia, Queensland and South Australia, have led relatively low case numbers, and are currently in a period of loosening restrictions as the number of case numbers continues to diminish. Queensland removed its border restrictions in July, except in the case of Victorian residents, given that state's problematic spike in numbers, and in respect of 'hotspots' in New South Wales, but then partly reimposed them. At the time of writing, Western Australia has persisted with its interstate border restrictions, though it has lifted its restrictions on intrastate movement.

These recent and current examples of border restrictions raise a fundamental constitutional question. Section 92 of the *Australian Constitution* ('*Constitution*') states that trade, commerce and intercourse among the states is to be 'absolutely free'. At the time of writing, legal challenges have been commenced, arguing in particular that Western Australia's current border restrictions infringe s 92 of the *Constitution*. It is expected that the challenge will focus on both the trade and commerce aspect, on the one hand, and the intercourse aspect, on the other hand, of s92. This article will consider the likely prospects of such a challenge.

II STATE BORDER RESTRICTIONS

The relevant regulations are found, in the case of Western Australia, in the *Quarantine (Closing the Border) Directions* ('*Directions*') issued in April 2020, following on from the declaration of a state of emergency under the *Emergency Management Act 2005* (WA) in March. That Act confers very broad powers on public officials in the case of such an emergency, including placing restrictions or prohibitions on the movement of individuals.[1] The *Directions* were issued pursuant

[1] *Emergency Management Act 2005* (WA) s 67.

to that legislation. They state simply that their purpose is to limit the spread of COVID-19.[2] Given space restrictions, I discuss only the essential provisions here.

Section 4 of the *Directions* states that a person must not enter Western Australia unless they are an exempt traveller. An exempt traveller is defined in s 27 in terms of various categories of individual. The list includes senior government officials, army personnel, members of the Commonwealth Parliament, someone carrying on responsibilities of the federal government, the State Premier and staff, a person who enters at the request of the Western Australian Chief Medical Officer, and those working in the field of transport, freight and logistics, those with certain specialist skills, those engaged on a fly-in fly-out employment contract and their families, emergency service workers, judicial officers, and those travelling for compassionate and/or medical or carer reasons. This is similar to regimes that previously operated in some other states.[3] Section 11 permits Western Australian residents to return to the state, provided they have been under supervised quarantine in another state for at least 14 days, are showing no symptoms of having contracted COVID-19, and agree to undergo another 14 day quarantine period upon returning to Western Australia. Breach of the *Directions* may attract a penalty of 12 months' imprisonment and/or a fine of $50,000 for an individual and $250,000 for an organisation.

Clearly, s 4 imposes a very significant restriction on the interstate movement of individuals (and, to some extent, trade and commerce) across the Western Australian border. It is also true that Western Australia has been very successful in containing the virus, with very few cases, and almost no community transmission. Of course, the Western Australian government will argue that its success has been due in no small part to it effectively isolating the state from the rest of Australia with the provisions the subject of this article.

---

[2] *Quarantine (Closing the Border) Directions 2020* (WA) s 1.
[3] Eg *Border Restrictions Direction No 5*, issued under the *Public Health Act 2005* (Qld) s 362B.

This question of possible cause and effect is important, and will be considered later in the article. It will be relevant to the question of the constitutionality of the relevant provisions, to which this article now turns.

III THE AUSTRALIAN CONSTITUTION

I will turn specifically to s 92 of the Constitution, the specific provision under which the Western Australian legislation is being challenged, shortly. However, at the macro level, the nature of the *Constitution* must be acknowledged. It reflected an attempt to bring together the people of six disparate colonies, separated by the tyranny of distance, and beset by limited communication opportunities and means among them, and limited transportation options. It attempted to forge one nation from a loose collection of colonies. This attempt to bring together people into one nation is noticeable in several different sections of the *Constitution*. Apart from s 92, it is reflected in s 117 of the *Constitution*, prohibiting a state law from subjecting an out of state resident to disability or discrimination on that basis. It is reflected in s 51(2), prohibiting the Commonwealth Parliament from discriminating in terms of taxation between states, and in s 99, prohibiting trade and commerce laws that preference one state or part of a state over another state or part of state.

This aspect of the *Constitution* was reflected upon in several of the judgments of the High Court in a leading s 117 case, *Street v Queensland Bar Association*.[4] Though the specific constitutional context there differed from the present, it is submitted that some of the macro-level expressions of the purpose of the *Constitution* are of universal application in regards its interpretation, including s 92. That section has some analogies with s 117 in terms of its concern over the retention of 'walls' (thankfully, figuratively only, but still of concern) between states.

Mason CJ in that case spoke of the object of federation being to

---

4 (1989) 168 CLR 461.

'bring into existence one nation and one people'.[5] He referred to the framers of the Australian *Constitution* wishing to 'bring into existence a national unity and a national sense of identity transcending colonial and state loyalties'.[6] The other important lesson in Street for current purposes is that members of the court favoured a substantive and broad, rather than formal and narrow, approach to constitutional freedoms. This led members of the court to reject an approach to s 117 based on whether the legislation applied an impermissible 'criterion' (relating to the interstatedness of the interest),[7] in favour of a consideration of how the legislation applied in fact. Three other justices specifically held that the section had to be applied in a practical, not technical, matter.[8] This is of importance here because there is evidence of a 'criterion' approach to s 92 questions, and there is also evidence of narrowness in approach, which sometimes eschews practical operation of legislation, as opposed to its prima facie appearance. The *Street* case is a reminder that this should not occur in the constitutional law realm.

Brennan J was also conscious of the undesirability of 'barrier(s) to the legal and social utility of the Australian people'. He would only permit them, in relation to the purposes of the *Constitution*, in cases involving 'the need to preserve the institutions of government and their ability to function'.[9] Dawson J said that states were constitutionally required to operate on the basis there was 'one nation and that the citizens of that nation carry their citizenship with them from state to state'.[10] McHugh J referred to the 'single economic region which is a prime object of federation'.[11] The intent of the founding fathers of the Australian Constitution in melding together one nation is very clear.

---

[5] Ibid 485.
[6] Ibid 485; and a constitutional object of Australian nationhood and national unity: at 492-493.
[7] Ibid 487.
[8] Ibid 488 (Mason CJ), 569 (Gaudron J) and 581 (McHugh J)
[9] Ibid 513.
[10] Ibid 548.
[11] Ibid 589.

III SECTION 92 OF THE AUSTRALIAN CONSTITUTION

Section 92 of the Australian *Constitution* is absolutely integral to the founders' plan. That section states quite starkly that on the imposition of uniform duties of customs, trade commerce and intercourse among the states of Australia is to be absolutely free. Uniform customs duties were first implemented in 1901.[12] It is one of the most litigated provisions in the *Constitution*. It is often said that two factors motivated federation in the colonies, that of perceived threats to border security, and dissatisfaction with trade among the colonies, with some states such as Victoria pursuing protectionist agendas, incurring the ire of other states such as New South Wales, which was generally more committed to free trade. It was argued that the colonies should join together to create both a customs union and 'common market', removing the economic borders that had been assembled at the physical borders between states, in order to get the benefit of free trade which was by this stage of human knowledge very evident.[13] These economic goals are reflected in ss 90 and 92, the former section removing the ability of colonies/states to impose excise duties on goods, and the latter preventing them from imposing taxes and charges on goods travelling from interstate. Members of the High Court have described the free trade and intercourse guarantee in s 92 as 'perhaps the most notable achievement of the *Constitution*'.[14] Its importance was noted by the person known as the 'father' of federation in Australia, Henry Parkes, at one of the Constitutional Conventions.[15]

---

[12] Peter Lloyd 'Customs Union and Fiscal Union in Australia at Federation' (2015) 91 *Economic Record* 155, 160.

[13] *Street v Queensland Bar Association* (1989) 168 CLR 461, 589 where McHugh J refers to the creation of the 'single economic region which is the prime object of federation'.

[14] *Ex Parte Nelson* (No1)(1928) 42 CLR 209, 218 (Knox CJ Gavan Duffy and Starke JJ).

[15] 'I seek to define what seems to be an absolutely necessary condition of anything like perfect federation, that is, that Australia shall be free ... free on the borders, free everywhere – in its trade and intercourse between its own people, that there should be no impediment of any kind – that there shall be no barrier of and kind between one section of the Australian people and another; but, that the trade and the general communication of these people shall flow on from one end of the continent to the other, with no one to stay in its progress or to call it to account: *Official Report of the Nation-*

Of course, there is a compelling economic argument underpinning s 92. The benefits of free trade were most obviously noted in the work of Adam Smith[16] and David Ricardo.[17] They spoke of the advantages of a country specialising in producing particular goods or services, in the production of which they might enjoy a comparative advantage, and trading with other countries which have specialised in the production of other goods or services in which they enjoy a comparative advantage. This would maximise efficiencies. Though these economists were speaking of the advantages of free trade globally, clearly such thinking could also be applied to free trade within a nation, across state borders.

Of course, the movement of people across borders is intrinsically linked with the movement of goods and services. The movement of goods and services could be effectively precluded or hampered if restrictions on the movement of individuals (for example, owners or distributors of the goods, providers of the services) were permitted. This spells trouble for an interpretation of s 92 that apparently imposes different tests for the trade and commerce part of s 92, on the one hand, and the intercourse aspect of s 92, on the other. This is explained further below, as will be a way to remove this differentiation.

As well as being linked to movement of goods and services, there is also a non-economic argument in favour of freedom of intercourse among the states. It is clear that the founding fathers wanted to create a unified nation, where individuals would see themselves as Australians first, and residents of a state second. One essential means of unifying the nation was to break down, literally and figuratively, borders between the states.[18] It is, for many, an unfortunate consequence of

---

al Australasian Convention Debates (Sydney, 2 March 1891–9 April 1891), 24-25.

[16] Adam Smith, *The Wealth of Nations* (1776) 485-486.

[17] *The Works and Correspondence of David Ricardo* (1952) 128-149; Alan Sykes 'Comparative Advantage and the Normative Economics of International Trade Policy (1988) 1 *Journal of International Economic Law* 49.

[18] *Harris v Wagner* (1959) 103 CLR 452, 476-477 (Windeyer J): 'the effect for the Australian economy which s92 was designed to secure is that, for purposes of trade, commerce and intercourse, State boundaries should not exist. For the flow of trade

the current COVID crisis that these borders have been reconstructed, more than 100 years after a document was agreed upon that apparently sought to see them vanish, at least in relation to trade, commerce and intercourse around Australia. The boundaries themselves have become somewhat difficult to defend. They were drawn up in the early 19th century, apparently by someone who had never visited the Australian continent. They do not, as some federal boundaries elsewhere do, reflect strong regional differences, whether of culture, religion, belief or other kind.[19] They never did. Their imposition was always a matter of administrative convenience, not a reflection of deep-seated difference. Modern technology, including very fast transport and communication links, arguably has made them redundant. The spectre of state premiers 'pulling up the drawbridge' is, for many, a regrettable throwback and backward step. It is not what Australia is, or should be. It does not reflect the nation that the founding fathers thought they were creating in, and surely would be proud to see today – a modern, integrated nation of one people, people who can seamlessly move around Australia, with seamless trade and commerce activity within Australia, for the benefit of all, and a rejection of narrow-minded parochialism.

Regarding the history of s 92 interpretation, there have been many attempts to have declared invalid various statutory schemes, typically involving licensing or other kinds of business regulation. The High Court endured periods of chronic disagreement as to the purpose/s of the section, and (sometimes, relatedly) the correct approach to its interpretation. Perhaps fortuitously, much of that case law was effectively removed when the High Court appeared to settle upon a new approach to interpretation of s 92. In the landmark decision in *Cole v Whitfield*,[20] ('Cole') the court swept away much of the previous case

---

and commerce among the States, Australia is one place and in their comings and goings among the States, Australians are one people. In this sense and for this purpose, s92 obliterates state boundaries'.

[19] Anthony Gray *Excise Taxation in the Australian Federation*, PhD Thesis, University of New South Wales (1997) 36-37; Leslie Crisp *Australian National Government* (1970) 4; Gerard Carney *The Story Behind the Land Borders of the Australian States*, Public Lecture Series, High Court of Australia (2013).

[20] (1988) 165 CLR 360, 394-395 (all members of the Court).

law. It settled upon a two-stage test to assess the validity of most laws challenged under s 92. It considered (a) whether the relevant provision discriminated against interstate trade, compared with intrastate trade and, if so, (b) whether it was passed for a protectionist purpose. If the answer to both of these questions was 'yes', the challenged measure was constitutionally invalid.

There is support for the adoption of a non-discrimination norm in this context in comparable jurisdictions. The United States *Constitution* does not contain an express provision like s 92. It simply provides Congress (the federal parliament) with power with respect to interstate and overseas commerce. However, the Supreme Court has interpreted that provision to include a 'negative' or 'dormant' aspect. This aspect precludes states from enacting provisions which discriminate against interstate trade and commerce, compared with intrastate trade and commerce.[21] There is evidence that the founding fathers who constructed Australia's *Constitution* were heavily influenced by the United States *Constitution*, including its arrangements regarding commerce regulation.[22] Sir Owen Dixon acknowledged this.[23] This makes

---

[21] *Guy v Baltimore* 100 US 434, 449 (1879): 'no state can, consistently with the Federal *Constitution*, impose upon the products of other states ... or upon citizens because engaged in the sale therein, or the transportation thereto, of the products of other states, more onerous public burdens or taxes than it imposes upon the like products of its own territory (Harlan J).

[22] Henry Parkes specifically spoke to the *Guy v Baltimore* decision at the 1890 Constitutional Convention in Melbourne: 'the case seems to put at rest, in the most emphatic manner, what is sometimes disputed – the question of existence of entire freedom throughout the territory of the United States. As the members of the Conference know, she has created a tariff of a very severe, and in some cases almost prohibitive character against the outside world, but as between New York and Massachusetts, and as between Connecticut and Pennsylvania, there is no customs house and no tax collector. Between any two of the States – indeed from one end of the States to the other – the country is as free as the air in which the swallow flies. We cannot too fully bear in mind that doctrine of the great republic, a doctrine supported in the most convincing manner by the case to which I have alluded': *Official Record of the Proceedings and Debates of the Australasian Federation Conference* (Melbourne, 10 February 1890) 46.

[23] 'The framers of our own federal Commonwealth *Constitution* ... found the American instrument of government an incomparable model. They could not escape from its fascination': *Jesting Pilate* (1965) 44; 'to Australians no small part of the consti-

sense, given that the United States adopts a federal structure which was also adopted in Australia. In turn, the concern of the United States with free trade makes sense given its strong attachment to capitalism, as well as deep memory of, and unpleasant experience with, the United Kingdom *Navigation Acts* in pre-revolutionary times, and disastrous interstate trade wars upon which the American confederation largely foundered.[24] Similarly, the European Union is built around non-discrimination norms in relation to goods, services, capital and people.[25]

The High Court had effectively adopted the suggestion of an esteemed Australian constitutional lawyer, Michael Coper, as to how the section should be interpreted, consistent with the original intent behind the section.[26] There has been much academic discussion of the new test, including some criticism.[27] I have suggested some ways in which the new test might insufficiently protect the fundamentally important consideration of free trade.[28] In particular, the requirement that a purpose of protectionism be shown may give the restriction less scope than it otherwise would. Such a requirement does not appear in equivalent provisions elsewhere. I will return to these criticisms near the end of this article.

Although it is said that the current challenge to the Western Australian provisions will deal with both the trade and commerce aspect and the intercourse aspect of s 92, I believe that the chances of a successful challenge are much greater under the intercourse aspect of s 92 than the trade and commerce aspect of s 92. As a result, I will focus this article mainly on the intercourse aspect of s 92.

---

tutional law of the United States must be of first importance ... lawyers whose work calls for any consideration of Australian constitutional questions cannot neglect the decisions of the Supreme Court of the United States': at 180-181.

[24] *The Federalist No 22* (Alexander Hamilton).

[25] *Treaty on the Functioning of the European Union* (2012) art 28, 45-48.

[26] *Freedom of Interstate Trade Under the Australian Constitution* (1983).

[27] Gonzalo Villalta Puig *The High Court of Australia and Section 92 of the Australian Constitution: A Critique of the Cole v Whitfield Test* (Lawbook Co, 2008).

[28] Anthony Gray 'Section 92 of the Australian *Constitution*: The Next Phase' (2016) 44(1) *Australian Business Law Review* 35, 44-48.

There are two main reasons why I view the possible challenge under the trade and commerce aspect of s 92 as being less likely to succeed. The first is based on an assumption that the High Court would continue to apply the two-stage test agreed upon in *Cole v Whitfield*. This appears to be reasonable, given there has been no suggestion to the contrary in the s 92 case law determined since then. Given this assumption, a challenge will be very difficult. The challenger will need to show that the provision discriminates against interstate trade and commerce, compared with intrastate trade and commerce. This might be possible – the provision only applies to travel across state lines. This would overwhelmingly, if not totally, apply to interstate trade and commerce, rather than intrastate trade and commerce. On the other hand, the prohibition contains an exemption for transport and logistics movement across state lines, provided the person only remains in Western Australia for as long as necessary to perform those duties. On balance, it would be possible to demonstrate that the provision is relevantly discriminatory, because it subjects interstate goods to greater restrictions than local goods.

However, it would be extremely difficult to demonstrate that the law is 'protectionist'. Now, protectionist in this sense means that the law is designed to, or has the effect of, protecting local trade and commerce from competition, as compared with interstate trade and commerce. It is rare that the High Court has found that a law has a protectionist purpose; in those cases where it has occurred, the evidence is very strong that the object of the law was to reduce competition from an interstate provider.[29] The fact that a law might have been passed in order to 'protect' Western Australians from the virus does not mean the law is 'protectionist' in the sense in which it informs s 92 analysis.

This would be extremely difficult for the challenger to show. The government could demonstrate quite convincingly that the purpose of the provision was to protect Western Australians from COVID-19. It was not to protect local industry from competition, as in *Castlemaine*

---

[29] *Castlemaine Tooheys Ltd v South Australia* (1990) 169 CLR 436; *Betfair Pty Ltd v Western Australia* (2008) 234 CLR 418 ('*Castlemaine Tooheys*').

Tooheys and *Betfair* where s 92 was offended, but to protect the health and welfare of local people. That is a purpose quite consistent with the trade and commerce aspect of s 92. The government could also demonstrate that its Directions contain an exception for transport and logistics, thus reinforcing its argument that its aim is not to keep interstate trade and commerce away, but to keep the virus at bay. It is not a case where the scope of the law, being larger than necessary in order to achieve the claimed legitimate objective, betrays an agenda of protecting local traders from interstate competition, like in *Castlemaine Tooheys*.

As a result, it is considered that any s 92 challenge based on the trade and commerce aspect is likely to fail. I will devote most attention to the question whether a challenge based on the intercourse aspect of s 92 might have a greater chance of success. The court in *Cole v Whitfield* indicated that the intercourse aspect of s 92 might be protected to a greater extent than the trade and commerce aspect of s 92.[30] It also recognised, without much elaboration, that it may not be appropriate to apply concepts such as discrimination and protectionist purpose to the intercourse aspect of the section.[31]

IV INTERCOURSE ASPECT OF SECTION 92

The intercourse aspect of s 92 has been considered on only a small number of occasions. The first case was *R v Smithers; Ex Parte Benson*[32] ('*Smithers*'). The case involved a challenge to the validity of New South Wales legislation. The legislation made it an offence for a person, other than a resident of that state, to enter New South Wales if, within the past three years, they had been convicted of a crime which carried a maximum possible punishment of 12 months' imprisonment or more. The challenger was convicted of a crime against the

---

[30] (1988) 165 CLR 360, 393 (all members of the Court).

[31] Ibid 394: 'There is no reason in logic or commonsense for insisting on a strict correspondence between the freedom guaranteed to interstate trade and commerce and that guaranteed to interstate intercourse'.

[32] (1912) 16 CLR 99.

New South Wales legislation because he entered that state. He was not a resident of New South Wales, and had a conviction within the past three years of a crime which carried a maximum punishment of 12 months' imprisonment. The High Court declared the New South Wales legislation to be invalid, contrary to s 92 of the *Constitution*.

Griffith CJ said that the past power that colonies had to prohibit others from entering the colony was now circumscribed by s 92 of the *Constitution*. Citizens now enjoyed the right to move around the nation to engage in business or to access government facilities and services. Griffith CJ suggested the right was not absolute, but any limitation would have to be based on a test of 'necessity'.[33] Here New South Wales had not shown the necessity to keep out non-residents who wished to travel to the state but who had been convicted of criminal activity. Barton J took a similar view.[34] Isaacs J viewed s 92 as an 'absolute' prohibition on state and federal governments using state borders as barriers to intercourse among Australians.[35] This word typically means that no exceptions would be permitted. Higgins J said that it was the fact that the provision was 'pointed directly at' the movement into the state that was constitutionally problematic.[36] He declined to consider the question of any possible powers in state governments to control border movement along the lines contemplated by Griffith CJ or Barton J.

The matter was next considered in *Gratwick v Johnson* (*'Gratwick'*), probably the factual scenario closest to the current situation. During wartime, federal regulations were passed stating that a person should not without a permit travel by rail or passenger vehicle from one state to another. A Commonwealth official could approve or deny permits. The regulations did not provide criteria by which an application for a permit would be assessed. Dulcie Johnson was charged

---

[33] Ibid 109; further confirmation that the intercourse aspect of s 92 is not absolute appears in *W and A McArthur Ltd v State of Queensland* (1926) 28 CLR 530, 550 (Knox CJ Isaacs and Starke JJ).

[34] (1912) 16 CLR 99, 110-111.

[35] Ibid 117.

[36] Ibid 118.

with an offence against the regulation. It was alleged she crossed the state border between South Australia and Western Australia on a train, without a valid permit. She had been travelling to Perth to visit her fiancé. She had sought to obtain a permit, but was advised that her reason for travel did not warrant one. The fact that the events occurred during war time is significant, because it is typically the case that during such times, the Court is more deferential to claims by government of a need to deny individuals fundamental rights.

Despite this, all members of the High Court declared that the relevant provision was invalid, as being contrary to s 92 of the *Constitution*. Latham CJ drew a distinction between mere restrictions on interstate movement, on the one hand, and outright prohibitions, on the other.[37] He said prohibitions on interstate movement were invalid.[38] He viewed the regulation at issue here as a prohibition. He took a similar position to that of Higgins J in *Smithers*, noting that the regulation was 'directed at' interstate trade and commerce. This also suggested its invalidity. Latham CJ also expressed concern that the regulation did not state what criteria were relevant to an assessment of an application for a permit.[39] Rich J said the offensive provision was a 'direct and immediate' invasion of the s 92 freedom.[40] Starke J agreed that legislation pointing directly at interstate intercourse was invalid. He seemed also to take an absolutist view:

> It is immaterial … that the object or purpose of the legislation … is for the public safety or defence of the Commonwealth or any other legislative purpose if it be pointed directly at the right guaranteed and protected by the provisions of s 92 of the *Constitution*.[41]

Dixon J agreed that the legislation was directed at the interstatedness of the journey and did not seem to be related to any specific de-

---

[37] (1945) 70 CLR 1, 14.
[38] Ibid 14.
[39] Ibid 15.
[40] Ibid 16.
[41] Ibid 17.

fence purpose of the movement of troops, munitions manufacture or war supplies. This seems to suggest he did not view the freedom in s 92 as absolute in nature, that a legislature might be able to restrict the freedom, for precise and justified reasons, where the regulation clearly related to those reasons.[42] McTiernan J agreed the provisions were invalid, being directed at interstate trade.[43]

If we pause the consideration of cases at this point, it seems as if those challenging the current border restrictions would have a strong case based on s 92. This is for a range of possible reasons:

- Because, according to Isaacs J in Smithers and Starke J in *Gratwick v Johnson*, the right to interstate intercourse is absolute in nature, admitting of no exceptions;

- Because, according to Higgins J in *Smithers* and Latham CJ, Starke, Dixon and McTiernan JJ in *Gratwick v Johnson*, the measures are 'pointed at' or 'directed at' interstate trade;

- Because, according to Latham CJ in Gratwick v Johnson, the provision prohibits, rather than regulates, interstate intercourse; and

- Because, according to Rich J in *Gratwick v Johnson*, the provision impacts interstate intercourse 'directly and immediately'.

Clearly, s 4 of the Western Australian regulations, forbidding a person from entering Western Australia unless they are exempt, would fall foul of these arguments. Argument (a) needs no elaboration. In terms of argument (b), s 4 is clearly pointed at or directed at interstate trade. In terms of argument (c), if Latham CJ concluded that the regulations in *Gratwick* amounted to a prohibition as opposed to regulation on the facts there (a prohibition unless the person had a government-issued permit), no doubt he would conclude the same regarding the current Western Australian regulations. And in terms of (d), the regulations impact interstate intercourse directly and immediately.

---

[42] Ibid 19.
[43] Ibid 21.

This conclusion is subject to two qualifications. The first is that, particularly in the earlier case, there is evidence of a clearly non-absolutist interpretation of the section. Griffith CJ and Barton J, Higgins J reserving his judgment on this aspect, clearly stated in dicta that a law might survive s 92 challenge to the extent it could be shown to have been passed based on 'necessity'. The Western Australian Government might rely on this exception, arguing that their aim was to prevent spread of a highly infectious, deadly disease, so that their measures were 'necessary'. I will return to this argument below.

The second qualification is that the law on s 92 was substantially reformed in 1988 when the High Court rendered its decision in *Cole v Whitfield*. This means that great care must be taken with any precedent on s 92 decided prior to *Cole*. It does not mean that the pre-Cole cases contain nothing of value in terms of the law today; however, at the very least, great care must be taken with precedents decided prior to *Cole*, since their reasoning may well have been substantially undercut by the High Court's 1988 decision.

Specifically, all members of the High Court in *Cole* rejected the so-called 'criterion of operation' test for determining whether or not a law was vulnerable to s 92 challenge. According to this test, the question of constitutional validity turns upon a close consideration of what particular thing is targeted by the legislation. So, for instance, a law that targets the 'interstatedness' of intercourse (or trade and commerce) would fail the test, and be liable to be held invalid due to s 92. An example of this reasoning appears in *Grannall v Marrickville Margarine Pty Ltd*:

> If some fact or event or thing which itself forms part of trade, commerce or intercourse or forms an essential attribute of that conception (essential in the sense that without it you cannot bring into being that particular example of trade, commerce or intercourse among the States) is made the subject of the operation of a law which by reference to it or in consequence of it imposes some restriction or burden or liability it does not matter how circuitously it is done or

how deviously or covertly. It will be considered sufficiently direct or immediate in its operation or application to inter-State trade, commerce and intercourse. Provided the prejudice is real or the impediment to inter-State transactions is appreciable, it will infringe upon s92. But generally speaking it will be quite otherwise if the thing with reference to or in consequence of which the law operates or which it restricts or burdens is not part of inter-State trade or commerce and in itself supplies no element or attribute essential to the conception.[44]

If this approach were applied, the Western Australian provision would likely be held invalid because the law operates by virtue of the very fact of the interstate intercourse. In this sense, the extract above is really another way of conveying the same ideas found in the judgments in *Smithers* and *Gratwick*, considering whether the provisions are 'pointed at' or 'directed at' interstate intercourse, have a 'direct and immediate' impact upon them etc.

However, in *Cole v Whitfield* all members of the High Court rejected this approach to s 92.[45] The effect of this is that, at the very least, of the four arguments made above as a result of *Smithers* and *Gratwick*, two of them (arguments (b) and (d)) are no longer tenable. This is according to the actual decision in *Cole*. However, the position is slightly more complicated than this, because subsequent decisions appear to backtrack from some of what was said in *Cole*, as we will see shortly.

While *Cole v Whitfield* was primarily focussed on the 'trade and commerce' aspect of s 92, and the actual factual scenario presented in that case concerned that aspect, the High Court made obiter dicta remarks about the intercourse aspect of s 92. These remarks effectively mean that argument (a) above is no longer tenable. The High Court stated that the intercourse aspect of the section was not absolute. It gave an example:

---

[44] (1955) 93 CLR 55, 78 (Dixon CJ McTiernan Webb and Kitto JJ).
[45] Ibid 400-402.

> Although personal movement across a border cannot, gener-
> ally speaking, be impeded, it is legitimate to restrict a pedes-
> trian's use of a highway for the purpose of his crossing or to
> authorize the arrest of a fugitive offender from one state at the
> moment of his departure into another state.[46]

Unfortunately, the High Court left the discussion there. It gave an example. It did not provide a principle, of which the example was merely an illustration. It did not provide a test. These (admittedly obiter comments) are inconsistent with any notion that the freedom of interstate intercourse is absolute in nature, so argument (a) above is no longer tenable. And since arrest of a fugitive seeking to leave the state would amount to a 'prohibition', not merely a 'restriction', on interstate trade, it is likely that argument (c) above is no longer tenable either. This effectively means that the precedent cases of *Smithers* and *Gratwick* are effectively useless in supporting a constitutional challenge to the Western Australian border restrictions, unless they are resurrected (which is not beyond the realms of possibility). But as the law currently stands, if the challenge is to succeed, it must be based on other precedents, or other arguments.

Though most of the case was concerned with the 'trade and commerce' aspect of s 92, and the new test for determining constitutionality under those limbs, the High Court in *Cole* made limited comments on the intercourse aspect of s 92. It made it clear that the new tests for the trade and commerce aspect of s 92 could not be applied to the intercourse aspect of s 92. The High Court was correct, with respect, to do so. It would simply not make sense to test restrictions on interstate intercourse based on whether they were discriminatory against interstate commerce and protectionist. The High Court suggested that the protection to be accorded interstate intercourse, as opposed to trade and commerce, might be stronger, though it was not an absolute right.[47] However, the Court did not indicate which test should be used

---

[46] Ibid 393.

[47] Ibid 393-394. That freedom of intercourse was stronger in nature than freedom of trade and commerce was confirmed in *Cunliffe v Commonwealth* (1994) 182 CLR 272, 395 (McHugh J).

to determine whether a law impacting interstate intercourse was valid or not. Given that the factual context of the case was elsewhere, this is understandable, if not entirely satisfactory.

Of course, as was subsequently pointed out, a differential test for the trade and commerce aspect of s 92, on the one hand, and the intercourse aspect, on the other, is also problematic. It is axiomatic in constitutional law that legislation can be characterised in more than one way, and it is quite possible that legislation might be characterised as both relating to trade and commerce, and intercourse.[48] If different tests are being applied to the 'trade and commerce' aspect of the section compared with the 'intercourse' aspect, this raises the spectre of a different answer depending on which of the aspects is applied. Thus the answer to a constitutional challenge might turn very sharply on which limb is argued to apply, or which limb the High Court places more focus on in determining the outcome, when on particular facts, both might reasonably be argued. This is problematic when the text of the *Constitution* does not reflect a difference in how the aspects are to be applied. This is an unhappy consequence of the High Court's decision in *Cole*, but at the end of this article, I suggest a possible way out.

Subsequently, members of the High Court accepted that laws of general application with an incidental, indirect impact on freedom of interstate trade, commerce or intercourse were consistent with s 92. This appears in *Nationwide News Pty Ltd v Wills*,[49] *Australian Capital Television Pty Ltd v Commonwealth*,[50] and *Cunliffe v Commonwealth*.[51]

---

[48] *APLA Limited and Others v Legal Services Commissioner of New South Wales and Another* (2005) 224 CLR 322, 457 (Hayne J).

[49] (1992) 177 CLR 106, 194-195.

[50] Ibid 58-59, where Brennan J stated that s 92 did not make interstate intercourse immune from laws of general application which were not aimed at interstate intercourse. Brennan J concluded that laws enacted 'for the purpose of burdening interstate intercourse' breached s 92, but a law passed for another purpose, provided it was reasonably appropriate and adapted for that purpose, the fact it incidentally impacted interstate intercourse did not mean it infringed s 92: at 57. He referred to the apparently discredited 'criterion of the imposition of the burden' (59) as determinative of liability. In a case where a multitude of purposes existed, Brennan J believed that the 'chief' purpose would be critical: at 59.

[51] (1994) 182 CLR 272.

There the court appeared (once again) to distinguish between direct and indirect burdens on interstate intercourse. Mason CJ said:

> A law which in terms applies to movement across a border and imposes a burden or restriction is invalid. But a law which imposes an incidental burden or restriction on interstate intercourse in the course of regulating a subject matter other than interstate intercourse would not fail if the burden or restriction was reasonably necessary for the purpose of preserving an ordered society under a system of representative government and democracy and the burden or restriction was not disproportionate.[52]

This was somewhat perplexing, with respect, for at least two reasons. Firstly, there is the suggestion, replicated in other judgments in the case,[53] that in applying the s 92 prohibition, a distinction should be drawn between measures that 'directly', and measures that 'indirectly' burden interstate trade. Judges like Mason CJ and Deane J (with whom Gaudron J agreed) use the word 'incidentally'. There is a clear strong link between a burden that is indirect and a burden that is incidental. This is problematic, because the joint reasons in *Cole v Whitfield* had rejected the past distinctions between direct and indirect burdens as being too formalist. Yet, just a few short years later, some version of the reasoning was apparently being resurrected. Different terms were utilised, to be sure, but essentially the same concept.

Secondly, the test espoused by Mason CJ seems to be based on whether the impugned measure was 'necessary for the purpose of preserving an ordered society'. Other justices suggested similar tests. Deane J, with whom Gaudron J agreed,[54] focussed on whether the measure was 'necessary or appropriate and adapted for the preser-

---

[52] Ibid 307-308 McHugh J agreed that a law which incidentally impacted freedom of intercourse, rather than directly, would be easier to justify. He applied a test considering whether the law was 'reasonably necessary for the government of a free society regulated by the rule of law': at 396.

[53] Ibid 346 (Deane J)(with whom Gaudron J agreed), 366 (Dawson J) and 396 (McHugh J).

[54] Ibid 392.

vation of an ordered society or the protection or vindication of the legitimate claims of individuals in such a society'.[55] McHugh J considered whether the measures were 'reasonably necessary for the government of a free society regulated by the rule of law'.[56] In contrast, Brennan J contrasted laws of general application, and laws aimed to interstate intercourse, the latter being likely invalid due to s 92.[57] Dawson J said the test was whether the measures were 'inappropriate or disproportionate',[58] in respect of laws not directed at interstate intercourse. Similarly, Toohey J pointed out the challenged provision was a law of general application.[59]

Further clarity on this matter was obtained in the 1999 decision of *AMS v AIF*.[60] This case again directly raised the question of the 'intercourse' aspect of s 92. It involved a family law dispute. Both of the parents of a child had been living in the Northern Territory, but moved to Western Australia. After the couple separated, the mother indicated she wished to move back to the Northern Territory with the child. Relevant family law provisions imposed an obligation of joint custodianship of children, and operated with a presumption that both parents would spend significant time with a child. One issue was whether a court might be able to restrict the ability of the mother to move back to the Northern Territory with the child, which would impact the father's contact with the child, or whether such a restriction would offend the freedom of intercourse aspects of s 92.

Gleeson CJ, McHugh and Gummow JJ suggested that the family court in such matters might be able to restrict the movement of the mother where such an order could be shown to be 'reasonably required by the object of the legislation'.[61] Gaudron J applied the view taken by Deane J in *Cunliffe*, considering whether the law incidentally

---

[55] Ibid 346.
[56] Ibid 396.
[57] Ibid 333.
[58] Ibid 366.
[59] Ibid 384.
[60] (1999) 199 CLR 160.
[61] Ibid 179, with whom Hayne J agreed: at 233.

impacted freedom of intercourse in pursuit of another legitimate objective and not beyond what is necessary to achieve that objective, or instead whether it was passed for the purpose of restricting interstate intercourse.[62] Kirby J took a similar position.[63] Callinan J did so as well, suggesting that McHugh J in *Cunliffe* had suggested a more restricted test of 'reasonable necessity' in terms of regulating interstate intercourse, as opposed to one of proportionality, but that either way, the regulation here was valid.[64]

The intercourse aspect of s 92 was also considered in *APLA Limited and Others v Legal Services Commissioner of New South Wales and Another*.[65] Gleeson CJ and Heydon J seemed to adopt a two-stage test in terms of the intercourse aspect of s 92.[66] They considered firstly whether the object of the legislation was to impede interstate intercourse. They determined that the legislation at issue in the case did not have such an object. Secondly, they considered whether the legislation imposed an impediment to interstate intercourse that went beyond what was reasonably required to achieve its objective. They determined that the legislation at issue did not exceed what was reasonably required. Gummow J adopted a similar approach, considering whether the object of the legislation was to impede interstate intercourse. Having determined it was not, Gummow J considered whether the legislation impacted interstate intercourse to a greater extent than was reasonably required by the object of the legislation. He also phrased this test in terms of whether the impact of the legislation on interstate intercourse was 'inappropriate and disproportionate'.[67]

Hayne J was critical of aspects of the reasoning of Mason CJ, Deane J (with whom Gaudron J agreed) and McHugh JJ in *Cunliffe*, in particular their reference to permitting the validity of legislation to be determined based on resort to concepts such as 'ordered society'. He

---

62 Ibid 193.
63 Ibid 215-216.
64 Ibid 249-250.
65 (2005) 224 CLR 322.
66 Ibid 353.
67 Ibid 393-394.

said that such a test was subjective. He preferred the position of the other justices in that case, and of the justices in *AMS*, in basing a test on more objective criteria focussed on the object of the legislation. He expressly adopted the position taken in AMS.

V SECTION 92 AND QUARANTINE CASES

Section 92 has been specifically considered in the context of quarantine. However, these cases have tended to focus on the 'trade and commerce' aspect, rather than the intercourse aspect of s 92. Further, they were all decided prior to the s 92 'revolution' announced in *Cole v Whitfield*. These present significant limitations on the utility of such cases to the present facts, but they are considered to shed some light, and therefore worthy of note.

In *Ex Parte Nelson (No1)*[68] the High Court (by statutory majority) validated New South Wales regulations permitted the Governor of the State to make an order prohibiting the importation of stock into the state where it was believed that the stock was infected with an infectious or contagious disease. Exceptions existed where it could be shown that the relevant stock had been appropriately dipped, and a relevant permit had been obtained. Knox CJ Gavan Duffy and Starke JJ stated that s 92 had not stripped states of their ability to protect their citizens from infections from elsewhere. The joint reasons determined that the relevant question was the 'true nature and character' of the challenged legislation. If its true nature and character was of a kind, for example, of prevention of disease importation, the fact that it had 'incidental' effects on interstate trade, commerce and intercourse did not make it offensive to s 92.[69] The absolutist position of Isaacs J in relation to s 92 is clearly evident in his (dissenting) decision: 'any legislative constraint whatsoever on those subjects (trade, commerce and intercourse) by the state is a derogation of the guaranteed immunity'.[70] He dismissed any suggestion of a health exception, on the basis it

---

[68] (1928) 42 CLR 209.
[69] Ibid 218.
[70] Ibid 242.

would create a slippery slope of immunity from s 92.[71] Higgins J stated that the provision was 'pointed at' the interstate movement of stock.[72] Powers J expressly agreed with Isaacs and Higgins JJ, noting the offensive provision directly affected and prevented interstate trade and commerce, and was invalid.[73]

The matter was considered again in *Tasmania v Victoria*.[74] There Victorian legislation permitted the state's Governor to prohibit the importation of any tree, plant or vegetable into the state which, in the Governor's opinion, was likely to introduce a disease into Victoria. The legislation made it an offence to import such material into the state contrary to a declaration by the Governor. The Governor declared that, in his opinion, the importation of potatoes from Tasmania was likely to introduce disease into Victoria, and prohibited it. A majority of the High Court declared that the Victorian legislation was unconstitutional, being contrary to s 92.

Gavan Duffy CJ, Evatt and McTiernan JJ noted that the Governor's discretion was quite unbounded, in contrast with that considered in *Ex Parte Nelson*. The provision here could impose a total prohibition, as opposed to a permit-type system involved in Nelson. The link, if any, between disease and the introduction of potatoes was, according to the joint reasons, 'far too remote'.[75] Rich J stated that test was whether the impact of the challenged provision was 'direct and immediate', or merely consequential. Here the regulation operated directly on importation, thus it was invalid.[76] The 'criterion' for the operation of the legislation was the source of the product.[77] This was offensive to s 92.

---

[71] Ibid 236: 'If we could admit "health" to be a legitimate ground of exception from the unqualified language of s92, we could find no halting place'.

[72] Ibid 246.

[73] Ibid 253.

[74] (1934) 52 CLR 157.

[75] Ibid 169.

[76] Ibid 173. This test of whether the measure 'directly' restricted interstate trade and commerce, as opposed to 'remotely' or 'incidentally', was adopted by the Privy Council in *Commonwealth v Bank of NSW* (*Bank Nationalisation Case*)(1949) 79 CLR 497, 637 (Lord Porter, for the Council).

[77] (1934) 52 CLR 157, 173.

Dixon J, also in the majority, strongly criticised the reasoning of the statutory majority in *Ex Parte Nelson*. He took issue with the reference in that reasoning to the 'true nature and character' of challenged legislation, in determining whether or not it was valid according to s 92. There the majority characterised the legislation as relating to health and the prevention of contagion and infectious disease. The majority there found the challenged legislation was not in itself regulation of interstate trade and commerce, though it was affected by the legislation.

Dixon J expressed strong disagreement with this reasoning:

> I find myself unable to regard this mode of reasoning as relevant to s92. It assumes that, because the legislation relates to disease in cattle, it cannot relate to trade in cattle. It appears to be quite plain that the statute stopped inter-state trade in cattle as a measure of precaution against the spread of disease. When a state by legislation forbids importation from another state of an ordinary commodity, it is difficult to understand what are the further considerations which must be inquired into under the description 'grounds and design of the legislation' … if the words mean that it is always necessary to ascertain why it does (what it does), the answer is that the terms of s92 admit of no excuses or justifications for abrogating the freedom of trade in a commodity … section 92 withdraws from the parliament of the state any power to detract from the absolute freedom of trade, commerce and intercourse between the states. Whatever purpose may be disclosed by state legislation … it may not restrict this freedom … what possible doubt can there be that, when it forbids the introduction into the state of a commodity produced in another state, it does restrict freedom of trade between the states.[78]

VI PROPORTIONALITY

There has been an increase in the use of proportionality in Australian constitutional law in recent years. While it is not an unfamiliar doc-

---

[78] Ibid 180-181.

trine in constitutional law jurisprudence, utilised sometimes in determining whether or not a Commonwealth head of power supports particular legislation,[79] its use has become more widespread. The concept of proportionality is significantly utilised in European human rights law, and it may have originally hailed from Germany.[80] It enjoys the strong support of the current Chief Justice of the High Court of Australia.[81] Its most ubiquitous use in recent constitutional law cases in Australia has occurred in relation to the implied freedom of political communication, where five of the current members of the High Court use it in order to determine whether or not legislation is consistent with the implied freedom.[82]

In that context of proportionality, the High Court has stated that there are three components of a proportionality analysis. The court must consider whether the law is suitable, necessary and adequate in its balance. A law will be suitable if rationally connected to its purpose. It will be necessary if there is no obvious and compelling alternative reasonably practical means to achieve the same purpose in a manner less restrictive of the freedom. The question of adequacy in the balance involves a weighing of the impact of the restrictions on the affected freedom, having regard to the importance of the objective.[83]

Application of a proportionality approach to a constitutional right or freedom is in sharp contrast to an absolutist approach to a constitutional right or freedom. As discussed above, there have been occasions in earlier s 92 decisions where an absolutist approach is

---

[79] For example, in the context of s51(29), see *Commonwealth v Tasmania* (1983) 158 CLR 1, 260 (Deane J); regarding s 51(6) *Polyukovich v Commonwealth* (1991) 172 CLR 501, 592 (Brennan J); and regarding the inherent nationhood power, *Davis v Commonwealth* (1988) 166 CLR 79, 99 (Mason CJ Deane and Gaudron JJ).

[80] Mosie Cohen-Elija and Iddo Porat 'Proportionality and the Culture of Justification' (2011) 59 *American Journal of Comparative Law* 463.

[81] Susan Kiefel 'Proportionality: A Rule of Reason' (2012) 23(2) *Public Law Review* 85.

[82] Proportionality was accepted in *McCloy v New South Wales* (2015) 257 CLR 178, 194-195 (French CJ Kiefel Bell and Keane), and was subsequently accepted by Nettle and Edelman JJ. Gordon and Gageler JJ do not accept the proportionality approach to the implied freedom of political communication.

[83] 195.

clearly evident. However, the trend seems to be away from an absolutist approach to interpretation of rights enshrined in the *Constitution*, although the particular provision might be written in absolute terms. So, for example, s 117 of the Australian *Constitution* prohibits states from discriminating on the basis of residence. Yet, the High Court has not interpreted this provision in the absolutist, literal terms in which it appears. It has allowed exceptions, where states can point to legitimate reasons for a provision that would otherwise fall foul of the prohibition.[84] One criticism of the development along these lines is that, of the seven justices in the relevant decision, *Street v Queensland Bar Association*, there are seven different articulations of precisely what the exception is.[85] This is not desirable.

The same might be said of s 99. That section appears to absolutely preclude Commonwealth laws from giving preference to states or parts of states. No exceptions appear. However, in *Permanent Trustee Australia v Commissioner of State Revenue*,[86] the joint reasons accepted that a law which had this effect could be valid if 'the differential treatment and unequal outcomes that are involved ... (were) the product of distinctions that are appropriate and adapted to a proper objective'. Thus, there are clear trends in relation to constitutional interpretation away from a literalist position of simply applying the words in the *Constitution* as written, and permitting exceptions to apparently strict rules, where they can be clearly justified by the enacting authority.

---

[84] *Street v Queensland Bar Association* (1989) 168 CLR 461.

[85] Mason CJ expressed it in terms of a 'compelling justification': 493 (and he specifically rejected a test based on the 'criterion of operation': at 487; Brennan J said it would be enough that the differential treatment 'has a rational and proportionate connection with a legitimate objective': at 511-512; Deane J based an exception on discrimination that flowed naturally from the nature and scope of state government responsibilities: at 529; Dawson J referred to a test based on the 'ordinary and proper administration of the state': at 548; Toohey J referred to a discrimination which was a natural consequence of legislation aimed at protecting the legitimate interests of the 'state community': at 560; Gaudron J stated that discrimination based on a relevant difference and appropriate to that difference: at 572-573; McHugh J stated the exception must relate to something arising by necessary implication from the assumptions and structure of the *Constitution*': at 584.

[86] (2004) 220 CLR 388.

Of course, this could be part of a much broader debate about constitutional interpretation, including the suggested virtues of literalism, as opposed to a flexible and/or 'living tree' approach. It is not possible to enter this debate here, but it is part of the milieu in which consideration of (implied) exceptions to apparently absolute provisions in the *Constitution* are considered.

The immediate question is the extent to which this kind of 'exception' might be applicable regarding s 92. Specifically, whether proportionality (as one kind of exception) might or should be utilised in s 92 cases, in particular those involving the intercourse aspect of the section. Once the High Court accepted that the freedoms with which s 92 was concerned were not absolute in nature, a position all members of the High Court arrived at in *Cole v Whitfield*, it became inevitable that a test would be needed to determine which measures would be valid, and which would be invalid. If some restrictions were compatible with s 92, how would a court determine which ones? The High Court had already in *Cole* rejected the past distinction between direct and indirect restrictions, although as indicated above, there has been evidence since *Cole* that this distinction might be creeping back into the analysis.

Enter the concept of proportionality. Though it was not referred to in the Cole decision, it was referred to in the decision *Castlemaine Tooheys Ltd v South Australia*.[87] It must be acknowledged that that case involved the trade and commerce, not intercourse, aspect of s 92. This means it was focussed on an application of the tests of discrimination and protectionist purpose, and it has already been indicated above that these concepts cannot easily be applied to the intercourse aspect of the section. That concession having been made, comments made there regarding proportionality are considered to be of possible relevance to any future cases involving intercourse.

The main joint reasons of Mason CJ, Brennan, Deane, Dawson and Toohey JJ stated that a law would be consistent with s 92 if it imposed a burden upon interstate trade and commerce that was incidental, or

---

[87] (1990) 169 CLR 436.

not disproportionate, to the attainment of the law's legitimate objective.[88] The main joint reasons denied that s 92 had the effect of extinguishing burdens on interstate trade that were 'necessary or appropriate and adapted to the protection of the people of the state from a real danger or threat to its wellbeing'.[89] The Court noted that it would be deferential to an assessment by a state government that particular measures were or were not necessary to deal with a particular problem.[90]

Members of the High Court in *Betfair Pty Ltd v Western Australia* discussed the suggestion that proportionality was relevant (again, in the context of the trade and commerce, not intercourse, aspect of the power), but seemed to prefer a test of 'reasonable necessity'.[91] It will be recalled that this was the limit on s 92 freedom accepted by Griffith CJ and Barton J in R v Smithers.

VII APPLICATION OF VARIOUS TESTS TO CURRENT WESTERN AUSTRALIAN LEGISLATION

I will now apply each of the above tests that have been discussed and applied in relation to s 92 to the current Western Australian *Quarantine (Closing the Border) Directions.*

If the absolutist approach, favoured by Isaacs J and others, were taken, the Western Australian directions would be invalid, because they clearly impose on the movement of trade, commerce and intercourse across the border dividing Western Australia from South Australia and the Northern Territory.

Some judges have considered whether the legislation is 'pointed at' or 'aimed at' or 'directed against' interstate trade and commerce. Legislation that does so is, according to Higgins J in *Smithers*, and Rich, Starke and Dixon JJ in *Gratwick*, invalid due to s 92. This came to be known as the 'criterion of operation' test. As noted above, this test

---

88 Ibid 473.
89 Ibid 473.
90 Ibid 473.
91 (2008) 234 CLR 418, 477 (Gleeson CJ Gummow Kirby Hayne Crennan and Kiefel JJ).

was apparently rejected by the High Court in *Cole v Whitfield*, who dismissed its formality, technicality and narrowness.[92]

However, somewhat unexpectedly, since the sharp rejection of this approach in *Cole*, shortly thereafter members of the High Court began to distinguish circumstances where a law directly impacted interstate trade, commerce and intercourse, and where the law only incidentally did so.[93] It seems that a law of the first kind will be unconstitutional due to s 92, whereas the second may not be. Respectfully, it is somewhat confusing that the High Court apparently rejected the criterion of operation test in *Cole*, only to apparently re-assert its substance (though not by name) in subsequent cases, by considering whether the law directly impacted trade, commerce and intercourse.

Another way of expressing this sentiment is to ask whether the object of the legislation is to impede interstate trade, commerce and intercourse. This is more difficult than it sounds, because it is not entirely clear whether the fact that legislation has this effect will be sufficient. And legislation is often passed for multiple purposes.

Putting these difficulties to one side for the present, the application of these tests to the existing Western Australian directions suggest grave difficulties. The Directions clearly do directly impact, and have the object of impacting, interstate intercourse. Thus, on this approach, the legislation would be invalid. The current authorities have generally adopted a two stage approach, considering firstly whether (a) the challenged legislation has an object (or the object or predominant object[94] – it is not always clearly articulated in the judgments

---

[92] (1988) 165 CLR 360, 401-403.

[93] For example, *Nationwide News Pty Ltd v Wills* (1992) 177 CLR 1, 58-59 (Brennan J); *Cunliffe v Commonwealth* (1994) 182 CLR 272, 307-308 (Mason CJ) referring to the invalidity of a law 'which in terms applies to movement across a border'; Deane J(with whom Gaudron J agreed) used the concept of 'incidental' burdens: at 346, and McHugh J stated that laws which 'directly' restricted or burdened interstate trade and commerce were more likely to be invalid: at 396.

[94] One rare example of clarity on this point appears in the judgment of Brennan J in *Nationwide News Pty Ltd v Wills* (1992) 177 CLR 1, 59 where he stated that the 'chief' purpose was the relevant one, in cases of multiple purposes.

which of these it is)[95] of impeding intercourse; and (b) if not, whether the legislation can be defended on reasonable necessity/proportionality grounds. Though it has not been specifically spelled out, it is surely a logical premise from this two-stage approach that a law which fits into category (a) is invalid, without further inquiry. In other words, the High Court adopts an essentially absolutist prohibition on laws which have the object of impeding interstate intercourse. It is only when laws are not in that category that the justifications for it are considered. This is considered to be the current state of the authorities.

On this basis, there is a strong argument that the Western Australian Directions are invalid because they have the object of impeding interstate intercourse, or have the predominant purpose of doing so.

Now, I may be wrong, and the High Court may find that the Western Australian Direction does not have the object, or the predominant object, of impeding interstate intercourse. If so, part (b) of the test becomes important. Here again, there seems to be some divergence of approach in terms of the test by which the validity of the measure will be assessed. I will apply each of the possible tests:

---

[95] The decision in *Castlemaine Tooheys Ltd v South Australia* (1990) 169 CLR 436 seems to sidestep this issue by apparently taking the position that a law has one purpose, which is either protectionist (seeking to protect local businesses) or non-protectionist (the state claimed an environmental rationale). Thus, the Court did not consider the resolution of a situation where a law has or may have multiple purposes. It may in such cases be necessary to consider the predominant purpose of the law. Other s 92 cases also seem to proceed on this premise – for example in *APLA Ltd v Legal Services Commissioner* (2005) 224 CLR 322, 355 Gleeson CJ and Heydon J asked whether 'the object' of the legislation was to impede interstate intercourse (again, implying legislation can only have one purpose and not clarifying what happens if legislation has more than one purpose), Gummow J did acknowledge the possibility of 'objects' of legislation, but similarly did not clarify how s 92 should apply in such cases: at 393. There is of course also a healthy debate about whether it is the effect of the law, rather than its purpose, that should decide questions about its constitutionality: Gonzalo Villalta Puig 'A European Saving Test for Section 92 of the Australian *Constitution*' (2008) 13(1) *Deakin Law Review* 99, 119: the reality is that it is only the effect of the law or measure that can be empirically quantified. Unlike purpose, effect is not measured in words but in actions. Effect is palpable and tangible. Purpose is not'; Christopher Staker 'Section 92 of the *Constitution* and the European Court of Justice' (1990) 19 *Federal Law Review* 322, 340.

A *What is reasonably required to achieve the object of the legislation (Gleeson CJ, McHugh and Gummow JJ in AMS, Gleeson CJ and Heydon J in APLA)*

The object of the legislation, to try to keep Western Australians as safe as possible from COVID-19, is clear enough. The question is whether a blanket prohibition, with limited particular exceptions, is 'reasonably required', or greater than that which is reasonably required to achieve legislative object/s. It is suggested that current rates of infection, in particular community transmission, are very low in almost all States in Australia, other than Victoria. Specifically, they are very low in the two jurisdictions that share a border with Western Australia, South Australia and the Northern Territory. Given the importance of freedom of movement around Australia in terms of a constitutional value, it is concluded that the Western Australian provisions go beyond what is reasonably required. A so-called 'hard border' with Victoria, prohibiting the movement of someone from Victoria and who had recently been in that state, might be reasonably required. It is very difficult to justify imposing similar draconian restrictions on those who have not been in that state.

B *Proportionality (Gummow J in APLA, Castlemaine Tooheys, Dawson J in Cunliffe), Implied Freedom of Political Communication*

It is not yet clear whether the High Court will apply a proportionality test to s 92 cases. While it suggested it might do so in *Castlemaine Tooheys*, it suggested another test in a subsequent decision in *Betfair*. If it does apply proportionality to s 92, it is similarly not clear whether it will use it as part of the same structured approach it applies to the implied freedom of political communication, considering whether the challenged measure is suitable, necessary and adequate in its balance.

On the assumption that the High Court will apply a proportionality analysis to s 92, and will apply it in the structured way that it does in relation to political communication, we must consider whether the Western Australian measures are suitable to achieving their objective, necessary and adequate in their balance.[96] These laws may be suitable, in that they are an understandable and defensible way of achieving their objective, in terms of seeking to quarantine the state from disease being transmitted from elsewhere. However, it is less clear that they are 'necessary', in particular given the very low rates of community transmission in all states and territories, other than Victoria. Measures that are less invasive of freedom of intercourse arguably would also achieve the same objective as that sought by the legislation, including border checks, taking contact details, taking the temperature of those seeking to enter, and only imposing a hard border on those coming from Victoria.

Further, they may for similar reasons not be held to be adequate in their balance, given the importance of the right that they significantly impede, and the threat to Western Australia. They directly target and attack one of the most fundamental freedoms of all that Australians possess, a freedom the founding fathers saw fit to emphatically enshrine in the *Constitution*, when they generally eschewed express rights protection. This freedom gives effect to the whole concept of Australia, and reflects one of the main reasons for the country's establishment and existence. While of course we must remain vigilant, Western Australia has had very low levels of the virus for many months now. Its neighbouring jurisdictions are in a similar position. It is hard to justify the hard border being applied currently in Western Australia to any traveller other than one from Victoria as being adequate in its balance, having regard to the serious impact on such a fundamental freedom.

C *Reasonable Necessity (R v Smithers per Griffith CJ and Barton, Callinan J in AMS)*

It is not entirely clear the extent to which this test would lead to tangibly different results than the first two tests. Callinan J in AMS suggested this test would be more difficult to justify than some of the others. If there is a difference, it would be more difficult, if anything,

---

[96] *McCloy v New South Wales* (2015) 256 CLR 178, 195 (French CJ, Kiefel Bell and Keane JJ).

for Western Australia to meet this test. It is hard to strongly argue the reasonable necessity for a hard border, given the low level of case numbers in most of the Australian states and territories. Measures that are less invasive of a fundamental constitutional right are readily available.

D *Measures Necessary for the Purposes of an Ordered Society/ Protection of Legitimate Claims of a State/Consistent with a Free Society and the Rule of Law (Mason CJ, Deane, Gaudron and McHugh JJ in Cunliffe, Gaudron and Kirby JJ in AMS)*

This test would be most advantageous to Western Australia. Some version of it appeared to enjoy majority support in *Cunliffe*, though the different ways in which different judges expressed it in that case weaken its precedent value. In any event, such broad-brush uncertain expressions of an exception did not enjoy majority support in *AMS* or *APLA*,[97] and was heavily criticised by Hayne J in the latter case. It is unlikely to enjoy support on the current High Court, which tends to favour tighter tests for constitutionality. Western Australia would have an argument that the measures are necessary to avoid public panic during the pandemic, that it is a legitimate interest for a state to seek to keep out a deadly disease. The measures are set out clearly in legislation, so may be compatible with the rule of law.[98] Adoption of this test is considered to be Western Australia's greatest chance of success.

---

[97] James Stellios 'The Intercourse Limb of Section 92 and the High Court's Decision in APLA Ltd v Legal Services Commissioner (NSW)(2006) 17 *Public Law Review* 10, 15.

[98] I do not pursue here an abstract argument that because the measures are seriously liberty-restricting, this aspect, per se, leads to a breach of the rule of law: see for example T R S Allan *Law, Liberty and Justice: The Legal Foundations of British Constitutionalism* (1993) 21. If there were evidence the measures were being applied in an arbitrary manner, arguments about breach of the rule of law might be stronger: Anthony Gray 'The Rule of Law and Reasonable Suspicion' (2011) 16(2) *Australian Journal of Human Rights* 53, 63-66. It has generally proven difficult to get the High Court to declare legislation constitutionally invalid on the basis it is said to be contrary to the rule of law.

In conclusion, on the likely tests to be applied to a current dispute involving the intercourse aspect of s 92, the reasonably required test, the proportionality test and/or the reasonable necessity test, Western Australia may well lose a s 92 challenge to its current border restrictions, in so far as they apply to travellers coming from any part of Australia other than Victoria.

VIII IMPLICATIONS FOR THE 'TRADE AND COMMERCE' ASPECTS OF SECTION 92

While this discussion is sufficient to deal with the current issue over borders, the discussion potentially has broader implications for the interpretation of the 'trade and commerce' aspect of s 92. As explained above, one impact of the *Cole v Whitfield* was to create (or rather suggest) a disjunct to the approach taken to the 'trade and commerce' aspect of s 92, compared with the 'intercourse' aspect of s 92. Hayne J has rightly criticised this. It is problematic, partly because there is often overlap between them. It seems anomalous and intellectually unsatisfactory that the Court could arrive at different results depending on whether it focuses on the goods or services affected by a restriction (ie the trade and commerce aspect of s 92) or the relevant individual (trader, distributor) etc.

There is a solution. The essential cause of the disjunct was the High Court's insistence that laws challenged under the trade and commerce aspect of s 92 had to be both (a) discriminatory against interstate trade and commerce; and (b) protectionist of local industry, compared with interstate industry. It is limb (b) that creates the disconnect, because it is unlikely that laws impacting interstate intercourse will be limited or even in most cases limited to those seeking to protect local trade and commerce.

As I indicated in an earlier article, the High Court's insistence that only laws with the relevant 'protectionist purpose' are invalid due to s 92 can be criticised.[99] *Cole v Whitfield* itself is internally contradictory, at times seeming to view protectionism as a separate requirement to

---

[99] Anthony Gray 'Section 92 of the *Constitution*: The Next Phase' (2016) 44(1) *Australian Business Law Review* 35, 44-48.

discrimination;[100] at others, to conflate them.[101] Other federations that seek to create and preserve a common market, such as the European Union and United States, do not limit their prohibitions to protectionist measures. It is enough (for invalidity) that they are discriminatory.

It is suggested that the High Court remove the requirement, in order for a law to be invalid due to the 'trade and commerce' aspect of s 92, that the measure be shown to be protectionist.[102] Rather, the test should focus on whether the impugned measure is discriminatory against interstate trade and commerce. If so, it is prima facie invalid, unless the legislation survives a proportionality analysis. In other words, although a law that discriminates against interstate trade and commerce is prima facie invalid, it will be valid if the enacting state can demonstrate that it is suitable to a legitimate objective, necessary in order to achieve that objective, and adequate in its balance, having regard to the importance of free trade and movement of goods around Australia.

This would have the effect of re-aligning the approaches to the interstate trade and commerce aspect of s 92, and the interstate intercourse aspect of the section. This is highly desirable. It would reduce the opportunity for states to erect barriers to free trade, contrary to the vision of the founding fathers. Rather than a challenger having to demonstrate that a particular law was passed for a protectionist purpose, something which has proven to be difficult to do, it would place the onus on the enacting state to demonstrate how its measures are compatible with the freedom of trade, commerce and intercourse that the Australian *Constitution* enshrines. It would not be an easy argument

---

[100] (1988) 165 CLR 360, 408: 'Where the law in effect ... discriminates in favour of intrastate trade, it will nevertheless offend against s92 if the discrimination is of a protectionist kind'.

[101] For example, a reference to a law whose 'effect is discriminatory in that it discriminates against interstate trade and commerce and *thereby* protects intrastate trade and commerce of the same kind': 407 (emphasis added).

[102] Anthony Gray 'Section 92 of the *Constitution*: The Next Phase' (2016) 44(1) *Australian Business Law Review* 35, 50 reached a similar conclusion: 'it is not worth the trouble to retain the requirement of a 'protectionism' finding in order to find a provision in breach of s92'.

for a state to make. Nor should it be. A state would be in a better position to have the necessary evidence to demonstrate how its measures are justified along these lines than for a challenger to try to demonstrate the existence of improper purposes.

IX CONCLUSION

The idea of freedom of trade, commerce and intercourse within the country's physical land mass was absolutely fundamental to the creation of the nation and its foundational legal document. In a document that is otherwise largely barren of express rights protection, s 92 is a standout example. The vision of a unified, connected nation is clearly evident. It must be maintained. Clearly the COVID-19 crisis has placed great strain on the nation. There are understandable attempts by governments to protect the safety of citizens, and respond to community concerns. Yet, the purpose of the *Constitution* is to place certain values above the day to day exigencies.

This article has charted developments in the High Court's interpretation of s 92. While it is by now accepted that the section does not confer absolute rights, it has proven somewhat problematic for the Court to properly articulate how a measure said to offend s 92 will be assessed. Tests such as reasonable necessity, proportionality and/or reasonable regulation to meet legitimate objectives seem to be the most likely to be applied. These tests are likely to apply quite similar principles, and lead to similar results in most cases. Applying these tests, it is considered likely that a s 92 challenge to the Western Australian Directions would be successful. The need for restrictions of that magnitude is far from clear. While some restrictions, particularly those on movement from Victoria, might well be justified, arguably the measures go well beyond that, and their impact on interstate movement is very significant. The measures are arguably disproportionate to achievement of their legitimate objective.

As important as that conclusion is, this article reaches a more important finding. The current s 92 case law is anomalous in applying a different test to the 'trade and commerce' aspect of the section compared with the 'intercourse' aspect. This is unsatisfactory. In considering the 'intercourse' aspect of the section in more detail, this article has suggested that one test be used for s 92. That test would consider whether the measure in question discriminates, on its face or in effect, against interstate trade, commerce and/or intercourse. If it does, it is prima facie invalid. It would be open to the enacting government to try to save the measure, by arguing it is designed to achieve a particular policy objective, and is proportional, reasonably necessary etc to achieve that objective. In this way, congruence in the interpretation given to the two aspects of the section would return. The test for a breach of s 92 would be easier to apply, and restrictions on interstate trade, commerce and intercourse harder to defend. That is as it should be, to give effect to the vision of the founding fathers regarding how the nation would operate.

Postscript: As this article was about to the published, the High Court announced that it would dismiss, at least by majority, Mr Palmer's s92 challenge to the Western Australian border restrictions. Kiefel CJ announced that the High Court had found that the Western Australian border restrictions '(did) not raise a constitutional question': *Palmer v State of Western Australia* [2020] HCA Trans 180. While we must await the publication of the reasoning of the members of the Court to more fully understand this position, this writer must respectfully disagree with it, for the reasons stated in this article.

7

Blurred Lines between Freedom of Religion and Protection of Public Health in the Covid-19 Era – Italy and Poland in a Comparitive Perspective

WERONIKA KUDLA* AND GRZEGORZ JAN BLICHARZ**

ABSTRACT

The COVID-19 pandemic caused a dramatic split between the right to protect one's health, which in current situation is effective by practicing 'social distancing' or even a complete isolation, and the liberty to participate in social life, which is essential for our mental health. While medicine and science grapple with coronavirus, trying to find an effective cure for the novel disease, government leaders aim to curb its spread by adopting preventive measures which often collide with many constitutional rights. The chapter analyses the impact of safety measures and limitations introduced by civil authorities of Italy and Poland on religious liberty, especially the right to religious gatherings in situations of health emergency caused by the outbreak of coronavirus pandemic. In both countries the relations between Church and State are based upon the cooperation, not separation, between both spheres. Thus, religion isn't confined to the private life of citizens, but constitutes a vital part of social life with Catholic Church as the majority religion. Taking into account temporary restrictions adopted into legal frameworks of these countries from the beginning of COVID-19 pandemic, it's interesting to observe their impact on in-person collective worship. Although Italy's and Poland's legal systems have many

* PhD, MArts, Jagiellonian University (Poland)
** PhD, MPhil, Assistant Professor at the Chair of Roman Law, Faculty of Law and Administration, Jagiellonian University (Poland).

points in common, the experience of pandemic in these countries is quite different with Italy being the first most affected European country by coronavirus crisis. For that reason, the assessment of restrictions imposed on religious worship in these countries can offer an instructive lesson with regards to adequacy and proportionality of measures aimed in first place to fight with the virus, and subsequently to co-exist with it.

I INTRODUCTION

The rapid spread of global pandemic caused by COVID-19 virus compelled the entire humanity to change or even totally abandon its existing regulations regarding human behavior in order to protect every human life from the novel and highly contagious disease. Lost in cacophony of changing rules regarding almost every dimension of our life, humanity had to give a humble look back at the history of past epidemics which despite the medical, social and economic progress still can offer an instructive lesson of survival. Striking similarities with the past can be discerned especially in the area of religious liberty as we notice that in situations of crisis, fear, imminent danger and death, people want to turn to God in search of comfort and consolation. The current pandemic of COVID-19 has only revived old schemes of human behavior in which the need of affinity between man and God becomes particularly strong. The essence of religious freedom is the right to practice one's religion or beliefs not only individually, but also collectively, not only in private, but also in public.[1] Although religious freedom is a fundamental human right, it's not absolute and in some circumstances it can be legitimately restricted. Undoubtedly, the coronavirus epidemic belongs to these extraordinary situations in which the protection of public health competes with the right to worship. Although the current health emergency doesn't undermine the freedom of conscience, which as an

---

[1] Franciszek Longchamps de Bérier, 'Law and Collective Identity. Religious Freedom in the Public Sphere' (2017) 10(1) *Krakowskie Studia z Historii Państwa i Prawa* 170. This paper is based on the legal situation as of September 2020. The authors inform that, as from November 2020, Poland is expecting to face more and far harsher governmental restrictions.

innate human right cannot be limited or forbidden as such, churches, religious organisations and individuals around the world are facing a significant limitation of their essential right as they cannot collectively attend faith services due to the COVID-19 preventive measures. Numerous questions arise regarding the extent, rationality and proportionality of limitations imposed both on believers and non-believers crossing the borders of countries affected by the virus which causes the COVID-19 disease. The right of individuals and churches to freely practice religion through collective participation and physical contact among the faithful clashes with the government's obligation to protect public health. The adoption of the most effective preventive measures – social distancing and reduction of individual mobility – significantly limits religious liberty. Scientific and medical data identify the coronavirus as highly contagious especially in large gatherings so limitations of them imposed by civil authorities also on religious entities remain a matter of grave concern and ferocious legal battles.

Courts around the world are being confronted with challenges brought by religious communities over the limitation or even a complete closure of their gatherings. These are regarded as discriminatory in comparison to measures imposed at the same time on secular gatherings. The most evocative example among this type of court cases comes from France's Council of State which, in a decision of 18 May 2020, forced the government to reopen churches for public religious gatherings arguing that:

> [u]nder these conditions [when] less strict control measures are possible, in particular with regard to allowing the gatherings of less than 10 people in public places, [...] the general and absolute prohibition of [...] any gathering or assembly in places of worship [...] is disproportionate to the objective of preserving public health and thus constitutes, given the essential nature of this component of freedom of worship, a serious and manifestly unlawful infringement of the latter.[2]

---

[2] *Order of the Council of State no 440366 of 18 May 2020*, point 34 <https://www. legifrance.gouv.fr/affichJuri Admin.do?idTexte=CETATEXT000041897157 (last access: 28.08.2020)>.

This article offers an analysis of extraordinary regulations implemented to curb transmission of COVID-19 by the governments of two European countries – namely Italy and Poland – with regards to restrictions on the religious freedom. In each of these countries religious liberty is a fundamental value under the Constitution.[3] Similarly, all churches and religious organisations have equal rights in them. In Italy as well in Poland the relations with the Roman Catholic Church, the prevailing religionamong citizens,[4] are defined by concordats with the Holy See. Moreover, unlike French and American models of separation between church and state, both in Italy and Poland relations between church and state are based upon their cooperation.[5] Church–state relations are to be resolved through negotiations rather than litigations. In fact, in both countries there were no legal claims against government filed by any religious group. Nevertheless, the lack of legal battles doesn't mean that the extent of restrictions wasn't contested by them since it indisputably constitutes a matter of great concern for churches and their faithful. Thus, the comparison between the decision-making process regarding hosting public religious events during the COVID-19 pandemic in these two legal systems may give relevant conclusions. The most important factor, however, which makes a difference is the public health emergency. Whereas Italy became the first focal point of the coronavirus outbreak in Europe, Poland still belongs

---

[3] See *The Italian Constitution* art 19 and *The Constitution of the Republic of Poland* art 53.

[4] According to the researches approximately 67 per cent of the Italian population identifies as Roman Catholic. See: US Department of State, 'Office of International Religious Freedom – 2019 Report on International Religious Freedom: Italy' <https://www.state.gov/reports/2019-report-on-international-religious-freedom/italy/>. The Polish Statistical Yearbook reports that 86 per cent of the population is Roman Catholic: Główny Urzą d Statystyczny, *Statistical Yearbook of the Republic of Poland* (Warszawa, 2019) Tabl 5 (129) 197.

[5] Joseph H Weiler, 'Lautsi: A Reply' (2013) 11(1) *International Journal of Constitutional Law* 233; Grzegorz Blicharz (ed), *Freedom of Religion. A Comparative Law Perspective* (Wydawnictwo IWS, 2019) 8–9; Weronika Kudła, *Wrogość wobec religii. Ostrzeżenia ze strony Sądu Najwyższego USA* (Księgarnia Akademicka, 2018) 332.

to countries with moderate number of positive cases of coronavirus.[6] The assessment of restrictions implemented in each of these countries cannot be in any case comparable between them due to the different development of the epidemic. However, with regards to the religious liberty it's interesting to observe how civil and religious authorities coped with the challenges regarding the limits on religious gatherings bearing in mind similarities of church–state relations. We are leaving aside discussions on the validity or appropriateness of legislative procedure launched to implement restrictions on religious liberty which sparked some discussions in both countries.[7] Under the Polish Constitution higher standards are set regarding limiting the freedom to manifest religion than other rights and freedoms (arts 53-7 *Constitution of Republic of Poland*, hereinafter: 'Polish Constitution'), yet still public health is a legitimate reason to interfere with the freedom of religion. How to weigh both constitutional values, to what extent religious liberty can be limited, and how to preserve exercise of religious freedom in the face of public health danger, is what this paper aims to analyse.

II ITALY'S RESPONSE TO COVID-19 CRISIS WITH RESPECT TO RELIGIOUS LIBERTY

Italy was the first European country which experienced a quick and steep increase in new COVID-19 positive cases (particularly in three northern regions: Lombardy, Emilia-Romagna and Veneto), becoming the epicenter of coronavirus and experimental field with regards

---

[6] As of 6 August 2020 the total number of positive cases of COVID-19 in Italy reaches 248,803 with 35,181 deaths, while Poland reports 48,789 with 1,756 deaths. See 'WHO Health Emergency Dashboard', *World Health Organisation* <https://covid19. who.int>.

[7] See, eg, Jerzy Kwaśniewski et al, 'Analysis of restrictions on freedom of religion and movement introduced in connection with counteracting the coronavirus epidemic in the light of the standards of the Polish Constitution and international law', *Ordo Iuris*, 16 April 2020 <https://ordoiuris.pl/wolnosci-obywatelskie/analiza-wprowadzonych-w-zwiazku-z-przeciwdzialaniem-epidemii-koronawirusa#_ftn25>; Fabio Adernò, 'L'emergenza "Coronavirus" in Italia: il Governo e la Chiesa', *Ius in Itinere*, 8 May 2020. <https://www.iusinitinere.it/lemergenza-coronavirus-in-italia-il-governo-e-la-chiesa-27827>.

to modes and measures aimed to extinguish the epidemic. The Italian Government declared the "state of emergency" for six months starting from 31 January 2020[8] (one day later after the WHO Director-General declared the novel coronavirus a public health emergency of international concern).[9] The first COVID-19 patient of Italy was diagnosed on 20th February in Codogno hospital (Lombardy) and as a quick answer to the possible health crisis, Italian authorities adopted on 23 February 2020 a decree-law[10] to combat and contain the COVID-19 virus. Regulations which went in force targeted only municipalities and areas of at least one new COVID-19 positive case. Among the emergency measures imposed in so-called "red zones" of northern Italy were the limitation of mobility, closure of all educational and cultural services and suspension of manifestations and meetings of any kind, taking place in public or private places (also of cultural, recreational, sporting and religious nature).

The subsequent dramatic surge of new positive cases of COVID-19 and deterioration of the sanitary situation led to the extension of preventive measures through the entire territory of Italy. The Prime Ministerial Decree of 8 March 2020[11] described as *#ImStayingHome Decree* provided far-reaching limitations only for Lombardy and 14

---

[8] 'Dichiarazione dello stato di emergenza in conseguenza del rischio sanitario connesso all'insorgenza di patologie derivanti da agenti virali trasmissibilim', *GU Serie Generale*, n 26, 1 February 2020.

[9] 'WHO Director-General's statement on IHR Emergency Committee on Novel Coronavirus (2019-nCoV)', *World Health Organization* <https://www.who.int/dg/speeches/detail/who-director-general-s-statement-on-ihr-emergency-committee-on-novel-coronavirus-(2019-ncov)>.

[10] 'Decreto-Legge 23 febbraio 2020, n. 6: Misure urgenti in materia di contenimento e gestione dell'emergenza epidemiologica da COVID-19', *GU Serie Generale*, n 45, 23 Feburary 2020) converted with modification into 'Legge 5 marzo 2020, n 13: Conversione in legge, con modificazioni, del decreto-legge 23 febbraio 2020, n 6, recante misure urgenti in materia di contenimento e gestione dell'emergenza epidemiologica da COVID-19', *GU Serie Generale*, n 61, 9 March 2020.

[11] 'Decreto del Presidente del Consiglio dei Ministri 8 marzo 2020: Ulteriori disposizioni attuative del decreto-legge 23 febbraio 2020, n 6, recante misure urgenti in materia di contenimento e gestione dell'emergenza epidemiologica da COVID-19', *GU Serie Generale*, n 59, 8 March 2020.

surrounding provinces, but in a Decree[12] signed by the Prime Minister one day later, on 9 March 2020, all necessary measures were confirmed and extended to the whole territory of Italy, initially till 3 April 2020 and with the adoption of new decrees remained in force until 3 May 2020. The ban on travel and movement from home, except for work requirements, reasons of absolute urgency or health needs, which had to be proved by means of a self-certification, had been correlated with the suspension of civil and religious ceremonies, funerals included.[13] In the explanation notes provided by the Government it was precisely indicated that places of worship may remain open and can be visited:

> [P]rovided that interpersonal distancing of at least one meter is observed at all times and keeping in mind that all gatherings of any kind are banned. You should visit the place of worship closest to home, or, if traveling to work or moving for any other reason of absolute necessity, the place of worship closest to your workplace or destination or along the way there and back, so that you are justified by your self-certification if you're stopped for checking by law enforcement officers.[14]

As to the ban on religious ceremonies it was specified that 'the celebration of religious services before a gathering of faithful or of other religious rites, regardless of the religion, such as Friday prayer in mosques, Saturday service in synagogues, and Sunday services in

---

[12] 'Decreto del Presidente del Consiglio dei Ministri 9 marzo 2020: Ulteriori disposizioni attuative del decreto-legge 23 febbraio 2020, n 6, recante misure urgenti in materia di contenimento e gestione dell'emergenza epidemiologica da COVID-19, applicabili sull'intero territorio nazionale' GU Serie Generale, n 62, 9 March 2020.

[13] The Prime Ministerial Decree of 8 March 2020 stated in art 2 that 'v) the opening of places of worship is conditioned by the adoption of organisational measures in order to avoid gatherings of people, considering the dimension and characteristic of places and with the aim to guarantee participants the possibility to keep distance of at least one meter indicated in the Appendix 1 letter d). Civil and religious ceremonies are suspended, including those funeral'.

[14] 'FAQs on the Italian Government's #ImStayingHome Decree', Ministero degli Affari Esteri e della Cooperazione Internazionale <https://www.esteri.it/mae/it/ministero/normativaonline/decreto-iorestoacasa-domande-frequenti/faqs-on-the-italian-government-s-imstayinghome-decree.html>.

churches is banned'.[15] As a result, individuals and faith-based communities operating in Italy experienced an unprecedented after World War II restriction of their religious freedom. Given that the *Constitution of the Italian Republic* in art 7 states that: 'The State and the Catholic Church are independent and sovereign, each within its own sphere'[16] and in art 8 confirms that 'denominations other than Catholicism have the right to self-organisation according to their own statutes',[17] the extraordinary regulations concerning suspension of religious ceremonies have directly interfered with their internal autonomy, depriving every religious group of control over the organisation of public religious services. In theory, for Italian faithful it was allowed to enter the church, temple or mosque only for personal prayer. Although the nature of preventive measures was indisputably legitimate as they were adopted to protect public health, their extent might have seemed too wide and disproportionate. Restrictions imposed by the Decree which went in force on 9 March 2020 on the territory of Italy treated every religious denomination on equal, non-specific terms due to the prioritisation of compelling national's interest in protecting health and life. Undoubtedly, the coronavirus crisis brought to the collision of two fundamental freedoms – the right to practice one's religion and the right to protect one's life. The dramatic outbreak of coronavirus in Italy which called for immediate actions under time pressure, left no time for bilateral negotiations between civil authorities and religious leaders regarding possible exemptions from imposed restrictions. During the worst month of COVID-19 crisis in Italy, which brought the peak of new confirmed cases on 22 March 2020 (6557 daily new infections)[18] and the highest number of confirmed deaths on 28 March 2020 (971 deaths reported on that day),[19] religious communities operating in Italy strict-

---

[15] Ibid.

[16] *The Constitution of the Italian Republic* art 7.

[17] Ibid art 8.

[18] Our World in Data, 'Italy: Coronavirus Pandemic' <https://ourworldindata.org/coronavirus/country/italy?country=~ITA>.

[19] Ibid.

ly adhered to the extraordinary laws without any objection[20] and declared complete co-responsibility and cooperation to curb the spread of the novel coronavirus.[21] The major difficulties experienced Catholics who constitute the largest religious group in Italy. The suspension of public Masses forced them to receive pastoral and spiritual assistance virtually through live broadcasts and social media platforms. Despite the fact that churches remained open and individuals could visit them for a prayer taking necessary precautions, they couldn't participate in the celebration of liturgy which is the central part of their faith. Practically, a worshipper who entered a church for individual prayer was obliged to leave it once the liturgy started, even when social distancing rules were obeyed. The reason for such severe preventive measures, which definitely undermined the importance of public religious rites, was the necessity to avoid any gatherings of people. These regulations considered religious events on the same level as cultural, entertainment and sporting manifestations, which cannot be accepted on a long-term basis by religious communities.

---

[20] It should be pointed out that on 12 March 2020 Cardinal Angelo De Donatis issued a decree closing all churches of the Diocese of Rome, but under sharp criticism of Catholics headed by Pope Francis who described the decree as too drastic, it has been modified one day later leaving all parochial churches open for individual prayer. See *Decree Prot. n. 468/20 of Cardinal Vicar Angelo De Donatis of 12 March 2020* <http://www.diocesidiroma.it/decreto-del-cardinale-vicario-angelo-de-donatis-del-12-marzo-2020/> and modified version of the Decree from 13 March 2020 <http://www.diocesidiroma.it/decreto-del-cardinale-vicario-angelo-de-donatis-del-13-marzo-2020/?fbclid=IwAR0u_O2WuLagW1HczoGMiR99jIDVcQDq9h2m9om T5c8vyYwZ4NaSjenWnNI>.

[21] See, eg, 'Note from the the Episcopal Conference of Italy', 8 March 2020 (Decreto 'coronavirus': la posizione della CEI)' <https://www.chiesacattolica.it/decreto-coronavirus-la-posizione-della-cei/>; 'Disposition of Coronavirus Emergency Measures in Muslim Communities', *Union of Italian's Muslim Communities*, 8 March 2020 (*01/2020 – Disposizioni Emergenza Coronavirus per le comunità islamiche*), at https://ucoii.org/2020/03/05/01-2020-disposizioni-emergenza-coronavirus-per-le-comunita-islamiche/ (23.07.2020); 'The statement of Rabbi Alberto Somekh', Jewish Community of Milan, 12 March 2020 (*Talmud: 'Se in città c'è una pestilenza ritira i tuoi passi", cioè: chiuditi in casa').* <https://www.mosaico-cem.it/vita-ebraica/ebraismo/talmud-se-in-citta-ce-una-pestilenza-ritira-i-tuoi-passi-cioe-chiuditi-in-casa>.

The Note,[22] released on 27 March 2020 by the Italian Ministry of the Interior and delivered upon request to the Undersecretary of the Italian Conference of Bishops, contained several detailed clarifications regarding the liberty to worship in churches. First of all, it was highlighted that except for any autonomous decision of ecclesiastical authorities, the closure of churches wasn't foreseen. Moreover, with regards to travel restrictions, the access to the church was made available only on the occasion of movements determined by 'proven working needs' or 'situations of necessity', provided that the church is located along the route and in case of the control by Police Forces the required self-certification is being exhibited or a declaration regarding the existence of these specific reasons made. In light of the government's compelling interest in protecting public health, regulations suspending religious ceremonies and funerals didn't prohibit ministers celebrating liturgy without the presence of people. The ratio of this provision was to avoid gatherings which potentially could become new clusters of COVID-19 infections.

With regards to the Holy Week rites, the note explained that among participants allowed to enter the church for celebration of them were: celebrants, deacon, reader, organist, singer and operators for the transmission. Both ministers and lay participants of the liturgy were required to fulfill the self-certification form indicating the day and time of the celebrations, as well as the address of the church in which the celebration took place. Civil authorities justified these outings as for the purposes similar to "proven working needs" and as such free from penalties for breaching public health orders. Similar considerations applied to the rite of marriage which could take place, provided that the allowed number of five attendees (the celebrant, the married couple and the witnesses) respected safe distance between them.

These extremely stringent limitations of religious liberty remained

---

[22] Ministry of the Interior, the Department for Civil Liberties and Immigration, *'Questions regarding the containment and management of the epidemiological emergency from Covid-19. Needs determined by the exercise of the right to freedom of worship'*, Ministry of the Interior, the Department for Civil Liberties and Immigration, ' <https://www.interno.gov.it/sites/default/files/allegati/specifiche-chiese.pdf>.

in force till 17 May 2020. For the first time in history of Italy, believers of three main monotheistic religions – Jews, Christians and Muslims were forced to celebrate their most significant celebrations of Passover, Easter and Ramadan in complete social isolation from community and with no exemptions made for their spiritual needs.

A *The Violation of Funeral Religious Rites During Pandemic*

Another interfaith challenge for religious liberty during COVID-19 pandemic, which still raises some concerns, concerned the prohibition of funeral ceremonies which usually are carried out according to religious rites. As the death toll from COVID-19 rises around the world, the inability to mourn the death becomes another wrenching disruption and as for now it's still impossible to estimate its long-lasting and surely devastating psychological effects as we bear in mind that the gathered community plays an important role in funeral rituals. Coronavirus pandemic raging across the globe triggered modification of burial procedures which affected almost every religious confession.

Italy became the first European country which was inundated with coffins of victims who died for COVID-19. In a country with such strong Catholic values it was particularly difficult for all believers to adapt to the new restrictions around funerals. The Prime Ministerial order declaring the suspension of funeral ceremonies along with indications[23] issued by the Italian Ministry of Health for healthcare providers, mortuary staff and burial team subjected religious rites and traditions to the new conditions laid down by civil authorities. The complete isolation of people dying from coronavirus in sealed-off hospital wards taken together with the quarantine of people who stayed close to them made it impossible for family members and friends to visit them and participate in their final moments of life. Regulations prohibiting any physical contact with hospitalized patients caused an emotional trauma for them and the only way of communication was

---

[23] See Ministero della Salute, Direzione Generale della Prevenzione Sanitaria Ufficio 4, *Oggetto: Indicazioni emergenziali connesse ad epidemia COVID-19 riguardanti il settore funebre, cimiteriale e di cremazione*. <http://www.ancicampania.it/wp-content/uploads/2020/04/Circolare-servizi-funebri-e-gestione-salme-DEF-2-Copia.pdf>.

possible through a system of video-conference. Nevertheless, following health protocols instituted by hospital authorities, in some of them the chaplains were admitted to continue their mission in bringing the patients pastoral care and sacraments (Eucharist, confession or anointing of the sick), but in the majority of cases chaplains were also barred from entering the coronavirus units so they had to stop saying last rites over the dying persons.

In the region of Lombardy which witnessed the highest mortality rate in Italy,[24] especially in the most infected province of Bergamo, procedures regarding the burial or cremation were accelerated due to the increased flux of deaths from COVID-19.[25] With funeral ceremonies suspended, the burials consisted of a direct transport of the coffin or urns to the cemetery, possibly with a brief blessing offered by the priest and sometimes only in presence of the undertaker and a maximum of five relatives provided that they weren't sick or under quarantine. Thus, under the new funeral procedures the traditional role of religious communities to pay respect to the body, offer consolation to the family members and help to handle the grief have been all undermined as it's still impossible to perform some religious practices after the death. Family members are barred from preparing body of the deceased before burial. For that reason, some religious communities adapted their end-of-life rites to new circumstances. The Islamic Center of Rome which serves the community of Muslims living in Italy issued a series of recommendations regarding funeral rites,[26] calling

---

[24] Statistics regarding number of deaths from COVID-19 in Italy show that Lombardy accounts for more than 50% of deaths of the entire country, counting as of 3 August 2020 the number of 16.818 deaths. See Statista, 'Coronavirus (COVID-19) deaths in Italy as of 3 August 2020, by region' <https://www.statista.com/statistics/1099389/coronavirus-deaths-by-region-in-italy/>.

[25] Chico Harlan, Stefano Pitrelli, 'In an Italian city, obituaries fill the newspaper, but survivors mourn alone', *Washington Post*, March 16, 2020/ <https://www.washingtonpost.com/world/europe/coronavirus-obituaries-bergamo-italy/2020/03/16/6c342f02-66c7-11ea-b199-3a9799c54512_story.html>.

[26] 'Guidelines of the Italian Islamic Confederation regarding the funeral rites during COVID-19 emergency' <http://www.conf-islamica.it/confederazione-islamica-italiana/linee-guida-della-cii-in-materia-di-riti-funebri-nella-situazione-di-emergenza-covid-19/>.

the Muslims to strictly follow government's dispositions regarding the public health. Some traditional rites practiced by Muslims (eg bathing of the body by relatives — *Ghusl* and *Tayammun*) have been modified, others even suspended (eg the process of repatriation of the Muslim migrant's body to his homeland due to closed borders). In order to accommodate religious needs of the Muslims who still wish to repatriate bodies of their family remembers to the country of origin, Mayor of Milan issued an emergency decree[27] permitting for a temporary burial of Muslim bodies and their extraordinary exhumation when the coronavirus restrictions cease. Apart from the modification of religious rites, the Italian Muslim community was confronted with another difficulty pertaining to the short supply of burial spots for non-Catholics in cemeteries (in Italy there're only 76 Islamic cemeteries).[28] Under the Italian law[29] a person should be buried on the territory of the municipality in which he/she died or previously resided. Since in most of the cases public cemeteries in northern Italy didn't have enough burial space designed for Muslims, civil authorities struggled to find plots in more distant regions of Italy breaching not only the existing civil law, but also the Muslim law according to which Islamic burial should take place within 24 hours of death.[30]

The lack of funeral gatherings also resulted in some erroneous burials of victims of coronavirus in common graves when relatives of the deceased were hospitalized or quarantined thus unable to claim

---

[27] 'The Municipality of Milan, Ordinance of the Mayor Giuseppe Sala 18/2020 of 26 March 2020' <http://www.conf-islamica.it/confederazione-islamica-italiana/wp-content/uploads/2020/03/Ordinanza-Sindaco-Milano-n.-16_2020.pdf>.

28 Union of Italian's Muslim Communities, Islamic Cemeteries in Italy <https://ucoii.org/cimiteri-islamici-in-italia/>.

[29] '*Approvazione del regolamento di polizia mortuaria*', Decree of the President of the Republic, 10 September 2020, n 285: art 50 n 1 <http://presidenza.governo.it/USRI/ufficio_studi/normativa/D.P.R.%2010%20settembre%201990,%20n.%20285.pdf>.

30 The shocking example of a Muslim woman living in the province of Pisogne who died during the pandemic and whose coffin was stored at home for a week since she couldn't be neither buried in islamic cemetery, nor expatriated to her homeland shows the inefficacy of existing Italian laws relating to burials: 'Non possono seppellire la giovane mamma: la bara resta in casa una settimana', *Brescia Today*, 25 March 2020 <https://www.bresciatoday.it/attualita/coronavirus/sepoltura-mussulmani-.html>.

the body from hospital. The Italian law which normally gives family members 30 days to decide where the body should be buried, was dramatically reduced by Municipality of Milan to only 5 days.[31] For that reason unclaimed bodies of COVID-19 victims were buried by civil authorities in a special section of Milan cemetery "Campo 87". Recently, authorities of Milan have received an increased number of claims from families who initially couldn't even locate the graves of their family members who died in hospitals from COVID-19 and now demand to retrieve their bodies from lonely graves in order to give the deceased a proper funeral and bury them with other family members.[32] In light of current Italian provisions their requests have been refused as the remains of people who die of an infectious disease can be exhumed after two years from the date of death.[33]

Undoubtedly, Italy had implemented the most stringent lockdown measures to contain the coronavirus which remained in force for more than 60 days. Considering the decreasing number of both new confirmed COVID-19 cases and deaths, the Italian government started to lift some of the restrictions very cautiously since 4 May 2020.[34]

The ceremonies of funerals have been resumed from 4 May 2020 when Italy had already reported almost 29,000 deaths from COVID-19.[35] In accordance with the Prime Ministerial Decree[36] the allowed

---

[31] 'Ordinance of the Mayor Giuseppe Sala 12/2020' *The Municipality of Milan,* 13 March 2020 <https://www.comune.milano.it/documents/20126/78875953/Ordinanza+n.+12+del+13_03_2020+codiv19.pdf/622047d1-be05-af7c-e947-0e19397a93ee?t=1584180195630>.

[32] Angela Giuffrida, 'A proper funeral: families try to claim Covid-19 victims from Milan cemetery', *The Guardian,* 10 June 2020 <https://www.theguardian.com/world/2020/jun/10/it-was-chaotic-the-families-trying-to-claim-covid-19-victims-from-milan-cemetery>.

[33] 'Approvazione del regolamento di polizia mortuaria', *Decree of the President of the Republic,* 10 September 1990, n 285: art 84, n 1 lett b.

[34] 'Ulteriori disposizioni attuative del decreto-legge recante misure urgenti in materia di contenimento e gestione dell'emergenza epidemiologica da COVID-19, applicabili sull'intero territorio nazionale', *Decree of the President of the Council of Ministers,* 26 April 2020, n 6, (20A02352; GU Serie Generale n.108 del 27-04-2020).

[35] WHO Health Emergency Dashboard <https://covid19.who.int/region/euro/country/it>.

[36] *Ulteriori disposizioni attuative del decreto-legge 23 febbraio 2020, n. 6, recante*

number of participants couldn't exceed fifteen persons all wearing protective masks and respecting the safety distance of at least one meter.[37] Following the request of the Italian Conference of Bishops, the Ministry of the Interior released a note of explanation in which excluded the possibility to form a cortege, which is a common practice for funerals especially in small villages of southern Italy.[38] As to the liturgical form of funerals it was recommended to follow the sanitary regime previously implemented by church authorities on order to ensure the safety of all participants. However, the same preventive measures weren't applied to other religious ceremonies which still couldn't be celebrated.

B *Italy's Response to the Co-existence with the COVID-19 Virus*

The recovery plan announced by the Italian Prime Minister on 26 April 2020 still precluded religious groups from participating in Friday prayer in mosques, Saturday service in synagogues or Sunday services in churches. While other freedoms were gradually regained, the religious freedom still remained restricted with no potential date to restart the celebration of liturgy. In a dissent[39] issued by the Italian Conference of Bishops the church authorities admitted that despite long-lasting negotiations between church and state with reference to the organisation of the liturgical life in full compliance with safety protocols, the Prime Minister arbitrarily excluded the possibility to restart Masses celebrated in presence of the faithful. It also reminded that civil authorities should distinguish between their duty to deliv-

---

misure urgenti in materia di contenimento e gestione dell'emergenza epidemiologica da COVID-19, applicabili sull'intero territorio nazionale. Il Decree of the President of the Council of Ministers, 26 April 2020 (20A02352, GU Serie Generale n.108 del 27-04-2020).

[37] Ibid art 1 p 1 lett i.

[38] 'Question regarding the celebration of the funeral ceremony', *Ministry of the Interior, the Department for Civil Liberties and Immigration*, 30 April 2020 <https://www.interno.gov.it/sites/default/files/allegati/circolare_cerimonie_funebri_e_quesi-to.pdf> (last access 5 August 2020).

[39] Ufficio Stampa CEI, 'Fase 2: il dissenso della CEI', 26 April 2020 <http://www.settimananews.it/chiesa/fase-2-dissenso-della-cei/>.

er indications of a sanitary nature and Church's duty to organise the life of Christian community in full autonomy and in consistency with health protocols.

Eventually, representatives of the Italian government and respective confessions succeeded in signing safety protocols which allowed to resume religious ceremonies starting from 18 May 2020, provided that all necessary health measures and social distancing are enforced by religious authorities. The agreement[40] signed on 7 May 2020 between the government and the Italian Conference of Bishops reveals a series of dispositions which particularly describe: 1) the access to places of worship in occasion of the celebration of liturgy, 2) the regular disinfection of places and objects used for the celebration, 3) measures which must be undertaken during the celebration to ensure the safety of all participants with special attention to the distribution of Holy Communion, 4) the necessity to inform members of religious community about the new safety rules. Unlike the previous provisions regarding the celebration of funerals which could be attended by a maximum of 15 people, the current protocol introduces a more reasonable and universal safety criterion of one meter of distance between every faithful in every direction. The entry to the church is allowed only to people who wear protective face masks and in absence of any flu-like symptoms, high temperature or recent contact with coronavirus patients. The traditional exchange of "the sign of peace" by handshake continues to be omitted, while before the distribution of Holy Communion the priest or extraordinary minister must disinfect hands, then wear mask and gloves and avoid any close contact with the hands of the faithful.

Similar protocols lifting ban on religious services were signed with: 1) Jews,[41] 2) the Church of Jesus Christ of Latter-day Saints,[42] 3) Islam-

---

[40] 'Protocollo circa la ripresa delle celebrazioni con il popolo' <http://www.governo.it/sites/new.governo.it/files/Protocollo_CEI_GOVERNO_20200507.PDF>.

[41] 'Protocollo con le Comunità ebraiche italiane' <https://www.interno.gov.it/sites/default/files/2020.05.14_protocollo_ucei.pdf>.

[42] 'Protocollo con la Comunità della Chiesa di Gesù Cristo dei Santi degli ultimi giorni' <https://www.interno.gov.it/sites/default/files/2020.05.14_protocollo_ucei.pdf>.

ic communities,[43] 4) Hindu, Buddhist, Bahai, Sikh confessions,[44] 5) Protestant, Evangelical, Anglican churches[45] and 6) Orthodox communities.[46] For all of these confessions civil authorities applied the same sanitary standards as for the members of the Catholic Church with only one exception regarding the maximum capacity of 200 persons per one celebration. This criterion wasn't mentioned in the government's agreement with the Italian Conference of Bishops. Equality does not mean uniformity. In the case of Catholic Church, being the predominant religious community in Italy,[47] the government allowed higher limits to accommodate the factual needs of believers.

III POLAND'S RESPONSE TO COVID-19

Facing the growing epidemic threat in European countries, the first legal step to combat the possible spread of COVID-19 epidemic in Poland was made on 2 March 2020 by adopting a special law[48] which permitted the authorities to supervise and manage the epidemic by providing them with new administrative measures. The first Polish laboratory-confirmed case of coronavirus was reported on 4 March 2020 and the first death due to COVID-19 was reported eight days

---

[43] 'Protocollo con le Comunità Islamiche' < https://www.interno.gov.it/sites/default/files/2020.05.14_protocollo_comunita_islamiche.pdf>.

[44] 'Protocollo con le Comunita Induista, Buddista' *(Unione Buddista e Soka Gakkai), Baha'i e Sikhi* <https://www.interno.gov.it/sites/default/files/2020.05.14_protocollo_buddisti_induisti_msoka_sikh_bahai.pdf>.

[45] 'Protocollo con le Chiese Protestanti, Evangeliche, Anglicane' <https://www.interno.gov.it/sites/default/files/2020.05.14_protocollo_comunita_religiose.pdf>.

[46] 'Protocollo con le Comunità ortodosse' < https://www.interno.gov.it/sites/default/files/2020.05.14_protocollo_comunita_ortodosse.pdf.

[47] Beatrice Serra, 'Religious Symbols and Public Sphere: The Italian Experience' in Grzegorz Blicharz (ed), *Freedom of Religion. A Comparative Law Perspective* (Wydawnictwo IWS, 2019) 78.

[48] *The Act of 2 March on special arrangements for preventing, counteracting and combating COVID-19, other infectious diseases and crisis situations caused by them* <https://isap.sejm.gov.pl/isap.nsf/download.xsp/WDU20200000374/U/D20200374Lj.pdf>.

later. On 10 March 2020 WHO included Poland into the group of countries with active local transmissions of coronavirus.[49] In order to mitigate the spread of pandemic the Polish Minister of Health declared on 13 March 2020 the state of epidemiological threat on the territory of the Republic of Poland.[50] Among the temporary social distancing measures introduced by Polish legal order since 14 March 2020 was the limitation of religious worship in public places, including buildings and open spaces, which consisted in the necessity to ensure that during religious ceremonies in a given area or in a given facility there were no more that 50 people in total, both inside and outside the premises, including participants and religious ministers.[51] Practically, while all cultural and educational institutions closed their doors and started to operate remotely, religious services were still available, though with certain restrictions on the amount of people able to participate in public masses and other religious ceremonies. The same limit of up to 50 people engaged in religious gathering was maintained in the ordinance issued by the Minister of Health on 20 March 2020 which regarded the announcement of the state of the epidemic in the territory of the Republic of Poland.[52] At that time the number of active infections detected in Poland was relatively low compared to other European countries (eg on 14 March 2020 Poland reported only 64 active infections, while in Italy there were already 17660 confirmed cases).[53]

---

[49] World Health Organization, 'Coronavirus disease 2019 (COVID-19) Situation Report – 50', 10 March 2020 <https://www.who.int/docs/default-source/coronaviruse/situation-reports/20200310-sitrep-50-covid-19.pdf?sfvrsn=55e904fb_2>.

[50] 'Ordinance of the Minister of Health of 13 March 2020 on the declaration of an epidemic threat in the territory of the Republic of Poland', DzU 2020 poz 433.

[51] Ibid § 6.1.3.

[52] 'Ordinance of the Minister of Health of 20 March 2020 regarding the announcement of the state of the epidemic in the territory of the Republic of Poland', DzU 2020 poz 491, § 7.1.3.

[53] World Health Organization, 'Coronavirus disease 2019 (COVID-19) Situation Report – 54', Table 2. Countries, territories or areas outside China with reported laboratory-confirmed COVID-19 cases and deaths. Data as of 14 March 2020. <https://www.who.int/docs/default-source/coronaviruse/situation-reports/20200314-sitrep-54-covid-19.pdf?sfvrsn=dcd46351_8>.

Nevertheless, the existing regulations were changed only a couple of days later, on 24 March 2020, with the adoption of new and more drastic safety rules. In accordance with the new ordinance[54] starting from 25 March 2020 the possibility of movement was limited to four reasons relating strictly to: 1) performance of professional or official activities, 2) fulfillment of the necessary needs related to the current affairs of everyday life (medical and psychological help, shopping for necessities), 3) volunteering in the fight against COVID-19, 4) performing or participating in the performance of religious worship, including religious activities or rites.[55] It's evident that although the temporary laws provided religious exemptions for the liberty of move-ment, the ban on religious gatherings (masses and funerals included) which exceeded the number of five people (excluding religious minis-ters performing the religious worship) effectively restricted religious liberty in Poland. Preventive measures which initially remained in force between 25 March 2020 and 11 April 2020 were subsequently extended until 20 April 2020.[56] Eventually, in Poland, the most strin-gent restrictions of the liberty to practice one's religion collectively in public remained in force for the total number of 26 days. In practice, during that period of time religious groups, with the overwhelming majority of Roman Catholics were obliged to participate in collec-tive rites through live streaming. The concept to limit religious events to only five participants was not only slightly disproportionate when compared to safety rules adopted at the same time for public transport (allowing half of the seats to be occupied),[57] but also lacked any scien-tific or medical justification, especially with regards to large churches where the safe distance could be easily maintained. The Polish leg-islator allowed people to move from home for religious reasons, but

---

[54] 'The Ordinance of the Minister of Health of 24 March 2020 amending the ordinance on the announcement of the state of the epidemic in the territory of the Republic of Poland', DzU 2020 poz 522.

[55] Ibid § 1.2.

[56] 'The Ordinance of the Council of Ministers of 10 April 2020 regarding the estab-lishment of certain restrictions, orders and bans in connection with an epidemic state', DzU 2020 poz 658, § 7.1.3) in correlation with § 8.1.3).

[57] Ibid § 17.

didn't take into consideration that religious gatherings can also be effectively organized with the implementation of the same sanitary regime, which was put in place with regards to other public places (eg safe distance between pews and their regular disinfection, use of protective masks and gloves by the faithful). On the other hand, it is important to bear in mind that while religious gatherings were limited to five people, all other types of gatherings were banned if attended by more than two people (except for members of the same household). This is in line with the favorable approach towards religious organisations granted by the Polish Constitution. The emphasis on the mutual independence of churches and religious organisations evoked in the Polish Constitution (art 25-3) indicates that the relationship between the state and a given entity should be shaped separately, individually, and that churches and religious organisations are independent of the state. However, independence of faith-based communities isn't equivalent to their absolute autonomy. After all, every religious entity is subject to the state regulations of the country in which it operates. Similarly, the existence of religious organisations and their rules affects society. Here, 'the principle of respect for their autonomy and the mutual independence of each church and religious organisation in its own sphere' as well as 'the principle of cooperation for the individual and the common good' (art 25-3) are decisive.

Emergency measures implemented by Polish government were then less restrictive for churchgoers than in many European countries as they didn't lead the churches to a complete lockdown and suspension of religious ceremonies. Moreover, the priests celebrating religious services were exempted from legal obligation to cover nose and mouth. The decision as to whether continue celebrating public religious rites for a group of maximum five attendants was left entirely and independently to ecclesiastical bodies. At the beginning of epidemic, when no limits regarding public religious gatherings had been put in force in Poland, the President of the Polish Conference of Bishops on 10th March called for the increase of Sunday Masses in order to make it possible for believers to safely attend the Sunday liturgy without creating excessive crowds.[58] However, three days later and with the announcement of the state of epidemic threat on the territory of Poland, the President of the Polish Conference of Bishops released another statement which encouraged bishops of all dioceses to dispense believers from the obligation to attend Mass on Sunday. It was nevertheless unimaginable for both Polish authorities and believers to suspend religious services in churches. While in many European countries raged a significant clash between government's obligation to ensure health and safety and individual's fundamental right to freely practice the faith, in Poland it assumed the form of rather smooth and peaceful cooperation between religious groups and state's authorities from the early beginning till the end of lockdown restrictions. During the stage of lockdown the sacramental life of the Catholic Church, though with some unprecedented modifications, still continued as the restrictions imposed by state were not only accepted by church leaders, but in some cases they voluntarily suspended public liturgy within the autonomy of every diocese. Considering a rather stable dynamic of new COVID-19 cases and low death rate during the strict lockdown of Poland it should be stressed that measures undertaken by Polish government were effective. Although for some groups of believers such restrictions imposed on places of worship might seem too excessive, the low number of infections occurred daily in Poland through March and April is undoubtedly the merit of home isolation and social distancing, which were strongly recommended by all main faith groups of Poland. In addition to the Catholic Church which strongly advised believers to remain in spiritual connection with their parish communities, the Mufti of Muslim Religious Association[59] also cancelled all prayers in Polish mosques. The same strict adherence to state directives regarding the health crisis in Poland was expressed by the

---

[58] 'Statement of the President of Polish Conference of Bishops regarding the threat of coronavirus', 10 March 2020 <https://episkopat.pl/przewodniczacy-episkopatu-kosciol-stosuje-sie-do-zalecen-sluzb-sanitarnych-ws-koronawirusa-2/>.
[59] 'Statement of the Mufti of the Supreme Muslim College by the Muslim Religious Association of Poland', 12 March 2020 <http://mzr.pl/oswiadczenie-najwyzszego-kolegium-muzulmanskiego-muzulmanskiego-zwiazku-religijnego-w-rzeczypospolitej-polskiej/>.

Lutheran Church of Poland[60] whose representatives recommended its communities to consider the current epidemiological situation when taking decisions regarding the organisation of religious services in houses of worship. In order to maintain the social dialogue with parishioners the majority of churches took the opportunity to propagate their faith through digital platforms. Similar immersion into the digital world can be observed also in other countries affected by COVID-19 pandemic where religious gatherings have been temporarily restricted or prohibited. In Poland religious communities also witnessed an accelerated and massive digitalisation of religious services. The decision to celebrate Masses without the presence of the faithful was left entirely to ecclesiastical bodies. As a result, in some dioceses, particularly during Easter which is the most significant holiday for Roman Catholics, participation was made possible only through the media platforms, public radio and television.

A *Gradual lifting of lockdown restrictions in Poland*

On 16 April 2020 the Polish government announced a plan to gradually loosen the coronavirus restrictions in four stages, starting from 20 April 2020. As to religious liberty, in the first phase[61] civil authorities decided to increase access to places of worship by replacing the limit of 5 churchgoers with the provision that 15 square meters be provided for one participant during public worship. From that day on the number of attendants allowed to attend collective religious rites was correlated with the dimensions of the church building (excluding celebrants). With regard to funerals taking place in cemeteries the number of mourners was restricted to 50 persons (excluding the minister conducting the service and workers doing the burial). In addition, starting from 16 April 2020 it became compulsory to cover

---

[60] See 'Pastoral letter of the Bishop of the Lutheran Church of Poland of 13 March 2020' <https://www.luteranie.pl/nowosci/nabozenstwa_w_czasie_zagrozenia_koronawirusem,6596.html>.

[61] 'The Ordinance of the Council of Ministers of 19 April 2020 regarding the establishment of certain restrictions, orders and bans in connection with an epidemic state', DzU 2020 poz 697, § 9.1.3.

face and nose when entering the church or house or worship both for individual visit or for collective service. In regulations[62] concerning the second phase of lifting COVID-19 restrictions, the limit of 5 people was reinstated only with reference to church buildings smaller that 75 square meters, while in the bigger ones the same rules remained in force until 16 May 2020. In the third phase civil authorities decided to decrease dimensions of church building to only 10 square meters for every churchgoer while still limiting the number of funeral attendees in cemeteries to 50 people. At the same time capacity limit for restaurants was 1 person per 4 square meters. On the other hand, in food stores and in shopping malls still were allowed only 1 person per 15 square meters. The limit of 1 person per 10 square meters was applied only to churches (with size beyond 50 square meters) and casinos. As it was expressed by the Prime Minister, lifting the limits in churches was scheduled 'for the hundredth anniversary of the birth of our great fellow countryman John Paul II, who changed the fate of the world, changed the fate of Poland', and since main church celebrations were taking place on Sunday, 17 May 2020, the limits were relaxed on this day, whereas limits for all other secular activities were lifted the day after – on 18 May 2020.[63] It was a clear sign of cooperative arrangement between church and state. Eventually, limits regarding religious gatherings on the church premises and at funerals celebrated in cemeteries were entirely lifted on 30 May 2020[64] while the requirement to cover nose and mouth remains still in force.

Beginning from 8 August 2020 certain restrictions were partially reintroduced in specific districts of Poland (categorized as "yellow" and "red" zones) with increased number of new infections larger than

---

[62] 'The Ordinance of the Council of Ministers of 2 May 2020 regarding the establishment of certain restrictions, orders and bans in connection with an epidemic state', DzU 2020 poz 792, § 8.1.3.

[63] 'The Ordinance of the Council of Ministers of 16 May 2020 regarding the establishment of certain restrictions, orders and bans in connection with an epidemic state', DzU 2020 poz 878.

[64] 'The Ordinance of the Council of Ministers of 29 May 2020 regarding the establishment of certain restrictions, orders and bans in connection with an epidemic state', DzU 2020 poz 792, § 15.8.

in other areas of Poland.[65] The list of districts with special requirements is subjected to permanent monitoring and updates. With regards to religious gatherings taking place in "red" zones there was announced a new participants' capacity limit of 50 per cent in houses of worship or churches. Additionally, unlike at the beginning of pandemic, in "red" zones religious events are allowed to take place outside provided that attendees keep a distance of 1.5 meters between them or cover the mouth and nose (excluding persons leading the religious services), and a maximum of 150 people can participate, which is a general restriction for all public gatherings in these zones. The new way of introducing restrictions on religious gatherings has been shaped by previous experience and scientific recommendations. It follows limits introduced in other countries: based not on the criterion of "one person per square meter", but on the percentage of the capacity of building. Moreover, the limit of 50 per cent capacity is applied almost universally across various secular and non-secular gatherings except for shopping facilities.

Interestingly enough, whereas in "yellow" zones there are no limitations imposed on the number of participants in religious gatherings, most secular activities are burdened with such limits, eg fitness clubs may accept one person per 7 square meters, cinemas are allowed to fill only 25 per cent of their capacity and restaurants, just like in "red" zones, welcome only one person per 4 square meters. On the other hand, both in "yellow" and in "red" zones there're no limits on the number of customers remaining at the same time in stores, marketplaces and post offices. The lack of restrictions on the operation of shopping malls and shopping centers obviously is tailored to restore the economy and protect against social and financial crisis, but on the other hand rises some concerns over the consistency of adopted provisions. As far as we consider the economic recovery from COVID-19 essential for the state's welfare, we shouldn't underestimate the im-

---

[65] 'The Ordinance of the Council of Ministers of 7 August 2020 regarding the establishment of certain restrictions, orders and bans in connection with an epidemic state', DzU 2020 poz 1356 § 25.8.

portance of unlimited access for public religious services which contributes to the personal well-being. Anyway, we should remember that balancing values and navigating through a current uncertain situation of pandemic is not a piece of cake for any government. That is why the state is allowed to make specific and even controversial tradeoffs for the public health or national economy reasons. However, there is always a bottom line that cannot be crossed – it's the discrimination against religion. In Poland we have seen bright, but not flawless, pictures of state's cooperation with churches and barely one would border upon discriminatory treatment of religious gatherings by the government. No church or religious organisation complained on legal grounds against restrictions imposed by the government. As arts 53–5 of the Polish Constitution reads: 'The freedom to publicly express religion may be limited only by means of statute and only where this is necessary for the defence of State security, public order, health, morals or the freedoms and rights of others'. Limitations of religious freedom are allowed if 'necessary in a democratic state' and do not 'violate the essence of this freedom' (arts 31–3). That is why such limitations have to be proportionate. The Polish government have been gradually loosing limits on religious gatherings and never violated the essence of freedom to publicly express religion, allowing collective religious worship albeit in smaller groups. In fact, in Poland the cooperation between state and church meant also that religious communities understood the seriousness of COVID-19 related problems and challenges which the government has faced and they adhered to the guidelines and policies of the state by providing their own sanitary and safety rules.

In order to distinguish the difference between civil and religious gatherings and the importance of the last ones for the citizen's life it's important to point out that Polish authorities decided to lift restrictions pending on religious ceremonies already in the first place, while mass gatherings up to 150 persons were prohibited till the beginning of the fourth stage. During the lockdown phase in Poland limitations regarding public worship neither targeted religious groups, nor privileged them by letting them to gather for religious services. Although church attendees are still obliged to wear protective masks, the minister who celebrates the Mass is exempted from that requirement. Unlike in Italy, there are also no specific provisions regarding the access to the church and distribution of Holy Communions – the church's 'own sphere' par excellence (art 25–3). Religious groups are invited to respect health directives but are allowed to organise religious service within its full autonomy.

IV FINAL REMARKS

As the coronavirus continues its tragic journey around the globe, Europe settles into the era of the evaluation of damages inflicted by the general lockdown. Among the damage, which for a long time will be difficult to access, remain the psychosocial effects in connection with the restriction of constitutional rights. As soon as the first scientific data evidenced the character of the novel virus and released the first sanitary guidelines to curb the spread of the virus, it was clear that its most fundamental and still the most effective rule apart from the sanitisation – the social distancing – would complicate and change every aspect of human life. While many social aspects of our life were effectively transitioned into virtual platforms, it is still impossible to digitalise religion. For that reason, the restrictions imposed on collective forms of worship are among the most debated ones. While the modern world tends to overuse the word "unprecedented" with reference to social distancing restrictions caused by COVID-19 pandemic, it must be emphasized that similar measures had already been undertaken in the past centuries. Attentive Italians living in the north of the country, who were the first European nation affected by the current pandemic in the worst possible way, quickly discerned many similarities between current coronavirus disease and the great pestilence of the 1630 which haunted Lombardy and had been vividly described by Alessandro Manzoni in an Italian classic novel The Betrothed ("Promessi Sposi"). His historical description of human behavior in situation of health emergency leaves the reader no illusions as to the fact that humanity hasn't changed a lot from that time sharing the same habits, fears and expectations regarding the uncertain days.

Passersby visiting one of the oldest districts of Milan – Porta Venezia – probably will stumble upon a small Renaissance church of San Carlo al Lazzaretto which also served as a backdrop for Manzoni's Milanese tale. The building, now deeply tucked between modern residential blocks, has already lost its special meaning for the old world. Only a few might recall that four centuries ago this church constituted the central part of a large, rectangular leper hospital. Its special construction of eight open arches, commissioned by the Saint Archbishop of Milan – Charles Borromeo, permitted all patients to follow, from a safe distance of their own private beds, the religious rites from every angle of the hospital. The now symbolic presence of this church in Milan on one hand may rise some concerns about the present role of religion amid the pandemic crisis which in some countries has been marginalized. If in the sixteenth century it was unthinkable to deprive the infected people of participation in religious practices, one might abruptly conclude that the same access should be granted to people nowadays. On the other hand, the same church reminds us that even in the past the access to religious worship was also conditioned by safety rules as the lack of them always contributed to the spread of new infections. The ill couldn't come closer to the altar, but were advised to watch the celebration from safe distance. That's all we're required to do also nowadays.

The public health crisis that has been sparked around the globe clearly shows that both in Poland and in Italy, local religious groups transitioned quickly to offer the believers virtual meetings, while still providing physical assistance for people in need. Moral and legal dilemmas regarding the onerous limitations on the right to freely profess one's religion collectively in public will still be strong, but it's quite evident that if faith-based institutions had defied orders not to gather in churches we would have seen more COVID-19 infections with coronavirus clusters tied to churches.

Before we cast the final vote over the legitimacy, rationality and proportionality of anti-epidemic restrictions imposed on religious groups, we should consider the value of public health and safety over the interest of religious groups. As the current pandemic reveals, most of them tried to adapt their rituals and practices to the new circumstances. However, the willingness to change or suspend religious rites in situations of public health emergency should not be interpreted as a pretext to abandon religious practices by the faithful in the name of public interests. As much as we appreciate the effort of religious groups to sacrifice their spiritual needs in order to curb the spread of COVID-19 pandemic, this situation cannot be used to intentionally target religion. Examples of Poland and Italy show how cooperation between church and state based on mutual understanding and respect may help either to keep collective exercise of religion going on or to reopen religious gatherings as soon as possible without unnecessary delay and without unfair treatment comparing with secular gatherings. History and comparative experience teach that any freedom may face limitations, but we may take the best out of any challenges and give the best of us to work for the common good which means also to find ways of protecting freedom of religion.

8

The Dictatorship of the Health Bureaucracy: Governments Must Stop Telling Us What Is for Our Own Good

ROCCO LOIACONO*

ABSTRACT

Much has been written over the last few months about how unelected bureaucrats, with the unquestioning acquiescence of our politicians, have acquired incredible and unparalleled power over the everyday lives of Australians. This had led to such bureaucrats, revelling in their new-found power, seemingly making policy on the run and treating us like fools who need to be told on a daily basis what is good for us (or else!). It is a dangerous time for our democracy, where the 'dictatorship of the health bureaucracy' has emerged, whereby a virus, labelled as a pandemic, is being used to take away fundamental rights and freedoms, handed down to us by our great Westminster tradition, with the stroke of a pen. Recent events have demonstrated the potential for health officials to enact policies that will exert even more control over our lives, which could have serious implications for the principle of informed consent – fundamental in the administration of any medical treatment.

I INTRODUCTION

Over the course of 2020, the extent to which various governments have become nothing but elected dictatorships has become extremely evident. These dictatorships have been aided and abetted by a now all-powerful health bureaucracy, whose don't-trust-people-to-know-

* Rocco Loiacono is a Senior Lecturer in the Curtin University Law School,

what's-best-for-themselves authoritarian instincts are have a deleterious effect on our fundamental rights and freedoms. Following his announcement of 19 August 2020 that a letter of intent had been signed with AstraZeneca to produce the Oxford vaccine in Australia, should it be successful, the Prime Minister suggested that any coronavirus vaccine be "as mandatory as possible". He also entertained a "no jab, no play" type policy to "encourage" as many people as possible to take it.[1] While Scott Morrison backtracked somewhat on this "mandatory" stance later the same day,[2] the following morning the Federal Health Minister, Greg Hunt, in an interview give to Channel 7's *Sunrise*, did not rule out taking measures to make it difficult to refuse the vaccine, including a denial of government welfare payments to those who did not vaccinate.[3] This was followed by the Deputy Health Officer, Dr Nick Coatsworth, postulating that without the coronavirus vaccine jab Australians would not be allowed to go to restaurants, use public transport or travel overseas.[4] This has serious implications for the principle of *informed consent* – fundamental in the administration of any medical treatment. Leaving to one side for a moment the ugly spectacle of the government and its *Politburo* of medical officers proposing to further and more brazenly and egregiously restricting the rights and freedoms of Australians, such a draconian approach is simply not warranted on the basis of the evidence.

II INFECTION RATE AND LOCKDOWNS – FAILED POLICY OF THE HEALTH BUREAUCRACY

In an interview on 3AW on 19 August 2020 (when Scott Morrison first suggested he wanted any vaccine to be mandatory) he added that

---

[1] Richard Ferguson, 'Future Vaccine Should Be Mandatory, Says PM', *The Australian*, 19 August 2020 <https://www.australian.com.au/nation/coronavirus-australia-live-news-fears-grow-of-sydney-hotel-breach-outbreak/news-story/cf35fb9ae-2901600276fa78ee89a2dc5>.

[2] 'Prime Minister rejects compulsory COVID-19 vaccine', 19 August 2020 <https://www.2gb.com/prime-minister-rejects-compulsory-covid-19-vaccine/>.

[3] Channel 7 News, *Sunrise*, <https://7news.com.au/sunrise/greg-hunt-refuses-to-rule-out-consequences-for-anti-vaxxers-refusing-covid-vaccine-c-1252235>.

[4] Ibid.

the aim was for a 95% take up of the vaccine, since this is the level of immunity that is required.[5] The Health Minister said the same thing on Channel 7's *Sunrise* the following day.[6] What they may have chosen to ignore is that, for most viruses, herd immunity is achieved if 60 to 70 percent of the population is immune. In fact, in an article in *Newsweek* on 24 June 2020, it was reported, quoting from an article in the journal *Science*, that the herd immunity threshold for coronavirus could be as low as 43%.[7] There have been studies published since then that suggest the immunity threshold could be even lower.[8] In fact, far from having no immunity, the evidence shows the vast majority of the population has pre-existing, crossover T-cell immunity, developed through exposure to coronaviruses such as the common cold. This explains why most people have a mild or asymptomatic response.[9]

What also seems to have been conveniently ignored is the rate of infection when compared to the general population. The Prime Minister, in justifying a mandatory approach, on 19 August 2020, referred to the number of coronavirus-related deaths and infections around the world.[10] As has been pointed out many times elsewhere, when compared to other pandemics, these numbers are actually quite small. At the time of writing, the World Health Organisation has certified a total number of 32,048,333 infections and 979,454 deaths. The current

---

[5] 'Scott Morrison expects COVID-19 vaccine will be 'as mandatory as you can possibly make it', 19 August 2020 <https://www.3aw.com.au/scott-morrison-expects-covid-19-vaccine-will-be-as-mandatory-as-you-can-possibly-make-it/>.

[6] Above n 3.

[7] Kashmira Gander, 'Herd Immunity Threshold for COVID-19 Could Be Just 43 Percent', *Newsweek*, 24 June 2020 <https://www.newsweek.com/herd-immunity-threshold-covid-19-could-just-43-percent-1512978>.

[8] See, for example, this report on the Brazilian city of Manaus: Terrence McCoy and Heloisa Traiano, 'In the Brazilian Amazon, A Sharp Drop in Coronavirus Sparks Questions Over Collective Immunity', *The Washington Post*, 24 August 2020 <https://www.washingtonpost.com/world/the_americas/brazil-coronavirus-manaus-herd-immunity/2020/08/23/0eccda40-d80e-11ea-930e-d88518c57dcc_story.html>.

[9] Rebecca Weisser, 'Once Upon a Time There Was a Wicked Virus...', *The Spectator Australia*, 19 September 2020 <https://www.spectator.com.au/2020/09/once-upon-a-time-there-was-a-wicked-virus/>.

[10] Above n 1.

population of the world is 7.8 billion. Thus we have an infection rate of 0.3% and a death rate of 0.01%, with the vast majority of these being people aged over 80. This is far smaller when compared to other pandemics, such as the 14th Century Bubonic Plague (where the death rate was 1 in 3) and the 1918-1919 Spanish Flu (where the estimates of death range between 40 to 50 million, many of whom were women of child bearing age). As Professor James Allan noted recently in *The Spectator Australia*, the Hong Kong flu epidemic of 1969 killed around 100,000 Americans.[11] At the time of writing, corona-related deaths in America stood at 187,000 (according to the Centre for Disease Control), therefore about the same percentage of the population in historical terms. Yet in 1969, 'there were no lockdowns, and Woodstock was not cancelled'. Professor Allan also noted that coronavirus is not even in the top 50 causes of death in Australia.[12] As Paul Murray detailed on 19 August 2020, the Australian Bureau of Statistics released a report in early August of the total number of deaths in Australia for the first half of 2020. The number was 55,047, and top of the list was cancer (18,959), followed by respiratory illnesses (7,540), dementia (5,794), heart disease (5,175), and cerebrovascular disease (3,497). Flu and pneumonia have taken the lives of 974 Australians up until that time, considerably more than the total number of coronavirus-related deaths,[13] which for the same period was 611.

The adoption of lockdown policies with alacrity by governments and their all-powerful health bureaucrats has occurred notwithstanding several renowned epidemiologists, including Professor Sunetra Gupta of Oxford University,[14] stating that the policies of these bu-

---

[11] James Allan 'One of the most colossal failures of the century' *The Spectator Australia*, 8 August 2020 <https://www.spectator.com.au/2020/07/one-of-the-most-colossal-failures-of-the-century/>.

[12] Ibid.

[13] Paul Murray, 'Thousands die unrelated to COVID and 'none have resulted in lockdowns', Sky News Australia, 19 August 2020 <https://www.skynews.com.au/details/_6182532977001>.

[14] Jacquelin Magnay, 'Oxford epidemiologist pushes herd immunity', *The Australian*, 3 July 2020 <https://www.theaustralian.com.au/nation/oxford-epidemiologist-pushes-herd-immunity/news-story/cf019113ea52916f64a16dcad96095a8>.

reaucrats such as lockdowns are actually causing more harm than the virus itself. Professor Mark Woolhouse, epidemiologist at Edinburgh University and adviser to the UK government told *The Sunday Express* on 24 August 2020 that attempting to control coronavirus through lockdown measures causes unnecessary panic, noting that 'history will say trying to control COVID-19 through lockdown was a monumental mistake on a global scale, the cure was worse than the disease'.[15]

A similar opinion was expressed by Dr David Katz, founding director of Yale University's Yale-Griffin Prevention Research Center and former president of the American College of Lifestyle Medicine. As early as 20 March 2020 Dr Katz, in an opinion piece for *The New York Times*, warned that extreme measures to fight coronavirus 'may end up being worse than the disease'. He stated that the "unique" nature of corona is that it results in only "mild" symptoms in 99 per cent of cases and that it appears to only pose a high risk to the elderly.[16] According to Dr Katz, it is deeply concerning that 'the social, economic and public health consequences of a near total meltdown of normal life – schools and business closed, gatherings banned – will be long-lasting and calamitous, possibly even graver than the direct toll of the virus itself.' Economies will bounce back in time, he says, 'but many businesses never will. The unemployment, impoverishment and despair likely to result will be public health scourges of the first order.'[17]

Dr Katz and Professor Woolhouse are not alone. Professor Michael Levitt from Stanford University, a Nobel Laureate, has been tracking coronavirus since January 2020, and, as a result of his research,

---

[15] Lucy Johnston, 'UK Lockdown Was A "Monumental Mistake" And Must Not Happen Again – Boris Scientist Says', *The Sunday Express*, 24 August 2020 <https://www.express.co.uk/life-style/health/1320428/Coronavirus-news-lockdown-mistake-second-wave-Boris-Johnson>.

[16] David L Katz, 'Is Our Fight Against Coronavirus Worse Than the Disease?', *The New York Times*, 20 March 2020 <https://www.nytimes.com/2020/03/20/opinion/coronavirus-pandemic-social-distancing.html>.

[17] Ibid.

has consistently argued against lockdowns.[18] Further, on 1 September 2020, senior doctors across Melbourne urged politicians not to support a state of emergency extension, saying the move threatens to "destroy" the health and wellbeing of fed-up Victorians. Box Hill Hospital urologist Dr Geoff Wells told NCA Newswire that in a letter to Premier Daniel Andrews, he and 12 other medical practitioners outlined their concerns about the Victorian Government's response to the COVID-19 pandemic. He hoped the letter would convince the government to lift harsh stage four restrictions on 13 September 2020. In the letter the doctors wrote: 'It is our professional opinion that the stage 4 lockdown policy has caused unprecedented negative economic and social outcomes in people, which in themselves are having negative health outcomes.'[19]

'When I see my patients and ask them how they're coping, the number one response is the sadness at not being able to see their grandchildren for three, four or five months and the ones who live on their own are extremely isolated,' he said.

> The mood of the population has changed dramatically in the past two weeks – there seems to be one half that is getting angrier and angrier and the other half which has just lost all hope – these policies are effecting the general psyche of the community. We just want to have significant input into this response instead of a blanket approach that is harming the general population.[20]

In the letter, the doctors said specialist referrals from GPs had fall-

---

[18] See, for example: 'Michael Levitt on why there shouldn't be a lockdown, how he's been tracking coronavirus', *The Stanford Daily*, 2 August 2020 <https://www.stanforddaily.com/2020/08/02/qa-michael-levitt-on-why-there-shouldnt-be-a-lockdown-how-hes-been-tracking-coronavirus/>.

[19] Anthony Piovesan, 'Victorian doctors pen desperate letter to Dan Andrews about controversial State of Emergency Bill', 1 September 2020 <https://www.news.com.au/lifestyle/health/health-problems/victorian-doctors-pen-desperate-letter-to-dan-andrews-about-controversial-state-of-emergency-bill/news-story/477352005ec852b6dd4b0e8f31f97441>.

[20] Ibid.

en dramatically as a result of patients fearing they would get sick if they went out. 'As a direct consequence of this delay, many will have poorer prognoses. This has especially been the case with three consultants who treat cancer,' they wrote in the letter. 'We now know that whilst COVID-19 is highly contagious, it is of limited virulence. We are told that since March 2020, 565 Victorian patients have died either with or from the virus (numbers as at 31 August). This compares with annual Victorian deaths of approximately 10,000 patients with cardiovascular disease and 11,000 with cancer.'[21]

The doctors go on:

> Accordingly, the COVID-19 deaths are a relatively small proportion of the 114 deaths per day that are normally seen in Victoria. In comparison, since the start of March COVID-19 has been associated with 3 of the 114 deaths per day. Most of the 565 deaths have occurred in nursing homes which according to doctors currently working in this environment have described causal factors related not only to the virus but to other care related issues, including isolation, loneliness, and related diminished nutritional intake.

The letter also states, tellingly:

> Since June 2020, the death rate has risen sharply in aged care facilities where the risk of transmission of COVID-19 has been unacceptably high. However, the government, and the doctors advising it, have not reviewed their policy in order to focus on this vulnerable segment of the population. Instead, stage 3-4 lockdowns for the whole community have continued for no apparent scientific reason.[22]

Of course, the Victorian Government ignored this advice from those on the "front line", preferring instead to hide behind its cadre of unelected bureaucrats and extend the "state of emergency" until March 2021.

---

[21] Ibid.

[22] Ibid.

III CORONA DEATH RATE AND OTHER POTENTIAL TREAT-MENTS TO VACCINES

However, the coronavirus death rate is now coming under increasing scrutiny. As Adam Creighton reported in *The Australian* on 1 September 2020, the US Centre for Disease Control and Prevention said only a fraction of US deaths from or with COVID-19 were attributed solely to coronavirus. 'For 6 per cent of the US deaths, COVID-19 was the only cause mentioned. For deaths with conditions or causes in addition to COVID-19, on average, there were 2.6 additional conditions or causes per death,' it said. In other words, the corona death rate should actually be revised down.[23]

As far back as 8 August 2020, *Newsweek* reported that a Mississippi county coroner, Joshua Pounder, said his state's death count could be incorrect, telling residents that possible misreporting has led to 'unnecessary fear in the public'. Newsweek reported that in an 'average month in DeSoto County', despite the ongoing coronavirus pandemic, the coroner's office recently completed reports for 144 deaths in July 2020. Pounder attributed the highest number of deaths to heart conditions, lung or vascular diseases and strokes, with 67 reported deaths. Pounder wrote that cancer was the second-highest, causing 30 reported deaths in the county.[24]

Of the 11 causes of death Pounder listed, coronavirus was not among them. Instead, the 24 DeSoto County residents who had a positive COVID-19 test at the time of their death were included in the count of total deaths and attributed to causes other than the novel coronavirus, Pounder said.

'All of the individuals who have died that were [positive] for CO-

---

[23] Adam Creighton, 'The COVID-19 Panic Is Unnecessary — It Is Much Less Threatening Than We Think', *The Australian*, 1 September 2020 <https://www.theaustralian.com.au/nation/politics/the-covid19-panic-is-unnecessary-it-is-much-less-threatening-than-we-think/news-story/b9246d82046820000686a18ec03e2580>.

[24] Jocelyn Grzeszcak, 'Mississippi Coroner Says State's Coronavirus Death Tally Is Misleading, Causing "Unnecessary Fear In The Public"', *Newsweek*, 8 August 2020 <https://www.newsweek.com/mississippi-coroner-says-states-coronavirus-death-tally-misleading-causing-unnecessary-fear-1523791>.

VID at some point have all had major medical problems prior to contracting COVID', Pounder wrote, adding that the majority of them were older than 75 and many of the people who died already had a terminal diagnosis of some kind.[25]

However, the Mississippi State Department of Health, "demands" that anyone who has a positive coronavirus test at the time of their death is reported as a "COVID death" without acknowledging the fact that 'many of them were terminal prior to a [positive] test],' Pounder said, adding that this misrepresentation that has caused 'unnecessary fear in the public' and significant stress. The coroner stated that cardiovascular and pulmonary deaths were 'drastically up' in DeSoto, which Pounder attributed to stress caused by the pandemic and fear caused by listening to politicians and news reporters give 'false information'.[26]

On 31 August 2020 the inaccuracy identified above in counting coronavirus-related deaths was confirmed as having been the practice followed in Australia. In his daily coronavirus briefing, the Victorian Chief Medical Officer, Dr Brett Sutton, said this about the number of deaths: 'Anyone who is a confirmed case who dies is classified as a coronavirus death. It doesn't have to be definitively from coronavirus, and in some instances, you know, in aged care, there would have been some residents who would have already been receiving palliative care who became infected with coronavirus'.[27]

Even in the face of these figures, what is more serious is the utter stubbornness born out of an apparent "Trump Derangement Syndrome" which ignores the effectiveness of the potential treatments of hydroxychloroquine and invermectin, both with zinc. In the case of the former, over the weekend of 22 to 23 August 2020 the renowned Yale epidemiologist, Dr Harvey Risch, specified that: 'there have been 53 studies showing positive results of its use in COVID infections. There are 14 that show neutral or negative results. Of those, 10 were

---

[25] Ibid.

[26] Ibid.

[27] Andrew Bolt, 'The Victorian Government is Lethally Incompetent', *The Bolt Report*, Sky News Australia, 31 August 2020 <https://www.skynews.com.au/details/_6186189844001>.

conducted in the later stages of the illness where no anti-viral drug would be expected to have much effect.' Of the remaining studies, Risch asserts, 'two come from the same author. Then there is a faulty study from Brazil, and should be retracted. The other is also faulty, published in The Lancet, and was retracted.' Risch told *Newsweek* he:

> [C]annot believe that, in the midst of a crisis, he is fighting for a treatment that the data fully supports but for reasons having nothing to do with a correct understanding of science, it has been pushed to the sidelines. As a result, tens of thousands of patients with COVID-19 are dying unnecessarily. Fortunately the situation can be reversed easily and quickly.[28]

This seems to be completely in accord with the medical profession's *Hippocratic Oath*, that is, to do no harm. Yet the use of hydroxychloroquine as a potential treatment is shut down by the health commissars. Doctors Sutton and Coatsworth on 26 and 28 August 2020 respectively dismissed it once more with a level of haughtiness that takes one's breath away.[29] With regard to invermectin, as Rebecca Weisser reported in *The Spectator Australia*, Dr Kylie Wagstaff from Monash University is struggling to get any funding to conduct proper clinical trials. When the potential of these drugs was first announced, the COVID- related death toll was under 50.[30] At the time of writing it stands at 861. How many of those deaths could have been prevented? As Andrew Bolt identified, this is wilful blindness to 'what could be our best cure' in the fight against coronavirus.[31] Another potential

---

[28] Dr Harvey A Risch, 'The Key to Defeating COVID-19 Already Exists. We Need to Start Using It', *Newsweek*, 23 August 2020 <https://www.newsweek.com/key-defeating-covid-19-already-exists-we-need-start-using-it-opinion-1519535>.

[29] Andrew Bolt, 'Potential Coronavirus Treatments Are Being "Patronisingly Dismissed"', *The Bolt Report*, Sky News Australia, 26 August 2020 <https://www.sky-news.com.au/details/_6184621840001>.

[30] Rebecca Weisser, 'No Warp Speed For Aussie Covid Wonder Drug', *The Spectator Australia*, 8 August 2020 <https://www.spectator.com.au/2020/08/no-warp-speed-for-aussie-covid-wonder-drug/>.

[31] Andrew Bolt, 'I must call Prime Minister Scott Morrison to Account', *The Bolt Report*, Sky News Australia, 10 August 2020 <https://www.skynews.com.au/details/_6179768424001>.

treatment that is receiving little attention is that of research into production of antibodies.[32] So much for the Hippocratic Oath!

IV LACK OF TRUST

This brings me to the issue of trust, necessary not only between a doctor and patient but also between the people and their government. Given the track record of our politicians and medical officers over the last few months, which to say the least is dismal, it would seem that trust in them is dwindling. Yet they only have themselves to blame. Adam Creighton reported in *The Australian* on 22 June 2020 about the over-reliance of our health commissars on failed doomsday health forecast models.[33] Now it has emerged in the Aged Care Royal Commission that the Federal Government failed miserably at developing policies to protect residents of nursing homes, they being the most vulnerable and where the highest incidence of death has occurred.[34]

We've had the Chief Medical Officer in Victoria proselytise on coronavirus and climate change,[35] precisely at the time it seems he

---

[32] Australian researchers, among many around the world, are working on a coronavirus antibody program that could treat and prevent COVID-19, especially among the elderly and vulnerable. Associate Professor Wai-Hong Tham, from Walter and Eliza Hall Institute, said 'the antibody research targets the spike protein, which is what the killer virus uses to enter human cells. If successful, it will boost someone's immune response to fight off the virus.' See: Mark Saunokonoko, Channel 9 News, 'Australian researchers test breakthrough antibody therapy to defeat virus' 26 August 2020 <https://www.9news.com.au/national/coronavirus-victoria-antibody-therapy-how-it-could-stop-and-defeat-covid-19/a06207d0-85d9-44ce-b498-6f14857b5415?app=applenews>.

[33] Adam Creighton, 'Coronavirus Australia: Call For 'Failed' Doomsday Health Forecast Models To Be Abandoned', *The Australian*, 22 June 2020 <https://www.theaustralian.com.au/nation/coronavirus-call-for-failed-doomsday-health-forecast-models-to-be-abandoned/news-story/c7622e0584b4f07355e05082e428af8b>.

[34] Royal Commission into Aged Care and Safety, *Aged care and COVID-19: A special report*, 30 September 2020, Commonwealth of Australia, p. 11 <https://agedcare.royalcommission.gov.au/sites/default/files/2020-10/aged-care-and-covid-19-a-special-report.pdf>.

[35] Brett Sutton, Vanora Mulvenna, Daniel Voronoff and Tiernan Humphrys, 'Acting on Climate Change and Health in Victoria' (2020) 212 (8) *Medical Journal of Australia* 345; Rachael Dexer and Marissa Calligeros, 'Hotel Quarantine Problems?

ought to have been aware of the impending disaster in the hotel quarantine system in that State, believed to be principally responsible for the outbreak of community transmission there. His Deputy, in trying to display her woke credentials, also showed her lack of historical knowledge by getting Captain Cook and Captain Arthur Phillip mixed up.[36] After the Ruby Princess and Newmarch House debacles, how the New South Wales Health Minister, Brad Hazzard, still has a job is anyone's guess. Our State borders are shut, despite there being little to no community transmission in most States and both Territories, causing massive job losses and mental health issues to skyrocket. However, most tragically, this senseless politicking by State Premiers has also led to the death of an unborn child.[37] We cannot even leave the country except in "exceptional" circumstances, decided by an unelected bureaucrat with no right of judicial review. So Shane Warne gets an exemption to go to commentate on the cricket in England but other Australians are not permitted to leave to visit dying relatives.[38] Oh, and remember when the government tried to extort the Australian public, telling us the COVID-Safe app (later shown to be a complete flop) was the ticket to getting our freedoms back? Remember who was the face of that campaign? None other than Dr Nick Coatsworth!

"I found out in the media", says Sutton', *The Age*, 7 August 2020 <https://www.theage.com.au/national/victoria/hotel-quarantine-problems-i-found-out-in-the-media-says-sutton-20200807-p55jls.html>.

[36] 'Health Officer "Unfit For Office" After Comparing Cook's Arrival To Coronavirus', *Sky News Australia*, 1 May 2020 <https://www.skynews.com.au/details/_6153302690001>.

[37] Charlie Coë, 'Unborn Baby Dies After Heavily Pregnant Mum Was Forced To Wait 16 Hours For Emergency Surgery In Sydney After Being Turned Away At The Queensland Border', *The Daily Mail Australia*, 28 August 2020 <https://www.dailymail.co.uk/news/article-8672159/Baby-dies-mum-forced-wait-surgery-turned-away-Queensland-border.html>.

[38] James Bolt, 'Australia Has Returned To Being A Convict Nation', *Institute of Public Affairs*, 25 August 2020 <https://ipa.org.au/publications-ipa/australia-has-returned-to-being-a-convict-nation>.

V ETHICAL CONCERNS REGARDING CORONAVIRUS VACCINE

It seems this guy cannot help himself. On 24 August 2020, after the Catholic Archbishop of Sydney, Anthony Fisher raised serious ethical and moral considerations for his flock regarding the production of the Oxford coronavirus vaccine,[39] Dr Coastworth decided he was also an expert on Catholic moral theology. In a post on his Facebook page, Archbishop Fisher stated that he had written to the Prime Minister outlining his concerns that the Oxford vaccine, among others, is being produced from the cultured cell lines of an electively aborted foetus. This would present Catholics with a serious ethical dilemma, notwithstanding the cell-line is derived from an abortion that occurred in 1972. Dr Coastworth responded by stating that the vaccine was being produced by one of the world's leading universities and 'we can have every faith that the way they have manufactured the vaccine has been against the highest of ethical standards internationally.'[40] Further, Professor Colin Pouton from Monash University's Institute of Pharmaceutical Sciences chimed in, stating the cell line was developed decades ago and had been widely used around the world. 'It's not like people are using a new cell line,' he said. 'It's already there, so in many respects the ethical issue is in history'.[41]

I'm not sure what makes these two people think they know more about Catholic moral teaching than the Archbishop of Sydney. The Catholic Church has opposed the development of vaccines using unethically derived foetal cell lines for many years. The Congregation for the Doctrine of the Faith's 2008 Instruction *Dignitas Personae* provides that the use of foetal cell lines for developing vaccines 'gives rise to various ethical problems with regard to cooperation in evil and with regard to scandal' and that 'everyone has the duty to make known

---

[39] Alison Xiao, 'Oxford University Coronavirus Vaccine Has "Ethical Concerns", Sydney Archbishops Warn Followers', *ABC News*, 24 August 2020 <https://www.abc.net.au/news/2020-08-24/sydney-catholic-archbishop-warns-pm-against-coronavirus-vaccine/12588578>.

[40] Ibid.

[41] Ibid.

their disagreement and to ask that their healthcare system make other types of vaccines available.'[42] This is precisely what Archbishop Fisher has done, expressing a wish that other vaccine candidates which are not produced with the cell lines of aborted foetuses be explored. In this letter, which was also signed by Anglican Archbishop Glenn Davies and Greek Orthodox Archdiocese of Australia Archbishop Makarios, the Church leaders stated that they and their Churches are not opposed to vaccination. However, harvesting 'foetal tissue was deeply immoral' and thus, members of their congregations might consider their 'individual conscience' and refuse a vaccine even if no other alternative was available to them.

Notwithstanding a clerical leader raising legitimate ethical concerns regarding the possibility that many in his flock may naively consent to medical treatment being administered under effective duress (facing the threat of the loss of welfare payments, etc), this has received short-shrift from politicians. Shadow Federal Treasurer Jim Chalmers has no qualms about this issue and told the ABC on 24 August: 'My personal view is if and when a vaccine is available and it is rolled out, then as many people as possible should get vaccinated'. 'I say that as a Catholic that that's the best outcome for Australia because the vaccine is really what will get us to the other side'.[43] This smacks of the same extortionate approach adopted with respect to the COVID-Safe app. What is more, when it comes to Catholic teaching, Labor politicians are the last people who should be giving advice on the subject. Just ask Victorians – Daniel Andrews calls himself a Catholic!

Given governments' thirsty desire to erode fundamental rights and freedoms in the face of continuing failure, it is high time they now stopped telling people what is good for them and maybe asked them for a change. At the time of writing, a poll published on Channel 7's

---

[42] Congregation for the Doctrine of the Faith, *Dignitas Personae*, September 2008, [35] <http://www.vatican.va/roman_curia/congregations/cfaith/documents/rc_con_cfaith_doc_20081212_sintesi-dignitas-personae_en.html>.

[43] Above n 39.

website showed that 80% of respondents did not believe any corona-virus vaccine should be mandatory.[44] Further, efforts to link people's freedoms and welfare payments would strike me as constitutionally problematic. I am in fact surprised the 'no jab, no play' laws have not yet been challenged in this way. Section 51 (xxiiiA) of the *Australian Constitution* allows for the provision of various allowances and benefits by the Commonwealth Government, but not to the extent of authorising any civil conscription. It could thus be argued that no government is authorised to make the Australian people take any medication against their will, or force children to be vaccinated in order to maintain benefit payments.

However, over the days from 22 to 24 August 2020, some form of common sense appeared to be prevailing, with several doctors urging governments to abandon measures to compel Australians to accept a coronavirus vaccine. The President of the Australian Medical Association, Omar Khorshid, said making vaccinations compulsory 'sends the wrong message to the community' and is confident that the move won't be necessary anyway.[45] Dr Khorshid told the *Sydney Morning Herald* that tying vaccination to access to services such as childcare, school or social security payments, as State and Federal governments do with paediatric vaccines under 'no jab, no play' and 'no jab, no pay' laws, could not be justified with a brand new corona vaccine.

'We have to acknowledge it is a rushed approval process and even if the phase three trials on this Oxford vaccine go really well, it's still not absolutely proven that it is safe, not as proven as is normally the case'. He added: 'That does increase the risk that there might be rare side effects …that we just don't know about.' Dr Korshid also called for the Federal Government to establish a no-fault vaccine injury compensation scheme before rolling out a COVID-19 vaccine. 'If society

[44] *Channel 7 News*, 'Australian Medical Association Says Coronavirus Vaccine Should Not Be Mandatory', 24 August 2020 <https://7news.com.au/sunrise/on-the-show/australian-medical-association-says-coronavirus-vaccine-should-not-be-mandatory-c-1260248>.
[45] Ibid.

is asking everyone to get vaccinated to protect each other, we have a collective responsibility to look after the very rare and unfortunate individuals who are harmed by vaccines.'[46]

This gets back to the issue I raised at the start of this chapter, that of *informed consent*. Just because we are assured something is safe, or legal, it does not necessarily mean it is. Many people are still haunted by, and show the horrible effects of, thalidomide, a drug marketed as a sedative and given to pregnant women in the 1950s and 1960s as a treatment for morning sickness. The drug subsequently caused babies to be born with a range of deformities. An Australian obstetrician, William McBride, alerted the world to its terrible side effects and the drug was withdrawn. As recounted by his daughter Catherine in *The Australian* on 2 July 2018,[47] his initial attempt to do so was rejected by guess who? – *The Lancet* (even though the journal subsequently published a letter written by him on the issue, which sparked the investigations into the drug) – and he paid the price for this act of courage for years afterward.

VI CONCLUSION

Australians have been lectured constantly, in increasingly condescending tones, by politicians and their health apparatchiks over the last six months. It seems most of this lecturing has involved bad advice and led to unnecessary authoritarian-style policies with a complete failure to protect the most vulnerable. Now it is my turn to tell them something. Memo to the Prime Minister, the State Premiers and Territory Chief Ministers, the Federal, State and Territory Health Ministers, the

---

[46] Dana McCauley, '"No Jab, No Play" The Wrong Approach To COVID-19 Vaccine, Doctors Warn', *The Sydney Morning Herald*, 23 August 2020 <https://www.smh.com.au/politics/federal/no-jab-no-play-the-wrong-approach-to-covid-19-vaccine-doctors-warn-20200821-p55o70.html>.

[47] Charlie Peel, 'A Medical Whistleblower: William McBride Won World Recognition for Exposing the Dangers of Thalidomide but Incurred the Wrath of Pharmaceutical Firms', *The Australian*, 2 July 2018 <https://www.theaustralian.com.au/nation/inquirer/william-mcbride-paid-the-price-of-taking-on-pharmaceutical-giants/news-story/0a871168a10c163caeed93db96e9116e>.

Federal, State and Territory Attorneys-General, the Federal Minister for Home Affairs, and all Medical Officers around the country: **Do not** tell me anymore what is for my own good. I will work that out for myself. I always have. And, as far as taking any coronavirus vaccine is concerned, that will by MY DECISION, AND MINE ALONE, after I have taken the time to inform myself on ALL aspects regarding it, freely and fully. Get it? If not, refer once more to the above…

9

The Role of the State in the Protection of Public Health: The Covid-19 Pandemic

GABRIËL A. MOENS*

ABSTRACT

This chapter deals with the disrupting effect of the Covid-19 virus in Australia. It briefly describes the restrictions which were imposed on people by the Australian authorities to combat the virus. The chapter characterises these restrictions as an extreme version of "Nanny State" measures which are paternalistic in nature and have an enormous and deleterious effect on the rights of people, and even have unintended consequences for the protection of their health. The author considers the constitutional foundations of the Covid-19 laws and regulations and highlights the perceived weaknesses of the Government's actions. It is suggested that it is too early to make an accurate assessment of the lasting impact of the pandemic on the fabric of Australian society.

I THE COVID-19 PANDEMIC AS A DISRUPTOR

The year 2020 has thus far been dominated by one momentous event: the Covid-19 virus which dramatically changed the domestic and in-

---

* Gabriël Moens, JD, LLM, PhD, GCEd, MBA, MAppL is an Emeritus Professor of Law, The University of Queensland, and an Adjunct Professor of Law at the University of Notre Dame Australia, Sydney, and at Curtin University. He is the author of a fiction debut novel, entitled *A Twisted Choice* (Boolarong Press, 2020), which explores the origins of the Covid-19 virus.

ternational landscapes.[1] The highly infectious virus spread quickly throughout the world, resulting on 30 January 2020 in a declaration by The World Health Organization ('WHO') of a Public Health Emergency of International Concern, which soon after was recognised as a 'pandemic'. The pandemic generated an avalanche of laws and regulations in many countries, aimed at combating, controlling, or eradicating the disease. This unprecedented legislative activity necessitates a consideration of the role of the State in the protection of peoples' health.

I have always been interested, intellectually and practically, in the proper role of the State in society, but I have pursued this interest in the context of a coronavirus-free environment. Specifically, in 2015 I published a paper that dealt with the role of the State in the protection of peoples' health in which I argued that governments, rather than prescriptively prohibiting unwanted behaviour by the adoption of "Nanny State" measures, had recourse to more subtle, but equally effective, "Nudge State" measures that purported to maintain personal choice.[2]

However, the spread of the Covid-19 virus has completely changed this narrative and, hence, it is appropriate to revisit the proper role of the State in the protection of peoples' health in the light of the pandemic. In this chapter, I trace the journey of State interventionism involving the legislative adoption of behavioural rules to improve public health. In the pre-Covid-19 era, "Nudge State" interventionism was the preferred legislative approach to controlling the health of citizens. However, since the outbreak of the Covid-19 pandemic and the staggering rivers of cash thrown at its eradication, it is clear that an ex-

---

[1] Of course, there were other events that captured the attention of the world, for example, the Black Lives Matters Movement that started following the death of George Floyd in Minnesota at the hands of a police officer, and the protests against racism and refugees' detention, which led to the destruction of many historical monuments in the United States, the United Kingdom and Australia. On 26 June 2020, President Donald Trump issued an Executive Order on Protecting Monuments, Memorials, and Statues and Combating Recent Criminal Violence.

[2] Gabriël A. Moens and Rajesh Sharma, 'Improving Public Health Through Behavioural Rules: A Legitimate Legislative Project of a Nanny State or a Nudge State?' (2015) 57(4) *Journal of the Indian Law Institute* 474.

treme version of the "Nanny State" approach is prevalent and that any "Nudge State" measures are merely convenient smokescreens used in less challenging times to protect the health of a State's population.

In the next section of this chapter, I will briefly describe Australia's response to the spread of the Covid-19 virus, and the measures which have been taken to fight the disease. An evaluation of these measures requires a theoretical understanding of the "Nanny State" and "Nudge State" approaches to the protection of peoples' health. Specifically, it will be argued in the third section that the distinction between "Nanny State" and "Nudge State" measures is a distinction without a difference and, therefore the "Nudge State" approach does not really differ, in substance, from the "Nanny State" approach. In section four, I argue that the Covid-19 virus pandemic has resulted in the restoration of an extreme version of the "Nanny State" approach. Section five examines whether this version is compatible with the Commonwealth Constitution and focuses on the consequences of the implementation of this extreme version for the rule of law and the rights of people. Some concluding comments are offered in the last section.

II AUSTRALIA'S RESPONSE TO THE COVID-19 PANDEMIC

The Covid-19 virus apparently entered Australia sometime in January 2020, possibly by plane coming from Wuhan, Hubei Province, People's Republic of China.[3] The Government of Australia responded to this unprecedented virus threat to the health of people by instituting a National Cabinet, consisting of the Prime Minister and the Premiers of the States and the Chief Ministers of the Territories, assisted by the Chief Medical Officer, to design a joint and co-ordinated response to the spread of the virus.

The response involved the adoption of draconian restrictions on the free movement of people. The measures taken were, by any standard, severe. Australia, like many other countries, opted for a 'lockdown' without seriously considering the social and economic consequences of this measure. China had previously ordered a lockdown in the Wu-

---

[3] https://www.health.gov.au/news/chief-medical-officers-update-on-novel-coronavirus.

han region, affecting approximately 56 million people. This measure became the template for other countries. The authorities were able to justify their harsh lockdown measures by referring to the seeming inability of the New South Wales Health Service to contain the infection found on board an arriving cruise ship, the *Ruby Princess*. The virus also seemed to proliferate in an uncontrolled manner in aged care facilities. In one facility, the now notorious Anglicare Newmarch House Facility in New South Wales, nineteen people died from the virus, out of a total of 126 fatalities attributed to the virus, as at 25 July 2020. The occupants of the Facility were apparently not allowed to go into a hospital to have their viral infection treated.

States and Territories effectively closed their borders. Meetings of more than ten people were banned in some States. People over 70 and Aboriginals over 50 were deemed to be vulnerable groups; as such they were encouraged, if not ordered, to stay at home. Visitors to Australia were required to self-isolate for fourteen days or were compulsorily quarantined in city hotels or government facilities. Food and medicines were delivered to people's houses and physical contact, even with children and grandchildren, was discouraged. People were expected to practice "social distancing" which involved maintaining a distance of at least 1.5 metres from other people.

The closure of businesses was ordered by the National Cabinet. The Cabinet also cancelled events, stopped international travel and most of domestic travel, thereby creating an unemployment crisis of immense proportions. More than one million workers lost their jobs, at least temporarily, making it difficult for many people to pay their rents or mortgages, or to purchase food for their families. All the resources of Government were commandeered to fight the disease. The Government undertook to spend a staggering amount of money, AU$214 billion, to protect the sovereignty of Australia and to ensure that businesses could return to normal once the crisis passed. When adopting the Covid-19 legislation on 8 April 2020 the Prime Minister stated:

> Our sovereignty is measured in our capacity and freedom to
> live our lives as we choose in a free, open and democratic so-

ciety. Our sovereignty is enabled by having a vibrant market economy that underpins our standard of living that gives all Australians the opportunity to fulfil their potential. To have a go and to get a go. We will not surrender this.[4]

The Government's treasure chest was used to temporarily finance the JobKeeper scheme which provided monetary support for workers who became unemployed when businesses closed. Childcare centres were subsidised to ensure they stayed open, private hospitals were brought under public control, and many people were directed to now work from home. Elective surgery was suspended temporarily in the expectation that hospital beds would be needed for coronavirus patients and that all ventilators would be used by Covid-19 sufferers. This may have had the unintended consequence that some people died from other diseases, for example cancer, because the treatment of all other health conditions were subordinated to the fight of the Covid-19 virus.[5] The implementation of these restrictive measures raises the question as to whether the Government's response to the virus threat was proportionate to the dangers associated with the disease.

The lockdown measures were not without critics. An English medical scholar, Carlo Caduff, commented that, 'A crude, extreme and ultimately unsustainable version of the Chinese approach became the international norm.'[6] Some countries, rather than ordering a total lockdown, promoted a herd immunity approach, and concentrated from the beginning of the pandemic on increased testing and contact

---

[4] Phillip Coorey, 'Coronavirus measures are temporary: PM', *Financial Review*, 8 April 2020 <https://www.afr.com/politics/federal/morrison-coronavirus-a-threat-to-our-sovereignty-20200408-p54i3y>.

[5] It is ironic that the lockdown measures taken to protect the health of citizens may have had the unintended effect of diluting the quality of medical services in Australia. For example, the Government-approved medical service delivery by telephone has made it more difficult to secure a face-to-face appointment with a medical practitioner in a timely manner.

[6] Carlo Caduff, 'What Went Wrong. Corona and the World after the Full Stop', accepted for publication in a forthcoming issue of *Medical Anthropology Quarterly*. See also volume 10, issue 2 of *Migration Policy Practice* which contains many articles about the pandemic; Barrie Sander and Jason Rudall (eds), 'COVID-19 and International Law' (2020) March-April *Opinio Juris*.

tracing. However, the Australian authorities, in deciding on lockdown measures in response to the transmission of the virus, relied on mathematical disease modelling which appeared, for some time, to be the only tool used in the formulation of Government policy. The National Cabinet were thus guided by medical experts who used statistical modelling to predict the extent to which the disease would spread in Australia. A commentator, Professor David Flint, has argued that reliance on mathematical modelling 'has limited utility'. Specifically, he opined that, 'Relying on secret modelling, today's leaders concentrated on stopping the spread of the virus they had let in by destroying jobs and much of the productive part of the country and ... squandering billions of the next generation's inheritance on a succession of ill-thought and knee-jerk measures.'[7] For him, the science of mathematical modelling had yielded routinely wrong results in the past and, in the circumstances of the Covid-19 challenge, it irrationally overstated the number of infections and deaths.

Flint's point implicitly warns that the use of questionable scientific tools in the making of policy decisions is precarious and possibly dangerous. However, in Government circles, there appears to be an unquestioned belief in the accuracy of scientific findings and in the ability of people to explain everything in a scientific way, leaving no room anymore for common sense and even faith.[8] Current scientific achievements and developments, while impressive and promising, may reveal the existence of unexplained phenomena and mysteries which are not yet amenable to systematic investigation. Hence, there will always be room for, and a need of, common sense and faith.[9]

---

[7] David Flint, 'Recover Reparations, Restore Independence', *The Spectator*, 11 April 2020.

[8] In this context, Article 1, The Humanist Manifesto II, 1973 states that, 'We believe ... that traditional dogmatic or authoritarian religions that place revelation, God, ritual, or creed above human needs and experience do a disservice to the human species. Any account of nature should pass the tests of scientific evidence; in our judgment, the dogmas and myths of traditional religions do not do so.'

[9] However, scientific developments have now made it possible to manipulate the gender of our children, and cloning technology already exists. We have witnessed the adoption of same sex marriage as a legal institution in Australia. And increasingly, legislators around Australia promote euthanasia to enable people to determine how and when they die.

Larry P Arnn, President, Hillsdale College in Michigan similarly criticises the idea, that health experts and other people with scientific expertise should run the government. He emphasises the importance of common sense when he states that, 'If decisions are made ultimately according to common sense and if everyone can have it, then we are able as well as entitled to manage the affairs of the nation as citizens who deliberate together.'[10]

The Australian lockdown measures were eased as from the beginning of May 2020, but Western Australia and Queensland kept their borders shut. South Australia, which did not register any infections for some weeks, opened its border to some interstate traffic in June 2020. Queensland opened its border to interstate travellers, except from Victoria and some New South Wales hotspots on 10 July 2020. A second wave of infections hit Victoria in July 2020, which resulted in the complete lockdown of nine social housing towers. A bungled supervision of quarantined people in a Melbourne hotel considerably increased the rate of infections. By the end of July 2020, there were more than 600 new infections every day in Victoria. New South Wales, especially some hot spots around Sydney, experienced a second wave of infections. By 13 August 2020, 352 people had died from Covid-19 complications.

It is expected that some limited interstate travel might be possible in the second half of 2020, but international travel does not seem to be an option until at least the middle of 2021.

III THE "NANNY STATE" AND THE "NUDGE" STATE: A DISTINCTION WITHOUT A DIFFERENCE?

Since the Second World War, governments have intervened legislatively and administratively to ensure that citizens are properly protected against health risks. This intervention led to the creation of the "Nanny State"' which essentially replaced the free choice of individuals with the decision-making power of the government. In pre-Covid-19 days, this intervention generated a discussion about the extent to which governments should embrace paternalism as a principle of

---

[10] Larry P Arnn, 'Thoughts on the Current Crisis' (2020) 49(3/4) *Imprimis* 4.

legislation. The implementation of this principle resulted in the imposition of unpopular and burdensome health regulations because it validated the making of decisions which individuals should be allowed to make themselves. For this reason, supporters of "Nanny State" interventionism sought to moderate their approach through the medium of a "Nudge State", though in goal and philosophy they are similar. This similarity arises from the fact that the "Nudge State" seeks to achieve the same objectives, not by prescriptively controlling, forbidding or compelling the behaviour of individuals, as is usual under "Nanny State" interventionism, but by making this behaviour economically expensive, socially undesirable, or emotionally challenging.

The term "Nanny State" is a familiar description of the tendency of many modern governments to treat their 'citizens as children in a nursery',[11] supervising and influencing their choices according to the government's view of their well-being. Such an approach is 'authoritarian and paternalistic ... imposing on people what is good for them, for "nanny knows best".'[12]

In contrast, the supporters of the "Nudge State" approach seek to make Nanny less prominent by seeking to preserve free choice. They rather wordily define a "nudge" as 'any aspect of the choice architecture that alters people's behavior in a predictable way without forbidding any options or significantly changing their economic incentives'.[13] According to Richard Thaler, the "Nanny State" is coercive, for example by banning cigarettes, while the "Nudge State" seeks to goad people in a pre-determined direction that is favoured by the State, for example, by quitting smoking.[14] The "Nudge State" philosophy thus seeks to manipulate and influence peoples' choices, not by ban-

---

[11] R W Holder, *How Not To Say What You Mean: A Dictionary of Euphemisms* (Oxford University Press, 4th ed, 2007) 269.

[12] John Ayto and Ian Crofton, *Brewer's Dictionary of Modern Phrase and Fable* (Weidenfeld & Nicolson, 2nd ed, 2006) 520.

[13] Richard H Thaler and Cass R Sunstein, *Nudge: Improving Decisions about Health, Wealth, and Happiness* (Yale University Press, 2008) 5-6.

[14] Interview with Richard Thaler, *HARDtalk*, BBC World Service, 24 October 2012 <http://www.bbc.co.uk/podcasts/series/ht/all>

ning these choices, but by making it more difficult to freely choose or by making the choice economically prohibitive, socially undesirable, or emotionally challenging. As such, although Nanny does not make the decisions, for example, that people should not smoke, it nevertheless influences and manipulates individuals' choices to smoke.

The "Nudge State" approach is zealously paternalistic: 'At the core of nudging is the belief that people do not always act in their own self-interest.'[15] Underlying that philosophy is the notion that the State can make better choices for citizens than those citizens will make for themselves if left to their own devices. This worldview seeks to protect consumers even where they do not want protection, 'overriding consumer preferences to improve public health.'[16]

A patronising sense of entitlement to a guiding role over the lives of others pervades the policies of a "Nudge State". The "Nudge State" seeks to 'coax and cajole ... autonomous adults into healthier decision making'[17] and 'to steer citizens towards making positive decisions as individuals and for society.'[18] Although the changes to the choice architecture of society might appear to be minimal, their cumulative effect is to significantly shift the behaviour of people in the direction favoured by governments.[19]

The Nudge approach even made its presence felt in the formal structure of government. The British coalition Government, led by former Prime Minister David Cameron, established a Behavioural Insights Team, popularly known as the "Nudge Unit". This unit attempted to apply insights from behavioural psychology to the devel-

---

[15] Katrin Bennhold, 'The Ministry of Nudges', *New York Times*, 8 December 2013, BU1.

[16] Katherine Pratt, 'A Constructive Critique of Public Health Arguments for Antiobesity Soda Taxes and Food Taxes' (2012) 87 *Tulane Law Review* 73, 107.

[17] Jonathan Cummings, 'Obesity and Unhealthy Consumption: The Public-Policy Case for Placing a Federal Sin Tax on Sugary Beverages' (2010) 34 *Seattle University Law* Review 273, 294.

[18] Alberto Alemanno, 'Nudging Smokers: The Behavioural Turn of Tobacco Risk Regulation' (2012) 3(1) *European Journal of Risk Regulation* 32.

[19] Helen Lewis, 'Out of the Ordinary', *New Statesman*, 30 September-6 October 2016, 23.

opment of policy, seeking to influence individual behaviour to ensure its compatibility with government policy objectives. The State thus employed people who were actively charged with dreaming up new ways to interfere in the lives of ordinary people. The Unit's Internet blog ranged over the staggeringly wide field in which they offer their valuable insights: from obesity, tax compliance, literacy, numeracy, organ donation, household appliances, loft insulation, mobile phone theft, Christmas presents, plastic shopping bags, staircases, and penalty shoot-outs.[20] Similarly, in the United States, President Barack Obama issued an Executive Order mandating the use of behavioural science in policymaking.[21]

But in general, there is little difference in substance between the "Nanny State" and the "Nudge State". The "Nudge State" is simply an attempt to rebrand the way in which governments seek to influence the choices made by their citizens. As the "Nanny State" has been rejected by the citizenry because of its paternalistic characteristics, a "Nudge State" government seeks to promote its preferred choices by manipulating the choice. In doing so, "Nudge State" governments often adversely impact on the rights and interests of the suppliers of these choices. Thus, the "Nanny State" and the "Nudge State" legislative programmes are both based on, and inspired by, the same "nanny knows best" philosophy. Essentially, it is a distinction without a difference.

For example, government policymakers may assume, perhaps correctly, that people in general are addicted to soft drinks which contain a high level of sugar, which contributes to obesity. This, in turn, may facilitate the introduction of "Nudge State" measures, including the imposition of production specifications or additional taxes, that result in substantially increasing the price of these products. In this sense, a Nudge measure is a short cut which enables governments to achieve

---

[20] http://www.behaviouralinsights.co.uk/blog.

[21] Executive Order 13707, 'Using Behavioral Science Insights to Better Serve the American People', 15 September 2015. This order requires federal agencies to integrate behavioural insights into their policies and programmes; it also establishes the Social and Behavioral Sciences Team ('SBST').

policy objectives, and targets, in an expedient manner perceived social ills without having to rely on the cumulative effect of private choices which are made by people.

In contrast, a libertarian philosophy and approach provide an alternative to the implementation of the principle of paternalism. According to libertarian philosophy, it is not the role of the State to hold the hands of adults of full capacity as they make their way through commercial life. This libertarian philosophy emphasises both personal choice and acceptance of individual responsibility for the consequences of those choices: 'people should be free to choose whether to live in ways that are healthy or unhealthy and take personal responsibility for their own health.'[22]

Every time the government seeks to mould individual economic and social choices, personal freedom is diminished, so strong justifications should be proffered for such interventions. Intervention should be a last resort, not a reflex instinct. Most "Nanny State" or "Nudge State" interventions take place by way of legislation, rather than judge-made law. Many rules of the common law and equity have libertarian characteristics, generally holding parties to their bargains and resisting the temptation to abolish or revise obligations freely undertaken merely because their outcomes subsequently prove disadvantageous to a party. In contrast, the legislative and executive branches of many governments in Western countries appear to be faithfully devoted to "Nudge State" interventions.[23]

There are numerous policy objections to most paternalistic "Nanny

---

[22] Pratt, above n 16, 110, 129.

[23] One of the most controversial "Nudge State" interventions is the Australian federal law which provides that tobacco products may be sold only in generic packaging. The exterior of Australian cigarette packs must be "dark drab brown" in colour and have a matt finish. The executively mandated specific colour is reputed to be the world's ugliest colour. The interior of packs must be white. The legislation effectively strips valuable tobacco trademarks of any economic significance. Trademarks may not appear on cigarette packaging, other than a single use of the brand name. Even the size, typeface and colour of the brand name are regulated closely. Trademarks may not appear on the cigarettes themselves or the packet wrappers. Ugly graphic health warnings must take up 75% of the front of packets and 90 % of their reverse side.

State" and "Nudge State" interventions, for example, the ready alternative of promoting and accepting individual responsibility, the substitution of the targeted product by a different, but an equally satisfactory product, the probable circumvention of paternalistic laws, for example by buying a targeted product in a neighbouring state, the likelihood of unintended consequences, the availability of voluntary alternatives, the lack of public support for such measures and the likelihood of endless litigation challenging "Nanny State" and "Nudge State" impositions. As it is conceptually difficult to distinguish "Nudge State" and "Nanny State" measures, these objections may apply equally to both types of impositions.

IV THE RESTORATION OF THE "NANNY STATE" APPROACH: THE COVID-19 CHALLENGE

It was argued in the previous section that "Nudge State" interventionism in the field of public health is the functional equivalent of "Nanny State" interventionism. These interventions, regardless of the form they take, have effectively removed from individuals the power to make their own health decisions. In a Covid-19 context, the Australian authorities have determinedly embraced this interventionist policy, adopting measures aimed at maintaining peoples' health. Hence, it is not surprising that a staggering amount of legislation relating to the Covid-19 pandemic has already been adopted.[24]

This legislation reveals the irrelevance of any attempts to ascertain sophisticated differences between "Nudge State" and "Nanny

---

[24] See, for example, *Biosecurity Act 2015 (Cth)* (Compilation as at 1 March 2019); *Biosecurity (Human Biosecurity Emergency) (Human Coronavirus with Pandemic Potential) (Emergency Requirements for Remote Communities) Amendment (No. 1) Determination 2020*, 7 April 2020; *Biosecurity (Human Biosecurity Emergency) (Human Coronavirus with Pandemic Potential) (Overseas Travel Ban Emergency Requirements) Determination 2020*, 25 March 2020; *Biosecurity Repeal (Human Health Response Zones) Determination 2020*, 18 March 2020; *Biosecurity (Human Biosecurity Emergency) (Human Coronavirus with Pandemic Potential) (Emergency Requirements) Determination 2020*, 18 March 2020; *Biosecurity (Human Biosecurity Emergency) (Human Coronavirus with Pandemic Potential) Declaration 2020*, 18 March 2020; *Coronavirus Economic Response Package Omnibus Act 2020*, 24 March 2020.Bottom of Form

State" measures. Indeed, the Commonwealth Government, in adopting draconian legislation to combat the coronavirus, has once again resorted to conventional, prescriptive "Nanny State" measures which have the potential to seriously impact on the enjoyment of civil liberties, and generally, respect for the rule of law. This is because these measures have substantially increased the discretionary power of the police, who may well assume that people are presumed guilty of violating social distancing rules, non-essential travel restrictions, and isolation requirements, all of which might result in the imposition of hefty fines.

These unprecedented restrictions on the enjoyment of our civil liberties have been criticised, notably by Professor Augusto Zimmermann in *Quadrant Online*, on the ground that they involve decision making by diktat. In his comment, *Government by Virus and Executive Diktat*[25] of 8 April 2020, he deplores the diminished authority of the Parliament and the erosion of the separation of powers doctrine, and he describes the actions of governments as more suitable to totalitarian regimes:

> Because these extreme measures are dictated by the executive and have no deadline to expire, we are effectively experiencing government by executive decree. This is something akin to the actions of deeply authoritarian regimes, in particular when such executive measures are not properly scrutinised.

Professor Zimmermann, while admitting that sometimes emergency powers are needed, maintains that the current measures 'will dramatically increase the power of the state, thus allowing governments to arbitrarily exercise mass surveillance powers' involving an 'alarming restriction of civil liberties'. He further states that, 'any rush to embrace draconian measures in our response to the present crisis will give the state terrifyingly broad powers.' In using these powers,

---

[25] Augusto Zimmermann, 'Government by Virus and Executive Diktat', *Quadrant Online*, 8 April 2020 < https://quadrant.org.au/opinion/qed/2020/04/government-by-virus-and-executive-diktat/>.

governments have adopted measures which have devastated the entire economy. Potentially, the collapse of the economy has frightening concomitant consequences:

> Inevitably, job losses will lead to far more homelessness, with financial pressures leading to a much higher suicide rate, widespread marriage breakdown and to a dramatic growth in crime, which always increases in times of economic crisis.[26]

His assessment is clear:

> Yes, coronavirus poses a serious public health risk. But the key word here is proportion. These draconian measures provide a pretext for the authoritarian takeover of civil society that not only unleashes unprecedented economic mayhem, but also threatens our present way of life and what it means to live in a free and democratic society.[27]

Similarly, Professor David Flint has argued in *The Spectator* that the lockdown is a disproportionate response to the challenges posed by Covid-19 and is not cogently related to the objectives that the State wishes to achieve. He is critical of Australia's policymakers:

> What our morally corrupt political elites have done is to deliver even more evidence that they had, with reckless indifference, not properly examined whether they had the power to impose this totally unnecessary lockdown nor considered whether the resulting damage to millions of Australians would be justified. In brief, they had not properly considered whether their cure would far worse than the disease.[28]

He argued that the Government, in relying on the advice of scientists who believed in the infallibility of modelling science, was responsible for major economic dislocations in society. Most sacri-

---

[26] Augusto Zimmermann, 'In the State You Will Trust', *Quadrant Online*, 5 April 2020 <https://quadrant.org.au/opinion/qed/2020/04/in-the-state-you-will-trust/>.
[27] Ibid.
[28] David Flint, 'The Horse Has Bolted and the Emperor Has No Clothes', *The Spectator*, 13 June 2020.

fices had to be borne by businesspeople, not the bloated public service which was preserved and was able to make regulations to burden the productive sectors of the Australian economy. He claims that, 'There is too often a complete absence of common sense.'[29]

Carlo Caduff, in a recent article on Covid-19, agrees with Flint's analysis on the disproportionate response to the virus. He states:

> How was it possible for a virus to trigger such a massive response that continues to threaten society and the economy, with so little discussion about the costs and consequences of extreme measures? Why is there widespread agreement that aggressive interventions to 'flatten the curve' were necessary and justified? It seems that this unprecedented public health experiment occurred without sufficient consideration of the social, political and economic consequences.[30]

In his paper he criticises the reliance of many Western countries on the lockdown approach of the Chinese Government and the failure, in the early part of the pandemic, to rely on testing and contact tracing.

V A CONSTITUTIONAL LAW ASSESSMENT OF THE GOVERNMENT'S RESPONSE TO THE COVID-19 PANDEMIC

The commentators referred to above bemoan the Government's failure to fashion a response which is proportionate to the objectives it wanted to achieve, which is the protection of peoples' health by controlling or eradicating the disease. The concept of "proportionality" 'has often been advanced as a touchstone of constitutional validity' of legislative provisions.[31] "Proportionality" has been discussed by the High Court of Australia mainly in cases involving Commonwealth legislative powers that are purposive in nature. The majority of s 51 and s 52 powers of the *Commonwealth Constitution* are non-purposive, for example, a power to regulate external affairs, taxa-

---

[29] Ibid.

[30] Caduff, above n 6.

[31] Gabriël A Moens and John Trone, *The Constitution of the Commonwealth of Australia Annotated* (LexisNexis Butterworths, 9th ed, 2016) 35.

tion, and family law. However, some powers are purposive because they require the court to look, not only at the terms of the legislation but also at its purpose in advancing the subject matter of the power. For example, the defence power is a purposive power because any legislation that relies on this legislative power is for the purpose of protecting the sovereignty of Australia, and that purpose may vary in the light of the changing circumstances in which the Commonwealth may find itself.[32]

The case of *Davis v Commonwealth*[33] provides a good example of the application of the purposive approach. This case dealt with the incidental power to the executive power of s 61 of the *Commonwealth Constitution*, the nationhood power. As the executive power extended to the incorporation of an institution to promote the Bicentenary of European settlement in Australia, the incidental power would support legislation regulating that institution's procedures, giving it certain powers, and protecting its name and symbols. However, "proportionality" considerations came into the picture because the legislation went much further and prohibited the expression of ideas violating freedom of expression. Brennan J said that, 'it cannot be incidental to the organisation of the commemoration of the Bicentenary to prohibit, under criminal sanctions, the peaceful expression of opinions about the significance of the events of 1788.'[34]

Australia's response to the Covid-19 challenge involves the adoption of legislation which arguably has been based on the Commonwealth's nationhood power. In Australia, the legislative power to adopt emergency legislation belongs to the States and Territories.[35] Hence, each jurisdiction has adopted relevant emergency legislation.[36]

---

[32] Ibid 28.

[33] (1988) 166 CLR 79.

[34] Ibid at 117.

[35] Australian Institute for Disaster Resilience, 'Australian Emergency Management Arrangements', Department of Home Affairs, 2019, 4.

[36] See *Emergencies Act* 2004 (ACT); *State Emergency and Rescue Management Act* 1989 (NSW); *Emergency Management Act* 2013 (NT); *Disaster Management Act* 2003 (Qld); *Emergency Management Act* 2004 (SA); *Emergency Management Act*

However, it might be argued that the "nationhood" power which is based on s 61 of the *Commonwealth Constitution* according to which 'The executive power of the Commonwealth ... extends to the execution and maintenance of this Constitution, and of the laws of the Commonwealth' may also provide a justification for the introduction of Commonwealth-sponsored emergency measures. If so, the question of proportionality is squarely in issue. The problem is that only the principles are known, not their implementation. Although we know that the means must be cogently related to the end, for example, flattening the curve or even eradication of the Covid-19 disease in Australia, we do not know how far the legislator can go. Does the government have an unfettered discretion in the matter?

Economist Andrew Stone told *The Australian* that, 'Government led people to believe the virus would be like a Spanish flu; that's turned out not to be the case, and they will forgive it if it admits that, on new information, it was wrong and allows businesses to reopen.' He went on to say that, 'Most of all we need to avoid a situation whereby we're effectively printing money to pay people to do nothing.'[37] His latter comment refers to the government's signature $130 billion JobKeeper package, which commenced in May 2020.

It is likely that the emergency measures introduced by the Commonwealth are constitutional as suggested in *Pape v Federal Commissioner of Taxation*, decided by the High Court in 2009.[38] Pape dealt with the Global Financial Crisis of 2008-2009 and the economic stimulus law adopted by the Parliament. In *Pape*, the Commonwealth argued that such law was supported by an implied legislative "nationhood power". Although a majority of the High Court (French CJ, Gummow, Crennan and Bell JJ) found it unnecessary to consider this issue,[39]

2006 (Tas); *Emergency Management Act* 1986 (Vic); *Emergency Management Act* 2013 (Vic); *Emergency Management Act* 2005 (WA).

[37] Adam Creighton, *The Australian*, 23 April 2020, 6.

[38] 238 CLR 1 (2009). See on this case Gabriël A Moens and John Trone, *The Constitution of the Commonwealth of Australia Annotated* (LexisNexis Butterworths, 9th ed, 2016) 233.

39 *Pape v Federal Commissioner of Taxation* (2009) 238 CLR 1, 133.

it was held that the *Tax Bonus for Working Australians Act (No 2) 2009* (Cth), which authorised the appropriation of money from consolidated revenue to make stimulus payments to individual taxpayers was constitutionally valid under s 51(xxxix) of the *Commonwealth Constitution*, namely the incidental power to the exercise of the executive power. Gummow, Crennan and Bell JJ stated that, 'The Executive Government is the arm of government capable of and empowered to respond to a crisis be it war, natural disaster or a financial crisis on the scale here.'[40]

Nevertheless, there were moderating voices. For example, French CJ indicated that, 'the exigencies of "national government" cannot be invoked to set aside the distribution of powers between Commonwealth and States and between the three branches of government for which this Constitution provides, nor to abrogate constitutional prohibitions.' In his dissent, Heydon J pointed out that the mere fact that a matter is one of national interest does not mean that it necessarily falls within an implied nationhood power.[41] He opposed a substantial extension of Commonwealth powers in this interesting passage from his judgment:

> The truth is that the modern world is in part created by the way language is used. Modern linguistic usage suggests that the present age is one of "emergencies", "crises", "dangers" and "intense difficulties", of "scourges" and other problems. They relate to things as diverse as terrorism, water shortages, drug abuse, child abuse, poverty, pandemics, obesity, and global warming, as well as global financial affairs. In relation to them, the public is endlessly told, "wars" must be waged, "campaigns" conducted, "strategies" devised and "battles" fought. Often these problems are said to arise suddenly and unexpectedly. Sections of the public constantly demand urgent action to meet particular problems. The public is continually told that it is facing "decisive" junctures, "crucial" turning points and "critical" decisions. Even if only a

---

40 Ibid 89 (Gummow, Crennan and Bell JJ).
41 Ibid, 504.

narrow power to deal with an emergency on the scale of the global financial crisis were recognised, it would not take long before constitutional lawyers and politicians between them managed to convert that power into something capable of almost daily use. The great maxim of governments seeking to widen their constitutional powers would be: "Never allow a crisis to go to waste.'

Justice Heydon's sentiment is reinforced in a powerful comment, published in *Quadrant Online* by Professor Zimmermann:

[M]any Australians have developed an utterly distorted view of what governments can do for them. Such individuals now blindly worship at the altar of the all-powerful State, expecting it to be their almighty saviour, seeing in government the ultimate provider for all things. Perhaps this is a result of society's lost faith in the God of Christianity. Be that as it may, the undeniable truth is that far too many Australians have acquired an unshakable faith in their political class. Call it a form of idolatry if you wish.[42]

VI CONCLUDING COMMENTS

It will be interesting to see how the Covid-19 crisis unfolds and what the lasting consequences will be for the protection of citizens' civil rights and the rule of law in Australia. Justice Heydon's admonition that governments could convert emergency powers into 'something capable of almost daily use', and Professor Zimmermann's assessment that citizens have acquired an unrealistic view of what governments can do for them, are important reminders of the innate dangers associated with this pandemic.

But for now, it is undeniable that Nanny has triumphed!

---

[42] Above n 26.

10

Corona, Culture, Caesar and Christ

BILL MUEHLENBERG*

ABSTRACT

The coronavirus crisis has raised numerous questions, ranging from the medical and scientific to the social and political. I will argue in this piece that for the most part far too many governments have overreacted to this crisis, with the result that we have had too many infringements on individual liberties, and far too much unnecessary expansion of government. In particular I will examine the following six matters: how crises can lead to increasing powers of the state; how the nature of risk needs to be responsibly dealt with by individuals and states; how some government policies and programs entail a notion of the perfectibility of human nature; how far things like security and safety can be mandated and enforced by the state; how concerns about religious freedom interact with concerns about public health and safety; and how feasible or desirable something like just revolution might be if statist overreach becomes too onerous.

I INTRODUCTION

That the coronavirus crisis of 2020 heavily tested legal, political and social structures and institutions would be an understatement. All these and more were put under great strain and duress. As such, many

* BA with honours in Philosophy (Wheaton College, Chicago), MA with highest honours in Theology (Gordon-Conwell Theological Seminary, Boston). The author is currently completing a PhD in Theology. He has his own website called CultureWatch, which features commentary on the issues of the day: billmuehlenberg.com.

questions emerged as to how various social goods and values are to be balanced (including public health and safety), what the role and limits of government are, the value and reach of liberty, and the place of coercion and the force of law.

Very early on with this pandemic it became clear that in the face of so much social and cultural upheaval, various trade-offs would be required, and extensive cost and benefit analyses of different government actions and public policy decisions would be needed to help us successfully navigate through these largely uncharted waters. It is these options and approaches, especially as undertaken in Australia and America (the two nations I have lived the longest in), that I will look at here in a somewhat broad-brush fashion – but with various specifics mentioned along the way.

My thrust will be this: Generally speaking, too many governments overreacted to this virus crisis, resulting in too many infringements on individual liberties, and far too much statist overreach and aggrandisement. The issues I will examine here are these: the role of crises in the increasing role of the state; the nature of risk and how states deal with it; the perfectibility of human nature through government programs; how far the state should seek to work for universal safety and security; religious freedom concerns; and the desirability or feasibility of just revolution over against unjust statist overreach.[1]

II THE STATE AND CRISES

One of the earliest pieces I wrote on my own website on the coronavirus crisis had to do with the issue of public crises and emergencies, and how governments have tended to respond historically. While still early days back then, I did warn that this Covid-19 crisis could easily turn into yet another clear case of governments rapidly expanding

---

[1] While most essays in this collection will have focused on legal aspects, mine will include that, but will also look even further at other considerations, such as historical, ethical, philosophical, political, and even theological ones – all at the request of the editor. Indeed, it is an honour to have been asked by Professor Zimmermann to contribute a chapter to this set of essays, and I thank him now for his kind invitation.

their powers, with individual freedoms being radically curtailed. Of course, any student of history could have proffered similar concerns.

We know that in times of crisis, the power of the state can easily and rapidly expand while the freedoms of the individual can shrink dramatically. That is not to argue against the notion that in times of genuine crisis and emergency there is a place for the state to step in and act in a responsible and appropriate manner. But the key is to carefully discern what is a real and major crisis, what is a mild crisis, and what is just a manmade or fake crisis.

Real crises can and do result in these sorts of trade-offs. In times of war for example people will often happily and willingly put up with all manner of constraints and limitations on their liberty. They will put up with various restrictions, with blackouts, with rationing, and even with donating precious items to the war effort – be they various metals and minerals, or even their very lives.

Tough times call for tough responses. But the key is to know that the emergency is real, and that it warrants such harsh measures and such huge sacrifices. And it helps to know that our leaders have our best interests at heart. This is not always the case of course. It is all too easy to find numerous instances of bias, agenda-pushing, hype, deception, and misinformation in political circles. Politicians often have hidden agendas or ulterior motives in what they say and do. And the temptation for them to take even more power and control is always a clear and present danger.

While the state is often willing to seize control of things, it can be quite loth to give up control. A public health crisis is just the sort of thing that power-hungry politicians will latch onto in order to grab more control and more power. And that means much less liberty and freedom for ordinary citizens.

If politicians only had the best of intentions when it comes to its citizenry, we could all breathe much easier. But they often do not. Too often runaway government is the norm, as are unwarranted restrictions on liberty. One can simply offer any number of quotes from various conservative thinkers and leaders on this matter. Ronald Reagan for example spoke often about these harsh realities. Here are a few of his oft-heard thoughts:

- *'Either you will control your government, or government will control you'.*
- *'No government ever voluntarily reduces itself in size. Government programs, once launched, never disappear. Actually, a government bureau is the nearest thing to eternal life we'll ever see on this earth'.*
- *'Concentrated power has always been the enemy of liberty'.*
- *'The most terrifying words in the English language are: I'm from the government and I'm here to help'.*[2]

The American Founding Fathers of course spoke to these issues constantly. Thomas Jefferson's warning must be carefully considered: 'The natural progress of things is for liberty to yield and government to gain ground.'[3] And George Washington reminded us of this truth: 'Government is not reason; it is not eloquent; it is force. Like fire, it is a dangerous servant and a fearful master.'[4]

Many others have sounded the alarm about such dangers. One expert who has examined these truths in some detail is worth appealing to. The Austrian-British philosopher and economist F. A. Hayek (1899-1992), wrote much about freedom and its enemies. In the third volume of his classic *Law, Legislation and Liberty* he has a short section on "Emergency powers". The first half of that is well worth sharing here:

> The basic principle of a free society, that the coercive powers of government are restricted to the enforcement of universal rules of just conduct, and cannot be used for the achievement of particular purposes, though essential to the normal

---

[2] 'Ronald Reagan Quotes', *AZ Quotes*, <https://www.azquotes.com/author/12140-Ronald_Reagan>.

[3] Thomas Jefferson, 'From Thomas Jefferson to Edward Carrington, 27 May 1788', *Founders Online*, https://founders.archives.gov/documents/Jefferson/01-13-02-0120>.

[4] George Washington, 'Famous Quotes by George Washington', *Quotes,* < https://www.quotes.net/quote/36541>.

working of such a society, may yet have to be temporarily suspended when the long-run preservation of that order is itself threatened. Though normally the individuals need be concerned only with their own concrete aims, and in pursuing them will best serve the common welfare, there may temporarily arise circumstances when the preservation of the over-all order becomes the overruling common purpose, and when in consequence the spontaneous order, on a local or national scale, must for a time be converted into an organization. When an external enemy threatens, when rebellion or lawless violence has broken out, or a natural catastrophe requires quick action by whatever means can be secured, powers of compulsory organization, which normally nobody possesses, must be granted to somebody. Like an animal in flight from mortal danger society may in such situations have to suspend temporarily even vital functions on which in the long run its existence depends if it is to escape destruction.

The conditions under which such emergency powers may be granted without creating the danger that they will be retained when the absolute necessity has passed are among the most difficult and important points a constitution must decide on. 'Emergencies' have always been the pretext on which the safeguards of individual liberty have been eroded – and once they are suspended it is not difficult for anyone who has assumed such emergency powers to see to it that the emergency will persist. Indeed if all needs felt by important groups that can be satisfied only by the exercise of dictatorial powers constitute an emergency, every situation is an emergency situation. It has been contended with some plausibility that whoever has the power to proclaim an emergency, and on this ground to suspend any part of the constitution, is the true sovereign. This would seem to be true enough if any person or body were able to arrogate to itself such emergency powers by declaring a state of emergency.[5]

---

[5] F A Hayek, *Law, Legislation and Liberty* (University of Chicago Press, 1979) 124-125.

Let me highlight the key sentence from that second paragraph: "Emergencies' have always been the pretext on which the safeguards of individual liberty have been eroded – and once they are suspended it is not difficult for anyone who has assumed such emergency powers to see to it that the emergency will persist.'

One can see how easy it is for any political leader to milk a crisis for all its worth. The temptation is always there, and that for the simple reason that power is so seductive and so corrupting. Even the best of leaders are not immune from the destructive virus of escalating power grabs.

And we must also beware of good intentions – they easily can serve less than good ends. American essayist and satirist H. L. Mencken (1880-1956) once put it this way: 'The urge to save humanity is almost always a false-face for the urge to rule it.'[6] Or as the noted economist Milton Friedman (1912-2006) once said: 'Concentrated power is not rendered harmless by the good intentions of those who create it.'[7]

And some wise words by C. S. Lewis presented in a 1949 essay come to mind here:

> Of all tyrannies, a tyranny sincerely exercised for the good of its victims may be the most oppressive. It would be better to live under robber barons than under omnipotent moral busybodies. The robber baron's cruelty may sometimes sleep, his cupidity may at some point be satiated; but those who torment us for our own good will torment us without end for they do so with the approval of their own conscience.[8]

We have seen this occurring far too often during the coronavirus crisis. While some leaders did have good intentions, and did seek to offer a balanced and judicious use of state power on the one hand, while allowing for as much liberty as was sensible on the other, we had too many authorities who seemed to relish their new-found pow-

---

[6] H L Mencken, *Minority Report: H. L. Mencken's Notebooks* (Alfred A Knopf, 1956) 247.

[7] Milton Friedman, *Capitalism and Freedom* (University of Chicago Press, 1962) 201.

[8] C S Lewis, 'The Humanitarian Theory of Punishment' in Walter Hooper (ed), *God in the Dock* (Eerdmans, 1978) 292.

ers, and acted like mini dictators. If we need some names here, a few can be highlighted: Michigan Governor Gretchen Whitmer was a classic case in point here, as was the Australian Premier of Victoria, Daniel Andrews. As I write this piece, both jurisdictions are still under various restrictive measures, compared to their neighbours.

Plenty of contemporary commentators have spoken of the dangers inherent in all this. Just a few can be mentioned here. American economist Walter Williams said this: 'The biggest casualty from the COVID-19 pandemic has nothing to do with the disease. It's the power we've given to politicians and bureaucrats. The question is how we recover our freedoms.'[9]

And British commentator Brendan O'Neill wrote:

Britain is on the brink of the worst recession since the Great Frost of 1709, according to the Bank of England. Others are predicting an utterly unprecedented 13 per cent contraction in national output. Millions will lose their jobs. And that's just the UK. More than 100 million Indians have lost their jobs as a result of the global contagion of lockdown. Many will be plunged into hunger, and worse. The International Labor Organization says 1.5 billion people around the world are at risk of losing their livelihoods. The halting of economic life and production and transportation could lead to a global 'hunger catastrophe', says the UN. I hope the lockdown fanatics think about that next time they post a pic of their latest loaf of sourdough.But they don't think about it. Not seriously. They treat it as incidental. The economic devastation being wrought in the US, the UK and elsewhere gets a few column inches here and there or is an afterthought in the nightly news. But it is rarely the story. Lockdown fanatics are so convinced of their moral rectitude, so bound up in anti-Covid zealotry, so enjoying their part in the culture of fear and the culture of condemnation against anyone who breaks lockdown, that they

---

[9] Walter Williams, 'Williams: Pandemic affording politicians great powers' *Toronto Sun*, 25 May 2020. <https://torontosun.com/opinion/columnists/williams-pandemic-affording-politicians-great-powers>.

just zone out the terrible things that they are helping to bring about.Or, worse, they engage in a political sleight of hand. They say job losses, rising mental-health problems, lack of money and a global downturn that will hit the poor severely are also down to Covid. 'Covid-19 is giving rise to economic problems, too', they occasionally say. No. We cannot allow this. It is not Covid that is destroying livelihoods and liberties – it is our societies' historically unprecedented, ill-thought-through, contagion-like authoritarian response to Covid; it is lockdown fanaticism.They need to take some responsibility. Covid can be excused; it's a virus. The lockdown fanatics cannot be excused. Their extremism is hampering sensible government action, stymieing open public debate, and nurturing economic catastrophe. They must be held to account. More than that, they must be opposed. We need a return to reason, freedom and productivity.[10]

Another English author, Peter Hitchens put it this way:

It has not been much fun fighting this. In fact, it has been exhausting and dispiriting. I feel as if I am in a nightmare where I can see a terrible danger approaching but when I cry out in warning, nobody can hear me. Can't you see? I yell in the dream. If you don't defend your most basic freedom, the one to go lawfully where you wish when you wish, then you will lose it for ever.

And that is not all you will lose. Look at the censorship of the internet, spreading like a great dark blot, the death of Parliament, the conversion of the police into a state militia? Aren't you alarmed by the creation of a creepy cult of state-worship, celebrated every Thursday night – in a country where church services and normal public gatherings are banned? When did you last hear an anti-government voice on the BBC, now little more than a servile state broadcaster?

---

[10] Brendan O'Neill, 'Lockdown fanatics scare me far more than Covid-19' *Spiked* 2020. <https://www.spiked-online.com/2020/05/08/lockdown-fanatics-scare-me-far-more-than-covid-19/>.

And then can you not see the strangling of the prosperity on which everything we hold dear is based? I mentioned the other day to a hard-working small business owner that a shop well known to me was down to ten per cent of its normal takings. 'Lucky him!' exclaimed the businessman, 'I have had no income at all for weeks, and I have no hope of any. But I am still having to pay my rent and power bills, and interest on my loans.'[11]

III RISK ASSESSMENT AND MANAGEMENT

If people are not familiar with the term 'actuary' they should be. While specifically referring to those in the insurance industry who calculate insurance risks and premiums, the term can have a broader usage. Life itself is always about trade-offs. When you go to a restaurant – perhaps especially somewhere overseas – you take a risk of possibly getting food poisoning. When you fly somewhere, there is always the risk of a plane crash. Nuclear power stations may be good at generating much-needed energy, but some consider them to be too risky. Having numerous cameras mounted throughout public areas can be good in monitoring criminal activities, but there is the risk that this can lead to an unwanted police state.

Life is like that. There are no guarantees, and everything has its risks. So we speak about things like cost-benefit analysis. We try to weigh up the possible risks and costs of any given course of action to see if the benefits are worth it. Governments have to do this all the time. Consider just one area, already hinted at: Should governments go ahead with nuclear power plants? Should they stick with coal-fired generators? Should they put all their efforts into things like wind farms?

Life is risky. Every time we step outside, we risk possible death: We might get hit by a truck; a tree might fall on us; we might get

---

[11] Peter Hitchens, 'PETER HITCHENS: We're destroying the nation's wealth – and the health of millions' *Daily Mail*, 2 May 2020. <hitchensblog.mailonsunday.co.uk/2020/05/peter-hitchens-were-destroying-the-nations-wealth-and-the-health-of-millions.html>.

struck by lightning; someone might take us out in a drive-by shooting. Sure, some of these risks may be much less likely than others, but life is inherently risky. The question is, what risks are we willing to live with?

Taking the car to work which might result in a person getting in an accident is seen as a necessary risk in order to earn money to feed the family. Other risks are more a matter of personal choice. Some folks may love to go rock climbing, but there is always the risk of a fatal fall. One does not have to go rock climbing, but one does need to earn a living.

And bear in mind that risk assessment changes over time – partly as our knowledge increases. My dad was a house painter and early on he and other painters almost always used lead-based paint. It was quite good paint because the lead sped up the drying process, it was durable, and so on. But after a while we learned about the dangers of toxicity in lead, so now you cannot easily buy it– not in the West at any rate. The same with asbestos. It was once widely used in building materials because it added strength and was great as a fire retardant. But then later we learned about its negative cancer-causing properties, so it was banned from use in many countries.

Conditions can also change. When I was young, I played outside, often a long way from home. We mostly kept our house and car doors unlocked, as few people back then worried much about crimes like child abuse, home break-ins, and so on. Things have changed and the risks have gone up. So in my hometown – and elsewhere – parents now keep a much closer eye on their children, houses are locked, and so on.

A wise person will seek to minimise risk – but within reason. If we banned all cars in Australia, we would of course then have zero car accidents and fatalities. But most people would say that the price is far too high to pay for this. So as always, we deal with trade-offs. But there have always been some who seem to think that we must work to eliminate most, if not all, risk – no matter how costly this might be. Some governments seek to do this in various areas. And now with the corona crisis we see more of the same in play.

The cost and benefit assessment is obvious here: On the one hand, we want to keep people safe and keep the virus from spreading. But on the other hand, we also do not want to shut down the nation, utterly destroy the economy, and effectively take away all of our freedoms. Some sort of balance is needed.

How much government intervention is necessary, wise and helpful? How much is too much? How many liberties should we surrender, and for how long? When does the cure become worse than the disease? Yes, some infringements of individual liberties will be needed, and some strict state measures will be necessary – at least for a while. But we also must be concerned about government overreach, statist overkill, overzealous policing, and far too many draconian measures being implemented with far too many freedoms being taken away.

Again, we are talking about risk, and weighing up options. So how do we decide which way to go? Nearly four decades ago an important book was written dealing with these matters in general. I refer to the 1983 volume by Mary Douglas and Aaron Wildavsky, *Risk and Culture*. The authors discuss the issue of risk in the context of environmental protection versus technological development. But their discussion can just as readily be applied to the coronavirus crisis. Let me simply quote their opening paragraph to see how it ties in here:

> Can we know the risks we face, now or in the future? No, we cannot; but yes, we must act as if we do. Some dangers are unknown; others are known, but not by us because no one person can know everything. Most people cannot be aware of most dangers at most times. Hence, no one can calculate precisely the total risk to be faced. How, then, do people decide which risks to take and which to ignore? On what basis are certain dangers guarded against and others relegated to secondary status?[12]

Many will say at this point that we simply must trust the experts.

---

[12] Mary Douglas and Aaron Wildavsky, *Risk and Culture* (University of California Press, 1983) 1.

But of course, what happens when the experts get it wrong, or when they disagree amongst themselves? Then who do we believe? Politicians also have to listen to the various "experts" and decide the best policy options. But it is not just medical or scientific facts gleaned from others that can sway them. Their own political and ideological commitments will also come into play.

IV PROGRESS AND PERFECTABILITY

Related to the above is how we understand the ideal society and the best sort of government. Political philosophy deals with such matters, but it is based on an even more important foundational matter: how we understand and assess human nature. How we think about things like personhood and humanity will colour our thoughts on preferred public policy options and political choices.

Some views of human nature stress the malleability and even the perfectibility of the person. The thought is that if we apply the right social conditions, we can create the right sort of people. Karl Marx basically ran with this view, as did philosophers such as Jean-Jacques Rousseau. Much of this sprang from Enlightenment notions of progress and perfectibility which have in many ways become a defining feature of modernity. As modern science increased expectations, as modern medical advances have extended our lifespan, and as more recent bio-medical technologies promise a brave new world of possibilities (or a new eugenics as some have warned),[13] the notions of personhood, suffering and limitation have been altered dramatically.

Whereas most of mankind throughout most of human history have accepted the fact that life is 'poor, nasty, brutish, and short', to use Hobbes's phrase,[14] advances in science, medicine, technology and other areas have resulted in a redefinition of what it is to be human, and have altered our expectations immeasurably. Several hundred years ago most people accepted that life was full of suffering and woe, and

---

[13] See for example the essay by Richard John Neuhaus, 'The Return of Eugenics' *Commentary* (1988) April, 15-26.

[14] Thomas Hobbes, *Leviathan* (Oxford University Press, 1998) 84.

death was in fact sometimes welcomed as relief from the drudgery, hardship and tedium of day to day living. The ordinariness and harshness of daily life, coupled with the belief in a much better afterlife, meant that for many people, suffering, privation and misery were both bearable and acceptable.

But with the advances of modernity much of this has changed, and suffering is now seen as something to be eliminated, instead of something to be endured, even welcomed. Whereas suffering (from whatever cause) was once seen at best as a gift from God, or at worse, as a cross to bear,[15] today suffering in almost any form is a thing to be avoided altogether. And the more promises modern technology makes concerning the alleviation of misery and suffering, the higher our expectations grow.

Years ago, C S Lewis contrasted the wisdom of earlier ages with the modern technological vision. In his vitally important – and pre-scient – volume, *The Abolition of Man*, he said this: 'The serious magical endeavour and the serious scientific endeavour are twins: one was sickly and died, the other strong and throve. But they were twins. They were born of the same impulse.'[16] He continued:

> There is something which unites magic and applied science while separating both from the wisdom of earlier ages. For the wise men of old the cardinal problem had been how to conform the soul to reality, and the solution had been knowledge, self-discipline, and virtue. For magic and applied science alike the problem is how to subdue reality to the wishes of men: the solution is a technique; and both, in the practice of this technique, are ready to do things hitherto regarded as disgusting and impious — such as digging up and mutilating the dead.. . . . The true object is to extend Man's power to the performance of all things possible. He rejects magic because it does not work; but his goal is that of the magician.[17]

---

[15] The two ideas are by no means incompatible from a Christian viewpoint.
[16] C S Lewis, *The Abolition of Man* (Macmillan, 1976) 87.
[17] Ibid 87-89.

Briefly stated, the theocentric worldview of the pre-modern period was replaced by an anthropocentric worldview of modernism. Man was seen as the measure of all things in the Enlightenment. Man by himself, guided by human reason alone, would scale every mountain and solve every mystery. Some well-known quotes can be offered here:

Enlightenment essayist Alexander Pope expressed these concepts this way: 'Know then thyself. Seek not God to scan. The proper study of mankind is man.' Education, knowledge, and especially science, would save the day.[18] Pope again: 'Nature and nature's laws lay wrapped in night. God said 'Let Newton be!' and all was light.'[19] The French Enlightenment humanist, Nicolas de Condorcet, proudly put it this way: 'No bounds have been fixed to the improvement of the human race. The perfectibility of man is absolutely infinite.' Or as Francis Bacon put it, 'Conquer nature, relieve man's estate.'[20] Again, more recently, Bertrand Russell was to confidently exclaim, 'What science cannot tell us, mankind cannot know.'

Medical ethicist Daniel Callahan, in his volume on end of life health care, examines this shift in thinking, and discusses how modernism has elevated science and medicine to divine proportions. He is well worth quoting:

Medicine is perhaps the last and purest bastion of Enlightenment dreams, tying together reason, science, and the dream of unlimited human possibilities. There is nothing, it is held, that in principle cannot be done and, given suitable caution, little that ought not to be done. Nature, including the body, is seen as infinitely manipulable and plastic to human contrivance. When that conception of medicine is set in a social context of an individualism which is, in principle, opposed

---

[18] Cited in Barry L Callen, *Discerning the Divine: God in Christian Theology* (John Knox Press, 2004) 86.
[19] Cited in Roger E Olson, *The Mosaic of Christian Belief: Twenty Centuries of Unity and Diversity* (InterVarsity Press, 2nd ed, 2016) 172.
[20] Cited in Roger Masters, *The Nature of Politics* (Yale University Press, 1989) 147.

to a public consensus about any ultimate human good, it is a potent engine of endless, never-satisfied progress.[21]

I did mention eugenics just above. Much more could be said about this in relation to the push for perfection. Just one quote however is worth sharing here:

> If the fear of being swamped by biological defectives was a powerful motivator for eugenists, the hope of achieving biological perfection was equally inspiring. The eugenists' naïve faith in modern science spawned a virulent utopianism. Dressed up in quasi-religious terminology, the eugenics faith promised to create heaven on earth through the magic of human breeding. The utopian vision had been a key part of the eugenics crusade from its inception. Francis Galton had promoted the goal of "gradually raising the present miserably low standard of the human race to one in which the Utopias in the dreamland of philanthropists may become practical possibilities."[22]

To help flesh out this notion of perfection a bit more, two important works (of many possible) can be briefly mentioned. American sociologist Robert Nisbet wrote a number of important works, many of which bear on this issue. One book in particular is well worth mentioning. His 1980 volume, *History of the Idea of Progress*, does a careful job of tracing this concept of progress. Several clear themes emerge from his incisive study. First, the idea of progress has been around for most of human history. Second, the idea of progress has been closely entwined with religious belief. Third, the idea of progress took a decidedly secular turn from the eighteenth century and beyond.[23]

In an equally ambitious and scholarly work, Australian philosopher John Passmore has traced the 300-year history of the concept of human perfectibility. His 1970 *The Perfectibility of Man*[24] is a lucid and

---

[21] Daniel Callahan, *Setting Limits: Medical Goals in an Aging Society* (Simon and Schuster, 1987) 60-61.

[22] John West, *Darwin Day in America* (ISI Books, 2007) 132.

[23] Robert Nisbet, *History of the Idea of Progress* (Basic Books, 1980).

[24] John Passmore, *The Perfectibility of Man* (Charles Scribner's Sons, 1970).

cogent discussion of the perennial attempt to not just better the human condition but to bring some form of utopia to earth. While Passmore describes a number of versions of perfectibility, from religious to secular, for our purposes, his later chapters on scientific progress, genetic and governmental perfectibility, social engineers like Marx, and other various personal and social utopians dovetail nicely with the insights of Nisbet. Both describe the yearning of the human heart to overcome obstacles, to better the human condition, and to solve every problem.[25]

While all this may seem a bit esoteric, or perhaps even off-topic, it does indeed figure into our discussion of government responses to corona. Some leaders, officials, bureaucrats and politicians have pushed the view that in order to fully protect humans, we must be willing to radically curtail social interaction and restrict various freedoms – until things are "safe."

The trade-offs discussed above were rather evident for these leaders: increased government control coupled with diminished individual freedoms must be the preferred option. What some have referred to as a police state regime was seen to the preferable option – much better than being too lax on a killer virus.

And we saw this played out quite clearly along political and ideological lines. For example, those cities and states that were the most restrictive, the harshest in lockdown measures, and the slowest to undo those restrictions, overwhelmingly tended to be run by those of the political left. That was largely true of Democrat mayors and governors in America, and Labor premiers in Australia.

These policies reflect two different types of views of humanity, the social order, and the public good. To use the thought of American economist Thomas Sowell, we have major differing visions at play here. Sowell has penned many dozens of first-rate books, but three volumes especially worth briefly mentioning are these: *A Conflict of*

---

[25] Along these lines, two other important works worth consulting are Thomas Molnar's *Utopia: The Perennial Heresy* (Sheed and Ward, 1967) and Michael Sandel's *The Case Against Perfection* (Harvard University Press, 2007).

Visions;[26] *The Vision of the Anointed;*[27] and *The Quest for Cosmic Justice.*[28]

Sowell argues that the left and right side or politics operate from fundamentally different premises. These premises really amount to differing worldviews, with differing ways of looking at the world, man, his predicament, and possible solutions. Thus the foundation, or vision, on which political ideas are built is hugely important.

The two main visions Sowell discusses are what he calls the constrained and the unconstrained visions. The constrained vision (the conservative worldview) acknowledges that there are limits. There are limits to human nature, limits to what governments can do, limits to what can be achieved in a society. The unconstrained vision (the radical or leftist worldview) tends to downplay limits. Mankind is seen as more or less perfectible; social and political utopia is to a large extent achievable; and evil is not endemic or inherent in the human condition, and therefore is able to be mostly eliminated.

The conservative vision tends to reflect the Judeo-Christian understanding that mankind is fallen, is limited, is prone to sin and self, and cannot produce heaven on earth, at least without the help of God. The left-liberal vision, by contrast, tends to see the human condition as innocent, malleable and perfectible, and tends to think that utopia on earth is achievable under the right social conditions.

Edmund Burke may best exemplify the former vision, and the American Revolution one of its main fruit. Rousseau may best exemplify the latter vision, with the French Revolution a key expression of it. Prudence and caution describe the first; radicalism and change the second. But these big picture themes have been discussed by others. What is of help is when Sowell provides specific examples of how these competing visions play themselves out in the social, political and economic arenas.

---

[26] Thomas Sowell, *A Conflict of Visions* (William Morrow, 1987).
[27] Thomas Sowell, *The Vision of the Anointed* (BasicBooks, 1995).
[28] Thomas Sowell, *The Quest for Cosmic Justice* (Simon & Schuster, 1999).

In *The Vision of the Anointed* Sowell puts it this way:

[T]he vision of the anointed is not simply a vision of the world and its functioning in a causal sense, but is also a vision of themselves and of their moral role in the world. It is a vision of differential rectitude. It is not a vision of the tragedy of the human condition: Problems exist because others are not as wise or as virtuous as the anointed.

The great ideological crusades of twentieth-century intellectuals have ranged across the most disparate fields... What all these highly disparate crusades have in common is their moral exaltation of the anointed above others, who are to have their very different views nullified and superseded by the views of the anointed, imposed via the power of government. Despite the great variety of issues in a series of crusading movements among the intelligentsia during the twentieth century, several key elements have been common to most of them:

- Assertions of a great danger to the whole society, a danger to which the masses of people are oblivious.

- An urgent need for action to avert impending catastrophe.

- A need for government to drastically curtail the dangerous behaviour of the many, in response to the prescient conclusions of the few.

- A disdainful dismissal of arguments to the contrary as either uninformed, irresponsible, or motivated by unworthy purposes.[29]

One can immediately see how the coronavirus responses fit in here. Indeed, we find similar things with the issue of climate change. Many on the left have taken this view: "We are all doomed, and the government must act NOW to solve all our problems." And if to save the climate the government must trample on our freedoms and punish dissenters, then so be it. Saving the planet trumps mere human liberties and freedoms. As if paying higher taxes to the government will somehow change the climate!

---

[29] Thomas Sowell, *The Vision of the Anointed* (BasicBooks, 1995) 5.

The same here with coronavirus: it appears that leftist politicians expect us to obey the state in all things; to not ask any hard questions; to be willing to surrender our freedoms for the good of 'society'; and above all, to simply follow orders. We certainly saw this played out massively throughout the crisis. How many people turned on their own neighbours, snitching on them, and reporting them to the authorities? The numbers were really quite frightening. Consider just one media report during the height of Australia's crisis:

> More than 600 calls a day are flooding into the state's crime reporting hotline as Victorians rush to dob in neighbours who flout COVID-19 social-distancing rules. Victoria Police has seen calls to the relatively new police assistance line spike by 50 per cent in recent weeks, with people increasingly phoning to report mass gatherings and isolation breaches.
>
> The onslaught of calls has led police to employ more civilian staff, as wait times blow out to more than 15 minutes. Calls to the hotline doubled to 1442 on March 30, a day after hundreds of beachgoers flocked to Point Addis on the Surf Coast. Of the 22,500 COVID-19 related calls made to the hotline in the last fortnight, 3781 were to report mass gatherings, 2117 for isolation breaches and 1770 for business breaches.
>
> On Tuesday, 4500 calls were made to the line. Of those, 2350 were related to COVID-19. In February the hotline recorded close to 61,000 calls, which rose to a record 69,000 in March. Police said the rise was directly related to an influx of coronavirus-related calls. During the first seven days in April, the hotline has received more than 22,000 calls, putting April on track to exceed more than 80,000 reports.[30]

One recalls the shocking scenarios found so often in the former Soviet Union and eastern Europe where neighbour turned on neigh-

---

[30] Erin Pearson, 'Police hotline swamped with COVID-19 calls as Victorians dob in neighbours' *The Age*, 2020. <https://www.theage.com.au/national/victoria/police-hotline-swamped-with-covid-19-calls-as-victorians-dob-in-neighbours-20200408-p54i5g.html>.

bour, and even children turned on their own parents. Those sorts of scenes were replayed before our very eyes over the past few months in the West.

V THE ILLUSION OF SAFETY

All of the above can be seen in how so many adhered to the illusion and delusion of complete safety – for individuals and for societies as a whole. Far too many leaders and citizens seemed to prefer unlimited lockdowns and restrictions on freedom until safety was guaranteed – as if that is ever possible, or desirable. How often did we hear both politicians and the masses calling out those who questioned the severe lockdown strategies as 'grandmother killers' and the like?

As one commentator put it, 'It's not the government's job to protect my health. It's the government's job to protect my rights. It's my job to protect my health. When you trade liberty for safety you end up losing both' – attributed to Professor Jamie Lynn (but I am still trying to track down the actual source). It follows on from the famous quote of Benjamin Franklin: 'Those who would give up essential Liberty, to purchase a little temporary Safety, deserve neither Liberty nor Safety.'[31]

American commentator Dennis Prager spoke often and eloquently about the corona crisis and reactionary state overreach. He did numerous broadcasts and penned numerous articles, warning about the direction America was heading in all this. On the issue of safety and state responses, his short but cogent remark was right on the money: '"Until It's Safe" Means Never.'[32]

We never will have a completely safe and foolproof world to live in. Such a thing does not and cannot exist. We live in the real world where risks are all around us. Yes, individuals can do all they want in their vain search for a completely safe life: they can never go out-

---

[31] Benjamin Franklin, 'Pennsylvania Assembly: Rely to the Governor – November 11, 1755', in Leonard W. Labaree (ed.), *The Papers of Benjamin Franklin, Volume 6* (Yale University Press, 1963) 242.

[32] Dennis Prager, 'Ep. 132 — "Until It's Safe" Means Never' *PragerU* 2020. <https://www.prageru.com/video/ep-132-until-its-safe-means-never/>.

doors; they try to be totally self-sufficient and can grow their own food; they can refuse all visitors and contact with the outside world; they can seek to eliminate all risks; and so on. In other words, they can move out into the middle of a desert or into a cave and see how that works for them. If a virus does not get them, a snakebite might.

But for the rest of us, as well as for governments, we need to think sensibly and critically about how much safety we want or can expect, and at what cost. Indeed, the wise words of Sowell are again worth mentioning here. His reference to leftists is applicable to all leaders and politicians:

> There are three questions that will destroy most of the arguments on the Left:
>
> - *Compared to what?*
> - *At what cost?*
> - *What hard evidence do you have?*
>
> There are very few ideas on the left that can pass all three of those kinds of things.[33]

Those first two questions were not asked enough during the coronavirus crisis. And too often it seems that the last question was dodged or evaded. Many leaders and people simply ran on fear and emotion, and ignored the facts and evidence. And very early on it was becoming quite clear that coronavirus was nowhere near as dangerous as first predicted. Indeed, the experts and their various models and forecasts proved to be wildly off. The very draconian shutting down of nations was based on what was often extremely faulty and panicky information.

Indeed, I recall a discussion I had online with an Australian academic when this first became a matter of concern. I suggested that this was not looking to be very bad, at least here in Australia. He strongly rejected my more sanguine views, and actually stated that it is quite

---

[33] Thomas Sowell, 'The Difference Between Liberal and Conservative' *YouTube*, 2010. <https://www.youtube.com/watch?v=5KHdhrNhh88>.

likely that Australia would experience a million deaths because of coronavirus. The actual numbers, as of the time of this writing (July 14) are 10,250 confirmed cases, 108 deaths, and a 98.63 per cent recovery rate.[34]

It is a very long way from 108 deaths to one million. But this fellow was absolutely convinced, as were so many others, that Armageddon was just around the corner. And to deal with this fear and panic, so many leaders were willing to entirely shut down whole nations, with all the negative repercussions that such moves would of course bring: recessions, massive unemployment, and record numbers of job losses and all that goes with it: depression, mental health problems, suicide, and so on. Indeed, I often told those who were critical of my calls to ease the lockdowns that all lives matter. I pointed out various inconvenient truths, including this very sad fact: during the American Great Depression some 40,000 Americans took their own lives – and that just in 1937-38. The truth is, fatalities by suicide are just as important and just as much to be avoided as fatalities due to a virus.[35]

Numerous reports about suicide brought on by the lockdowns have been reported. As just one of them has said:

> The costs of the government responses to the 2020 COVID-19 pandemic have been severe. New evidence suggests they could be even worse than we imagined. An ABC affiliate in California reports that doctors at John Muir Medical Center tell them they have seen more deaths by suicide than COVID-19 during the quarantine. 'The numbers are unprecedented,' said Dr. Michael deBoisblanc, referring to the spike in suicides. 'We've never seen numbers like this, in such a short period of time,' deBoisblanc added. 'I mean we've seen a year's worth of suicide attempts in the last four weeks.' Kacey Hansen, a trauma nurse who has spent 33 years at the hospital, said she has never witnessed self-inflicted attacks

---

34 <https://www.worldometers.info/coronavirus/country/australia/>.
35 Elizabeth MacBride, 'Suicide and the Economy' *The Atlantic*, 26 September 2013 <https://www.theatlantic.com/health/archive/2013/09/suicide-and-the-economy/279961/>

on such a scale. 'What I have seen recently, I have never seen before,' Hansen said. 'I have never seen so much intentional injury.'[36]

The Australian situation is similar. The Australian Medical Association for example has said that as a result of these draconian lockdown measures and the resultant negative impact on the economy there will be an additional 750 to 1,500 suicides per year: 'We are facing a situation where between an extra 750 and 1500 more suicides may occur annually, in addition to the 3000 plus lives that are lost to suicide already every year.'[37]

But so many refused to listen to us as we warned about the very bad outcomes of these excessive restrictions and lockdown measures. We were told we do not care about life, that we were putting profit ahead of people, and that we were heartless grandma killers. I heard all this far too often.

So the projections and the guesstimates and the gloom and doom prognostications turned out to be way off. But I have yet to hear one apology from anyone making or promoting these false figures and reckless ruminations. But of course it is not just our leaders and politicians who can be faulted here. A major crisis can easily drive the masses into panic, fear, and hysteria, and they far too readily will then renounce their freedoms and hand the state a blank cheque to do as it likes – so long as it somehow guarantees their safety. They are far too easily turned into willing sheep who will do their masters' every bidding.

This has also been a clear lesson of history. Simply consider our recent tyrants, be they Joseph Stalin or Adolf Hitler or Mao Tse-tung

---

[36] Jon Miltimore, 'A Year's Worth of Suicide Attempts in Four Weeks': The Unintended Consequences of COVID-19 Lockdowns' *Foundation for Economic Freedom*, 2020 <https://fee.org/articles/a-years-worth-of-suicide-attempts-in-four-weeks-the-unintended-consequences-of-covid-19-lockdowns/>.

[37] Dr Tony Bartone et al, 'Joint Statement: Covid-19 Impact Likely to Lead to Increased Rates of Suicide and Mental Illness' *Australian Medical Association*, 2020 <https://ama.com.au/media/joint-statement-covid-19-impact-likely-lead-increased-rates-suicide-and-mental-illness>.

or Kim Jong-un: they have maintained total control over the masses by keeping them in a steady state of fear and uncertainty. Let me draw upon several articles here. One piece from a law professor says this:

> Thomas Jefferson is reported to have said: "When government fears the people, there is liberty. When the people fear the government, there is tyranny." I have investigated and prosecuted dictators and their henchmen for most of my professional life. I have studied their lives, personalities, their rise to power and how they governed once achieving that power. The one common theme in their theories of governance is fear. It is easier to govern and dictate to citizens through fear.

> As Hannah Arendt wrote in her book, The Origins of Totalitarianism: 'A fundamental difference between modern dictatorships and all other tyrannies of the past is that terror is no longer used as a means to exterminate and frighten opponents, but as an instrument to rule masses of people who are perfectly obedient.' The infamous dictators of the twentieth century, such as Stalin, Hitler, and Mao Tse-tung among others, understood this all too well. Their theory was that a frightened populace will allow their government to take drastic measures to protect them without protest, usually from perceived evil that threatens their society or country externally.[38]

That does sound familiar, doesn't it? Another article on political philosophy says this in part:

> Ruling classes for thousands of years have understood the power of intentionally invoking fear in their subjects as a means of social control. . . . The artificial construction and maintenance of fear in a population by a ruling class has remained pervasive from the time of Ancient Egypt up until the modern day. Oppressive governments often maintain their grip on a nation by continually invoking fear, and then pro-

---

[38] David Crane, 'Fear – A Dictator's Tool' *Jurist*, 29 January 2019 <www.jurist.org/commentary/2019/01/fear-a-dictators-tool/>.

ceeding to claim that only they, the ruling powers, have the means and ability to protect the population from such a threat: "The whole aim of practical politics", wrote HL Mencken, 'is to keep the populace alarmed (and hence clamorous to be led to safety) by menacing it with an endless series of hobgoblins, most of them imaginary.'[39]

Another authority can be appealed to here. The French political writer and historian Alexis de Tocqueville released his important two-volume work *Democracy in America* in 1835 and 1840. In a chapter on "Types of Despotism" he famously said this:

After having thus taken each individual one by one into its powerful hands, and having molded him as it pleases, the sovereign power extends its arms over the entire society; it covers the surface of society with a network of small, complicated, minute, and uniform rules, which the most original minds and the most vigorous souls cannot break through to go beyond the crowd; it does not break wills, but it softens them, bends them and directs them; it rarely forces action, but it constantly opposes your acting; it does not destroy, it prevents birth; it does not tyrannize, it hinders, it represses, it enervates, it extinguishes, it stupefies, and finally it reduces each nation to being nothing more than a flock of timid and industrious animals, of which the government is the shepherd.[40]

Indeed, the State is my shepherd, I shall not want... Also, a former judge from the UK has also warned about the dangers of a slide into a police state because of paranoia, fearmongering and panic. As one important interview said in part:

The former Supreme Court Justice Jonathan Sumption, QC, has denounced the police response to the coronavirus, saying the country is suffering 'collective hysteria'. Here is part of

---

[39] 'Fear and Social Control' *Academy of Ideas*, 29 November 2015 <academyofideas.com/2015/11/fear-and-social-control/>.

[40] Alexis de Tocqueville, *Democracy in America*, as accessed here: <https://www.academia.edu/10431803/Tocqueville_Democracy_in_America_1835_>.

an interview he was involved in from late March:

BBC interviewer Jonny Dymond 'A hysterical slide into a police state. A shameful police force intruding with scant regard to common sense or tradition. An irrational overreaction driven by fear.' These are not the accusations of wild-eyed campaigners, they come from the lips of one of our most eminent jurists Lord Sumption, former Justice of the Supreme Court. I spoke to him just before we came on air.

Lord Sumption The real problem is that when human societies lose their freedom, it's not usually because tyrants have taken it away. It's usually because people willingly surrender their freedom in return for protection against some external threat. And the threat is usually a real threat but usually exaggerated. That's what I fear we are seeing now. The pressure on politicians has come from the public. They want action. They don't pause to ask whether the action will work. They don't ask themselves whether the cost will be worth paying. They want action anyway. And anyone who has studied history will recognise here the classic symptoms of collective hysteria. Hysteria is infectious. We are working ourselves up into a lather in which we exaggerate the threat and stop asking ourselves whether the cure may be worse than the disease.

Dymond At a time like this, as you acknowledge, citizens do look to the state for protection, for assistance, we shouldn't be surprised then if the state takes on new powers if it responds. That is what it has been asked to do, almost demanded of it.

Sumption Yes that is absolutely true. We should not be surprised. But we have to recognise that this is how societies become despotisms. And we also have to recognise this is a process which leads naturally to exaggeration. The symptoms of coronavirus are clearly serious for those with other significant medical conditions, especially if they're old. There are exceptional cases in which young people have been struck down, which have had a lot of publicity, but the numbers are pretty small. The Italian evidence, for instance, suggests that only in 12 per cent of deaths is it possible to say coronavirus was the main cause of death. So yes this is serious and yes it's understandable that people cry out to the government. But the real question is: is this serious enough to warrant putting most of our population into house imprisonment, wrecking our economy for an indefinite period, destroying businesses that honest and hardworking people have taken years to build up, saddling future generations with debt, depression, stress, heart attacks, suicides and unbelievable distress inflicted on millions of people who are not especially vulnerable and will suffer only mild symptoms or none at all, like the Health Secretary and the Prime Minister.[41]

And progressive politicians have even sought to enact rights against fear. As Dinesh D'Souza reminds us in his new book on socialism, Franklin Delano Roosevelt called for this very thing – "freedom from fear" – in his famous January 1944 speech: 'Yes, freedom from fear. We have a right not to be afraid. And who can deliver that right? For FDR, there was only one answer to this question: the federal government. So in FDR's vision, the government, previously viewed by the founders as inimical to rights, now becomes the friend and guarantor of rights.'[42]

Finally, Georgetown University professor Joshua Mitchell nicely ties all this together. He argues that our search for complete safety, the eradication of fear, and perfectibility in a corona world is really a secular Great Awakening. It is a counterfeit – and political – redemption story:

> Identity politics is an American Awakening without God and without forgiveness. Like Christianity, it seeks to overcome the curse of death. Like Christianity, it seeks to overcome sin. Like Christianity, it recognizes that the problem of sin is deeper than the problem of death, and has precedence over it.

---

[41] 'Former Supreme Court Justice: "This is what a police state is like"' *The Spectator*, 30 March 2020 <https://www.spectator.co.uk/article/former-supreme-court-justice-this-is-what-a-police-state-is-like->.

[42] Dinesh D'Souza, *United States of Socialism* (All Points Books, 2020) 89.

Identity politics does not overcome death, as Christianity does, through faith in Christ, so that man may again have eternal life as he did in the Garden of Eden. Identity politics overcomes death by attempting to build an Edenic world protected from death. Augustine wrote that all reasonable beings understandably shrink from death. But that is not what is happening here. Citizens captivated by identity politics quarantine so that they may remain isolated from death until a vaccine arrives that will inoculate them from death. In the interim, they are content to be served by the least among us, service industry workers who cannot quarantine. This is not medical science doing triage in a world where death is always near; it is a religious longing to be saved from death, no matter the collateral damage done to the livelihoods of millions along the way.[43]

VI RELIGIOUS LIBERTY AND SOME CONCLUDING THEOLOGICAL REFLECTIONS

The numerous clampdowns on individual freedoms, including religious liberties, during the coronavirus crisis, have again raised questions about the role of the state, the place of religion, and the nature of individual liberty. Church closures were just one aspect of all this. A number of important questions arise here:

- How much can individual and/or organisational liberties be curtailed in the interests of public health and safety?

- Just what is an essential service? Are shopping malls? Abortion providers? Gun shops? Churches? Barbers?

- Are pastors being wise to defy these state orders? Are they putting their people at risk?

- Can reasonable alternate provision of such services take place? Does a virtual church service suffice – at least for a while?

- What happens when a right to freedom of worship clashes with

---

[43] Joshua Mitchell, 'A Godless Great Awakening' *First Things*, 2 July 2020 <https://www.firstthings.com/web-exclusives/2020/07/a-godless-great-awakening>.

other rights, such as the right to be safe, and protected from infectious diseases?

- How far can states go in shutting down economies and curtailing basic freedoms in the name of keeping the public safe?

Indeed, many critics rightly asked why crowds could go to hardware stores or Kmarts or, more recently, protest marches, but could not go to church services. They also asked why things like abortion clinics were still open for business while church services were deemed to be non-essential activities.

But religious freedoms are not an absolute, and there will be trade-offs with other community concerns. Sometimes religious beliefs and practices do conflict with the common good. I have in mind, for example, things like the tragic case reported some years ago of a Sydney woman and her unborn baby who died because she refused a blood transfusion.[44]

The woman was a Jehovah's Witness. This heterodox group, which began in the US during the mid-nineteenth century, denies many orthodox biblical teachings, such as the Trinity and the deity of Christ. But it also believes, because of faulty hermeneutics, that it is sinful to receive a blood transfusion. It all comes from a faulty understanding of passages such as Leviticus 17:10-14.[45]

We have had a number of cases of Jehovah's Witnesses dying over the years because of this erroneous belief about blood transfusions. If a patient chooses to refuse life-saving medical treatment, that is up to them. But when a second party – who often cannot give his or her consent – also faces death as a result, that is quite a different matter.

---

[44] Amy Corderoy, 'Pregnant Jehovah's Witness' decision to refuse treatment "harrowing" for hospital staff after mother and baby die' *Sydney Morning Herald*, 6 April 2015 <https://www.smh.com.au/national/nsw/pregnant-jehovahs-witness-decision-to-refuse-treatment-harrowing-for-hospital-staff-after-mother-and-baby-die-20150406-1mf570.html>.

[45] Bill Muehlenberg, 'Hermeneutics and Blood Transfusions' *CultureWatch*, 9 April 2015. <https://billmuehlenberg.com/2015/04/09/hermeneutics-and-blood-transfusions/>.

Then the state may need to intervene, and some religious beliefs may need to be overridden.

So there can often be genuine conflicts that will exist between church and state regarding such matters. Getting back to coronavirus: how far does religious freedom extend, especially during a time of a pandemic? Can the modern state simply trample on religious freedoms in the interests of public safety? American Columnist Matt Walsh has written specifically about the clampdown on churches. He says this at the close of his piece:

> I am trying to imagine a definition of "religious liberty" that includes the government closing churches indefinitely on the basis that they are not essential enough to remain open. I cannot think of one that would be at all cogent or meaningful. Indeed, it has become obvious (if it wasn't already) that our mainstream notions of "liberty" and "rights" and "freedom" are largely nonsensical, as evidenced by the people who normally assert these concepts as absolutes but now insist that the government has the unquestioned power to lock us in our homes and shut our businesses for as long as it pleases.
>
> Most of us, it turns out, do not have a governing philosophy or set of principles. We are slaves to our emotions. So, if the government scares us enough, we will rip the "Give me liberty or give me death" and "Don't tread on me" bumper stickers off of our cars and stuff them in the closet while we cower along side it. Then when the threat has passed – or at least we are told that it has passed – we will proudly affix the bumper stickers back on our bumpers again, and sing bravely about our love of freedom.[46]

A final point about church closures has to do with the glaring double standards that so many governments were involved in. Most the mass protests (and rioting) that occurred around the West after the

---

[46] Matt Walsh, 'WALSH: Pastors Are Being Arrested for Holding Worship Services. This Is Not "Health and Safety." This Is Tyranny' *The Daily Wire*, 2020. <www.daily-wire.com/news/walsh-pastors-are-being-arrested-for-holding-worship-services-this-is-not-health-and-safety-this-is-tyranny>.

death of George Floyd in Minneapolis on May 25 were effectively given the green light by far too many states, while churches were still being held in strict lockdown. Many pointed out the blatant duplicity on display here. For example, Perth Pastor Margaret Court sent a letter to *The West Australian* about this matter, which said this in part:

> If the Government of Western Australia allows thousands to rally on Saturday, why do churches have to obey all the rules of restricted numbers and social distancing (as we do) on Sunday? Victory Life Centre is multi-racial church with a common belief in the words of Jesus. Throughout COVID19 we have fed thousands of people in need (over 50 tonnes of food per week) and comforted them in these tough times. Churches across this great city have risen to the challenge to help in this time of need and yet the restrictions still stand for them. This is a double standard, I ask you to reconsider this.[47]

One more example: in New York some religious groups are suing the government over this. As one report puts it:

> New York's Governor Andrew Cuomo, his Attorney General Letitia James, and New York City Mayor Bill de Blasio are being sued by two Catholic priests from upstate New York and a trio of Orthodox Jewish congregants from Brooklyn for violation of civil rights by prejudicial orders and selective enforcement. The federal lawsuit, filed June 10, 2020, in United States District Court for the Northern District of New York, charges the governor, attorney general, and mayor with violating the plaintiffs' rights to free exercise of religion, freedom of speech, assembly and expressive association, and due process, under the First and Fourteenth Amendments to the U.S. Constitution. Governor Cuomo is also accused of acting against New York state law and the New York State Constitution. Senior Judge Gary L. Sharpe has ordered the defendants

---

[47] Rourke Walsh, 'Tennis legend Margaret Court slams "double standard" for Black Lives Matter rally amid restrictions for churches' *The West Australian*, 31 March 2020 <https://thewest.com.au/news/wa/tennis-legend-margaret-court-slams-double-standard-for-black-lives-matter-rally-amid-restrictions-for-churches-ng-b881575478z>.

to file a response by noon (Eastern) on June 15, 2020.

Thomas More Society Special Counsel Christopher Ferrara explained the key points of the lawsuit: 'These orders, both the emergency stay-home and reopening plan declarations, clearly discriminate against houses of worship. They are illegally content based, elaborate, arbitrary and pseudo-scientific. The governor and his agents, along with New York City's mayor have employed favoritism and political platforms against people of faith.'[48]

And a U.S. District Court has just agreed with this:

Catholic League president Bill Donohue comments on a judicial decision just handed down that is of utmost importance to people of faith: Protesters can take to the streets, some violently, and that is okay by Mayor Bill de Blasio and Gov. Andrew Cuomo—the mob does not have to abide by social distancing rules—but religious New Yorkers cannot congregate in their houses of worship lest they imperil the public health.

Well, the jig is up. U.S. District Court Judge Gary Sharpe issued a preliminary injunction on June 26 saying that de Blasio and Cuomo (as well as Attorney General Letitia James) exceeded their authority by putting restrictions on people of faith while simultaneously condoning the protests.[49]

In sum, these issues can be rather complex, and a number of pro and con arguments can be made here. My take on this should be clear by now: we should not act foolishly and presumptuously as Christians. While we are not to succumb to paralysing fear, neither are we to be reckless and stupid in ignoring sound health and safety advice and practice. But standing up for religious freedom when it seems clear

---

[48] 'Priests sue NY governor, NYC mayor for oppressing churches in COVID reopening' *LifeSiteNews*, 12 June 2020 <https://www.lifesitenews.com/news/new-york-governor-nyc-mayor-sued-for-pseudo-scientific-coronavirus-response>.

[49] Bill Donohue, 'De Blasio and Cuomo Get Creamed in Court' *Catholic League*, 26 June 2020. <https://www.catholicleague.org/de-blasio-and-cuomo-get-creamed-in-court/>.

that it is being violated is also an important obligation not just of religious persons, but of all concerned about the fair and just administration and enforcement of law.

More can be said on these issues, however. Back in 2005 Mathew Staver, the president and general counsel for Liberty Counsel, penned a volume on religious freedom in America entitled *Eternal Vigilance*. What he said in the preface to his book is relevant here. He tells us that before he went into law school he was a pastor, and during that time he learned this: 'We lose our religious liberties for three primary reasons: (1) ignorance of the law, (2) hostility toward religion, and (3) apathy. . . . In this battle over religious liberty, I frequently encounter a great deal of apathy among Christians and people of faith. Most people would rather run than fight and lose their rights rather than struggle for them.'[50]

This has been the case with so many believers both in America and Australia during the coronavirus crisis. Far too many simply surrendered their religious freedoms without a fight – indeed, without a whimper. Many of us were quite alarmed by that reaction – or lack of reaction. A meme making the rounds on the social media during this time was certainly as telling as it was humorous. In the first panel one Christian says to another, "When persecution comes, we will remain faithful to gather for worship." In the second panel the man replies, "Like you did with COVID-19?"

Many did speak out on this, and some churches did defy the guidelines. And many questioned how believers could simply run with virtual church services for indefinite periods of time. While this essay is not primarily about Christianity, let me offer a few quotes from just one piece on this matter. Rev Dr Joe Boot said this about how evangelical Christians should consider such restrictions:

> I should add, whilst the Bible has important things to say about quarantining the seriously sick, I have yet to find the scriptural text where Christ or his apostles hid from the dis-

---

[50] Mathew Staver, *Eternal Vigilance* (Broadman & Holman, 2005) xvl.

eased and destitute, the lonely, depressed or dying in the interest of loving and saving them. If ever Christians should be wearied by empty evangelical platitudes to justify our inaction, it's now....

Civil authorities can lock down a business, but they cannot switch off the essence of human nature. We are cultural beings made specifically to work (Gen. 1:28; 2:15) and social beings made for fellowship; most especially fellowship with the living God (Gen 2:18, 21-23; Ex. 29:45; Jn. 1:3, 5-7; Jn. 14:23; Rev. 21:3-4). To deny human beings these things, even amidst the risk of infection or sickness, is to deny part of the essence of their humanity and fundamentally undermine their life and wellbeing. Work and corporate worship are both pre-political; they are part of the normative structure of human life and existence. Human governments do not bestow on people a right to worship and work, they are merely called to recognise and protect that right. It is God himself who commands human beings to rule and subdue, to work and serve (and observe a sabbath rest).[51]

Catholic philosopher Edward Feser looks at the coronavirus lockdowns from a wider perspective, dealing with some matters I have already briefly touched on. He says that early on he did support the lockdown, but as of the time of writing, (May 22) he no longer could morally support it. He examined a number of key areas, but let me just feature one of his concerns: "The natural right to earn a living." He says this:

The basic natural law grounds for this judgment are straightforward. Breadwinners have a natural right to labor in order to provide for themselves and their families. Hence, governing authorities may not prevent them from doing so unless strictly necessary for preserving the common good. Now, a strong case could be made at the beginning of the lockdown that preventing such labor was indeed strictly necessary. But

---

[51] Joe Boot, 'The Way is Shut: Evangelical Silence and the Illusion of Virtual Church' *Christian Concern*, 28 May 2020 <https://christianconcern.com/comment/the-way-is-shut-evangelical-silence-and-the-illusion-of-virtual-church/>.

such a case cannot be made now. Hence, while a total lockdown was justifiable at the beginning, it is no longer justifiable, and governing authorities have a strict duty in justice to relax it. The details of how this might be done in this or that locality are debatable, but the general principle is clear.

One reason this is not more widely recognized is because of the seriously misleading way in which the issue is routinely framed, viz. as a matter of balancing "the economy" against "saving lives." First of all, what is in jeopardy is not some abstraction called "the economy." What is in jeopardy is the basic natural human right to earn a living. To talk about how the lockdown affects "the economy" tends to disguise the true moral situation, because it makes it sound as if public authorities are merely tinkering with the operation of some impersonal mechanism.

What they are actually doing is preventing millions of human beings from exercising their fundamental right to support themselves and their families. And the vast majority of them are people who live paycheck to paycheck and cannot afford to have their life savings depleted. Chatter about the effects of the lockdown on "the economy" can give the false impression that government officials may decide what to do about the situation at their leisure. Keeping in mind that what we are really talking about is interference with a basic human right reminds us of the situation's true urgency.[52]

VII JUST REVOLUTION?

One final consideration can be raised here – one as much theological as political. The question arises – certainly for the Christian thinker – as to whether a state can become so tyrannical and so obsessed with power and control that the citizen has a right and a duty to rebel.

Obviously it is a big leap from something like resistance to church

---

[52] Edward Feser, 'The lockdown is no longer morally justifiable' *Edward Feser Blog-site*, 22 May 2020 <https://edwardfeser.blogspot.com/2020/05/the-lockdown-is-no-longer-morally.html>.

closure laws and other lockdown measures – such as opening up your barber shop or beauty salon to earn some income to feed one's family (as happened in the US) – to full blown revolution. So I am not equating the two. But the biblical and/or theological principles found in the one can also be found in the other.

And of course it will be apparent that my biases are on display here, since I am an American, and my country of origin was founded by rebellion against England – a revolution against powers perceived to be tyrannical. So perhaps I have such views in my blood!

Be that as it may, it is quite clear obviously that the American Founding Fathers had a strong view on the need to resist tyranny. A few representative and well-known quotes will suffice here:

> 'Resistance to tyranny becomes the Christian and social duty of each individual. ... Continue steadfast and, with a proper sense of your dependence on God, nobly defend those rights which heaven gave, and no man ought to take from us.' – John Hancock (1st Signer of the Declaration of Independence)[53]

> 'When the government violates the people's rights, insurrection is, for the people and for each portion of the people, the most sacred of the rights and the most indispensable of duties' – Marquis de Lafayette (French-born American military commander during Revolutionary War)[54]

> 'The Revolution was effected before the War commenced. The Revolution was in the minds and hearts of the people; a change in their religious sentiments of their duties and obligations ... This radical change in the principles, opinions, sentiments, and affections of the people, was the real American Revolution.' – John Adams (Second US President)[55]

---

[53] Cited in Maryann Brickett, *Yes We Are A Christian Nation* (Xulon Press, 2011) 43-44.

[54] Marquis de Lafayette, 'To Constitutional Assembly, February 20, 1790', in George Seldes (ed), *The Great Thoughts* (Ballantine Books, 1996) 57.

[55] John Adams, 'Letter to H. Niles, February 13, 1818', in Charles Francis Adams (ed), *John Adams, Second President of the United States, With A Life Of The Author – Volume 10* (Little, Brown and Co, 1856) 282.

'The spirit of resistance to government is so valuable on certain occasions, that I wish it to be always kept alive. It will often be exercised when wrong, but better so than not to be exercised at all. I like a little rebellion now and then.' – Thomas Jefferson (from a letter to Abigail Adams, February 27, 1787)[56]

'Give me liberty or give me death.' – Patrick Henry (from a speech given at Saint John's Church in Richmond, Virginia on March 23, 1775)[57]

'Rebellion to Tyrants is obedience to God.' – Benjamin Franklin[58]

But how have Christian thinkers throughout the centuries thought about such matters? Since I am a Protestant, I will here confine my remarks to what some key Protestants have taught on this over the past 500 years. Let me start with a brief historical overview. The Reformers of course spoke to this issue in various places. For example, Martin Luther believed that we must respect the office of the magistrate. Because civil government is established by God, people must not resist it. However, he also said that obedience to the state is not unconditional.

He said for example, 'There are lazy and useless preachers who do not denounce the evils of princes and lords…. Some even fear for their skins and worry that they will lose body and goods for it. They do not stand up and be true to Christ!' Appealing to Acts 5:29 he taught that we must obey God rather than man when tyrannous rulers violate God's laws. But his insistence that we resist such magistrates was to

---

[56] Thomas Jefferson, 'Letter to James Madison, January 30, 1787', cited in Dustin Gish and Daniel Klinghard, *Thomas Jefferson and the Science of Republican Government* (Cambridge University Press, 2017) 283.

[57] Patrick Henry, *Give Me Liberty Or Give Me Death* (Independently Published, 2020) 43. This was a speech he made to the Virginia Convention. It was given on 23 March 1775, at St John's Church in Richmond, Virginia.

[58] Cited in Brahm French, *Why Christians Must Be Right* (WestBow Press, 2012) 39. Benjamin Franklin coined this phrase in 1776. He was comparing the Exodus of the Hebrews from Egypt to the overthrowing of the English rule in the thirteen colonies that eventually formed the United States of America.

be understood as more of a passive resistance or civil disobedience as opposed to active revolt.

John Calvin, in his *Institutes of the Christian Religion* said that private revolution was not allowable but proper representatives of the people could and should resist the tyranny of kings. Appealing to Daniel's refusal to obey the king's decree (Dan 6:22), Calvin said this: 'We are subject to the men who rule over us, but subject only in the Lord. If they command anything against Him let us not pay the least regard to it.'

The book *Lex, Rex* (1644) by Scottish Presbyterian Samuel Rutherford is of course perhaps the most important and most detailed discussion of all this. The title, simply meaning 'The Law, the King' refers to the biblical truth that the law is king, and the king is subject to the law, which is under the law of God.[59]

Very simply stated, Rutherford argued that there are limits to monarchies, since everyone, from kings to the common man, are subject to the rule of law – God's law. When a king or magistrate violates God's law, he loses his authority, and people may then have the right to overthrow this ruler. Tyrannical governments are immoral and can and must be opposed. Indeed, tyrannic government is satanic government, and the believer must resist it. To oppose tyranny is to honour God. The office of the magistrate demands our respect, but we need not blindly respect the ruler in that office.

His important book of course deals with far more than the place of revolution against unjust authorities. It is a comprehensive discussion of key issues such as the rule of law, the case against royal absolutism, the importance of constitutionalism and limited government, and the nature of political theory based on biblical law and natural law. The book was certainly a volatile volume, and was later burned in Edinburgh. But it was hugely influential, not only in refuting the then widely-accepted notion of the divine right of kings, but paving the way for resistance to government tyranny, most notably as found in the American Revolution.

---

[59] Samuel Rutherford, *Lex Rex, Or the Law and the Prince* (Hess Publications, 1999).

Let me here offer a few commentaries on these themes from some key contemporary Christian thinkers. One such figure is well known, at least in evangelical circles. The noted Christian apologist Francis Schaeffer is worth looking at more closely here. He spent the last four chapters of his important 1981 volume, *A Christian Manifesto* looking at this issue in some detail. He sided with Rutherford and believed that just revolution is the duty of the Christian. He argued that we are getting very close in the West today to seeing the need for such revolt to be carried out.

He appealed to historical and political grounds, as well as to biblical principles: "Simply put, the Declaration of Independence states that the people, if they find that their basic rights are being systematically attacked by the state, have a duty to try to change that government, and if they cannot do so, to abolish it."[60] To say we cannot resist an unjust and tyrannical state means that we are elevating the state above God and his law: 'If there is no final place for civil disobedience, then the government has been made autonomous, and as such, it has been put in the place of the Living God.'[61]

And again: "It is time we consciously realise that when any office commands what is contrary to God's Law it abrogates its authority. And our loyalty to the God who gave this law then requires that we make the appropriate response in that situation to such a tyrannical usurping of power."[62]

And the use of force is morally licit in the face of tyrannical regimes:

> There does come a time when force, even physical force, is appropriate. The Christian is not to take the law into his own hands and become a law unto himself. But when all avenues to flight and protest have closed, force in the defensive posture is appropriate. This was the situation of the American Revolution. The colonists used force in

---

[60] Francis Schaeffer, *A Christian Manifesto* (Crossway Books, 1981) 128.
[61] Ibid 130.
[62] Ibid 131-132.

defending themselves. Great Britain, because of its policy toward the colonies, was seen as a foreign power invading America. The colonists defended their homeland. As such, the American Revolution was a conservative counter-revolution. The colonists saw the British as the revolutionaries trying to overthrow the legitimate colonial governments.[63]

Such rebellion against authority was also appropriate in Hitler's Germany: 'A true Christian in Hitler's Germany and in the occupied countries should have defied the false and counterfeit state and hidden his Jewish neighbors from German SS troops. The government had abrogated its authority, and it had no right to make any demands.'[64]

But Schaeffer also said, 'When discussing force it is important to keep an axiom in mind: always before protest or force is used, we must work for reconstruction. In other words, we should attempt to correct and rebuild society before we advocate tearing it down or disrupting it.'[65] He again appeals to Rutherford here:

> Rutherford offered suggestions concerning illegitimate acts of the state. A ruler, he wrote, should not be deposed merely because he commits a single breach of the compact he has with the people. Only when the magistrate acts in such a way that the governing structure of the country is being destroyed – that is, when he is attacking the fundamental structure of society – is he to be relieved of his power and authority. That is exactly what we are facing today. The whole structure of our society is being attacked and destroyed. It is being given an entirely opposite base which gives exactly opposite results. The reversal is much more total and destructive than that which Rutherford or any of the Reformers faced in their day.[66]

---

[63] Ibid 117.
[64] Ibid 117-118.
[65] Ibid 106.
[66] Ibid 101-102.

Another Christian commentator – who does have a legal background – is worth drawing upon here. Back in 1982 the American constitutional attorney and religious freedom specialist John Whitehead wrote an important volume called *The Second American Revolution*. After examining how America is being undermined and destroyed by secularism, immorality, and anti-Christian government, he asks how Christians should respond to this.

He writes, 'The battle for Christian existence may be upon us. As the state becomes increasingly pagan, it will continue to exert and expand its claims to total jurisdiction and power over all areas, including the church. . . . Strong biblical grounds serve for a foundation for Christian resistance to state paganism.'[67]

Whitehead also appeals to Rutherford. 'Citizens have a moral obligation to resist unjust and tyrannical government. Unfortunately, this has long been overlooked in churches, as a whole. While we must always be subject to the office of the magistrate, we are not to be subject to the man in that office, if his commands are contrary to the Bible.'[68] He continues:

> Rutherford was not an anarchist. In Lex, Rex he does not propose armed revolution as a solution. Instead, he sets forth three levels of resistance in which a private person may engage. First, he must defend himself by protest (in contemporary society this would usually be by legal action). Second, he must flee if at all possible; and, third, he may use force, if absolutely necessary, to defend himself.... Christian resistance does not mean that Christians should take to the streets and mount an armed revolution.[69]

However, there 'does come a time when force, even physical force, is appropriate. When all avenues to flight and protest have closed,

---

[67] John Whitehead, *The Second American Revolution* (Crossway, 1985) 149-150.
[68] Ibid 154.
[69] Ibid 155-156.

force in the defensive posture is appropriate. This was the situation of the American Revolution.'[70]

This article is not primarily about resisting the state from a theological point of view. But the concerns raised here about statism and the restriction of fundamental freedoms does raise the matter, and since many of the readers here will come from the Christian tradition, a brief look at these matters has been worth exploring.[71]

VIII CONCLUSION

As stated at the outset, this essay was intended to be a rather broadbrush look at the many key issues involved in the coronavirus crisis and how various states have responded to it. My aim was to demonstrate that this international crisis certainly highlighted a number of important considerations, ranging from the political, legal and social to the ethical, philosophical and theological.

My main concern has been to suggest that far too often government overreach and alarming statist expansionism was the normal response, resulting in diminished liberties and restrictions on freedoms. In the light of all this, one can rightly ask: If a virus like this could result in so much growth in Big Brother statism and alarming clampdowns on individual freedoms, what will an even greater and more fearsome crisis bring about?

---

[70] Ibid 158. One other book can be mentioned here: the 1984 volume by Lynn Buzzard and Paula Campbell, *Holy Disobedience: When Christians Must Resist the State* (Servant Books, 1984). This helpful volume carefully looks at the issue of civil disobedience more so than just revolution. But it contains many helpful insights and observations, examining biblical, historical and political matters.

[71] For more on these matters, see my two-part article: Bill Muehlenberg, 'Is Revolution Ever Justified?' *CultureWatch*, 11 July2013 <https://billmuehlenberg.com/2013/07/11/is-revolution-ever-justified-part-one/>, <https://billmuehlenberg.com/2013/07/11/is-revolution-ever-justified-part-two/>.

11

The Age of Covid-19: Protecting Rights Matters

MONIKA NAGEL*

ABSTRACT

Covid-19 ('C-19') has created uncertainty around the world; human rights ('HRs') as stated in the Universal Declaration of Human Rights ('UDHR'), regulations and morals got dismantled. Established HRs have been curbed in the interest of saving lives. Activities people were accustomed to, and took for granted, have been greatly restricted by worldwide lockdowns and social distancing regulations. What motivated the writing of this chapter is our global economic, social and political environment at the 21st century, and today's role of HRs. Why has globalisation, a process of integration and interaction among individuals, companies, and governments, worked extremely well for economic and political gains since the early 1980s, yet failed in its capacity for responding to a global health crisis? Furthermore, this chapter brings to light our decline of values, the rising propaganda for identity and people's strong opinions about their rights, and why the thinking of today's societies and global and social changes must be considered for protecting FRs. Previous cartas were created out of circumstances at the time. And that is not less true for protecting FRs in the age of C-19. Subsequently, this paper moves away from using HRs as stipulated in the UDHR as the key construct for protecting FRs. FRs are defined here as human intrinsic needs essential for a person's development ranging from basic needs to self-ac-

---

* Cert Ed, B Psych, PhD (Org Psych). Former educator; Advocate for Values; Public Speaker; Author of book *Fatal Cocktails*.

tualization. Not surprisingly, some of these needs overlap with the definition of rights contained in the UDHR. This chapter revisits human rights in changing societies to ensure that they continue to protect all people equally in these unprecedented, unexpected, and vulnerable times. The argument is presented that it is difficult to protect FRs, both in the age of Covid-19 and in the future, when the rights defined by the UDHR can lead to the pursuit of personal benefits which are not in the public interest. Furthermore, it brings to light the importance of responsibility and respect when leaders make tough decisions and people have to feel bounded to new norms.

I INTRODUCTION

Protecting fundamental rights ('FRs') in the age of COVID-19 ('C-19') is complex: to save lives, rights as stated in the *Universal Declaration of Human Rights* ('UDHR') have been curbed; social responsibility is declining; and identity activism is on the rise. With the outbreak of this vicious and deadly virus in China, restrictions have affected the rights people had previously taken for granted. Their strong volition to freely do what they want has been shattered by strict regulations.[1] These have also impeded people's innate needs. Above all, the rights of individuals to be warned about health risks was compromised by the sparsity and vagueness of information about C-19.

It is a challenge to find a way to protect FRs when rights that have been the pillars of our civilisation – fostered especially in Westernised but also other countries, and manifested in rules and laws for millennia – were overruled to save lives. Moreover, individuals and minority groups do not necessarily respect these restrictions any longer but insist on what they believe it is their right to have. These ways of thinking, these attitudes and behaviours, put at risk the well-being and lives of others around the world.

The age of C-19 is the latest and most horrendous example of what

---

[1] 'Novel Coronavirus – China', *WHO* (Web Page, 12 January 2020) <https://www.who.int/csr/don/12-January-2020-novel-coronavirus-china/en>.

happens when a lack of responsibility prevails in society. Humanity is in crisis; societies must acknowledge that rights cannot protect humanity without responsibility.

At the beginning of 2020, radical changes to normal daily living were imposed because of the fast spread of a new, deeply infectious and deadly virus.[2] Globalisation and international travel were ideal conditions for C-19 to spread quickly. Strict sanctions on people's daily lives created uncertainty, and people were tested by the unexpected need to manage life under unfamiliar conditions. Adding even more tension to these unprecedented circumstances were the many unknowns concerning the virus outbreak.[3] With C-19 spreading so viciously, people were asked to avoid social contact with others in order to reduce transmission.[4] Regulations to this effect were announced, but the new, life-saving restrictions interfered with human rights ('HRs').

The first section of this chapter discusses the virus, how the outbreak was handled and the impact of C-19 on the world. The main section brings to light the effect C-19 has had on people's lives and their rights to fulfil their innate needs and to be warned about health hazards. The chapter uses Maslow's theory of human motivation to argue for the significant role of FRs in the age of C-19. The term people's rights is commonly associated with HRs, as defined in the UDHR; however, this paper makes a distinction between the HRs stipulated in the UDHR and FRs, which are defined here as human needs essential for one's development, ranging from basic physiological needs

---

[2] Catherine Cadell, 'Global coronavirus cases top 1 million: Johns Hopkins tally', *The Sydney Morning Herald* (Web Page, 3 April 2020) <https://www.smh.com.au/world/asia/global-coronavirus-cases-top-1-million-johns-hopkins-tally-20200403-p54gnj.html>.

[3] Lauren M Sauer, 'What Is Coronavirus?' *John Hopkins Health* (Web Page, 31 July 2020) <https:// www.hopkinsmedicine.org/health/conditions-and-diseases/coronavirus>.

[4] 'Coronavirus disease (COVID-19) advice for the public', *WHO* (Web Page, 4 June 2020) <https://www.who.int/emergencies/diseases/novel-coronavirus-2019/advice-for-public>.

to self-actualisation. Some of these needs overlap with the definition of rights contained in the UDHR. The differentiation between the two definitions is a prerequisite for the discussion of protecting FRs in the age of C-19.

The last section concerns the political, monetary and economic benefits of globalisation and its failings during the outbreak of C-19, in addition to emphasising the difficulties in protecting FRs when societies are preoccupied with their own interests and hold strong views on identity and personal rights. The concluding comments highlight the significance of protecting FRs, draw attention to the predicaments that arise from attempting to do so, and propose that FRs must be for the common good and cannot be challenged with current legislation for reasons pertaining to personal interests in the midst of a global crisis.

II THE KNOWN AND THE UNKNOWN

A *The Confusion*

The new virus, which originated in Wuhan, in China's Hubei Province, began its spread without warning.[5] In its early weeks, C-19 was compared to the flu because both are infectious respiratory illnesses with similar symptoms.[6] This may have created misconceptions about the danger it poses to human life and health; human beings also tend to live in denial when an enemy cannot be seen, as in the case of C-19. Somewhat more serious attention was paid to the disease two months into the outbreak when the media revealed a rapid increase in transmission and early fatalities in Italy at the end of February.[7]

---

[5] 'China didn't warn public of likely pandemic for 6 key days', *The Associated Press* (Web Page, 15 April 2020) <https://apnews.com/68a9e1b91de4ffc166acd6012d82c2f9>.

[6] Lisa L Maragakis, 'Coronavirus Disease 2019 vs. the Flu', *John Hopkins Medicine* (Web Page, 30 July 2020) <https://www.hopkinsmedicine.org/health/conditions-and-diseases/coronavirus/coronavirus-disease-2019-vs-the-flu>.

[7] Ciro Indolfi and Carmen Spaccarotella, 'The Outbreak of COVID-19 in Italy: Fighting the Pandemic', *JACC Journals* 2(9) (Web Page, 15 July 2020) <https://casereports.onlinejacc.org/content/2/9/1414>.

With C-19, too much was new, and so it was not possible to fully respond using knowledge and skills gained in the past. Day by day, medical teams and scientists learned about the disease through the rapidly rising number of infected people, fatal cases and laboratory work. C-19 was identified as a new virus causing severe respiratory symptoms – unlike flu, which is triggered by strains of influenza-like viruses.[8] Its effects on human health after recovery could only be gathered over time.[9] Protection measures were limited to washing hands, using hand sanitiser and social distancing;[10] no consensus was reached on wearing masks after more than six months. In overpopulated and poor countries, even these simple safety measures were difficult to meet.[11]

Reactions to the outbreak of C-19 were diverse among leaders on national, state and district levels,[12] and a global response was lacking when compared to other world-endangering diseases such as Ebola.[13]

Countries followed their own assessments. What people were looking for was global solidarity in leadership and a consensus on how

[8] 'Similarities and Differences between Flu and COVID-19', *Centre for Disease Control* (Web Page, 27 July 2020) <https://www.cdc.gov/flu/symptoms/flu-vs-covid19.htm>.

[9] Lisa L Maragakis, 'Coronavirus Disease 2019 vs. the Flu', *John Hopkins Medicine* (Web Page, 30 July 2020) <https://www.hopkinsmedicine.org/health/conditions-and-diseases/coronavirus/coronavirus-disease-2019-vs-the-flu>.

[10] 'Coronavirus disease (COVID-19) advice for the public', *WHO* (Web Page, 4 June 2020) <https://www.who.int/emergencies/diseases/novel-coronavirus-2019/advice-for-public>; 'How to protect yourself and others from coronavirus (COVID-19)', *Australian Government Department of Health* (Web Page, 30 July 2020) <https://www.health.gov.au/news/health- alerts/novel-coronavirus-2019-ncov-health-alert/how-to-protect-yourself-and-others-from-coronavirus-covid-19>.

[11] Farrah Tomazin, "Tsunami' of cases as coronavirus spreads where social distancing is a privilege', *The Sydney Morning Herald* (Web Page, 4 April 2020) <https://www.smh .com.au/national/tsunami-of-cases-as-coronavirus-spreads-where-social-distancing-is-a-privilege-20200403-p54gr0.html>.

[12] Paul Kelly, 'Coronavirus: Virus exposes weak global leadership', *The Australian* (Web Page, 31 July 2020) <https://www.theaustralian.com.au/inquirer/coronavirus-virus-exposes-weak-global-leadership/news-story/5d980f57f22f212cc1e9078cd8b76 5b9>.

[13] 'Key events in the WHO response to the Ebola outbreak', *WHO* (Web Page, January 2015) <www.who.int/csr/disease/ebola/one-year-report/who-response/en/>.

to deal with the global health, humanitarian and economic problems. People wanted cohesion, and this evoked questions and uncertainty about how well they were informed. However, humans have a strong sense of and need for the known.[14]

Hundreds of thousands became infected, and both the young and old died. Personal anguish and financial misery were seen on an unprecedented scale. Economic stimulus packages were announced, also on scales previously unimaginable. Financial losses escalated for individuals and in the private and public sectors. Normal daily expectations were reduced to meeting basic physiological needs. What gave people meaning in life before became less relevant when they had lost loved ones and their jobs, were close to becoming destitute or consistently heard devastating news.

B *The Beginning of the Age of C-19*

The prosperity seen throughout the world in the 21st century stopped by the middle of March 2020, when C-19 was declared a pandemic. Drastic restrictions were enforced on individuals, small companies and large organisations regarding how to maintain their daily businesses or compelling them to close. People had to adjust to the unknown. Concerns about future economic and financial crises became evident. Most importantly, people's basic human needs and freedom to do what they pleased were impeded since they were asked to stay at home, unless leaving the house for necessary food shopping, medical reasons and limited exercise. These restrictions were put into place to stop the new virus from spreading. In addition, facts about the virus were limited at the time the lockdowns were implemented.

Two Chinese tourists in Rome tested positive for the virus on 31 January 2020, and one week later, an Italian man returned to Italy from the city of Wuhan and was hospitalised.[15] Italy reported a cluster

---

[14] Abraham H Maslow, *A Theory of Human Motivation* (BN Publishing, 2015).

[15] 'Italian man dies from coronavirus as number of confirmed cases jump in Italy', *ABC News* (Web Page, 21 February 2020) <https://www.abc.net.au /news/2020-02-22/italian-tests-positive-for-coronavirus-two-more-cases-suspected/11990454>. Elisa Anzolin and Angelo Amante, 'First Italian dies of coronavirus as outbreak flares

of 16 cases on 21 February 2020,[16] but only two days later, *The Guardian* wrote about 76 infected patients and the first deaths related to C-19.[17] By early March, the virus had spread from Lombardy, a province in the northern part of Italy, to every region of the country.[18] The World Health Organization ('WHO') reports that the Wuhan Municipal Health Commission in China reported a cluster of pneumonia cases in Wuhan on 31 December 2019.[19] Chinese governmental records include data going back to 17 November 2019.[20] In France, also, cases were traced back to 16 November 2019.[21]

Regular reports about C-19 were seen in the media in connection with peak travelling around Chinese New Year; however, no international travel restrictions were announced.

Later information was disturbing. As early as 30 December 2019, Dr Li Wenliang warned his former schoolmates that a new coronavi-

---

in north', *Reuters* (Web Page, 21 February 2020) <https://www.reuters.com/article/us-china-health-italy/coronavirus-outbreak-grows-in-northern-italy-16-cases-reported-in-one-day-idUSKBN20F0UI>.

[16] Anzolin Elisa and Amante Angelo, 'Coronavirus outbreak grows in northern Italy, 16 cases reported in one day', *Thomson Reuters* (Web Page, 21 February 2020) <https://news.trust.org/item/20200221165731-rzbol>.

[17] 'Coronavirus: northern Italian towns close schools and businesses', *The Guardian* (Web Page, 23 Feb 2020) <https://www.theguardian.com/world/2020/feb/23/coronavirus-northern-italian-towns-close-schools-and-businesses>.

[18] 'Coronavirus. Colpite tutte le regioni. La Protezione civile: ecco i numeri aggiornati', *Avvenire.it* (Web Page, 5 March 2020) <https://www.avvenire.it/attualita/pagine/coronavirus-aggiornamento-5-marzo-2020>; 'Coronavirus: Fears over rapid spread in Italy's south', *BBC News* (Web Page, 26 March 2020) <https://www.bbc.com/news/world-europe-52048919>.

[19] 'Archived: WHO Timeline – COVID-19', *WHO* (Web Page, 27 April 2020) <https://www.who.int/news-room/detail/27-04-2020-who-timeline---covid-19>.

20 Helen Davidson, 'First Covid-19 case happened in November, China government records show – report', *The Guardian* (Web Page, 13 March 2020) <https://www.theguardian.com/world/2020/ mar/13/first-covid-19-case-happened-in-november-china-government-records-show-report>.

[21] 'Coronavirus: France's first known case 'was in December'', *BBC News* (Web Page, 13 March) <https://www.theguardian.com/world/2020/mar/13/first-covid-19-case-happened-in-november-china-government-records-show-report>.

rus infection had been confirmed.[22] His alerts were not appreciated by everyone – he was called a whistle-blower and criticised for making untrue comments.[23] He was diagnosed with the disease on 20 January 2020 and died on 7 February 2020. Eight people, including Dr Li, were disciplined by officials for cautioning people about the health risks of the newly discovered C-19.[24] According to the mayor of Wuhan, quick action at the early stage, which would have been crucial, was not taken.[25]

Some two months into the outbreak, on 22 January 2020, the WHO issued a statement to the effect that there was evidence of human-to-human transmission of the virus.[26] On the following day, an Emergency Committee under the International Health Regulations was set up to assess the seriousness of the outbreak and whether it was of international concern.[27] A consortium of independent members from around the world could not reach a consensus, based on the evidence provided, that the outbreak constituted a public health emergency.[28] By 30 January 2020, this opinion was revised, and it was concluded that the novel virus constituted a Public Health Emergency of International Concern.[29]

---

[22] 'Li Wenliang: Coronavirus kills Chinese whistle blower doctor', *BBC News* (Web Page, 7 February 2020) <https://www.bbc.com/news/world-asia-china-51403795>.

[23] 'Coronavirus whistle blower doctor Li Wenliang dies from infection in Wuhan, local hospital says', *ABC News* (Web Page, 7 February 2020) <https://www.abc. net. au/news/2020-02-07/doctor-who-warned-of-coronavirus-dies-in-china/11941948>.

[24] 'Coronavirus China: Dr Li Wenliang treated 'inappropriately' before death from COVID-19, Chinese officials admit', *News.com.au* (Web Page, 20 March 2020) <https://www.news.com.au/lifestyle/health/health-problems/coronavirus-china-dr-li-wenliang-treated-inappropriately-before-death-from-covid19-chinese-officials-admit/news-story/15517ef9476314352afc15dd5ab5d7da>.

[25] Rebecca Ratcliffe and Michael Standaert, 'China coronavirus: mayor of Wuhan admits mistakes', *The Guardian* (Web Page, 27 Jan 2020) <https://www.theguardian. com/science/2020/jan/27/china-coronavirus-who-to-hold-special-meeting-in-beijing-as-death-toll-jumps>.

[26] 'Archived: WHO Timeline – COVID-19, *WHO* (Web Page, 27 April 2020) <https:// www. who.int/news-room/detail/27-04-2020-who-timeline---covid-19>.

[27] Ibid.

[28] Ibid.

[29] Ibid.

People formalise views and make decisions based on their percep-tions. However, in this case, the global public became confused by mixed information and were doubtful whether they knew everything they needed to know. The announcements by the WHO, a body of professionals with expertise and responsibility for public health, did not ease their minds.

When disasters occur, experts and the public want to know whether the tragedy could have been prevented. With C-19, the question is asked, what could have been done to stop the virus from spreading and why did globalisation – a process of international connections and cooperation – enable this deadly virus to spread throughout the world?

C The Costs of Saving Lives

The main solution to the pandemic was seen to be isolation and social distancing. However, these restrictions constituted drastic changes to people's normal lives and the normal operation of businesses. With such restrictions, governments and organisations put people's health first, and HRs[30] and the economy second.[31] International and domestic flights were cancelled; schools, places of worship, shops, shopping malls and restaurants were closed; and businesses, small and large, were asked to organise arrangements whereby their employees could work from home. When the UDHR was adopted by the United Na-tions on 10 December 1948, it unequivocally proclaimed the inherent rights of all human beings – to live in a world in which human be-ings shall enjoy freedom and are free and equal in rights.[32] But with C-19, societies were no longer free; business and private lives were harshly restricted by the new regulations to ensure that people would stay apart and not transmit C-19.

---

[30] United Nations, 'Universal Declaration of Human Rights', 10 December 1948 <https://www.un.org/en/universal-declaration-human-rights/>.
[31] 'Australia: Legal Responses to Health Emergencies', *Library of Congress* (Web Page, 24 July 2020) <https://www.loc.gov/law/help/health-emergencies/australia.php>.
[32] See United Nations (n 30).

III C-19: AN ATTACK ON HUMANITY

A *Silent and Invisible Attack on Life and Achievements*

Our ancestors fought wars and wrought destruction upon one another in ancient times. Not surprisingly, the world's first charter of human rights goes back to 539 BC. At that time, Cyrus the Great – the first king of Persia, who freed the slaves – declared that all people had the right to choose their own religion, in addition to also establishing racial equality.[33] Despite these early ideas and rulings on equality, we do not know of any other significant documents on human rights issues, until 1215, when the Magna Carta first set out the right of habeas corpus. It established a tradition of civil rights that still exists today.[34]

Still, neither our charters nor the miseries caused by war could prevent humans from taking advantage of and interfering with the rights of others. Warriors went to war to conquer land in antiquity; the king of the Visigoths, Alaric, conquered Rome in 410 with the help of rebelling slaves who opened the city's gates;[35] and the World Wars and the Vietnam War were long and costly.[36] Concerns about the danger of nuclear weapons led to the signing of the Nuclear Test Ban Treaty between the United States, the Soviet Union and Great Britain on 7 October 1963;[37] and there was the inspection of weapons of mass destruction by United Nations officials in Iraq (2002–2003).[38] Modern

---

[33] 'History of Natural Law & Basic Freedoms, Cyrus the Great', *United for Human Rights* (Web Page, 2014-2020) <http://www.humanrights.com/what-are-human-rights/brief-history/cyrus-cylinder.html>.

[34] A Davis and J L Hancock, 'The Uniqueness of the Magna Carta in Human History' (Web Page, 13 June 2015) <https://www.americanthinker.com/articles/2015/06/the uniqueness of the uniqueness_of_the_magna_carta_in_human_history.html>.

[35] Richard Cavendish, 'The Visigoths sack Rome', *History Today* (Web page, 8 August 2010) 60(8) <https://www.historytoday.com/archive/months-past/visigoths-sack-rome>.

[36] 'Vietnam War', *A&E Television Networks* (Web Page, 29 October 2009) <https://www.history.com/topics/vietnam-war/vietnam-war-history>.

[37] 'Nuclear Test-Ban Treaty', *A&E Television Networks* (Web Page, 9 November 2009) <https://www.history.com/topics/cold-war/nuclear-test-ban-treaty>.

[38] Julian Borger, 'There were no weapons of mass destruction in Iraq', *The Guardian* (Web Page, 7 October 2004) <https://www.theguardian.com/world/2004/oct/07/usa.iraq1>.

chemical engineering has given rise to concerns that chemicals could be used for fatal attacks on humanity.

In the past, attacks were on tribes, groups and nations; C-19 has attacked the entire world, as well as its humanity and achievements. C-19 causes people to fall ill, interferes with their psychological state, deprives them of things they fundamentally need and have a right to, and kills them; it depresses the economy and renders individuals, private businesses, multinational companies and nations bankrupt.

Globalisation was developed to enhance cooperation between nations, companies and governments in order to facilitate business worldwide; it has raised the world market to new heights. However, globalisation appears not to function at its best during global health emergencies. Could globalisation become a process of attacking humanity and destroying its accomplishments?

Around the world, nations announced localised or national lockdowns at different times and for weeks or months while some tightened restrictions after lifting them.[39] Nothing else should or could have been done because of the importance of protecting life.[40] However, when restrictions have a significant effect on people's normal lives, one might ask whether all decisions were optimal. The question is whether these decisions were made on valid grounds and whether alternative decisions would have been less effective.

B *Lockdowns: Interference with People's Needs*

How people have coped with the sudden, strange and horrendous new circumstances has depended on factors such as financial circumstances, whether they lost their jobs or businesses, family and government support, education, general health, life experiences and personal resilience. However, everyone's needs have changed, to varying degrees.

---

[39] 'Coronavirus: The world in lockdown in maps and charts', *BBC News* (Web Page, 7 April 2020) <https://www.bbc.com/news/world-52103747>.

[40] 'Right to life: Public sector guidance sheet', *Australian Government Attorney-General's Department* (Web Page,) <https://www.ag.gov.au/rights-and-protections/human-rights-and-anti-discrimination/human-rights-scrutiny/public-sector-guidance-sheets/right-life>.

People possess a strong drive to fulfil their needs. A person might often think of their 'needs' as what they like to shop for. Taking action to obtain a desired purchase is only part of what makes people behave as they do. The real driving force behind human behaviour and ambitions is their distinctive, inborn need. These kinds of need have been identified through research such as that carried out by Abraham Maslow in the 20th century and are evident through evolution and reflected in the growing refinement of human behaviour through civilisation.[41] Our cultures, art and advanced science reflect what people are capable of achieving when they feel the need to actualise their potential.

C Maslow's Work on Human Needs

Abraham Maslow, an American psychologist, developed with a hierarchy of needs that humans want to have fulfilled.[42] His theory proposes that these needs greatly determine people's behaviour – namely, what people do and why, what their patterns of behaviour are and what becomes habit or high achievement. His work also implies that a person's psychological health is dependent on the fulfilment of their innate needs. This is important to note when millions of people have lost their jobs or have been required to take leave or pay cuts – ie when their needs abruptly change through no fault of their own.

Maslow's Theory of Motivation comprises five main types of need.[43] Each consists of individual needs, which are universal and significant because they give people satisfaction whenever they are fulfilled. The theory also implies that people become motivated to achieve a higher levels of need when they are satisfied that the goals in the lower part of the hierarchical order have been achieved.

So, what does Maslow's theory have to do with C-19? Maslow's principal findings – namely, how a person's behaviour, motivation and psychological health depend on how an individual is satisfied with

---

[41] Abraham H Maslow, *Toward a Psychology of Being* (Wilder Publications, 2011).
[42] Ibid.
[43] Ibid.

their needs – is relevant to understand the impact of lockdowns and uncommon regulations on humans. His studies provide valuable insight into the predicament that millions of people have experienced. During the first lockdown, they struggled with financial issues and staying positive and motivated, but then businesses had to close again when transmission rates began to increase again. Some businesses have closed for good, and many people have lost their jobs.

Maslow's studies help us to understand what people have gone through during the lockdowns and how they must have felt when they lost their jobs and began to struggle to meet urgent basic needs.

At the bottom of Maslow's hierarchy of needs are the basic or physiological needs, such as food, water, breathing and sleep. These protect the body from physical harm. One who lacks everything in life will most likely crave food and water above anything else and will also be motivated most by a lack of food. Safety ranks the second highest of the human needs; if the physiological needs are gratified, the body is absorbed in seeking and maintaining safety. Societies are preoccupied with their members' health and the well-being of their bodies, families, homes and regular jobs. What people also look for, and what they mean when they say they want safety, is stability in the world and the ability to see and maintain that which is familiar. Moreover, people have a preference for the known over the unknown.

Work with children has found that an undisrupted routine – an orderly world – is a requirement if young people are to feel safe. However, children feel anxious and unsafe if they experience unfairness, inconsistency and conditions that give the impression of an unreliable and unpredictable world. In society, adults learn to camouflage their innate feelings and reactions, whereas children and particularly babies become unsettled and show this when they sense danger or insecurity. On the other hand, young children seem to thrive when kept to schedules and when there is something they can count on. We can say that a child needs an organised world rather than an unstructured one, as well as parents who protect them from harm.

If the first two levels of needs are satisfied, then people focus on social needs such as a desire for love, belonging and affection. People will have a yearning for relationships – a partner and groups of friends. Being social, interacting with others and communicating are typical behaviours that humans want to engage in. Isolation and loneliness, by contrast, lead to depression.

The second highest category pertains to what we do to esteem and think highly of ourselves and to have an impact on others to gain their attention and respect. Needs that relate to a person's aims for achievements, high self-esteem, self-respect, confidence, freedom and independence – but also respect for others – fall under the umbrella of esteem needs. Being satisfied with one's self-esteem is about feeling adequate and useful in the world; a lack of these needs creates feelings of inferiority, weakness and helplessness and leads to discouragement. In the worst circumstances, severe traumatic neurosis can result.

Maslow's first four categories capture the basic conditions that concern coping with life. At the fifth and highest level of human needs, people are occupied with actualising what they are capable of becoming. Needs in this category are also known as cognitive needs. At this level, people generally seek purpose in their own lives, knowledge, a sense of purpose in being there for others and the ability to explore mindfulness. The need to reach out to others involves a readiness for caring and helping, empathy and compassion. Societies may also derive satisfaction from advocating ideologies such as justice, tolerance, education and moral issues.

The five levels of needs drive humans to develop and actualise their full potential. Achieving and maintaining the various conditions – and feeling ambitious enough to conquer the next level of needs – depends on factors such as education, culture, environment, age and opportunities. The needs are related to each other and are hierarchically ranked. A person can fall back and work on needs at a lower level. As life goes on, people may no longer think about previous needs because they take them for granted; ie those needs no longer dominate their conscious mind. What is important to acknowledge from empirical studies is that human beings have an innate desire to satisfy individual needs and to

fulfil higher needs. In normal life, the average person is partially satisfied and partially unsatisfied in the totality of what they want.

D *Human Needs: Lost in the Age of C-19*

Eleven days after C-19 was declared a pandemic,[44] Australia, Canada
and Japan already had over 1,000 cases and Bondi Beach in Sydney,
along with pubs, restaurants and gyms, was closed. Millions of people
in the US were placed under strict quarantine, and individual states
asked all non-essential businesses to close. Jordan announced a strict
nationwide curfew, and Syria banned visitors from all affected countries.

The news was received with concern and scepticism. People re-
alised that they had been living with a deadly virus for almost three
months. Maslow, as noted earlier, talks about humans' fundamental
need for safety – a natural wish to be healthy and to know.[45] The latter
desire was now barely, if at all, met.

On 19 April 2020, the Australian Foreign Minister, Marise Payne,
asked for a global investigation into the origins of C-19 and its outbreak.[46] The response from China was not in favour of the request.[47]
China moved to re-visit the mandate for an investigation after the pandemic.[48]

---

[44] Rebecca Ratcliffe, 'Coronavirus: 21 March at a glance', The Guardian (Web Page,
21 March 2020) <https://www.theguardian.com/world/2020/mar/21/coronavirus-at-
a-glance>.

[45] Maslow, above n 14.

[46] Brett Worthington, 'Marise Payne calls for global inquiry into China's handling
of the coronavirus outbreak', *ABC News* (Web Page, 19 April 2020) <https://www.
abc.net.au/news/2020-04-19/payne-calls-for-inquiry-china-handling-of-coronavirus-
covid-19/12162968>.

[47] Graeme Smith, 'Murky origins: why China will never welcome a global inquiry
into the source of COVID-19', *The Conversation* (Web Page, April 22 2020) <https://
theconversation.com/murky-origins-why-china-will-never-welcome-a-global-inqui-
ry-into-the-source-of-covid-19-136713>.

[48] Rob Picheta, 'China backs coronavirus investigation but says it should wait until pandemic is contained', *CNN* (Web Page, May 18 2020) <https://edition.cnn.
com/2020/05/18 /health/world-health-assembly-china-inquiry-intl/index.html>.

In the meantime, people continued to face the unfolding difficulties in their own and other countries. The bleak outlook for a vaccine has amplified people's anguish. Their need for safety has been jeopardised twofold: first, by the uncertainty surrounding the unknown, i.e. the virus, how to protect themselves and the personal unfamiliar circumstances; second, people's fundamental right to know and be warned about the health risks of C-19 has been compromised.

By 10 January 2020, when the WHO was not recommending restrictions for international traffic and precautions for international travellers, 41 cases were reported by Chinese authorities.[49] When the WHO announced that there was a Public Health Emergency of International Concern on 30 January 2020, the number of cases in mainland China was almost 9,700, with at least 213 deaths.[50] However, when C-19 was declared a pandemic on 11 March 2020, there were 118,000 cases in 114 countries and 4,291 fatalities.[51]

C-19 changed the world profoundly and rapidly. By the end of April, the International Labour Organization reported a significant drop in working hours (10.5%) compared to the last quarter of 2019.[52] Upper-middle-income countries were hit most in the first quarter (8.8%), while a drop in employment in lower-middle-income (11.4%) and high-income (12.2%) countries was predicted in the second quar-

---

[49] 'WHO advice for international travel and trade in relation to the outbreak of pneumonia caused by a new coronavirus in China', *WHO* (Web Page, 10 January 2020) <https://www .who.int/news-room/articles-detail/who-advice-for-international-travel-and-trade-in-relation-to-the-outbreak-of-pneumonia-caused-by-a-new-coronavirus-in-china>.

[50] Helen Regan et al, 'January 30 coronavirus news', *CNN* (Web Page, 31 January 2020) <https://edition.cnn.com/asia/live-news/coronavirus-outbreak-01-30-20-intl-hnk/h_ccc67e9d3ac64e126fd44f219fec0e0b>.

[51] 'WHO Director-General's opening remarks at the media briefing on COVID-19', *WHO* (Web Page, 11 March 2020) <https://www.who.int/dg/speeches/detail/who-director-general-s-opening-remarks-at-the-media-briefing-on-covid-19-11-march-2020>.

[52] 'ILO: As job losses escalate, nearly half of global workforce at risk of losing livelihoods', *ILO* (Web Page, 29 April 2020) <https://www.ilo.org/global/about-the-ilo/newsroom/news/WCMS_743036/lang--en/index.htm>.

ter.[53] CNBC reported on 30 March 2020 that the downturn in the economy could cost 47 million jobs and increase unemployment to over 32% in the US.[54] Analysts worried about particularly high layoffs in high-risk jobs.[55] BBC News reported on 7 April 2020 that a total of 81% of the global workforce of 3.3 billion had seen their workplaces partially or fully closed.[56] In this meltdown of the labour market, the ILO also warned that almost half of the global economy – 1.6 billion employees in informal jobs – could be out of work due to the decline in working hours and lockdowns, with people under the age of 25 being hit particularly hard because of working in informal employment sectors.[57]

The loss of employment caused significant changes in people's needs. Those previously in good positions, with high salaries and the ability to actualise their full potential in their work, faced grief, embarrassment, a lack of self-esteem and a loss of coveted reputation. Those who overspent because they had become used to high incomes may have struggled with bills after redundancy. Having no income leads to guilt, despair and helplessness for wage earners regardless of past or current work. Living with less was something many people had never had to deal with, and they were learning about it for the first time. Families had to lower their expectations and needs; of the 1.6 billion people employed in the informal economy, many were unable to earn a living to fulfil their most basic needs such as food, clean water

---

[53] 'ILO Monitor: COVID-19 and the world of work', *ILO* (Web Page, 27 May 2020) <https://www.ilo.org/wcmsp5/groups/public/---dgreports/--dcomm/documents/briefingnote/wcms_745963.pdf>.

[54] Jeff Cox, 'Coronavirus job losses could total 47 million, unemployment rate may hit 32%, Fed estimates', *CNBC* (Web Page, 30 March 2020) <https://www.cnbc.com/ 2020/03/30/coronavirus-job-losses-could-total-47-million-unemployment-rate-of-32percent-fed-says.html>.

[55] Ibid.

[56] 'Coronavirus: Four out of five people's jobs hit by pandemic', *BBC News* (Web Page, 7 April 2020) <https://www.bbc.com/news/business-52199888>.

[57] 'ILO: As job losses escalate, nearly half of global workforce at risk of losing livelihoods', *ILO* (Web Page, 29 April 2020) <lo.org/global/about-the-ilo/newsroom/news/WCMS_743036/lang--en/index.htm>.

and a place to sleep.[58] The changes to employment worldwide were in stark contrast to what we might understand from art 13 in the UDHR, which states that, 'everyone has the right to work, to free choice of employment'.[59]

Humans are social beings. In the age of C-19, it would have been natural and important for people to reach out to friends; however, the lockdowns forced them to stay in isolation or with members of their households only. Such interference with private lives has been widely accepted because of the fear of C-19, but it is not in line with art 12, which states that, 'no one shall be subjected to arbitrary interference with his privacy, family, home...'.[60] It is unnatural for human beings to avoid social contact, to sense other human beings, to talk and to listen, and to touch and be touched. People require love and affection – to both receive and give these.[61] People in relationships but not living under the same roof were separated for weeks or months.

In addition, people could not attend weddings or funerals, visit loved ones in hospitals or care homes, or give them comfort in their final hours. Travelling any distance to see relatives or friends, or for pleasure or business, was also restricted. art 23.1 states that, 'everyone has the right to freedom of movement and ... the right to leave any country, including his own, and to return to his country'.[62]

Education was interrupted by the closure of educational institutions for weeks or months, and families were asked to homeschool and extend holidays. The disruption for learners was significant. According to a publication by UNESCO, as of 24 April 2020, 1.5 billion children and youth from pre-primary to higher education have been

---

[58] Peter Kemny, 'ILO raises global job loss forecast to 305M amid virus', *Economy* (Web Page, 29 March 2020) <https://www.aa.com.tr/en/economy/ilo-raises-global-job-loss-forecast-to-305m-amid-virus/1823051>.

[59] UDHR art 13.

[60] UDHR art 12.

[61] Maslow A, *A Theory of Human Motivation* (BN Publishing, 2015).

[62] UDHR, above n 29, art 23.1.

affected by school closures.[63] Figures were even higher on 30 March 2020 (1.6 billion or 90.3%). Four months later, on 23 July 2020, over 1 billion or 60.9% of young children and youth were still unable to attend school. Nations with country-wide closures dropped from 191 to 107 between the end of March and July 2020.[64] However, school closures also brought high social and economic costs for people across communities. Underprivileged learners were disadvantaged; children from poor families suffered malnutrition if they relied on meals provided by schools; and parents were unprepared for home learning and incurred costs when staying at home with their children. Neither should we ignore the fact that pre-schoolers and students missed the social contact they could enjoy at school. Under these conditions, social problems such as child labour, sexual exploitation and early marriages and pregnancies erupted. Yearly assessments were thrown into disarray, and students were stressed because their plans became uncertain. According to art 26.1, 'everybody has the right to education...'[65] However, in the age of C-19, this right was greatly curbed.

Our learners were also disadvantaged by the interruption to their routines, which are important for older students but especially for the young, who need stability and an orderly world. They may also have felt insecure because of their parents' change in work or employment status, or the different family dynamics.

Article 18 of the UDHR states that everyone has the right to manifest their religion or belief in teaching, practice, worship and observance.[66] However, worshippers could not attend churches, temples, mosques, synagogues or shrines for prayer because they were closed world-wide. Worship is a tradition that has been cultivated throughout

---

[63] '1.3 billion learners are still affected by school or university closures, as educational institutions start reopening around the world, says UNESCO', *UNESCO* (Web Page, 29 April 2020) <https://en.unesco.org/news/13-billion-learners-are-still-affected-school-university-closures-educational-institutions>.

[64] 'From Disruption to Recovery', *UNESCO* (Web Page, 1 August 2020) <https://en.unesco.org/covid19/ educationresponse>.

[65] UDHR art 26.1.

[66] UDHR art 18.

history. In the age of C-19, when people would have been drawn to prayers for comfort, strength and solutions to the global dilemma, they could not fulfil this intrinsic need. The last point concerns needs, which Maslow listed in his hierarchy of human motivation under esteem and self-actualisation. As mentioned earlier, a person's needs on these two levels include the need for relationships with oneself and others, personal interests, spirituality and ideologies. To protect FRs, these needs, which are beyond the physiological, are important because desires that lead to actualising one's potential can advance not only one's personal growth but also the growth of humanity – what societies have achieved and who we have become. However, with C-19, all of these innate and legitimate needs of our societies were infringed upon by novel circumstances. People were required to stay at home, faced uncertainty about their future and were even prevented from enjoying nature and attaining fulfilment through its beauty.

IV FUNDAMENTAL RIGHTS AND RESPONSIBILITY IN PERSPECTIVE

The intense sensitivity that societies display towards HRs and what they believe they are entitled to makes it difficult to develop a scheme to protect FRs. Today's focus on identity rather than responsibility adds to the dilemma of identifying FRs, which are universal, valid and indisputable in the age of C-19 – and in other crises, which we hope will never occur.

The two previous sections presented accounts of C-19's impact on humanity and my argument that draws on Maslow's theory of human motivation to protect FRs in the age of C-19. Both sections shed light on our time – a time in which regulations and established rights are protested against and misused for individual gain – and examine why our HRs may be less effective today and how human behaviour (specifically, a lack of responsibility) has led to a pandemic that seems out of control.

What follows does not provide a clear-cut path to a solution, but they do attempt to offer thoughts on protecting FRs in the age of C-19, providing detail on what must be protected and how.

As already stated, this paper sets FRs apart from HRs and proposes protecting FRs by drawing on humans' natural needs; for some, however, notions of FRs and HRs may be the same or similar. FRs, in my conception, are concerned with humans' innate needs, which are achieved by people through their development and over their lifetimes and are found through evolution. They are true, intrinsic, natural desires to strive for: food, safety, health, work, housing, family, being with others, and actualising one's potential in areas of individual choice. HRs, in contrast, were drafted by humans for a purpose.

The UDHR and earlier charters of human rights were created with wisdom and in the interest of humanity, with the aim of establishing equality among people at a certain time. Wars and unfair treatment of people of different cultures, races and religions occurred during the times the charters were written.

In the age of C-19, we must consider our global economy and politics, values and social movements. What was previously a reason to mandate the protection of rights may no longer be of the same significance today. One must ask why existing rights are not working. People's perceptions of their rights have changed, as has their respect for rights and laws; people now enforce individual views. This diversity makes it difficult to define FRs in a way that is widely accepted. One must be clear why particular FRs should be protected in preference to others, and one must question whether protecting FRs in the age of C-19 will also be helpful to humanity in other crises.

The FRs that it seems essential to protect would be the innate human needs that constitute the UDHR, such the right to employment, education, worship, privacy, freedom from aggression and the idea that people should act towards one another in a spirit of brotherhood. In other words, FRs that would have to be protected would be those that are concerned with what people need, not what they believe they should have. A paper that discusses the protection of FRs should also include a mandate for the right to investigate the cause of any disaster without delay in order to avoid further harm to humanity.

The argument for using Maslow's research on human needs in preference to the UDHR should not be viewed as disregard for the UDHR, but it does appear that the UDHR can be used for personal gain. In crises, when difficult decisions must be made, people should not be able to find a loophole in the UDHR to gain what they believe is their right.

Everyone's FRs should be protected equally; however, we know that the decisions of politicians and professionals have not been unified or equal but have placed various countries and states in better or worse positions in the age of C-19. Then again, it was not possible to lean on experience during this crisis, and leaders around the world have had dissimilar economic and social conditions and populations to deal with. Restrictions following the outbreak of C-19 did not make sense when they varied between political leaders and were impractical in some parts of the world.

The purpose of protecting FRs is to serve the people. However, for this to happen, FRs must resonate with the public and must be accepted and followed; people must see that these rights are in their best interests. People must understand why rights and restrictions are put in place and know that they should be fair to everyone and treat everyone equally. Furthermore, protecting FRs not only serves the individual and humanity but also assures that what societies have accomplished will be maintained: advanced knowledge of science, technology and medicine, and our cultures. Only through self-actualisation has humanity developed to the point at which we currently find ourselves.

Not everyone is equally credible. This is important for two reasons: first, FRs should be drafted by a body with credibility; second, authorities that have the power to make decisions should have special qualities such as competency, credibility, integrity, expertise, honesty, knowledge, responsibility and unbiased and lateral thinking. People who have the privilege of making critical decisions must weigh the consequences of their decisions in terms of their effects on people's lives. Even though unexpected circumstances may prompt urgent decisions, they must be scrutinised and responsible.

Protecting FRs must be seen in relation to today's world market and how companies and politicians are conducting business because it is here that rights are upheld or neglected. Globalisation, a process that began in the early 1980s, has prevailed in terms of connecting the world. Cooperation between organisations, political leaders and individuals has brought lucrative returns; however, while global cooperation worked well for financial profit, it failed during the outbreak of C-19. A prompt response in the form of cooperation and global leadership was missing. Why? Article 1 of the UDHR reminds us that, 'all human beings ... are endowed with reason and conscience and should act towards one another in a spirit of brotherhood'.[67] Has this fundamental wisdom been lost in the age of globalisation? Is it a sign that power through business can create its own culture, disassociated from people's right to live?

The age of C-19 provides impetus to formulate new FRs that can protect everyone equally, particularly in world crises such as C-19. It is important that these FRs cannot be challenged by individuals or minority groups for personal reasons. Restrictions on FRs in emergencies must be sound, sensible and in the interest of humanity.

V CONCLUDING COMMENTS

In the age of C-19, values and policies are too often ignored, but the rights to which people feel they are entitled prevail. When these are the general sentiments, it is difficult to formulate FRs that will be respected as tools to protect humanity.

Protecting FRs matters. It is the difference between humanity prospering and not surviving. It gives guidance and opportunities to people, in private lives and in business, to do the right thing and ensure a better future for the next generations. However, if we place personal interests on pedestals, humanity is in trouble. This is why the battle to protect FRs is vital.

---

[67] UDHR 29 art 1.

My comments are directed towards people who are interested in the future of humanity and are in a position to make changes. The present world crisis of C-19 is unprecedented. Disrespect for rights beyond an individual's interests has become dangerously widespread. It is time to remind people of their responsibilities and the fact that responsibility counts. To be responsible also means to respect rules and regulations that one may not personally like. FRs that protect our civilisation are timely in an age when people too often ignore the idea that they should act towards others in a spirit of brotherhood,[68] and when individuals believe they are entitled to their desires and take action that is to the detriment of others, or even of humanity.

---

[68] UDHR 29 art 1.

12

Molinism, Covid-19 and Human Responsibility

JOHNNY M SAKR*

ABSTRACT

Coined after Roman Catholic Jesuit Luis de Molina,[1] Molinism is a philosophical tool that attempts to explain how a provident God can exercise sovereign control over his world while honouring the genuine freedom He has bestowed upon His creatures.[2] While Molinism holds that all things that happen in the actual world are part of God's decree,[3] it does not remove human responsibility. This chapter will show how the Christian-Molinist perspective promotes human efforts to prevent epidemics, cope with them, and change the way of life to lower their impact.

I INTRODUCTION

With the current COVID-19 epidemic, it's only natural for detractors of religious ideology to argue for the irreconcilability of 'evil' (be it man-made or natural evil) with the existence of God(s), and how theological convictions interact with practical applications.

---

* LLB, Grad Dip. Leg Prac, LL.M. (Commercial Transactions), MPhil. (Law), PhD (Law) (*candidate*). Adjunct Lecturer in Law at the University of Notre Dame Australia, Sydney.

[1] Alexander Aichele and Matthias Kaufmann, 'Introduction' in Alexander Aichele and Matthias Kaufmann (eds), *A Companion to Luis de Molina* (Brill, 2014) xiv.

[2] Thomas P Flint, 'Molinsm' (2015) *Oxford University Press* 1 <https://www.oxfordhandbooks.com/view/10.1093/oxfordhb/9780199935314.001.0001/oxfordhb-9780199935314-e-29>.

[3] Luis De Molina, *Foreknowledge*, 4.14.15.53.3.17. See also; Kirk MacGregor, *Luis de Molina: The Life and Theology of the Founder of Middle Knowledge* (Zondervan Academic, 2015) 115-121.

While there is a myriad of views on this issue, this chapterwill present the Molinist-Christian attitude regarding epidemics, particularly COVID-19. The first section of this chapter will briefly explain what Molinism is and the elements within this belief system. Given Molinism is a system of theological thought concerning God's omniscience and it's attempt to reconcile this with human freedom, the second section will address the inevitable question 'but, if God is omniscient and thus, knows all our decisions, how do we possess free will?' The last section will illustrate how Molinism can be applied to this epidemic. In particular, how Molinism, taking into consideration its theological roots, can be used to promote humanitarian efforts to prevent outbreaks, cope with them, and change the way of life to lower their impact.

II MOLINISM

Molinism is named after Luis de Molina,[4] a Spanish Jesuit theologian[5] who has become well-known among philosophers of religion for his doctrine of middle knowledge (Latin: *scientia media*).[6] *Scientia media* is knowledge of all true counterfactual propositions, including counterfactuals of creaturely freedom. That is to say; God knows what contingent states of affairs would obtain if certain antecedent states of affairs were to obtain. God knows what any free creature would freely do in any set of freedom permitting circumstances.[7]

Molinism is a philosophical theory that seeks to reconcile God's divine foreknowledge, sovereignty, and human freedom.[8] On Molin-

---

[4] Aichele and Kaufmann (n 1) xiv. See also; Edward Craig, *Concise Routledge Encyclopedia of Philosophy* (Psychology Press, 2000) 588.

[5] Thomas P Flint, *Divine Providence: The Molinist Account* (Cornell University, 1998) 2.

[6] MacGregor (n 3) 9. See also; Tim Stratton and Jacobus Erasmus, 'Mere Molinism: A Defense of Two Essential Pillars' (2018) 16(2) *Perichoresis* 18.

[7] William Lane Craig, '"No Other Name": A Middle Knowledge Perspective on the Exclusivity of Salvation Through Christ' (1989) 6(2) *Faith and Philosophy* 177.

[8] Edward Craig, *Routledge Encyclopaedia of Philosophy* (Taylor & Francis, 1998) 465. See also; Jerry L Walls and Joseph Dongell, *Why I Am Not a Calvinist* (InterVarsity Press, 2004) 134.

ism, 'human freedom' is freedom in the libertarian sense, otherwise known as contra-causal freedom.[9] Quoting Hasker, Hamilton explains, a human agent contains contra-causal or libertarian freedom with respect to a particular action if at the time the choice is made 'it is within the agent's power to perform the action and also in the agent's power to refrain from the action'.[10]

The action performed by the agent is free from all causally determining external and internal factors, 'no antecedent conditions and/or causal laws determine that he will perform the action or that he won't'.[11]

In his book, *The Recalcitrant Imago Dei: Human Persons and the Failure of Naturalism*, J P Moreland offered four essentials of libertarian free will:

1. P is a substance that has the active power to bring about e;

2. P exerted power as a first mover (an 'originator') to bring about e;

3. P had the categorical ability to refrain from exerting power to bring about e; and

4. P acted for the sake of reasons, which serve as the final cause or teleological goal for which P acted.[12]

It is this libertarian sense of freedom that allows human beings to be responsible for their actions.[13] It is not within the scope of this chapter to argue that moral responsibility requires libertarianism.

---

[9] Kenneth Perszyk, *Molinism: The Contemporary Debate* (Oxford University Press, 2011) 262. See also; Kenneth Perszyk, 'Molinism and Compatibilism' (2000) 48(1) *International Journal for Philosophy of Religion* 11; Stratton and Erasmus (n 6)18; Jonathan Glover, *Responsibility* (Humanities Press, 1970) 34.

[10] Robert L Hamilton, *Philosophical Reflections on Free Will* (2000) 2, citing William Hasker, 'A Philosophical Perspective' in *The Openness of God*, Pinnock (ed), (Downers Grove, 1994) 137.

[11] Alvin Plantinga, *God, Freedom and Evil* (Grand Rapids, 1977) 29.

[12] James Porter Moreland, *The Recalcitrant Imago Dei: Human Persons and the Failure of Naturalism* (Hymns Ancient and Modern Ltd, 2009) 44.

13 William O'Donohue and Kyle E Ferguson, *The Psychology of B F Skinner* (SAGE, 2001) 165. See also; George Berkeley and Jonathan Dancy (ed), *A Treatics Concerning the Principles of Human Knowledge* (Oxford University Press, 1998); Thomas Reid, *Essays on the Active Powers of the Human Mind* (MIT Press, 1969).

Molinism describes God's knowledge in three logical moments – God's natural knowledge, middle knowledge, and free knowledge.[14] As William Lane Craig explains:

> Although whatever God knows, He has known from eternity, so that there is no temporal succession in God's knowledge, nonetheless there does exist a sort of logical succession in God's knowledge in that His knowledge of certain propositions is conditionally or explanatorily prior to His knowledge of certain other propositions. That is to say, God's knowledge of a particular set of propositions depends asymmetrically on His knowledge of a certain other set of propositions and is in this sense posterior to it.[15]

The term logically should not be understood in the sense of chronological progression. For example, the axioms of a mathematical theory are logically, not chronologically, prior to the theorems derived from them.[16] Therefore, there was no point in time where God contained middle knowledge and lacked natural and free knowledge.[17]

The following section will discuss God's natural knowledge, the first logical moment in God's knowledge.[18]

---

[14] For Molina's doctrine, see Ludovici Molina, *De liberi arbitrii cum gratia donis, divina praescientia, providentia, praedestinationae et reprobatione Concordia* 4. This section has been translated by Alfred J Freddoso, 'Introduction', in Luis de Molina, *On Divine Foreknowledge*, tr Alfred J Freddoso (Cornell University Press, 1988). See also; William Lane Craig, *The Only Wise God: The Compatibility of Divine Foreknowledge and Human Freedom* (Wipf and Stock Publishers, 2000) 131; John David Laing, 'Molinism and Supercomprehension: Grounding Counterfactual Truth' (PhD Thesis, Southern Baptist Theological Seminary, 2000) 154; Kenneth Keathley, *Salvation and Sovereignty: A Molinist Approach* (B&H Publishing Group, 2010) 16-17.

[15] William Lane Craig, *Divine Foreknowledge and Human Freedom: The Coherence of Theism: Omniscience* (Brill, 1990) 237.

[16] Douglas Amedeo and Reginald G Golledge, *An Introduction to Scientific Reasoning in Geography* (Wiley, 1975) 34. See also; William Richard Connolly, *The Given and the a Priori: Some Issues in the Epistemology of C. I. Lewis* (Michigan State University, 1973) 145; Arthur Newell Strahler, *Understanding Science: An Introduction to Concepts and Issues* (Prometheus Books, 1992) 243.

[17] Keathley (n 14) 40.

[18] William Lane Craig, 'God Directs All Things: On Behalf of a Molinist View of

A *Natural Knowledge*

Molina called God's pre-volitional knowledge of necessary truths as natural knowledge.[19] That is, 'every logical possibility is an object of God's knowledge, which depends only on his intellect'.[20]

These truths are metaphysically necessary because they could not have been false[21] and are true in all possible worlds.[22] For example, the laws of logic and the laws of mathematics.[23] As John Laing notes, 'God has no control over the truth of the[se] propositions'; they are independent of His will.[24] Molina explained:

Through this type of knowledge He knew all the things to which the divine power extended either immediately or by the mediation of secondary causes, including not only the natures of individuals and the necessary states of affairs composed of them, but also the contingent states of affairs-through this knowledge He knew, to be sure, not that the latter were or were not going to obtain determinately, but rather that they were indifferently able to obtain and able not to obtain, a fea-

---

Providence' [in Dennis Jowers and Stanley N Gundry (eds), *Four Views on Divine Providence* (Zondervan, 2011) 82-83. See also; Kevin Timpe, *Arguing About Religion* (Routledge, 2009) 335.

[19] Luis de Molina, *Concordia: Disputations* 52 sec 9. See Flint (n 5) 38.

[20] Jean-Pascal Anfray, 'Molina and John Duns Scotus' in Alexander Aichele and Matthias Kaufmann (eds), *A Companion to Luis de Molina* (Brill, 2014) 336.

[21] Thomas P Flint, 'Two Accounts of Providence' in Michael C Rea (ed), *Oxford Readings in Philosophical Theology: Providence, Scripture, and Resurrection* (Oxford University Press, 2009) 25. See also; Molina (n 14) 11.

[22] Richard A Fumerton, *Realism and the Correspondence Theory of Truth* (Rowman & Littlefield, 2002) 51. See also; Robert Nozick, *Invariances: The Structure of the Objective World* (Harvard University Press, 2001) 129.

[23] Geoffrey Scarre, *Logic and Reality in the Philosophy of John Stuart Mill* (Springer Science & Business Media, 2012) 141. See also; Mark A Olson, 'Descartes' First Meditation: Mathematics and the Laws of Logic' (1988) 26(3) *Journal of the History of Philosophy* 408.

[24] Laing (n 14) 125 (emphasis mine). See also; Michael J Murray and [Michael C Rea, *An Introduction to the Philosophy of Religion* (Cambridge University Press, 2008) 59; Michael V Griffin, *Leibniz, God and Necessity* (Cambridge University Press, 2013) 114.

ture that belongs to them necessarily and thus also falls under God's natural knowledge.[25]

The truths known in His natural knowledge are necessary and independent of God's free will.[26]

Although God's natural knowledge is knowledge of all possible worlds, not all possible worlds are actualisable. Before further elaboration on God's knowledge is discussed, it is important to briefly discuss three concepts – actualisation, creaturely world-types, and possible world semantics.

B *Actualisation*

It is semantically improper to assert that God created the 'world' because the term world (as used in this chapter), is not an thing that was established at a point in time, but rather one of numerous complete sets of attuned states of affairs which have subsisted in the mind of God for all eternity.[27] Plantinga explains:

---

[25] Luis de Molina, *Concordia* 4.52.9 in Molina (n 14) 168.

[26] Thomas P Flint, 'Two Accounts of Providence' in Thomas V Morris (ed), *Divine and Stanley N Gundry* (eds), *Four Views on Divine Providence* (Zondervan, 2011) 82-83. See also; Kevin Timpe, *Arguing About Religion* (Routledge, 2009) 335.

Luis de Molina, *Concordia: Disputations* 52 sec 9. See Flint (n 5) 38.

Jean-Pascal Anfray, 'Molina and John Duns Scotus' in Alexander Aichele and Matthias Kaufmann (eds), *A Companion to Luis de Molina* (Brill, 2014) 336.

Thomas P Flint, 'Two Accounts of Providence' in Michael C Rea (ed), *Oxford Readings in Philosophical Theology: Providence, Scripture, and Resurrection* (Oxford University Press, 2009) 25. See also; Molina (n 14) 11.

Richard A Fumerton, *Realism and the Correspondence Theory of Truth* (Rowman & Littlefield, 2002) 51. See also; Robert Nozick, *Invariances: The Structure of the Objective World* (Harvard University Press, 2001) 129.

Geoffrey Scarre, *Logic and Reality in the Philosophy of John Stuart Mill* (Springer Science & Business Media, 2012) 141. See also; Mark A Olson, 'Descartes' First Meditation: Mathematics and the Laws of Logic' (1988) 26(3) *Journal of the History of Philosophy* 408.

Laing (n 14) 125 (emphasis mine). See also; Michael J Murray and Michael C Rea, *An Introduction to the Philosophy of Religion* (Cambridge University Press, 2008) 59; Michael V Griffin, *Leibniz, God and Necessity* (Cambridge University Press, 2013) 114.

Luis de Molina, *Concordia* 4.52.9 in Molina (n 14) 168 and *Human Action* (Cornell University Press, 1988) 157.

[27] Laing (n 14) 147.

We speak of God as creating the world; yet if it is α [the actual world] of which we speak, what we say is false. For a thing is created only if there is a time before which it does not exist; and this is patently false of α, as it is of any state of affairs. What God has created are the heavens and the earth and all that they contain; he has not created himself, or numbers, propositions, properties, or states of affairs: these have no beginnings. We can say, however, that God actualises states of affairs; his creative activity results in their being or becoming actual.[28]

James Baillie put it more succinctly, 'the actual world is made up of the facts corresponding to the set of true propositions',[29] or as Van Inwagen wrote, 'for the Abstractionist (if he thinks of worlds as states of affairs), actuality is just obtaining: the actual world is the one world – the one among possible states of affairs maximal with respect to the inclusion of other state of affairs – that obtains'.[30]

Philosophers have distinguished between two kinds of actualising activity to aid in discussing how God can actualise a world while preserving a strong view of freedom.[31]

C Strong Actualisation

The first kind of actualisation is called *strong actualisation*. Strong actualisation refers to 'the efforts of a being when it causally determines an event's obtaining'.[32] Flint and Freddoso write, 'an agent S strongly actualises a state of affairs p just when S causally determines

---

[28] Alvin Plantinga, *The Nature of Necessity* (Clarendon Press, 1974) 168 (emphasis mine).

[29] James Baillie, *Contemporary Analytic Philosophy* (Prentice Hall, 2003) 25. See also; David Sanford, *If P, Then Q: Conditionals and the Foundations of Reasoning* (Routledge, 2011) 156; Alexander R Pruss, 'The Leibnizian Cosmological Argument' in William Lane Craig and J P Moreland (eds), *The Blackwell Companion to Natural Theology* (John Wiley & Sons, 2009) 37.

[30] Peter van Inwagen, 'Two Concepts of Possible Worlds' in Peter van Inwagen, *Ontology, Identity, and Modality: Essays in Metaphysics* (Cambridge University Press, 2001) 211.

[31] See Plantinga (n 28) 172-173; Roderick Chisolm, *Person and Object* (Open Court, 1976) 67-69.

[32] Laing (n 14) 148.

p's obtaining'[33] or as Morriston wrote, 'a person P strongly actualises a state of affairs S if, without relying on help from any indeterministic processes, P causes S to obtain'.[34]

An example of strong actualisation is that of a potter making a vessel.

D *Weak Actualisation*

The second kind of actualisation has been coined *weak actualisation*. Weak actualisation refers to a being's contribution to an event's obtaining by placing a creature in circumstances in which the creature will freely cause the event. Flint and Freddoso explain, 'in such cases the agent in question, by his actions or omissions, strongly brings it about that another agent S is in situation C, where it is true that if S were in C, then S would freely act in a specified way',[35] or as Morriston wrote, 'P weakly actualises S if P strongly actualises some other state of affairs S*, such that if P were to actualise S*, some indeterministic process would bring about the actualisation of S'.[36]

For example, God could weakly actualise an event by placing person P in circumstances C knowing P would do action A in C.

The distinction between strong and weak actualisation assist in understanding the relationship between human freedom and divine providence. However, in Molinism, there are limitations on the possible worlds that God can actualise. For example, as Laing notes, 'God cannot strongly actualise counterfactuals of freedom because that would involve a contradiction [because counterfactuals of creaturely freedom are not causally determined by God (thus forming a creaturely world-type) and strong actualisation involves God causally determin-

---

[33] Thomas P Flint and Alfred J Freddoso, 'Maximal Power' in Alfred J Freddoso (ed), *The Existence and Nature of God* (University of Notre Dame Press, 1983) 139.

[34] Wes Morriston, 'Omnipotence and Necessary Moral Perfection: Are They Compatible?' (2001) 37(2) *Religious Studies* 145.

[35] Flint and Freddoso (n 33) 140.

[36] Morriston (n 34) 145.

ing a state of affairs]. God is also limited in the states of affairs He can weakly actualise'.[37]

In summary, strong actualisation occurs when God causally brings about some effect directly by His action whilst weak actualisation arises when God places agents in a set of circumstances knowing that the person would freely choose to produce an effect.

Creaturely-world types and their relationship to feasible worlds will be discussed in the following section.

E *Creaturely World-Type*

If God has middle knowledge, a concept that will be further elaborated, then God knows all true counterfactuals of creaturely freedom (if P was in C, P would do A), and knows them logically prior to the divine decree.[38] Thus, limiting the type of God can bring into existence. Flint explains as follows:

> For example, if God knows a counterfactual of creaturely freedom which we might symbolize as (C→A), then he knows that he cannot make a world in which circumstances C are actual but action A is not performed. For to make such a world, he would have to bring it about that C is actual; but, since (C→A) is prevolitionally true, God knows that his bringing about C would as a matter of fact lead to A's being performed. Hence, since any complete set of counterfactuals of creaturely freedom which God might know to be true would restrict God to making a certain type of world, let us refer to such a set as a *creaturely world- type*.[39]

---

[37] Laing (n 14) 149 (emphasis mine).

[38] Craig (n 15) 267. See also; Timpe (n 18) 335; Kirk R MacGregor, *A Molinist-Anabaptist Systematic Theology* (University Press of America, 2007) 39; William Lane Craig, 'Middle Knowledge, Truth–Makers, and the "Grounding Objection"' (2001) 18 *Faith and Philosophy* 338-339.

[39] Flint (n 5) 48. World-type terminology was first introduced in Flint's dissertation, 'Divine Freedom' (PhD Thesis, University of Notre Dame, 1980); Thomas P Flint, 'The Problem of Divine Freedom' (1983) 20(3) *American Philosophical Quarterly* 255-264.

In other words, 'a creaturely world-type is a complete set of counterfactuals'.[40] Otherwise, a more complicated explanation:

T is a creaturely world-type iff [41] T is a set such that, for any proposition s,

(i) s is a member of T only if either s or $\sim s$ is a counterfactual of creaturely freedom, and

(ii) if s is a counterfactual of creaturely freedom, then either s or $\sim s$ (but not both) is a member of i, and

(iii) if s is a counterfactual of creaturely freedom and s is not a member of T, then there exists a counterfactual of creaturely freedom $s*$ such that

(a) $s*$ has the same antecedent as s, and

(b) $s*$ is a member of T.[42]

There are three important characteristics of creaturely world-types that should be noted.

Firstly, 'whichever creaturely world-type is true is only contingently true'.[43] Given a creaturely world-type takes into consideration freedom in the libertarian sense, and since this type of freedom is not compatible with necessatarianism, creaturely world-types are only contingently true.

Secondly, 'God cannot cause a particular creaturely world-type to be true'.[44] A creaturely world-type highlights how an agent would freely act in any given circumstance; so God is only able to decide

---

[40] Laing (n 14) 150.

[41] 'if and only if'.

[42] Flint (n 5) 49. Flint also proposed two other possible descriptions:
(CWT3) T is a creaturely world-type iff for any counterfactual of creaturely freedom $(C \rightarrow A)$, either $(C \rightarrow A)$ or $(C \rightarrow \sim A)$ is a member of T; and
(CWT4) T is a creaturely world-type iff for any counterfactual of creaturely freedom $(C \rightarrow A)$, either $(C \rightarrow A)$ is a member of T or there exists a proposition $A*$ such that $(C \rightarrow A*)$ is a counterfactual of creaturely freedom and $(C \rightarrow A*)$ is a member of T.
See Flint (n 51) 49-50.

[43] Flint (n 39) 257.

[44] Flint (n 39) 257.

which creaturely world-type is true if He determines the truth value of counterfactuals of creaturely freedom. However, given the truth of libertarianism, God cannot do this as it's logically impossible to make someone do something freely.[45] Therefore, 'which creaturely world-type is true is a contingent fact not determined by God'.[46]

Thirdly, 'every creaturely world-type determines a unique galaxy'.[47] A galaxy is a group of possible worlds in which a specific creaturely world-type holds.[48] Understanding creaturely world-types aids in our understanding of what it is logically possible for God to do and what God has the power to do.[49]

Since creaturely world-types determine a galaxy, those being worlds consisting of counterfactuals that God did not determine; God is only able to actualise worlds which are members of this galaxy. These are called feasible worlds.[50]

With these concepts covered, the next concept to understand is possible world semantics.

F *Possible World Semantics*

The phrase 'possible world' is used by philosophers as 'a maximal description of reality, or a way reality might be'[51] that are governed, in general, by broad logical possibility.[52]

---

[45] Timothy R Phillips and Dennis L Okholm, *Christian Apologetics in the Postmodern World* (InterVarsity Press, 2009) 92. See also; Alvin Plantinga, 'Against Naturalism' in Alvin Plantinga and Michael Tooley, *Knowledge of God* (John Wiley & Sons, 2009) 3; John S Feinberg, *Theologies and Evil* (University Press of America, 1979) 71.

[46] Flint (n 39) 257.

[47] Flint (n 39) 257.

[48] Laing (n 14) 152.

[49] Plantinga (n 28_ 172-173, 180-184. See Flint (n 39) 257.

[50] Flint (n 39) 257. See also; Justin Mooney, 'Best Feasible Worlds: Divine Freedom and Leibniz's Lapse' (2015) 77(3) *International Journal for Philosophy of Religion* 225; Wierenga, 'Perfect Goodness and Divine Freedom' (2007) 48(3) *Philosophical Books* 208.

[51] William Lane Craig, *Reasonable Faith* (Crossway, 3rd ed, 2008) 183.

[52] Bob Hale, 'Absolute Necessities' (1996) 30(10) *Philosophical Perspectives* 93-117.

A possible world can either be 'feasible' or 'infeasible', depending on the truth value of counterfactuals.

As mentioned earlier, a feasible world is a description of those worlds which God has the power to actualise, while infeasible worlds are worlds that God cannot actualise. Craig explains:

> For although it is logically possible that God actualise any possible world (assuming that God exists in every possible world), it does not follow therefrom that it is feasible for God to actualise any possible world. For God's ability to actualise worlds containing free creatures will be limited by which counterfactuals of creaturely freedom are true in the moment logically prior to the divine decree.[53]

Although there may be an infinite number of possible worlds known by God by His natural knowledge, there is also an endless number of possible worlds that are not actualisable 'because the counterfactuals of creaturely freedom which must be true in order for Him to weakly actualise such worlds are in fact false'.[54] For example, there may be a possible world in God's natural knowledge where Peter does not deny Christ in the exact same circumstances ('C') in which he did.[55] Though this is logically possible, because there is no positive truth value for the counterfactual 'if Peter were in C, he would not deny Christ', God cannot use His middle knowledge to weakly actualise a world where Peter does not deny Christ in C, for the truth value of this proposition is false and thus, God cannot actualise a world where Peter does not deny Christ in C. As Craig remarks, 'this [delimitation] might be thought to impugn divine omnipotence, but in fact such a restriction poses no non-logical limit to God's power'.[56]

---

[53] Craig (n 7) 180, citing Flint (n 39) 257.

[54] Craig (n 7) 181, citing Alvin Plantinga, 'Self-Profile' in James Tomberlin and Peter Van Inwagen (eds), *Alvin Plantinga* (D Reidel, 1985) 50-52.

[55] See Matthew 26:31-75; Mark 14:29-72; Luke 22:33-66; John 18:15-27. See also; Roger David Aus, *Simon Peter's Denial and Jesus' Commissioning Him as His Successor in John 21:15-19: Studies in Their Judaic Background* (University Press of America, 2013) 170.

[56] Craig (n 7) 181, citing Flint and Freddoso (n 33) 93-98.

As Flint and Freddoso maintain:

> [t]here will be some state of affairs ... which even an omnipotent agent is incapable of actualising. And since this inability results solely from the logically necessary truth that one being cannot causally determine how another will freely act, it should not be viewed ... as a kind of inability which disqualifies an agent from ranking as omnipotent.[57]

In other words, actualising an infeasible world is logically impossible because it is a logically impossible act. But the infeasible world in and of itself is logically consistent and logically possible.[58]

On Molina's view, 'it could be said that it is up to God whether we find ourselves in a world which we are predestined' that is, God chooses which world to actualise, 'but that it is up to us whether we are predestined in the world in which we find ourselves', for the agent determined the truth value of counterfactuals of creaturely freedom.[59]

Logically posterior to natural knowledge is middle knowledge, the second logical moment.[60]

G *Middle Knowledge*

Middle knowledge is 'God's knowledge of what every possible free creature would do under any possible set of circumstances'.[61] As Laing explained, 'middle knowledge also proposes that God has knowl-

---

[57] Flint and Freddoso (n 33) 95.

[58] 'Molinism and Infallibility', *Religion & Spirituality Podcast* (Reasonable Faith, 2016).

[59] William Lane Craig, *The Problem of Divine Foreknowledge and Future Contingents from Aristotle to Suarez* (BRILL, 1988) 204, citing Theodore Regnon, *Bannesianisme et Molinisme* (Retaux-Bray, 1890) 48. See also; Edmond Vansteenberghe, *Le Dictionnaire de théologie catholique*, sv, "Molinisme" 10.2 cols 1028-9; Craig (n 59) 204.

[60] MacGregor (n 38) 71. See also; William Lane Craig, "Men Moved By the Holy Spirit Spoke From God' (2 Peter 1.21): A Middle Knowledge Perspective on Biblical Inspiration' in Michael C Rea (ed), *Oxford Readings in Philosophical Theology: Providence, Scripture, and Resurrection* (Oxford University Press, 2009) 180.

[61] Craig (n 14) 130.

edge of counterfactuals of creaturely freedom'.[62] Counterfactuals take the form, 'placed in situation C, A would do B'.[63]

Finally, Molina explained middle knowledge as follows: 'before any free determination of His will, by virtue of the depth of His natural knowledge . . . He discerns what the free choice of any creature would do by its own innate freedom'.[64]

William Hasker notes the following regarding Molinism and its use of middle knowledge:

> If you are committed to a 'strong' view of providence, according to which, down to the smallest detail, 'things are as they are because God knowingly decided to create such a world,' and yet you also wish to maintain a libertarian conception of free will – if this is what you want, then Molinism is the only game in town.[65]

Zagzebski sings similar praise, middle knowledge is '[p]erhaps the most ingenious solution to the dilemma of foreknowledge and freedom'.[66] Although some reject the doctrine of middle knowledge based on the grounding objection,[67] it is not within the scope of this

---

[62] Laing (n 14) 128.

[63] Francesco Piro, 'The Philosophical Impact of Molinism in the 17th Century' in Matthias Kaufmann and Alexander Aichele (eds), *A Companion to Luis de Molina* (BRILL, 2014) 372.

[64] Luis de Molina, *Concordia: Disputations* 49 (n 11). See Molina (n 14) 119. Cf Anfray (n 20) 358.

[65] William Hasker, 'Response to Thomas Flint' (1990) 60(1/2) *Philosophical Studies* 117-18.

[66] Linda Trinkaus Zagzebski, *The Dilemma of Freedom and Foreknowledge* (Oxford University Press, 1996) 125.

[67] Steven B Cowan, 'The Grounding Objection to Middle Knowledge Revisited' (2003) 39(1) *Religious Studies* 93-102; Alexander Zambrano, 'Truthmaker and the Grounding Objection to Middle Knowledge' (2001) 21(1) *Aporia* 19-34; Robert Adams, 'An Anti-Molinist Argument' (1991) 5 *Philosophical Perspectives* 343-353. William Lane Craig explains the grounding objection as follows: 'It is the claim that there are no true counterfactuals concerning what creatures would freely do under certain specified circumstances–the propositions expressed by such counterfactual sentences are said either to have no truth value or to be uniformly false–, since there is nothing to make these counterfactuals true. Because they are contrary–to–fact conditionals and

chapter to address this objection.[68]

Like natural knowledge, middle knowledge is pre-volitional and therefore its truth value is independent of God's will.[69] Likewise, middle knowledge is similar to free knowledge in that the truths known are contingent; they depend on creaturely will.[70]

Molina wrote:

> The third type is middle knowledge, by which in virtue of the most profound and inscrutable comprehension of each faculty of free choice, He saw in His own essence what each such faculty would do with its innate freedom were it to be placed in this or that or, indeed, in infinitely many orders of things--even though it would really be able, if it so willed, to do the opposite.[71]

Thus, the substance of God's middle knowledge can be understood as a nearly infinite number of propositions of the form,

If person, P, were in circumstance, C, then P would freely perform action, A.

It is important to highlight that the actual existence of P or C is not a necessary condition for God possessing this knowledge. Molina maintained that God not only knew of state of affairs that would obtain but also that would not obtain. Furthermore, Molina argued that God knew how free creatures would act if placed in non-actual state of affairs, '[i]t is clear from Sacred Scripture that the supreme God has

---

are supposed to be true logically prior to God's creative decree, there is no ground of the truth of such counterfactual propositions. Thus, they cannot be known by God.' [Citation from Craig (n 38) 338.]

[68] See responses by John Laing, *Middle Knowledge: Human Freedom in Divine Sovereignty* (Kregel Academic, 2012) ch 2; Craig (n 38) 337-352; Tyler Crown, 'Truth-Makers and the "Grounding Objection" to Molinism' (2018) 4(1) *The Liberty Undergraduate Journal for Philosophy of Religion* art. 2; Alvin Plantinga, 'Reply to Robert Adams' in James E Tomberlin et al (eds), *Alvin Plantinga* (D Reidel Publishing Company, 1985) vol 5 371-382.

[69] Laing (n 14) 127.

[70] Laing (n 14) 127. See also; Flint (n 26) 158.

[71] Luis de Molina, *Concordia* 4.52.9 in Molina (n 14) 168.

certain cognition of some future contingents that depend on human free choice, but that neither have existed nor ever will exist in reality and that hence do not exist in eternity either'.[72]

Molina's biblical support for God possessing counterfactual knowledge will not be discussed in this chapter,[73] nor will a philosophical defence of whether God has middle knowledge will be provided in this chapter.[74]

The third logical moment in God's knowledge is free knowledge.[75]

H *Free Knowledge*

Free knowledge refers to the part of God's knowledge which He knows by His decision to actualise the world. The content of this knowledge is of what actually exists (or will exist).[76] This knowledge is contingent, and contains 'only metaphysically contingent truths, or truths that could have been prevented by God if He had chosen to create different situations, different creatures, or to not create at all'.[77] Molina stated that, in His free knowledge, God knows 'absolutely and determinately, without any condition or hypothesis, which ones from among all the contingent states of affairs were in fact going to obtain and, likewise, which ones were not going to obtain'.[78]

The truths known in His free knowledge are contingent and dependent on God's free will.[79]

The diagram opposite illustrates the three logical moments in God's knowledge.

---

[72] Luis de Molina, *Concordia* 4.49.9 in Molina (n 14) 116. See also; Laing (n 14) 128.

[73] See Laing (n 14) 130-140; MacGregor (n 3) ch 3.

[74] See Craig (n 18) 95–100; Craig (n 15) 237–278; Daniel J Hill, *Divinity and Maximal Greatness* (Psychology Press, 2005) 111–125; Stratton and Erasmus (n 6) 17-29.

[75] Craig (n 18) 82-83. See also Timpe (n 18) 335.

[76] Laing (n 14) 125.

[77] Laing (n 14) 126. See also Keith E Yandell, *The Epistemology of Religious Experience* (Cambridge University Press, 1994) 112; Michael J Loux and Dean W Zimmerman, *The Oxford Handbook of Metaphysics* (Oxford University Press, 2005) 180.

[78] Luis de Molina, *Concordia* 4.52.9 in Molina (n 14) 168.

[79] Flint (n 26) 157.

Diagram 1.0:

MOMENT ONE:

··· ○   ○   ○   ○   ○   ○ ···

NATURAL KNOWLEDGE: *God knows the range of possible worlds*

MOMENT TWO:

··· ○   ○   ○ ···

MIDDLE KNOWLEDGE: *God knows the range of feasible worlds*

DIVINE CREATIVE DECREE

MOMENT THREE:

···   ○   ···

FREE KNOWLEDGE: *God knows the actual world*

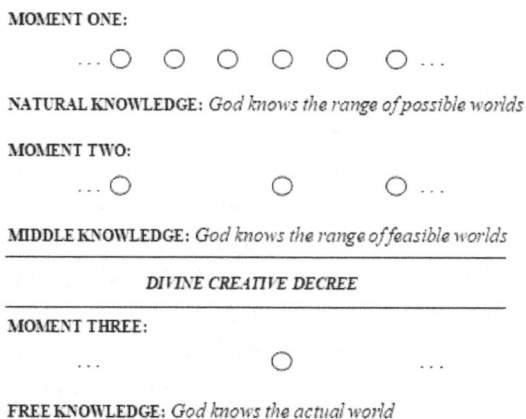

III BUT, IF GOD IS OMNISCIENT

'But, if God is omniscient and thus, knows all our decisions, how do we possess free will?' In response, some people have adopted a view called theological fatalism which holds that if God foreknows what you're going to do, then you are fated to do it and therefore, everything happens necessarily.80 The argument can be put in syllogistic form:

1. Necessarily if God foreknows x, then x will happen.

2. God foreknows x.

3. Therefore, x will necessarily happen.[81]

---

[80] Nelson Pike, 'Divine Omniscience and Voluntary Action' (1965) 74 *Philosophical Review* 27-46. See also the revised version in Nelson Pike, *God and Timelessness, Studies in Ethics and the Philosophy of Religion* (Routledge & Kegan Paul; Schocken, 1970) ch 4; Bernard B Poggi, 'Towards a Renewed Theology of Personal Agency: Origen's Theological Vision and the Challenges of Fatalism and Determinism' (2018) *Jesuit School of Theology Dissertation* i fn 1; Linda Zagzebski, "Recent work on Divine Foreknowledge and Freewill' in Robert Kane (ed), *The Oxford Handbook of Free Will* (Oxford University Press, 2002) 45.

[81] Craig (n 14) 72.

This has the logical form:

1. $\Box P \to Q$

2. P

---

3. $\Box Q$[82]

This however, commits an elementary logical fallacy because the conclusion – (3) – does not follow from the premises (1) – (2).[83] From (1) – (2), it only follows that x will happen, not that x will necessarily happen. Thus the necessity of God's knowledge being accurate and His knowledge of x happening do not necessitate x happening. Medieval philosophers identified this fallacy and coined it confusing the *necessitas consequentiae* (necessity of the consequences) with the *necessitas consequentis* (necessity of the consequent).[84] That is to say, the deduction of Q from the premises $\Box(P \to Q)$ and P is necessary in respect with *modus ponens*; but the consequent of the conditional $\Box(P \to Q)$, Q itself, is not itself necessary.[85]

In other words, although (2) 'God foreknows x' follows necessarily from (1) – 'necessarily if God foreknows x, then x will happen', the conclusion – (3) 'therefore, x will necessarily happen' – does not necessarily follow from (1).

A valid form of the argument is:

1. Necessarily if God foreknows x, then x will happen.

2. God foreknows x.

---

3. Therefore, x will happen.

---

[82] The letters 'P' and 'Q' are being used to represent propositions.

[83] J P Moreland and William Lane Craig, *Philosophical Foundations for a Christian Worldview* (InterVarsity Press, 2009) 71-2; Craig (n 14) 69-74.

[84] Moreland and Craig (n 83) 72. See also; Norman Kretzmann and Susan Linn Sage, *The Metaphysics of Creation: Aquinas's Natural Theology in Summa Contra Gentiles II* (Oxford University Press, 1999) 158; Parmenides and David Gallop (ed), *Parmenides of Elea: Fragments: A Text and Translation with an Introduction* (University of Toronto Press, 1991) 38 fn 70; Simo Knuuttila, *Reforging the Great Chain of Being: Studies of the History of Modal Theories* (Springer Science & Business Media, 2013) 174.

[85] Moreland and Craig (n 83) 72.

This has the logical form:

1. $\Box P \rightarrow Q$
2. P

_____

3. Q

This form of the argument does not preclude that x cannot be $\neg x$. It is entirely possible for x to fail to happen ($\neg x$). However, if $\neg x$ was true, then God would have not foreknown x. From the fact that God knows x will happen, we know with absolute certainty that x will happen. But x will not necessarily happen, $\neg x$ could be true.

What is impossible is that both God foreknows x and x fails to happen, for this is a logical contradiction. We cannot, however, construe that because both God knowing x will happen and x not happening cannot both be true, that this is a limitation on human freedom. Freedom, in this case, is the ability of either one being true. Although x can fail, x will not fail.

x will not happen because God foreknows x will happen; God knows x will happen because x will happen. This does not mean that x happening causes God's foreknowledge. The word 'because' here indicates a logical, not a causal relation. Similar to that articulated in the phrase 'four is an even number because it is divisible by two'. The word 'because' communicates a logical relation of ground and consequent.[86]

God's foreknowledge is chronologically prior to x happening, but x is logically prior to God's foreknowledge. x happening is the ground; God's foreknowledge is its logical consequent. x happening is the reason why God foreknows x $\neg x$ is possible, and if that were the case, God would have foreknown $\neg x$.[87]

Contemporary theological fatalists identify the modal fallacy presented in the previous argument, so an attempt has been made to make

_____

[86] Craig (n 14) 73-74.
[87] Craig (n 14) 74. See also; Paul Copan, *That's Just Your Interpretation: Responding to Skeptics Who Challenge Your Faith* (Baker Books, 2001) 82; MacGregor (n 38) 90.

the second premise as necessary to form a valid argument.[88] The argument is reformulated as follows:

    1. Necessarily if God foreknows x, then x will happen.

    2. Necessarily, God foreknows x.

---

    3. Therefore, x will necessarily happen.[89]

This has the logical form:

$$1. \ \Box P \rightarrow Q$$
$$2. \ \Box P$$

$$3. \ \Box Q$$

Because premises (1) and (2) are necessary, a necessary conclusion – (3) – follows.90 However, this does not mean that this is a sound argument. If (2) can be demonstrated to be false, then the conclusion is also false.

The content of God's foreknowledge isn't necessary. For God could have actualised a different world, and thus, the content of His foreknowledge would be different. Although it is necessary that whatever God foreknows is true, it does not logically follow that what God knows is necessary. To argue otherwise is to say that this is the only world God could create and that He created it necessarily.[91]

However, a different sort of necessity is often argued called the 'necessity of the past'. According to theological fatalists, unlike the future, the past is necessary. This is expressed as stating that the past is unalterable or unpreventable. And since God's foreknowledge is in the

---

[88] William Lane Craig, *Time and Eternity: Exploring God's Relationship to Time* (Crossway, 2001) 258. See also Calvin Pinchin, *Issues in Philosophy: An Introduction* (Springer, 2014) 169; J R Lucas, *The Freedom of the Will* (Oxford University Press, 1970) ch 14; Timpe (n 18) 337.

[89] Craig (n 14) 72.

[90] Moreland and Craig (n 83) 71.

[91] Craig (n 14) 75.

past (since He has always foreknown what He foreknows), the future likewise is necessary. Therefore, divine foreknowledge is incompatible with human freedom.

Craig offers a solution to this proposition – 'it is important to distinguish between changing the past or future and causing the past or future'.[92]

To alter the past would be to bring it about that an event that transpired did not transpire. To alter the future is to prevent a future act that will occur, from occurring. It is self-refuting to maintain that an event that occurred has not occurred; thus altering the past is impossible. Likewise, claiming to prevent an event that will occur from occurring is also logically impossible.[93]

As the British philosopher A J Ayer explained:

> The past is closed in the sense that what has been has been: if an event has taken place there is no way of bringing it about that it has not taken place; what is done cannot be undone. But it is equally true, and indeed [definitional], that what will be will be; if an event will take place there is no way of bringing it about that it will not take place; . . . for if it were prevented it would not be something that will be done.[94]

However, to cause ('C') the past, an event must be produced in the past so that the effect ('E') occurs before the cause. Thus, causing the past requires E → C, while causing the future requires C → E. That is, causing the future requires the cause to precede the effect. Therefore, causing the past or future is not synonymous with altering the past or future. Because in the case of causation, the effect remains unchanged

---

[92] Craig (n 14) 76.

[93] Moreland and Craig (n 83) 520. See also; Margarita Vázquez Campos and Antonio Manuel Liz Gutiérrez, *Temporal Points of View: Subjective and Objective Aspects* (Springer, 2015) 297; John Roy Burr and Milton Goldinger, *Philosophy and Contemporary Issues* (Pearson, 2004) 446; Peter Streveler, 'The Problem of Future Contingents: A Medieval Discussion' (1973) 47 *The New Scholasticism* 241; Brian Garrett, 'Fatalism: A Dialogue' (2018) 17(49) *Think* 77; John Martin Fischer and Patrick Todd, *Freedom, Fatalism, and Foreknowledge* (Oxford University Press, 2015) 264 fn 39.

[94] A J Ayer, *The Problem of Knowledge* (Macmillan; 1956) 189.

However, if the future cannot be changed, doesn't this entail fatalism? By no means, what has been has been and what will be will be necessarily. However, 'fatalism holds that what has been has necessarily been and that what will be will necessarily be'.[95]

Unalterability does not imply fatalism. According to Ayer, 'if [the fatalist's] only ground for saying that an event is fated to occur is just that it will occur, or even that someone knows that it will, there is nothing more to his fate than the triviality that what happens at any time happens at that time, or that if a statement is true it is true'.[96] Even fatalist's like Taylor admit, 'all these seemingly grave observations are really utterly trivial, expressing only what is definitionally true'.[97]

So while both the past and future are unalterable, this does not imply fatalism.

Although we cannot change the future, we can cause the future, freely. Our present actions aid in determining future outcomes. It is our ability to cause the future that provides us with freedom, and the idea that the future is open. Can we, however, cause the past? Whilst this is certainly an interesting question, it falls outside the scope of this chapter.[98]

So then, how can we cause the future?

When God chose to actualise a world, through His middle knowledge, He took into consideration the counterfactuals of creaturely freedom. That is, if P were in C, P would do A.

---

[95] Craig (n 14) 78.

[96] Ayer (n 94) 191.

[97] Richard Taylor, 'Prevention, Postvention, and the Will' in Keith Lehrer (ed), *Freedom and Determinism* (Humanities, 1976) 73.

[98] For papers on backward causation see Craig (n 14) 78-82, ch 7; Craig (n 15), ch 6; Jan Faye, 'Backward Causation' in Edward N Zalta (ed), *The Stanford Encyclopedia of Philosophy* (2018) <https://plato.stanford.edu/archives/sum2018/entries/causation-backwards>; Michael Dummett and Antony Flew , 'Symposium: ""Can An Effect Precede Its Cause?"' (1954) 28(1) *Aristotelian Society Supplementary* 27–62; Max Black, 'Why Cannot an Effect Precede Its Cause?' (1956) 16(3) *Analysis* 49–58.

This pre-volitional knowledge occurs logically prior to the divine decree. Once God chooses to actualise a world, then future-tense truth makers become actual. That is, there is a transition from the hypothetical, 'P would do X in C' to 'P will do X in C'.

So the truth value of the counterfactual – if P were in C, P would do X – has a catalyst effect of future consequences. For example, God knew Judas would betray Christ in a specific state of affairs, which would have the result of Judas leading the soldiers to arrest him.[99]

The truth-value of what Judas would do caused the future event – the arrest of Christ. Under Molinism, God knows all the outcomes of the free actions of creatures, including the free responses of other creatures to those actions. So, in this sense, what creatures would freely do in any given circumstance, in conjunction with the chains of causation and creaturely responses throughout history, is how we *cause* the future. In summary, our actions have consequences, and those consequences shape the future.

The final section will apply Molinism to the spread of COVID-19 and how human beings can be held responsible for their actions, albeit the event being foreknown and decreed by God.

IV MOLINISM AND COVID-19: A PRACTICAL APPLICATION

With Molinism explained, this section will demonstrate how the Molinist perspective promotes human efforts to prevent epidemics, cope with them, and change the way of life to lower their impact.

Molinism has been applied to various theological and non-theological issues such as scriptural inspiration,[100] salvation,[101] the perse-

---

[99] John 18:1-13; Luke 22:47-54; Matthew 26:47-56; Mark 14:43-50.

[100] See Craig (n 60) 45-52.

[101] See Craig (n 7) 172-188; Keathley (n 14); Ken Keathley, 'A Molinist View of Election, or How to Be a Consistent Infralapsarian' in Brad J Waggoner (ed), *Calvinism: A Southern Baptist Dialogue* (B&H Publishing Group, 2008) 195-215.

verance of the saints,[102] papal infallibility,[103] evolutionary theory,[104] Christology,[105] and the problem of evil.[106] The latter applies to the CO-VID pandemic.

A question understandably posed in this troubled time is, 'why does God allow something like COVID-19 to change everything? Why has God allowed a world in which a virus can run rampant in this kind of way?' This is the classic problem of suffering; however, it's a particular type of suffering. It's an event which could be argued that it's not necessarily because of human freedom that we see this virus having its impact, it's part of nature if you will.

I think in this pandemic, we probably have some suffering that is the fusion of both natural and moral evil because, although the epidemic is caused by a virus, it seems that human factors could have been, although disputed, involved in its initial careless handling in the laboratory in Wuhan, China.[107] The mishandling in the laboratory may have resulted in it being unintentionally released into the world. So there may have been both the human factor and the natural factor involved. At a minimum, human involvement has lead to the spread of

---

[102] William Lane Craig, "Lest Anyone Should Fall': A Middle Knowledge Perspective on Perseverance and Apostolic Warnings' (1991) 29 *International Journal for Philosophy of Religion* 65-74.

[103] Thomas P Flint, 'Middle Knowledge and the Doctrine of Infallibility' in James E Tomberlin (ed) *Philosophy of Religion* (Ridgeway, 1991) vol 5 373-93.

[104] Del Ratzsch, 'Design, Chance and Theistic Evolution' in William Dembski (ed), *Mere Creation* (InterVarsity Press, 1998) 289-312.

[105] Thomas P Flint, "A Death He Freely Accepted': Molinist Reflections on the Incarnation' (2001) 18(1) *Faith and Philosophy* 3-20.

[106] See Kenneth J Perszyk, 'Molinism and Theodicy' (1998) 44(3) *International Journal for Philosophy of Religion* 163-184; Kenneth J Perszyk, 'Free Will Defence with and without Molinism' (1998) 43(1) *International Journal for Philosophy of Religion* 29-64; Plantinga (n 54) 36-55; Plantinga (n 11); William Dembski, *The End of Christianity* (Broadman & Holman, 2009).

[107] Although disputed. See Anthony Galloway and Eryk Bagshaw, 'Australian Concern over US spreading Unfounded Claims about Wuhan Lab', *The Sydney Morning Herald* (online, 7 May 2020) <https://www.smh.com.au/politics/federal/australian-concern-over-us-spreading-unfounded-claims-about-wuhan-lab-20200506-p54qhp.html>; Peter Daszak, 'Ignore the Conspiracy Theories: Scientists Know COVID-19 Wasn't Created in a Lab', *The Guardian* (online, 9 June 2020) <https://www.theguardian.com/commentisfree/2020/jun/09/conspiracies-covid-19-lab-false-pandemic>.

the virus, either due to negligence, recklessness, or sheer ignorance.

One of the things that we might take away from this event is that it illustrates that, due to our cognitive limitations, we are simply not in a position to judge, with any sort of confidence, the probability for God having morally sufficient reasons for permitting the suffering to occur.[108] Seemingly trivial events in history can be amplified to have worldwide repercussions so that we have no idea whatsoever why a certain event might have been permitted by God to occur. And if indeed it's correct that this virus was unleashed on the world through the careless handling of a laboratory technician in Wuhan, this illustrates so well that a seemingly, isolated, inconsequential event can have truly worldwide repercussions as it's amplified. Irrespective of the genesis of this virus, we can see from this pandemic that seemingly insignificant events can have global ramifications. This ought to make us very cautious about saying of any particular evil or suffering that God cannot have, or that it is improbable that He has, morally sufficient reasons for allowing it to occur.

But, if God exists, then why are believers taking precautions? Don't they trust in God? Likewise, if the world has been decreed in such a way that everything that will happen, will happen, then why are precautions taken?

God does not exempt Christians from suffering in this world, we in fact ought to know that as we follow a crucified saviour who was innocently tortured and executed.[109] So, the idea that no precautions

---

[108] Moreland and Craig (n 83) 504. See also; James A Keller, 'The Problem of Evil and the Attributes of God' (1989) 26(3) *International Journal for Philosophy of Religion* 155-171; Henry J Schuurman, 'Two Concepts of Theodicy' (1993) 30(3) *American Philosophical Quarterly* 209-221; Nelson Pike, 'Hume and Evil' in Robert Merrihew Adams and Marilyn McCord Adams (eds), *The Problem of Evil* (Oxford University Press, 1990) 41; William Hasker, 'Defining 'Gratuitous Evil': A Response to Alan R. Rhoda' (2010) 46(3) *Religious Studies* 303-309.

[109] Matthew 27:1-54; Mark 15:1-40; Luke 23:1-48; John 19:1-30. See also; Ernest De Witt Burton, 'Sources of the Life of Jesus outside the Gospels' (1900) 15(1) *The Biblical World* 26-35; Tacitus, *Annals* 15.44; Lucian, 'The Death of Peregrine' in *The Works of Lucian of Samosata*, tr H W Fowler and F G Fowler (Clarendon Press, 1949) vol 4 11-13; Gary Habermas, *The Historical Jesus* (College Press Publishing Company, 1996) 206 and Michael Licona's monumental book *The Resurrection of Jesus:*

should be taken but trust in God is quite naïve. We take precautions because we know God has established a world that operates according to natural laws and that He is not going to preferentially exempt Christians from the consequences of those laws.

According to the Bible, God's overall purpose for the human race is to lovingly and freely bring them into an eternal saving relationship with Himself (1 Tim. 2:4, 2 Pet. 3:9).[110] This life is not all there is, and therefore, the purpose of life is not happiness in this life. Instead, God's purpose in history is to freely bring men and women into an eternal loving relationship with Himself, and that is an incommensurable good.[111] Not merely because it's eternal and everlasting, but because God is Himself infinite goodness and love. And so to be in a personal relationship with the infinite good is incomparable. So, when God permits horrible suffering in this life, it is only to accomplish His ultimate purposes, which is to bring people freely into a relationship with an incommensurable good, which far outweighs the shortcomings of this finite existence.

Although under the Molinism everything that happens in the world has been decreed by God,[112] human beings are still responsible for taking precautions because God took into consideration the counterfactuals of creaturely freedom to accomplish His will. Just as this chapter has established that foreknowledge is compatible with human freedom, likewise human freedom and responsibility are compatible with God's decree in the same manner.

God's decision to actualise this world took into consideration the counterfactuals of creaturely freedom. That is, what human beings would do in freedom permitting circumstances.

A New Historiographical Approach (IVP Academic, 2010).

[110] 1 Timothy 2:3-4 '3 This is good, and it is pleasing in the sight of God our Savior, 4 who desires all people to be saved and to come to the knowledge of the truth.'; 2 Peter 3:9 '9 The Lord is not slow to fulfil his promise as some count slowness, but is patient toward you, not wishing that any should perish, but that all should reach repentance.'

[111] John Calvin, *Commentary on Matthew 23:34*. See John Calvin, *Commentary on a Harmony of the Evangelists Matthew, Mark and Luke*, tr Rev William Pringle (The Edinburgh Printing Company, 1846) vol 3 101.

[112] Luis De Molina, *Foreknowledge*, 4.14.15.53.3.17. See also; MacGregor (n 3) 115-121.

Given that the truth value of counterfactuals of creaturely freedom are not determined by God,[113] and given this libertarian conception of freedom, the agent determines which counterfactuals are true;[114] though it's presumably up to God which (if any) antecedents to actualise.[115] Therefore, agents are held morally responsible.

On this basis, it can be argued that under Molinism, if a counterfactual represents an evil act, God merely *permits* evil to occur since He does not determine the truth value of counterfactuals.[116]

While God's sovereignty extends to everything that comes to pass, it does not follow that God wills everything that comes to pass. God wills the good, but does not will evil decisions, but merely permits. Molina explained,

> All *good* things, whether produced by causes acting from a necessity of nature or by free causes, depend upon divine predetermination . . . and providence in such a way that each is *specifically intended* by God through His predetermination and providence, whereas the *evil* acts of the created will are subject as well to divine predetermination and providence to the extent that the causes from which they emanate and the general concurrence on God's part required to elicit them are granted through divine predetermination and providence – though not in order that *these particular acts* should emanate from them, but rather in order that *other, far different*, acts might come to be, and in order that the innate freedom of the things endowed with a will might be preserved for their maximum benefit; in addition evil acts are subject to that same divine predetermination and providence to the extent that they cannot exist in particular unless God by His providence *permits them in particular* in the service of some greater good. It clearly follows from the above that all things

---

[113] See William J Wainwright, *Philosophy of Religion, Wadsworth Basic Issues in Philosophy Series* (Wadsworth Publishing Corporation, 1988) 28; Craig (n 15) 272.
[114] Craig (n 15) 273, 276.
[115] Perszyk (n 105) 170.
[116] Ibid.

without exception are *individually* subject to God's will and providence, which intend certain of them *as particulars* and permit the rest *as particulars*.[117]

Therfore, everything that happens occurs either by God's permission or His will.[118]

As previously discussed, although we can't *change* the future, we can cause the future. This *causation* occurred when God took into consideration the counterfactuals of human freedom when actualising the world. This is accomplished by Molinism's functional equivalence of backward causation; however, it does not possess the problems associated with backward causation.

Molinism's functional equivalence of backward causation works as follows, 'agent A can do non-B, even if God has fore[known or decreed] that A will do B, but at the moment in which he will have done non-B, it will have been true from eternity that God has fore[known] non-B'.[119]

It is worth quoting MacGregor at length, however, amending his words accordingly to fit into the pandemic narrative:

> To illustrate, suppose there was a [worldwide viral pandemic]. In his middle knowledge, God knows that if he were to permit this evil event (because he knows he could work through it to bring about a greater good), then when the [virus is] reported on the news ... a mother would freely pray that her son wasn't [infected]. Consequently, in his creative decree God decides to actualize a feasible world where God permits the [pandemic] but protects the son from [being infected]. But had God instead middle-known that if he were to permit the [pandemic], then when the [pandemic

---

[117] Molina, *On Divine Foreknowledge* 4.53.3.17. Cf. Moreland and Craig (n 83) 563 (emphasis from source).

[118] Moreland and Craig (n 83) 563.

[119] Piro (n 63) 394 citing Bernardo de Aldrete, *SI, Commentariorum et Disputationum in Primam Partem D. Thomae, de Visione et Scientia Dei, 2 vols.* (Lyon, 1662) vol 1 disp 23 305-15, disp. 27 389-406.

is] reported on the news the mother would not freely pray for her son, God in his creative decree may well decide to actualize a different feasible world with exactly the same history as the aforementioned world up to the moment of the [pandemic] but where the son is [infected]. Hence even though I cannot change the past, through prayer I can affect the past. I can pray in such a way that had I not prayed, the past would have been different than it in fact is. Even though this is not backward causation (making the past no longer the past), it is what I have called in another place a 'functional equivalent to backward causation'.[120] For it accomplishes, in a non-contradictory way, the aim of causally impacting the past without altering the past. The past cannot be altered, but the reason the past is the way it is consists in my divinely middle-known prayer in the present or future. Consequently, on Molinism, the past is not counterfactually closed, an observation Molina implied in reflecting on the scriptural truth that God knows the end from the beginning (Isa 46:10).[121] Through prayer, then, we do have some degree of counterfactual power over the past.[122]

Under the Molinist schema, we can have confidence that our actions, whether be past, present, or future, have been taken into consideration in God's decree. We can, therefore, be assured that our actions to prevent the spread of the virus are not done in vain, and they do cause the future.

Aquinas also echoed this principle:

When considering the problem of the usefulness of prayer, one must remember that divine providence not only disposes what effects will take place, but also the manner in which they will take place, and which actions will cause them.... [W]e do not pray in order to change the decree of divine providence, rather we pray in order to impetrate those things

---

[120] MacGregor (n 38) 89.
[121] Molina, *Concordia*, 5.19.6.2.1.
[122] MacGregor (n 3) 126-127, citing Flint (n 5) 243.

which God has determined would be obtained only through our prayers.[123]

Following Augustine and other Christian writers, Molina claimed that God would not permit an instance of evil if He couldn't (or wouldn't) bring about a greater good, 'though the evil may not itself be a necessary condition for that good'.[124]

Therefore, God's decree and plan for the world takes into consideration the counterfactuals of creaturely freedom. This includes evil that occurs as a consequence of human actions to bring about His purpose, the greater good.

It is through the Molinist's view of foreknowledge, divine providence, and human freedom that best promotes human efforts to prevent epidemics, cope with them, and change the way of life to lower their impact.

V CONCLUSION

In conclusion, this chapter has demonstrated how the Christian-Molinist perspective promotes human efforts to prevent epidemics, cope with them, and change the way of life to lower their impact. Furthermore, this philosophical system also provides a reconciliation between God's sovereignty, foreknowledge and human freedom.

The first section of this chapter explained Molinism and the different elements within this belief system. Molinism holds to the presupposition that man has freedom in the libertarian sense and that God's knowledge can be understood in three logical moments – natural knowledge, middle knowledge, and free knowledge.

Natural knowledge is God's knowledge of all necessary truths – these truths are independent of His will; while the truths known in His free knowledge are contingent and dependant on His will. Middle knowledge is God's knowledge of counterfactuals, these truths are

---

[123] Thomas Aquinas, *Summa Theologiae*, 2a2ae, 83, 2. Cf Flint (n 5) 212.
[124] Perszyk (n 105) 170. See Luis de Molina, *Concordia*, disputation 53, part 3, ss 9 and 17.

contingent and, like the truths possessed in His natural knowledge, independent of His will.

Using God's middle knowledge, God can actualise any feasible world, also known as a creaturely world-type, He so desires to fulfil His will. The actual world possesses state of affairs that are both strongly and weakly actualised. The former being when God causally determines an event's obtaining whilst the latter involves God allowing an event to obtain.

Although God is omniscient, section II demonstrated how man still has free will and is responsible for his actions. Though the future is known from eternity past, the future is not faded to occur. While we can't *change* the future or past, we can cause the future, and as explained, the mechanics of Molinism allows a functional equivalence of backward causation; however, it does not possess the problems associated with backward causation.

The final section argued that Molinism promotes human efforts to prevent epidemics, cope with them, and change the way of life to lower their impact. This was done by revealing that, according to Molinism, God takes into consideration the counterfactuals of creaturely freedom to accomplish His purpose. God works *with* the will of man, not *on* the will of man.[125] In this way, our actions – past, present, and future – have a *real* impact in this world, and thus, our efforts to prevent, cope and change our way of life amid a pandemic are not without warrant, albeit being foreknown and decreed.

---

[125] This is also known as divine (or simultaneous) concurrence. For more information see Anfray (n 20) 348-352; Piro (n 63) 374-375, 398-403; Friedrich Stegmüller, *Geschichte des Molinismus. I: Neue Molinaschriften* (Aschendorff, 1935) 194-201; Moreland and Craig (n 83) 563-564.

13

Interposition: Magistrates as Shields against Tyranny

STEVEN ALAN SAMSON*

ABSTRACT

The conduct of politics proper, through the arts of persuasion, may be contrasted with despotism, which relies upon coercion. Historically, regimes that secure the rule of law, constitutional limitations, civil liberty, and self-government are a remarkable but often short-lived achievement. A crucial part of this history has been played by a form of resistance, or civil disobedience, known as interposition. Indeed, politics and freedom emerge from the often-brutal conflict of powerful stakeholders. Historical sketches, including precedents for interposition by lawful magistrates, lead into an essay on trends that enhance or threaten the well-being of communities as well as the institutions that enable human flourishing.

I FIRST CONSIDERATIONS

The political culture of the West emerged by fits and starts over a long span of time. Civic order arose independently in scattered places at various times as people's liberties and the rule of law periodically waxed and waned. What Francis Lieber referred to as 'civil liberty and self-government' has many ancestors and undergone countless

* B.A., M.A., PhD. Retired Professor of Government and former Department Chairman with the Helms School of Government at Liberty University, Virginia, U.S.A.

trials.[1] An outstanding part of this history has been played by acts of innovation, confrontation, even a form of resistance or civil disobedience known as interposition, by leaders in positions of authority. As Kenneth Minogue has emphasized, politics began as 'the business of the powerful: citizens, nobles, property-owners, patriarchs—all had power and status.'

> It was essential to the idea of the state, in all its forms, that it should be an association of *independent* disposers of their own resources. ... It was precisely because the state was composed of masterful characters that it could not turn into a despotism. Having projects of their own, powerful individuals of this kind had no inclination to become the instruments of someone else's project. This is the sense in which despotism and politics are precisely opposed, and the state was distinguished by the right of the individual to dispose of his (and in time her) own property.[2]

II HISTORICAL VIGNETTES

In 930 AD Iceland's Althing first met at the Law Rock in the fissure zone of a long rift valley where the Eurasian and North American tectonic plates slowly pull the volcanic island apart. In this stark setting the elected Lawspeaker recited the laws to the assembled chieftain-priests (the *godar* or godly ones). There in the year 1000 the Lawspeaker Thorgeir Ljosvetningagodi, a still-pagan chieftain-priest, declared Christianity to be the official religion, although certain pagan practices were retained.[3]

In that same millennial year in the Carpathian basin, the Grand Prince Stephen, adopting a German Christian custom, was crowned and consecrated as the first Hungarian king and presided over nearly

---

[1] Francis Lieber, *On Civil Liberty and Self-Government* (J B Lippincott, 3rd rev ed, 1877).

[2] Kenneth Minogue, *Politics: A Very Short Introduction* (Oxford University Press, 2000) 112.

[3] Gwyn Jones, *A History of the Vikings* (Oxford University Press, rev ed, 1984) 282-86.

forty years of relative peace. Nine centuries later the last bearer of the Crown of St Stephen, the young Emperor Charles acceded to the throne of the Dual Monarchy halfway through the First World War and died in exile on Madeira five years later, having tragically failed in his courageous and ultimately self-sacrificial bid to end the war, due in part to a series of betrayals on all sides.[4] Seen from one standpoint a heroic act of conscientious objection may be regarded as treason from another.

The Christian Middle Ages were the great seedtime of the liberties we enjoy today. In 1033 the humble monks of a Benedictine monastery at Thorn Ey, near King Canute's residence on the Thames, held a contested election that went through several ballots before a new abbot was formally elected. Before long King Edward the Confessor began expanding the monk's church into today's Westminster Abbey and built a palace that 'was eventually transformed into the Houses of Parliament.'[5]

Institutionally divided and limited power is the cornerstone of the western political tradition. The Decrees of León in 1188 made León the first kingdom to accord representation to the common people, along with the king, the clergy, and nobility. Kings John of England and Andrew II of Hungary were soon forced by their nobility to accept restraints on their power through Magna Carta (1215) and the Golden Bull (1222), respectively.[6] Magna Carta, drafted by Stephen Langton, the Archbishop of Canterbury, and imposed by the barons, was intended to restore 'what the barons claimed had formerly been the relationship between the King and the feudal magnates.'[7] It was subsequently reconfirmed at least forty times.

---

[4] See Gordon Brook-Shepherd, *The Last Habsburg* (New York: Weybright and Talley, 1968); Erik von Kuehnelt-Leddihn, *Leftism: From de Sade and Marx to Hitler and Marcuse* (Arlington House, 1974) 244-47.

[5] Charles Colson and Harold Fickett, *The Faith* (Zondervan, 2008) 212.

[6] See Helen Silving, 'The Origins of the Magnae Cartae' (1965) 3 *Harvard Journal of Legislation* 117; Helen Silving, *Sources of Law* (William S Hein and Co, 1968) 237-49.

[7] Sydney D Bailey, *British Parliamentary Democracy* (Houghton Mifflin, 2nd ed, 1962) 14.

Another baronial revolt demanded representation in the king's government, which led to the Provisions of Oxford in 1258 and the creation of the Privy Council. Simon de Montfort later called the Great Parliament of 1265 in order to strip King Edward III of his unlimited authority and even ruled for a time in his stead. It was the first representative assembly in England to include merchants as well as the landed nobility.[8] Limited government is the byproduct of usurpations as well as forcible interpositions – acts of intervention or resistance – by rulers, councils, and magistrates.

In 1628, as a result of disputes over customs duties and forced loans to finance the Thirty Years War, Parliament presented Charles I with the Petition of Right to compel him to consult it on matters of state and the purse. The King granted the petition as an act of grace but refused to be bound by its terms. The following year he dissolved Parliament and – supported by revenue from the Irish gentry – ruled by royal prerogative for eleven years until he needed funds for the Bishops' Wars in Scotland.

The King summoned the Short Parliament in the Spring of 1640, so named because it quickly deadlocked over longstanding grievances and opposition to an invasion of Scotland. He then turned to merchants for loans and raised an army in August, but it was repelled by the Scots within days, leaving the King with a mounting ransom bill and a Scottish army occupying northern England. In November he again summoned Parliament. This time Parliament's ultimate control of the purse strings strengthened its hand, enabling it to finally pass major reforms, which included the Triennial Act, which allowed this so-called Long Parliament to stay in session for many years, and abolition of the Star Chamber. A series of confrontations and protests culminated in the King's fruitless invasion of Parliament early in 1642 to seize five members he accused of treason.[9]

The ensuing Civil War and Interregnum inspired a remarkably

---

[8] Ibid 57.
[9] Conrad Russell, *The Crisis of Parliaments: English History, 1509-1660* (Oxford University Press, 1971) 326-29, 338-39.

fertile period of political and religious thought, including the West-minster Confession's chapter on liberty of conscience.[10] Precedents and models from what John Selden styled the Hebrew Republic were a major inspiration to reformers.[11] The lively Putney Debates held within Oliver Cromwell's New Model Army in 1647 gave voice to the grievances and perspectives of ordinary soldiers, whose lives were dominated by the ruling gentry.

Politics and freedom emerge from the often-brutal conflict of powerful interests.[12] They operate best within a relatively free market of persuasion rather than coercion.

III THE THREEFOLD RISE OF CIVIC ORDER

Cater-corner across the continent and two millennia earlier, the citizens of ancient Athens discussed public affairs in the marketplace and gathered forty times a year at the Pnyx as members of the Assembly (*ekklesia*), deciding issues up or down. The political agenda was set by the Council (*boule*) of 500 that served as the full-time government for a year. It was chosen by lot, as were members of its presiding committee (*prytanes*) for a given month.

In 406 BC the board of ten generals (*strategoi*) in charge of military operations intervened to save the Athenian fleet at the Battle of Arginusae but were prevented by a storm from rescuing drowning sailors or retrieving their bodies. So great was the public outrage that the generals were summoned to answer directly to the Assembly. In a courageous act of interposition, only Socrates, who had been appointed president (*epistates*) of the Assembly for that single day, used his office to stand against mob rule and for due process by opposing a mass trial. The following day hotter heads prevailed; the generals

---

[10] See Gai M Ferdon, *The Political Use of the Bible in Early Modern Britain: Royalists, Republicans, Fifth Monarchists and Levellers* (Jubilee Centre, 2013) <https://www.jubilee-centre.org/ebooks/political-use-bible-early-modern-britain-dr-gai-ferdon>.

[11] Gertrude Himmelfarb, *The People of the Book: Philosemitism in England, from Cromwell to Churchill* (Encounter, 2013) 26-27.

[12] In *Discourses on Livy*, Book One, chapters four and five, Machiavelli makes a similar observation about how conflicts between the people and the elites fostered liberty.

were found guilty and took the hemlock, adding a second disaster to the first.

After its final defeat by Sparta two years later, Athens fell under a reign of terror by the Thirty Tyrants, during which time Socrates again stood for the rule of law and refused to arrest an opponent of the Thirty. The general amnesty that followed their overthrow was disregarded by the enemies of Socrates, who pressed spurious charges against him a few years later. Socrates chose death over exile.[13] His memory was preserved by his students, notably Plato and Xenophon, as an embodiment of the classical *paideia*.

A century earlier, according to Livy's traditional account, the Romans overthrew a now despotic Etruscan monarchy in 509 BC and introduced a republic under the leadership of the tribune Lucius Junius Brutus, who was himself a member of the royal family. Although he was afterward elected consul, several of his in-laws and his two sons later conspired to restore the monarchy. Brutus and his fellow consul had them arrested and executed.[14]

Historically, despotism is the default position of worldly rule and may be just as descriptive of a democracy or a republic as of a monarchy.[15] It often takes time and considerable confrontation for freedom to filter down to the lower ranks of society. When the much-oppressed underclass of plebeians seceded from Rome in 494 BC and took sanctuary on the Sacred Mount, the ruling patricians introduced a series of reforms, including creation of Tribunes of the Plebs to protect them. Even so, discrimination persisted.[16]

According to tradition, the turbulent son of Lucius Quinctius Cincinnatus, a very able leader who served as consul, killed a plebeian

---

[13] Plato, *The Apology*, 32a-e, 42; Xenophon, *Conversations of Socrates*, trans. Hugh Tredennik and Robin Waterfield (Penguin, 1990) 72. See Bettany Hughes, *The Hemlock Cup: Socrates, Athens and the Search for the Good Life* (Alfred A Knopf, 2013) 59ff.

[14] Livy, *The Early History of Rome*, trans. Aubrey de Sélincourt (Penguin, 1960) bk 1, 57-60, bk 2, 4-5.

[15] See Minogue, above n.2, chapter one.

[16] Livy, above n 12, bk 2, 23-25.

and fled into exile. Cincinnatus was held liable and forced to sell his property to pay the heavy fine, then retired to a humble farm. One day, he was approached by a delegation from Rome while at work. He laid down his plow, put on his toga, and was greeted with the grant of a dictatorship in order to save Rome from an invading army. He accepted this open-ended offer of unlimited power and returned to Rome to raise an army. Fifteen days later he relinquished power and returned to his plow, having defeated the enemy and won their allegiance to Rome.

On another occasion, Cincinnatus was called upon to deal with Spurius Maelius, a wealthy patrician who allegedly sought to buy the people's support. The man who would be king died while resisting arrest.[17]

Democratic but often tyrannical Athens and republican but increasingly corrupt Rome soon enough went the way of all flesh. A third civil order was born out of the crumbling remains of the western Roman Empire through the spiritual challenge posed by the Christian faith and, earlier, by Judaism, both of which articulated world-and-life views based on divine revelation that were radically at odds with the imperial order and its classical ideals. To the cardinal virtues of wisdom, courage, temperance, and justice, the Christians added faith, hope, and caritas, translated alternatively as love and charity. A new civilisation began to emerge.[18]

IV THE GREAT SOURCEBOOK

As the Apostle Paul noted, all authority is delegated by God (Rom 13:1) for defined but limited purposes. The ideals of limited government – 'with malice toward none, with charity for all'[19] – are readily derived from the narratives of Scripture: indeed, from the necessary boundaries, divisions, and judgments that restrain, compartmentalize, and redeem errant individuals, institutions, and governing authorities.

---

[17] Ibid bk 2, 14, 26-30, bk 4, 13-16.
[18] See Minogue above n 2, ch 4.
[19] Abraham Lincoln, Second Inaugural Address, March 4, 1865.

The giving of God's commandments was accompanied by blessings for obedience and curses for disobedience (Deut 28).[20] 'In the Abrahamic Covenant, the covenantal blessing that God will be a God and a Father to us and our seed after us is linked with the covenantal command to "walk before me and be thou perfect."'[21] Failure to follow the Great Commandment (Matt 22:35-40) leads repeatedly to suffering, judgment, exile, and, sometimes, repentance.

The Bible remains a great sourcebook of practical political wisdom. Divine warnings and human responses to abuses of power are depicted, for example, in Jotham's parable of the trees (Jud 9:7-21), Samuel's speech to the people (1 Sam 8), the people's intercession on Jonathan's behalf (1 Sam 14:45), Azariah opposing Uzziah's usurpation of power (2 Chron 26:16-20), the people's resistance to an unjust ruler (1 Kings 12:1-14), Jeremiah's rescue by Ebed-Melech (Jer 38:4-13, 39:16-18), Peter's resistance to an unjust command (Acts 5:29), and Paul's appeals to both Roman law and Jewish faith (Acts 22:25-23:10).

In terms of worldview, philosophical insights and practical applications may be drawn from a careful reading of the scattering of nations (Gen 11:6-9), the tithe to Melchizedek (Gen 14:18-20), Jethro's recommendation of a federal division of governance (Ex 18:19-26), the gracious provision of God's Law (eg Ex 20-23, Deut 5-6), restraints on kings (Deut 17:14-20), the cities of refuge (Deut 19, Josh. 20), the revelatory witness of the Prophets (Jer 29:4-8; Hos 3:4-5), Jesus on servant leadership (Mark 9:35) and giving both God and Caesar their due (Matt 22:11), Paul's counsel to 'be subject to the governing authorities' (Rom. 13:1), and his practical definition of the love we owe (Rom 13:7-10). From such judicious examples one might reasonably

---

[20] The 9th century English King Alfred the Great prefaced his Laws with the Ten Commandments and otherwise drew upon the Bible as a source. See Harold J Berman, *Law and Revolution: The Formation of the Western Legal Tradition* (Harvard University Press, 1983) 65.

[21] Louis DeBoer, 'The Fundamental Biblical Tactic for Resisting Tyranny' Gary North (ed) *Christianity and Civilization*, 3: *Tactics of Christian Resistance* (Geneva Divinity School, 1983).

expect the development of a system of separate spheres of authority mediated by checks and balances to help restrain abuses of power.

The Bible dramatically reveals the full scope of human depravity on the historical stage and honestly portrays the way people, driven by envy and ambition, bear false witness, turn colleagues and families against each other, and deflect blame onto rivals. The child sacrifices practiced by apostate kings such as Ahaz (2 Kings 16:3) and Manasseh (2 Kings 21:6) resemble initiation rituals that bind, on pain of death, criminal conspiracies. The singular wickedness of Queen Jezebel, who criminally deprived a landowner of both his property title and his life, has made her name a byword down to the present day. Her treacherous but feckless husband, King Ahab, scorned Elijah as his enemy. Nevertheless, when Elijah confronted him with a crime akin to Cain's, Ahab repented of Naboth's murder and was reprieved (1 Kings 21:20).

V BIBLICAL REALISM

An examination of the evidence should make it evident that a heavy dose of Biblical realism is needed to strengthen wisdom generally and statecraft specifically in the face of social contagions and their consequences. One scholar who has done so, René Girard, characterizes the dynamic, transactional, underlying motive behind scandals and violent conflicts as "mimetic desire," which draws us into envy and rivalry.[22] In The One By Whom Scandal Comes, Girard singles out for analysis a familiar passage from the Sermon on the Mount (Matt 5:38-40) about turning the other cheek and handing over one's tunic:

> Most people today regard these injunctions as a utopian sort of pacifism, manifestly naïve and even blameworthy because servile, doloristic, perhaps even masochistic. ...
>
> This reading pays only glancing attention to St. Matthew's text, which presents us with two examples: someone who slaps us without provocation; and someone who sues us for

---

[22] René Girard, *I See Satan Fall Like Lightning*, trans James G Williams (Orbis, 2001) 10.

our tunic, the main article of clothing, often the only one, in Jesus's world. Gratuitously reprehensible conduct of this sort suggests the presence of an ulterior motive. We are dealing with people who wish to infuriate us, to draw us into a cycle of escalating conflict. They do everything they can, in other words, to provoke a response that will justify them in retaliating in turn; to manufacture an excuse for legitimate self-defense. For if we treat them as they treat us, they will be able to disguise their own injustice by means of reprisals that are fully warranted by the violence we have committed. It is therefore necessary to deprive them of the negative collaboration they demand of us.

Violent persons must always be disobeyed, not only because they encourage us to do harm, but because it is only through disobedience that a lethally contagious form of collective behavior can be short-circuited. Only the conduct enjoined by Jesus can keep violence from getting out of hand, by putting a stop to it before it starts.[23]

We see this principle illustrated by King Saul's repeated, unanswered provocations against David while David's refusal to harm God's anointed king led him to take refuge in the wilderness for a time (1 Sam 19, 24). Elijah, who stood against Ahab and the priests of Baal, similarly fled into the wilderness to escape the wrath of Jezebel before being sent back on a final errand (1 Kings 18-19). The Suffering Servant of Isaiah 53 is described as silent toward his oppressors. God spoke through Jeremiah to the exiles in Babylon: 'And seek the peace of the city where I have caused you to be carried away captive, and pray to the LORD for it; for in its peace you will have peace' (Jer 29:7). Captives and exiles like Joseph, Daniel and his friends, Mordechai, and Nehemiah suffered much in rendering service but, proving themselves faithful stewards, were elevated to offices of trust by foreign monarchs.

---

[23] René Girard, *The One by Whom Scandal Comes*, trans. M B DeBevoise (Michigan State University Press, 2014) 19-20.

Here a question naturally arises: How may we honor those in authority yet hold them accountable when they do not act the part of 'a minister to us for good' (Rom 13:4) or deliberately provoke us? For those of us who have been nurtured within representative institutions, what responsibility do we have to hold the governing authorities accountable? And through what procedures?

VI HARBINGERS OF LIMITED GOVERNMENT

The spread of Christianity and the institutional struggles between church and state – as empires receded and nation-states rose – increasingly brought the individual onto the historical stage. The independent status and Christian character of the English system of common law has had the long-term effect of restraining the powers that be.[24] As the cleric and lawyer Henry of Bracton put it at the outset:

> The king himself ... ought not to be under man but under God, and under the law, because the law makes the king. ... [F]or there is no king where will, and not law, wields dominion. That as a vicar of god he [the king] ought to be under the law is clearly shown by the example of Jesus Christ.[25]

The Germanic tradition of elective warrior kings was gradually Romanized and Christianized to the point where increasingly the king was expected to defend the faith without, however, exercising authority over it. Kings emerged as lords over the lords of realms. Government by consent emerged out of the king's right to counsel from his leading vassals, an ancestor of the 'advise and consent' function of the United States Senate.[26]

The growing recognition that ordinary people are beloved of God gradually transformed cultural norms and encouraged a restructuring of the civil order to ensure the rule of law, both civil and ecclesias-

---

[24] See Augusto Zimmermann, *The Christian Foundations of Common Law*, vol 1: *England* (Connor Court, 2008) ch 8.

[25] Herbert W Titus, 'God's Revelation: Foundation for the Common Law' (1994) 4 (Spring) *Regent University Law Review* 1.

[26] Henry A Myers, *Medieval Kingship* (Nelson-Hall, 1982) 155.

tical.[27] This enabled, first, the barons and bishops of the land to be represented in government (Magna Carta and the rise of Parliament) and, gradually, permitted individuals of all classes to win economic and civil liberty. All this led M Stanton Evans to conclude:

> On net balance, it is fair to say, the Catholic Church of the Middle Ages was the institution in Western history that did the most to advance the cause of constitutional statecraft. This resulted from its constant readiness, in the spirit of the Hebrew prophets, to challenge the might of kings and emperors if they transgressed the teachings of religion.[28]

Yet there is also a reciprocating aspect in which kings and emperors at times play a positive role as defenders of the faith and protectors of reformers while asserting their own prerogatives.[29] The Investiture Struggle over the appointment of bishops led to what Eugen Rosenstock-Huessy called the Papal Revolution of the eleventh century, soon followed by the reintroduction of Roman civil law (the Institutes and the Code of Justinian). The protracted contest between emperors and the church hierarchy had a restraining effect on both. It was the first of a series of clerical, then secular, revolutions that shaped the West.[30] Similar upheavals inspired the great landmarks of liberty, the rise of representative institutions, even, ironically, the divine right of kings idea developed by Jean Bodin. Each revolution institutionalized changes we now take for granted but whose terms are ever open to renegotiation.

---

[27] Many unbelievers cherish this transformation and acknowledge the West's dependence on Christianity. See Marcello Pera, *Why We Should Call Ourselves Christians: The Religious Roots of Free Should Societies*, trans L B Lappin (Encounter, 2011); Roger Scruton and Mark Dooley, *Conversations with Roger Scruton* (Bloomsbury, 2016) ch 11; Tom Holland, *Dominion: How the Christian Revolution Remade the World* (Basic Books, 2019).

[28] M Stanton Evans, *The Theme Is Freedom: Religion, Politics, and the American Tradition* (Regnery, 1994) 152 (italics omitted).

[29] See Eugen Rosenstock-Huessy, *Out of Revolution: Autobiography of Western Man* (William Morrow, 1938) 382.

[30] Ibid 519-45.

The Truce of God [limiting warfare], the free choice of a profession, the liberty to make a will, the copyright of ideas—
these institutions are like letters in the alphabet which we
call Western civilization. ... They have emancipated the
various elements of our social existence from previous
bondage. ... A police force means nothing less than the
emancipation of the civilian within myself; for without it, I
should be forced to cultivate the rugged virtues of a vigilant
man. To free the courts from the whims of changing government exalts my will and testament to a kind of immortality:
something will endure when I have passed away. And so
each of these institutions was hailed as a deliverance. Not
one of them came into existence without the shedding of
streams of blood.[31]

Divided power helps check tyranny and favors greater accountability. The great Scholastic philosopher, St Thomas Aquinas, dealt with
the issue of sedition while carefully distinguishing it from lawful resistance to tyranny in his *Summa Theologica*. The difference between
them turns on the correspondence of law with the common good. 'The
sin of sedition is first and chiefly in its authors ... and secondly it is
in those who are led by them to disturb the common good,' he wrote.
Those who resist such seditious parties, however, are not themselves
seditious:

A tyrannical government is not just, because it is directed,
not to the common good, but to the private good of the ruler.
... Consequently there is no sedition in disturbing a government of this kind. ... [I]t is the tyrant rather that is guilty of
sedition, since *he encourages discord and sedition among his
subjects*, that *he may lord over them more securely*; for this is
tyranny, since it is ordered to the private good of the ruler and
to the injury of the multitude.[32]

---

[31] Ibid 30-31.
[32] *The Summa Theologica of Saint Thomas Aquinas* (Encyclopædia Britannica, 1952)
vol 2 584. *Secunda Secundae*, qu 42, art 2. Italics added to illustrate the deliberate
provocation.

In fact, Christian theories of resistance to tyranny and even tyrannicide were already extant in the Middle Ages at least a century before Aquinas. At their heart was a dynamic tension and an admonition to honor the office even when a particular officeholder is found unworthy. Procedures for bringing offenders to account developed within this context. John of Salisbury, who had gone into exile for a time with Thomas à Becket (who was later murdered in the cathedral as Archbishop of Canterbury), was an early contributor to the literature.[33] Examples of such resistance abound: John Wycliffe's and William Tyndale's translations of the Bible, the French Huguenots, the English Pilgrims and Puritans, John Hampden, Algernon Sidney, and many others.

VII INTERPOSITION BY PUBLIC OFFICERS

One of the most sophisticated forms of resistance is the doctrine of interposition in which, usually, lesser magistrates intervene to protect people against the abuse of power by higher authorities. Without the practice of interposition, the Protestant Reformation would have been stillborn. In 1520 Martin Luther addressed his letter *To the Christian Nobility of the German Nation* and called for a general council for the purpose of reforming the church.[34] Such councils had been called for the same purpose at earlier times, as in the case of the Councils of Nicaea and Chalcedon. A year later Luther was summoned to appear before the imperial Diet and condemned for heresy, a capital offense. But he was spirited away and kept in hiding at Wartburg Castle for a year by his prince, the Elector of Saxony, Frederick the Wise.[35]

Almost three decades later the same emperor, Charles V, tried to force the Protestants into submission. While the magistrates of Magdeburg resisted, the pastors of the city drafted the Magdeburg Confession, an appeal to the emperor that stated the principle of defense by magistrates against tyranny. Charles placed Magdeburg under siege for more than a

---

[33] John of Salisbury, *Policraticus: Of the Frivolities of Courtiers and the Footprints of Philosophers*, Cary J Nederman (tr, ed) (Cambridge University Press, 1990) 201-05.

[34] J M Porter (ed), *Luther: Selected Political Writings* (Fortress Press, 1974) 37-49.

[35] Rosenstock-Huessy, above n 29, 380-81.

year before withdrawing. Four years later the Peace of Augsburg (1555) brought a truce between the Catholic and Lutheran parts of Germany.[36]

In the last chapter of the *Institutes*, John Calvin writes: 'The first duty of subjects towards their rulers, is to entertain the most honourable views of their office, recognising it as a delegated jurisdiction from God, and on that account receiving and reverencing them as the ministers and ambassadors of God.'[37] Here he stands on common ground with earlier theologians. Addressing the problem of bad rulers, Calvin notes that they may be God's means of bringing judgment on the iniquity of the people. He holds that rulers owe mutual duties to those under them, but this does mean 'that obedience is to be returned to none but just governors.' It is not for private persons to cure these evils but to implore the help of the Lord, who may raise up avengers from among His servants or, alternatively, use the fury of men who have their own motives.

> Let princes hear and be afraid; but let us at the same time guard most carefully against spurning or violating the venerable and majestic authority of rulers. ... Although the Lord takes vengeance on unbridled domination, let us not therefore suppose that that vengeance is committed to us, to whom no command has been given but to obey and suffer.[38]

Yet it is at this very point that Calvin introduces a subtle shift of emphasis for which he had carefully prepared:

> I speak only of private men. For when popular magistrates have been appointed to curb the tyranny of kings (as the Ephori, who were opposed to kings among the Spartans, or Tribunes of the people to consuls among the Romans, or Demarchs to the senate among the Athenians; and perhaps there is something similar to this in the power exercised in each

---

[36] 'The Magdeburg Confession' [1550] <http://magdeburgconfession.com/mag/>; see also <http://www.zum.de/whkmla/military/16cen/magdeburg1551.html>.

[37] John Calvin, *Institutes of the Christian Religion*, bk 4, ch 20, [22]. <https://www.biblestudytools.com/history/calvin-institutes-christianity/book4/chapter-20.html>.

[38] Ibid [31].

kingdom by the three orders, when they hold their primary diets), so far am I from forbidding these officially to check the undue license of kings, that if they connive at [ignore or fail to act against] kings when they tyrannize and insult over the humbler of the people, I affirm that their dissimulation is not free from nefarious perfidy, because they fraudulently betray the liberty of the people, while knowing that, by the ordinance of God, they are its appointed guardians.

xxxii. But in that obedience which we hold to be due to the commands of rulers, we must always make the exception, nay, must be particularly careful that it is not incompatible with obedience to Him to whose will the wishes of all kings should be subject, to whose decrees their commands must yield, to whose majesty their scepters must bow. And, indeed, how preposterous were it, in pleasing men, to incur the offence of Him for whose sake you obey men! The Lord, therefore, is King of kings. When he opens his sacred mouth, he alone is to be heard, instead of all and above all. We are subject to the men who rule over us, but subject only in the Lord. If they command anything against him let us not pay the least regard to it, nor be moved by all the dignity which they possess as magistrates—a dignity to which no injury is done when it is subordinated to the special and truly supreme power of God.[39]

Beginning with this opening wedge, the doctrine of interposition emerged by stages. John Knox, the founder of the Presbyterian Church of Scotland, appealed to the Scottish nobility over his condemnation by the bishops and clergy. His Appellation (1558) systematically advanced the doctrine of interposition as a principle of resistance by lesser magistrates.[40] The legal historian Harold J Berman wrote that, despite a positivism that 'finds the ultimate sanction of law in political coercion,' the Reformation built on the earlier Christianising of the

---

[39] Ibid [31]-[32].

[40] John Knox, 'The Appellation from the Sentence Pronounced by the Bishops and Clergy: Addressed to the Nobility and Estates of Scotland' (1558) <http://www.swrb. com/newslett/actualNLs/appellat.htm>.

law and assumed 'the existence of a Christian conscience among the people and a state governed by Christian rulers.'[41] He added that we owe 'to Calvinist congregationalism the religious basis of our concepts of social contract and government by consent of the governed.'[42]

Interposition was further developed a few years after Calvin's death in 1564 through various Huguenot tracts, such as *François* Hotman's *Franco-Gallia*, Theodore Beza's *Right of Magistrates*, and the anonymous *Vindiciae contra Tyrannos*.[43] Its articulation at that time reflects the Protestant experience with both royal and ecclesiastical persecution during the protracted religious warfare in France that only abated in 1598 with the Edict of Nantes. Specifically, the doctrine holds that when a ruler violates his oath of office – the 'covenants and contracts passed between him and the people'[44] – he is in a state of rebellion and forfeits his lawful authority. Other (perhaps lesser) magistrates may then raise their standard against him to restore constitutional rule.[45]

Drawing on Aquinas's discussion of tyranny, the anonymous Huguenot writer Junius Brutus, who is generally believed to be Philippe de Mornay, made a succinct case for interposition by officeholders in the *Vindiciae* (1579):

> [I]n this their action, we must not esteem them as private men and subjects, but as the representative body of the people, yea, and as the sovereignty itself, which demands of his minister an account of his administration. Neither can we in any good reason account the officers of the kingdom disloyal, who in this matter acquit themselves of their charge.
>
> There is ever, and in all places, a mutual and reciprocal obligation between the people and the prince; the one promises

---

41 Harold J Berman, *The Interaction of Law and Religion* (Abington Press, 1974) 67.

42 Ibid 68. See also 161 fn 16.

43 Julian H Franklin (tr, ed), *Constitutionalism and Resistance in the Sixteenth Century: Three Treatises by Hotman, Beza, & Mornay* (Pegasus, 1968).

44 Junius Brutus, *A Defence of Liberty Against Tyrants: or, Of the lawful power of the Prince over the People and of the People over the Prince* (Still Waters Revival, 1989) 147.

45 Franklin, above n 43, 86-87, 110-13, 196-97.

to be a good and wise prince, the other to obey faithfully, provided he govern justly. The people therefore are obligated to the prince under condition, the prince to the people simply and purely. Therefore, if the prince fail in his promise, the people are exempt from their obedience, the contract is made void, the right of obligation of no force. . . .

It is therefore permitted the officers of a kingdom, either all, or some good number of them, to suppress a tyrant; and it is not only lawful for them to do it, but their duty expressly requires it; and, if they do it not, they can by no excuse colour their baseness.[46]

Two kinds of officers are held eligible to interpose their authority to protect the people: general officers of the realm, which in America include Congress and the Supreme Court, and those who govern any province, city, or other governing unit, such as governors, mayors, and sheriffs. 'Private subjects, however, may not draw the sword against a tyrant by conduct [a lawfully installed ruler turned tyrant] since he was created not by all severally but by all together.'[47]

Early during the English Civil War, which Rosenstock-Huessy regarded as the true English Revolution, the Rev Samuel Rutherford, a Scottish Presbyterian pastor, left room for legitimate popular resistance and held that all rightful authority lies in law.[48]

Royalists say, a private man against his prince hath no way to defend himself but by flight; therefore, a community hath no other way to defend themselves but by flight. 1. The antecedent is false. Dr. Ferne alloweth to a private man supplications, and denying of subsidies and tribute to the prince, when he employeth tribute to the destruction of the commonwealth; which, by the way, is a clear resistance, and an active resistance made against the king (Rom. xiii. 6, 7) and against a commandment of God, except royalists grant tyrannous powers may be re-

---

[46] Brutus, above n 44, 134.

[47] Franklin, above n 43 (emphasis added).

[48] J F Maclear, 'Samuel Rutherford: The Law and the King' in George L Hunt (ed) *Calvinism and the Political Order* (Westminster Press, 1965) 77.

sisted. 2. The consequence is naught, for a private man may defend himself against unjust violence, but not any way he pleaseth: the first way is by supplications and apologies,--he may not presently use violence to the king's servants before he supplicate, nor may he use reoffending [attacking, retaliating], if flight may save. David used all three in order.[49]

In short, the procedural order – even for civilians – is petition, flight, and, as a last resort, fight.

Following these events and those of England's Glorious Revolution of 1688, the idea of interposition entered the common political parlance in part due to the Revocation of the Edict of Nantes in 1685, causing the entrepreneurial Huguenots to flee all over the Protestant world. One reason for their flight was the quartering of soldiers in private homes as a tool of provocation, a practice that continues today in Xinjiang. When Parliament passed a Quartering Act as one of several "Intolerable Acts" of 1774 directed at Massachusetts due to its resistance to parliamentary taxes, the colonists feared it could be used to billet soldiers in their own homes. These Coercive Acts, as Parliament itself called them, marked the point of no return. By the time of the Declaration of Independence, Benjamin Franklin proposed using the phrase 'Rebellion to tyrants is obedience to God' on the Great Seal of the republic, along with a scene of Pharaoh and his forces perishing as they pursued Moses and the freed Israelites.[50]

VIII ALBION'S SEED

Such avenues of resistance, self-governance, and exercising liberty of conscience[51] have resonated throughout American history, beginning

---

[49] Samuel Rutherford, *Lex, Rex, or the Law and the Prince* (Sprinkle Publications, 1982) 160; see also Daniel L Dreisbach, *Reading the Bible with the Founding Fathers* (Oxford, 2017) 123-35.

[50] Steve Straub, 'Rebellion to Tyrants is Obedience to God, Benjamin Franklin', 30 November 2012 <https://thefederalistpapers.org/founders/franklin/rebellion-to-tyrants-is-obedience-to-god-benjamin-franklin>.

[51] See L John Van Til, *Liberty of Conscience: The History of a Puritan Idea* (The Craig Press, 1972).

humbly with secret congregational meetings by religious separatists in England in defiance of the church establishment. Subsequent emigration by religious dissenters, defeated royalists, and a variety of other outcasts was organized through agreements and covenants for colonial self-government and, in some cases, royal charters.

Beginning in the 1620s, the significance of the Pilgrims and Puritans of New England for the self-understanding of later generations of Americans is difficult to overstate but easy to misrepresent. Colonial New England became a lively experiment: indeed, a laboratory of political innovation, including formal agreements and covenants, Bible-based law codes, citizenship oaths, a long tradition of election sermons, bicameral legislatures, and written constitutions with a separation of powers and federalism as organising principles.[52] To a long tradition of Anglican liberty, as Francis Lieber called it, self-governing, self-taxing colonists contributed imaginative blends of a uniquely American liberty and the basic political symbols that define the American experiment.[53]

Many of the great themes and issues of American history have been described or defined in language drawn from the Bible, such as 'city upon a hill,' 'garden' and 'wilderness,' 'covenant,' the 'house divided,' the 'grapes of wrath,' and the 'chosen people.' The sense of divine superintendence cherished by these early colonists remains powerful in some quarters. The spiritual aspirations of the Puritans and dissenters have colored the American mind more than is generally acknowledged.[54]

---

[52] On federalism, see Daniel J Elazar, 'Religious Diversity and Federalism' International Conference on Federalism, October 1999 <http://www.forumfed.org/library/religious-diversity-and-federalism/>.

[53] Donald Lutz (ed) *Colonial Origins of the American Constitution* (Liberty Fund,1998) xv-xix; Lieber above n 1, chs 5-23; Francis Lieber, 'Anglican and Gallican Liberty' *Miscellaneous Writings, vol 2: Contributions to Political Science, Including Lectures on the Constitution of the United States and Other Papers* (J B Lippincott, 1880) 371-88.

[54] See Erik von Kuehnelt-Leddihn, 'The Western Dilemma: Calvin or Rousseau?' in George A Panichas (ed), *Modern Age: The First Twenty-Five Years: A Selection* (LibertyPress, 1988) 520-31.

The historian Perry Miller, who was impressed by the Puritans' realism about human nature, wrote eloquently of the faith that could produce so firm a character:

> Puritanism would make every man an expert psychologist, to detect all makeshift "rationalizations," to shatter without pity the sweet dreams of selfenhancement in which the ego takes refuge from reality. A large quantity of Puritan sermons were devoted to ... exposing not merely the conscious duplicity of evil men, but the abysmal tricks which the subconscious can play upon the best of men. The duty of the Puritan in this world was to know himself – without sparing himself one bit, without flattering himself in the slightest, without concealing from himself a single unpleasant fact about himself.
>
> In the course of this sustained and unmitigated meditation, he perpetually measured himself by the highest imaginable excellency. The Puritan was taught to approve to approve of no act because it was good enough for the circumstances, to rest content with no performance because it was the best that be done in this or that situation. He knew indeed that life is imperfect, that the purest saints do not ever entirely disentangle themselves from the meshes of corruption, but though perfection was unattainable – even more because it was so – he bent every nerve and sinew to attempting the attainment.[55]

Other colonies were likewise practical expressions of a reforming – and often – religious purpose. George Calvert was granted a proprietary charter for Maryland to pursue his vision of Catholics and Protestants living in harmony. Quakers and Anabaptists found a haven in Pennsylvania, a proprietary colony begun by William Penn and assisted by George Fox. The Lords Proprietors of Carolina employed Lord Ashley's secretary, John Locke, to help draft a constitution. The last was Georgia, which like Rhode Island, became a refuge for outcasts, including Huguenots, Scottish Covenanters, and defaulting debtors who were offered a second chance. Such was

---

[55] Perry Miller and Thomas H Johnson (eds) *The Puritans: A Sourcebook of Their Writings* (Harper Torchbooks, 1963) vol 1, 284.

the diversity from which a common resistance against British colonial policies and practices was forged. David Hackett Fischer has identified four major British folkways, drawn from different parts of the United Kingdom, that shaped the American cultural landscape.[56] Daniel Elazar and Wilbur Zelinsky noted comparable political and geographical patterns.[57]

Taken together, these were the cultural and political seeds that germinated, over the first century and a half, into town meetings and colonial legislatures; the New England Confederation; unchartered New Haven's aid to two regicides and eventual annexation by Connecticut, which had been granted a charter; and the forced consolidation of several colonies into the short-lived Dominion of New England and resistance to Gov Edmund Andros as symbolized by the story of Connecticut's charter oak. The Glorious Revolution of 1688 restored the colonies but the Puritan experiment came to an end.

After a long period of "salutary neglect," the colonies' relationship to the Crown changed during the long reign of King George III that began in 1760. Some of the characteristic developments of this period include the Benjamin Franklin's proposed Plan of Union at the Albany Congress (1754) near the start of the French and Indian War; postwar boycotts against the Sugar Act, Stamp Act, and other protests against mercantilist restrictions and taxes; Samuel Adams's committees of correspondence between towns, counties, and provinces to exchange information; two continental congresses to knit a common response, including declarations of rights and a trade boycott; the Declaration of Independence; the Articles of Confederation; and the Constitutional Convention of 1787.

---

[56] See David Hackett Fischer, *Albion's Seed: Four British Folkways in America* (Oxford University Press, 1989) 783-898.

[57] Daniel J Elazar, *American Federalism: A View from the States* (Thomas Y Crowell, 1966) 85-140; Wilbur Zelinsky, *The Cultural Geography of the United States* (Prentice-Hall, rev ed, 1992) 117-28.

IX THE DISSIDENCE OF DISSENT IN THE AMERICAN COLONIES

Echoing John Adams,[58] Francis Grund, a nineteenth century Austrian émigré, believed that the character associated with 'the domestic virtue of the Americans' provided the key to understanding why the experiment with constitutional self-government succeeded as it had at the time he wrote (1837):

> The American Constitution is remarkable for its simplicity; but it can only suffice a people habitually correct in their actions, and would be utterly inadequate to the wants of a different nation. Change the domestic habits of the Americans, their religious devotion, and their high respect for morality, and it will not be necessary to change a single letter in the Constitution in order to vary the whole form of their government.[59]

In the eighteenth century, the patriot-pastors of the American colonies further developed a Bible-based literature of resistance even before the issue of taxation without representation became a central public question following the French and Indian War of 1754-1763. Earlier controversies over religious reform and revivalism helped set the stage for a deepening debate over and commitment to the principles of constitutional government, as Alice Baldwin illustrated in her pathbreaking study, *The New England Clergy and the American Revolution* (1928).

> The years from 1743 to 1763 were prolific in sermons, pamphlets, and petitions in which constitutional rights, civil and religious liberty, the right to resistance, etc., were more clearly defined and more positively asserted than ever before. Laymen as well as clergy, poor and unlearned as well as those of higher estate expressed their conviction in no uncertain terms, and again the Bible, natural law, the rights of Eng-

---

[58] John Adams, 'Letter to Massachusetts Militia, 11 October 1798 <https://founders. archives.gov/documents/ Adams/99-02-02-3102>.

[59] Francis J Grund, *The Americans in Their Moral, Social, and Political Relations* (Longman, Rees, Orme, Brown, Green, & Longman, 1837) vol 1, 307.

lishmen, covenants, charters, and statutes were drawn upon for arguments. ... The phrase "unalienable right" grew more common and the references to Locke, Sydney, and other radical theorists more frequent.[60]

The seeds of independence may be found scattered through the history of the colonies. But some of the key issues – such as taxation without representation, abuse of power, political and ecclesiastical tyranny – came to the fore during and immediately after the French and Indian War and led to acts of interposition by legislative assemblies, counties, and judicial bodies. Virginia, Massachusetts, Pennsylvania, and New York emerged as the major players in the struggle that led to independence.

The pulpit and the independent press were the most effective instruments for spreading republican political ideas during this period. While the relative influence of the American Puritan tradition of preaching in comparison with Whig political journalism is still a debated point among historians, Mark Noll acknowledges the seminal role played by Puritanism:

> [W]ithout the fertile soil of the American religious tradition, without particularly Puritan preoccupations with original sin, the ongoing battle against Satan, and the "liberty wherewith Christ hath made us free," Whig ideology would not have exerted such a powerful sway in leading the thought and guiding the actions of the Patriots. Similarities between the view of life in the world developed by American Christianity and Real Whig conceptions of political reality imported from England were responsible for the sense of cosmic importance and the fervent religiosity that permeated the Whig expressions of many Christians.[61]

---

[60] Alice M Baldwin, *The New England Clergy and the American Revolution* (Frederick Ungar, 1958) 65. Other good sources on the role of the clergy in the development of the American constitutional tradition include Gai M Ferdon, *A Republic If You Can Keep It* (Foundation for American Christian Education, 2008); Franklin P Cole, *They Preached Liberty* (LibertyPress, 1977); and Ellis Sandoz (ed), *Political Sermons of the American Founding Era, 1730-1805* (Liberty Press, 1991).

[61] Mark A Noll, *Christians in the American Revolution* (Christian University Press, 1977) 150.

Edmund Burke was perhaps the most insightful member of Parliament on this score. In his "Speech on Conciliation with the Colonies" (March 22, 1775), given before the first battles of the War for Independence, Burke spoke out against the use of force, which could only damage both sides and render them vulnerable to outside meddling. He extolled the colonists' devotion to 'Liberty according to English ideas, and on English principles,' noting that the 'great contests for freedom in this country were from the earliest times chiefly upon the question of Taxing.' The colonists were well versed in this history: 'The Colonies draw from you, as with their life-blood, these ideas and principles. Their love of Liberty, as with you, fixed and attached on this specific point of taxing.'[62]

Burke addressed his fellow parliamentarians in the name of these common principles, which had earlier been cited by Americans as in, for example, the Fairfax County Resolves of July 18, 1774 and other complaints.

[The] share of the people in their ordinary governments never fails to inspire them with lofty sentiments, and a strong aversion from whatever tends to deprive them of their chief importance. If anything were wanting to this necessary operation of the form of government, religion would have given it complete effect. Religion, always a principle of energy, in this new people is no way worn out or impaired; and their mode of professing it is also one main cause of this free spirit. The people are protestants; and of that kind which is the most averse to all submission of mind and opinion. This is a persuasion not only favourable to liberty, but built upon it. ... The dissenting interests have sprung up in direct opposition to all the ordinary powers of the world; and could justify that opposition only on a strong claim to natural liberty. Their very existence depended on the powerful and unremitted assertion of that claim. All protestantism, even the most cold and passive, is a sort of dissent. But the religion most prevalent in our Northern Colonies is a refinement on the principle

---

[62] Edmund Burke, *Select Works* (Liberty Fund, 1999) vol 1, 238.

of resistance; it is the dissidence of dissent, and the protestantism of the protestant religion.[63]

This is nowhere more evident than in the systematic but measured resistance of the colonists to taxes and regulations imposed by a Parliament that never consulted them. A year after Burke's appeal to Parliament and a few months after George III insisted upon passage of the American Prohibitory Act, which declared the American people to be outside the king's protection, Chief Justice William Drayton, who had been trained at the Inns of Court, echoed the indictment against James II nearly a century earlier in his charge to a South Carolina grand jury declaring formal independence from the Crown.[64] In July Congress passed its own Declaration of Independence.

In the *Oxford History of the American People,* Samuel Eliot Morison relates one soldier's account of the reasons for the separation:

> What made the farmers fight in 1775? Judge Mellen Chamberlain in 1842, when he was twentyone, interviewed Captain Preston, a ninetyoneyearold veteran of the Concord fight: 'Did you take up arms against intolerable oppressions?' he asked.
>
> 'Oppressions?' replied the old man. 'I didn't feel them.'
>
> 'What, were you not oppressed by the Stamp Act?'
>
> 'I never saw one of those stamps. I certainly never paid a penny for one of them.'
>
> 'Well, what then about the tea tax?'
>
> 'I never drank a drop of the stuff; the boys threw it all overboard.'
>
> 'Then I suppose you had been reading Harrington or Sidney and Locke about the eternal principles of liberty?'
>
> 'Never heard of 'em. We read only the Bible, the Catechism, Watt's Psalms and Hymns, and the Almanac.'
>
> 'Well, then, what was the matter? And what did you mean in going to fight?'

---

[63] Ibid 239-40.
[64] Evans, above n 28, 243-44.

'Young man, what we meant in going for those redcoats was this: we always had governed ourselves, and we always meant to. They didn't mean we should.'[65]

X 'THE MISCHIEFS OF FOREIGN INTRIGUE'

The Constitution of 1787 was the product of a special convention of delegates from all but one of the future states. It was subsequently ratified by each of the states that composed the new union. Suggested amendments were soon ratified together as the Bill of Rights, which, among other things, reserved to the states and the people those powers that had not been delegated to the central government. The resulting decentralized federal system depended on a practical consensus – a deliberate sense of the community, as the Federalist Papers put it, rather than any temporary majority vote. This resolve was soon tested by the French Revolution and the war it launched against the monarchies of Europe in 1792.

President Washington issued a Neutrality Proclamation in May of 1793, shortly after the arrival of Edmond Charles Genêt, the new ambassador of the French Republic. Citizen Genêt, as he was known, sought to raise a private navy to attack British and Spanish territories from American bases. Breaking a promise to Jefferson, he openly defied the Administration by appealing to the people for support. But before he could be recalled, the Committee of Public Safety came to power in France and instituted the infamous Terror. The now-regnant Jacobin faction sent a new ambassador with orders to arrest Genêt, who sought and was granted refuge.[66]

Agitation by Jacobin supporters and the spread of their 'revolutionary faith'[67] drove an ideological wedge into American politics. Cit-

---

[65] Samuel Eliot Morison, *The Oxford History of the American People* (New American Library, 1972) vol 1, 284.

[66] Richard B Morris (ed), *Encyclopedia of American History* (Harper & Brothers, 1950) 125-26.

[67] See James H Billington, *Fire in the Minds of Men: Origins of the Revolutionary Faith* (Basic Books, 1980).

ing 'the mischiefs of foreign intrigue,' George Washington's Farewell Address counseled against taking sides in international 'quarrels and wars.'[68] A second French incident, known as the XYZ Affair, might have led to war except for the opposition of President John Adams, who had to fight a radical faction within the Federalist Party.[69]

A more serious controversy grew out of the Adams's support of the Alien and Sedition Acts of 1798. Sponsored by a group of High Federalists from Massachusetts, the laws seemed to have little other purpose than to stifle political dissent. Jefferson and Madison regarded them as unconstitutional. Each drafted a set of resolutions introduced into the Kentucky and Virginia legislatures, respectively. Jefferson's Kentucky Resolutions set forth a theory of nullification, by which the states could overrule unconstitutional actions. James Madison's less far-reaching Virginia Resolutions merely stated a theory of interposition by which a state could intercede on behalf of its citizens to block an unconstitutional action by a higher authority. Both states also declared their loyalty to the Union and both deliberately avoided taking any action either to nullify or to obstruct enforcement of the Alien and Sedition Acts.[70]

The United States were more of a coalition of rival geographical and cultural regions than a full union of states. Even today, a fear of conspiracy remains one of the consistent features not only of wartime politics but often of domestic politics, as well.

XI INTERPOSITION IN NEW ENGLAND

Interposition and nullification continued to exacerbate sectional divisions in the years leading to the Civil War. The next confrontation began nearly a decade after the Alien and Sedition Acts when the Jefferson and Madison Administrations introduced economic sanctions to keep the country from being drawn into the war between Britain and Napoleonic France. The greatest public outcry was directed against

---

[68] https://avalon.law.yale.edu/18th_century/washing.asp.
[69] Morris, above n 65, 128-29.
[70] Ibid 130.

Britain because the royal navy, which needed help to man a naval blockade against France, pressed able-bodied seamen into its service, claiming they were deserters.[71]

In a series of Non-Importation, Embargo, and Non-Intercourse Acts, Congress restricted overseas commerce, penalising New England merchants while profiting smugglers. It would not be the last time that a moralistic foreign policy would be cynically manipulated and defeated.[72] New England towns and legislatures sent resolutions challenging the constitutionality of these laws. Gov Jonathan Trumbull of Connecticut declared that state legislatures were dutybound 'to interpose their protecting shield between the rights and liberties of the people and the assumed power of the general government.'[73]

Urged by Southern and Western War Hawks, President Madison pushed for a declaration of war against Britain in June 1812. The Federalist governor of Massachusetts declared a public fast and, along with the governor of Connecticut, refused to supply militia forces. In New Hampshire, Daniel Webster condemned the war in the Rockingham Memorial, suggesting that if the Union were ever to dissolve it might occur 'on some occasion when one portion of the country undertakes to control, to regulate, and to sacrifice the interest of another.'[74]

After President Madison called for conscription, a convention was called to meet at Hartford late in 1814 to consider a joint course of action.[75] Several resolutions were passed, including limits on trade restrictions, requiring a supermajority for declarations of war and the admission of new states, and ending the three-fifths representation advantage of the Southern states. By the time the delegation it sent

---

[71] Ibid 134-36.

[72] See Colin Dueck, *Reluctant Crusaders: Power, Culture, and Change in American Grand Strategy* (Princeton University Press, 2006) 2-5; Angelo M Codevilla, *To Make and Keep Peace Among Ourselves and with All Nations* (Hoover Institution Pres, 2014) 67-69.

[73] Morris, above n 65, 136-37.

[74] Ibid 145-46.

[75] Tom Rose, 'On Reconstruction and the American Republic' (1978) 5(1) *Journal of Christian Reconstruction* 25.

arrived in Washington, DC, however, news of the Treaty of Ghent that ended the war and Gen Andrew Jackson's victory at the Battle of New Orleans dashed any opportunity it might have had to succeed.[76] It was the last hurrah of the Federalist Party.

XII THE TARIFF OF ABOMINATIONS

As the election of 1828 approached, candidate Jackson's supporters on the House Committee on Manufactures decided to embarrass the Administration by reporting out a tariff on raw materials so high that all sections of the country would oppose it on the floor. President John Quincy Adams could then be blamed for its defeat, thus alienating his protectionist supporters in the middle states. The plot backfired when New England supported the bill and it passed. John Randolph of Roanoke grumbled that the law 'referred to manufactures of no sort or kind, but to the manufacture of a President of the United States.'[77]

The exacerbation of regional disagreements and political rivalries led to decades of recriminations. The impasse over the tariff persisted for four years. During his reelection campaign in 1832, Jackson supported a new tariff that did not appreciably change the situation. South Carolina Gov James Hamilton called for an extraordinary session of the legislature following state elections, leading to a special convention, which adopted an ordinance nullifying the two tariffs, prohibiting the collection of duties within the state, imposing a test oath on state executive officials, forbidding appeal to the US Supreme Court of any case arising under the law, and threatening secession if force were used against the state. Jackson replied by placing the forts in Charleston harbor on alert. Jackson issued his Proclamation to the People of South Carolina on December 10, which called nullification an 'impractical absurdity' and held that 'disunion by armed force is treason.'[78]

---

[76] Morris, above n 65, 153.

[77] Ibid 166.

[78] Ibid 172; see Rose, above n 75, 28-29.

In January, Jackson asked Congress for extraordinary powers to enforce the tariff by military force if necessary. Webster and former Vice President Calhoun, who had resigned to take a seat in the Senate, debated the issue in the Senate. Meanwhile, Henry Clay led a compromise tariff through to passage. South Carolina rescinded its ordinance.[79]

The lines of discord were thus already deeply drawn nearly three decades before the War between the States erupted. The centralisation that followed the war left the Early Republic far behind. Opportunistic political empire-builders have never looked back.[80]

XIII THE ADMINISTRATIVE STATE

In America, the post-Civil War Reconstruction led to Progressivism, New Deal liberalism led to the Great Society's entitlements revolution,[81] civil service reform and federal regulatory agencies led to a centralized administrative state, the Constitution of Rights yielded to the Constitution of Powers.[82] In *Cooper v Aaron*, 1958, the Supreme Court rejected nullification and interposition by states against federal laws. Yet some aspects of the older practice are reasserted when, for example, county commissions pass Second Amendment Sanctuary resolutions,[83] sheriffs refuse to enforce facemask regulations,[84] or judges enjoin onerous COVID-19 lockdown restrictions on business or religious activity.[85]

---

[79] Ibid 172-73.

[80] See Felix Morley, *The Power in the People* (Nash, 1972) 120-28.

[81] Christopher Caldwell, *The Age of Entitlement* (Simon & Schuster, 2020).

[82] Edward S Corwin, *Total War and the Constitution* (Alfred A Knopf, 1947) 170-72.

[83] See 'Updated Map of American Pro Second Amendment/2A Sanctuary Counties', 3 April 2020 <https://sanctuarycounties.com/2020/03/04/updated-map-of-american-second-amendment-sanctuary-counties-3-4-2020/>.

[84] See Amanda Prestigiacomo, 'Sheriff Slams Democrat Governor in Viral Post, Says He Won't Enforce Lockdown: "I Can No Longer Stay Silent"', *Daily Wire*, 22 April 2020 <https://www.dailywire.com/news/sheriff-slams-democrat-governor-in-viral-post-says-he-wont-enforce-lockdown-i-can-no-longer-stay-silent>.

[85] Andrew Mark Miller, 'Judge Rules in Favor of Michigan Judge, Allowing Him to Stay Open Despite Lockdown Order' *Washington Examiner*, 21 May 2020, <https://

As the modern administrative state extends its operations into all areas of social life, it breaches the constitutional safeguards that have traditionally kept society and its various institutions free from intrusive regulation by civil authorities.[86] The essence of the original decentralized federal system is constitutionally divided and limited power, as expressed philosophically by Abraham Kuyper's 'sphere sovereignty' and Pope Leo XIII's 'subsidiarity.'[87] Constitutional discipline is the hard-won reward of the Puritan experiment – a moderator of the historical drama of clashing interests and passionate convictions.

In *The City of God*, St Augustine asks: 'Justice being taken away, then, what are kingdoms but great robberies?'[88] He punctuates his point with Cicero's tale of a lowly pirate who was seized by Alexander the Great.

> When asked by the king what he thought he was doing by infesting the sea, he replied with noble insolence, "What do you think you are doing by infesting the whole earth? Because I do it with one puny boat, I am called a pirate; because you do it with a great fleet, you are called an emperor."[89]

The story illustrates Frederic Bastiat's observations on the corrupting character of the lust for power (Augustine's *libido dominandi*). What Bastiat called 'legal plunder'[90] – the abuse of power or office for personal gain – is akin to what Gordon Tullock identified and

---

www.washingtonexaminer.com/news/judge-rules-in-favor-of-michigan-barber-allowing-him-to-stay-open-despite-lockdown-order>.

[86] See John Marini, *Unmasking the Administrative State: The Crisis of American Politics in the Twenty-First Century* (Encounter, 2019), especially ch 9.

[87] See J Budziszewski, *The Revenge of Conscience: Politics and the Fall of Man* (Spence, 1999) 118-19.

[88] St Augustine, *The City of God*, bk 4, ch 4. St Augustine, *Political Writings*, tr Michael W Tkacz and Douglas Kries (Hackett, 1994) 30-31.

[89] See Cicero, *The Republic* and *The Laws*, tr Niall Rudd (Oxford University Press, 1998) 66, 74.

[90] Frederic Bastiat, *Selected Essays on Political Economy*, tr Seymour Cain, George B. de Huszar (ed) (Foundation for Economic Education, 1964) 64. <http://bastiat.org/en/the_law.html>.

Anne Krueger designated as 'rent-seeking.'[91] The law is backed by force. We should carefully consider where the use of force is both appropriate and accountable – and where it is not. Prerogative power, entitlement, and privilege often degenerate into power- or plunder-enhancing turnstile operations, a form of rent-seeking. Like the Prussian model of public education,[92] the introduction of administrative law in the 19th century German tradition superimposed a foreign body onto the constitutional system for which adequate antibodies to resist insidious abuses of power and influence have yet to develop.[93] The delegation of the law- and rule-making power to administrative agencies – where it is not accountable to the whole body politic – threatens basic civil liberties, such as procedural rights, by introducing an element of continental absolutism into the system. The Declaration of Independence contains complaints of comparable practices.[94]

Today, resistance to the COVID-19 lockdowns by sheriffs, mayors, judges, and citizens merge with the struggle between divergent visions of the American future.[95] Sheriffs refuse to enforce gun control laws and the closure of public recreation areas; judges overrule the closure of businesses and overly broad or inconsistent lockdown orders. Many states reacted to the spread of the disease by closing churches and stopping "elective surgeries" while keeping abortion facilities open as "essential" services.[96] Many of the institutions, groups, business-

---

[91] See David R Henderson, 'Rent Seeking', *The Library of Economics and Liberty* <https://www.econlib.org/library/Enc/RentSeeking.html>.

[92] See Paolo Lionni and Lance J Klass, *The Leipzig Connection: The Systematic Destruction of American Education* (Heron Books, 1980); Lawrence A Cremin, *The Transformation of the School: Progressivism in American Education, 1876-1957* (Alfred A. Knopf, 1961) ch 1.

[93] See Philip Hamburger, *Is Administrative Law Unlawful?* (University of Chicago Press, 2014) ch 24.

[94] See Philip Hamburger, *The Administrative Threat* (Encounter, 2017) 4-7, 42-47, 50-52.

[95] Thomas Sowell, *A Conflict of Visions: Ideological Origins of Political Struggles* (William Morrow, 1987) ch 2; *The Vision of the Anointed: Self-Congratulation as the Basis for Social Policy* (Basic Books, 1995) ch 5.

[96] Rabbi Michael Barclay, 'Now Is the Time for Al People of Faith to Come Together and Support Rob McCoy', *PJ Media*, 8 August 2020 <https://pjmedia.com/culture/

es, and practices targeted in such an authoritarian manner were often already under pressure, even censure or reprisal. Churches had long been targeted by various regulatory agencies. Similarly, universities that were once at the epicenter of free speech and antiwar protests are now being hamstrung by byzantine speech codes and administrative procedures.[97]

XIV FINAL CONSIDERATIONS – LOOKING AHEAD

Since late May, the pace of change has accelerated from sporadic crises into a more settled state of endemic political antagonism.[98] It is a pattern we have seen, a refrain we have heard, down through history. In 1838, following the murder of an abolitionist newspaper publisher and other instances of mob violence, a young Illinois legislator described a similar 'increasing disregard for law which pervades the country; the growing disposition to substitute the wild and furious passions, in lieu of the sober judgment of Courts; and the worse than savage mobs, for the executive ministers of justice." When a gaslighting media and political class characterizes months of looting and burning as peaceful protests, reality itself is brought into question.[99] As with the Great Fear that followed the storming of the Bastille on July 14, 1789, people

---

rabbi-michael-barclay/2020/08/08/now-is-the-time-for-all-people-of-faith-to-come-together-n766828>.

[97] Joshua T Katz, 'A Declaration of Independence by a Princeton Professor', *Quillette*, 8 July 2020 <https://quillette.com/2020/07/08/a-declaration-of-independence-by-a-princeton-professor/>; see also David French, 'A Eulogy for a Friend, a Lament for Our Nations', *The Dispatch*, 26 July 2020. <https://frenchpress.thedispatch.com/p/a-eulogy-for-a-friend-a-lament-for?utm_campaign=post&utm_medium=web&utm_source=facebook&fbclid=IwAR121ZzCz1dQqKGdPb81aQ33ZeSqDBNWYGgoOIIlpa5qZSW7wWPPqWeKZxc>.

[98] See Robert Higgs, *Crisis and Leviathan: Critical Episodes in the Growth of American Government* (Oxford University Press, 1987); Guillaume Groen van Prinsterer, *Unbelief and Revolution*, Harry van Dyke (tr, ed) (Lexham Press, 2018).

[99] See Stephanie A Sarkis, '11 Warning Signs of Gaslighting' *Psychology Today*, 22 January 2017 <https://www.psychologytoday.com/us/blog/here-there-and-everywhere/201701/11-warning-signs-gaslighting>; for a political application, see Larry Alex Taunton, 'Understand What Is Happening in America: A Christian Response' <https://larryalextaunton.com/2020/07/understanding-what-is-happening-in-america-a-christian-response/>.

are unsettled by doubt, even despair. Power abhors a vacuum. When elected and appointed officials fail to govern, a new constabulary – perhaps akin to Mao's Red Guard[100] – will simply install itself.[101] We would do well to heed Abraham Lincoln's warning:

> [T]he innocent, those who have ever set their faces against violations of law in every shape, alike with the guilty, fall victims to the ravages of mob law; and thus it goes on, step by step, till all the walls erected for the defense of the persons and property of individuals, are trodden down, and disregarded. But all this even, is not the full extent of the evil. – By such examples, by instances of the perpetrators of such acts going unpunished, the lawless in spirit, are encouraged to become lawless in practice; and having been used to no restraint, but dread of punishment, they thus become, absolutely unrestrained.—Having ever regarded Government as their deadliest bane, they make a jubilee of the suspension of its operations; and pray for nothing so much, as its total annihilation. While, on the other hand, good men, men who love tranquility, who desire to abide by the laws, and enjoy their benefits, who would gladly spill their blood in the defense of their country; seeing their property destroyed; their families insulted, and their lives endangered; their persons injured; and seeing nothing in prospect that forebodes a change for the better; become tired of, and disgusted with, a Government that offers them no protection; and are not much averse to a change in which they imagine they have nothing to lose. Thus, then, by the operation of this mobocractic spirit, which all must admit, is now abroad in the land, the strongest bul-

---

[100] See Jeff Sanders, 'Five Common Threads Between China's Red Guard and Antifa' *PJ Media*, 14 September 2017 <https://pjmedia.com/culture/jeff-sanders/2017/09/14/five-common-threads-chinas-red-guard-antifa-n168889>.

[101] A confrontation by Antifa provocateurs degenerated into a Maoist struggle session in which an elderly woman was doused with paint, wrapped with crime scene tape, and denounced as a non-person. See Victoria Taft, "Day 70: Portland Woman Attacked as She Stands up to Antifa Trying to Set Precinct on Fire," *PJ Media*, August 7, 2020. https://pjmedia.com/news-and-politics/victoria-taft/2020/08/07/day-70-portland-woman-attacked-as-she-stands-up-to-antifa-trying-to-set-precinct-on-fire-n763960

wark of any Government, and particularly of those constituted like ours, may effectually be broken down and destroyed
– I mean the *attachment* of the People.[102]

Interposition as a doctrine is the product of an explicitly Christian
civilisation and is not simply a political tactic. While the foundations
of that civilisation remain in place, this is less evident to the eye.[103] We
borrow from the accumulated capital of a thousand years of Christen-
dom while we increasingly plunder it, root and branch. Even though
elements of interposition may be found at other times and places, the
practice really belongs to an Age of Faith, a time of resolute convictions and not mere preferences. Today, instead, we struggle to navigate
the treacherous crosscurrents of a politics of fear and rage that is now
spinning wildly into a frenzy of vandalism. The cancel culture[104] associated with our social media is being redirected to cancel the West.
The duplicitous guardians of our citadels of learning long ago began
abandoning their calling as trustees of our intellectual treasury in order to settle ideological scores and earn political points.[105] The upstart
Silicon Valley tech empires of the last three decades are now the ar-

---

[102] Abraham Lincoln, Lyceum Address, January 27, 1838 <http://www.abrahamlin-
colnonline.org/lincoln/speeches/lyceum.htm>; see Daniel McCarthy, 'The Mock
Revolution of the Elites', *Spectator USA*, 28 July 2020 <https://spectator.us/mock-
revolution-elites-protests-amazon/?fbclid=IwAR0ydSAzfp9deBrdBVMAoVJSiX_3
ENLqEu8fHcSnysH9LCx__a2-9745dhw>.

[103] The pervasiveness of Christian presuppositions in the West is often most readily
discerned by nonbelievers. See Tom Holland, *Dominion: How the Christian Revolution Remade the World* (Basic Books, 2019); Evan Osnos, Interview with Zhao Xiao
(Television Interview, 2011) <http://www.pbs.org/frontlineworld/stories/china_705/
interview/xiao.html>.

[104] Brooke Kato, 'What Is Cancel Culture? Everything to Know About the Toxic Culture Trend', *New York Post*, 10 July 2020 <https://nypost.com/article/what-is-cancel-
culture-breaking-down-the-toxic-online-trend/>; see also David T Katz, 'I Survived
Cancellation at Princeton', *Peckford42*, 27 July 2020. <https://peckford42.wordpress.
com/2020/07/27/i-survived-cancellation-at-princeton/>.

[105] See David Gelernter, *America-Lite: How Imperial Academia Dismantled Our Culture (and Ushered in the Obamacrats)* (Encounter, 2012); Kenneth Minogue, 'How
Civilizations Fall' (2001) 19(8) *The New Criterion* <http://www.ejfi.org/Civiliza-
tion/Civilization-18.htm?fbclid=IwAR0JChzdgdMgdzLNAoH7VIMWPyaRZEzIP
mVgnk3oDyx93mVsKsn5zb3SRrs#fall>.

biters of politically-correct sentiments and permissible expression.[106] Increasingly, all that remains evident of the great fountainhead of our common culture is a lingering 'whiff of the empty bottle.'[107]

James Chowning Davies's J-curve theory offers some insight as to what triggers political violence: 'Revolutions are most likely to occur when a prolonged period of objective economic and social development is followed by a short period of sharp reversal.'[108] Following the long period of rising expectations, a sudden reversal of fortunes during the economic lockdown may have created a sense of 'relative deprivation.'[109] So it should not be surprising under these circumstances that counterfeit forms of resistance to tyranny should also arise. Following the death of George Floyd in Minneapolis while in police custody, widespread protests quickly devolved into revolutionary violence. A subversive postmodern nihilism has long sought to dismantle the institutions that undergird the increasingly post-Christian West.[110]

Just as the French Revolution underwent a pell-mell of institutional upheavals, and the 1960s spawned a hedonistic counterculture, so today we see a network of well-organized shock troops and saboteurs that seek to overturn the constitutional system through the conversion of its own liberties and defences into weapons.[111] Amidst a climate of

---

[106] Anjana Susarla, 'Algorithms Are Making Cancel Culture Even Worse', *Fast Company*, 3 February 2020 <https://www.fastcompany.com/90458174/hate-outrage-and-cancel-culture-are-snowballing-thanks-to-this>.

[107] See Francis Stuart Campbell (pseud Erik von Kuehnelt-Leddihn), 'The Whiff from the Empty Bottle' (1945) 62 *Catholic World* 20.

[108] James C Davies, 'Toward a Theory of Revolution' (1962) 6(1) *American Sociological Review* 5.

[109] Ted Robert Gurr, *Why Men Rebel* (Princeton University Press, 1970) 23.

[110] See Steven Alan Samson, 'A Strategy of Subversion' (2020) 25 *The Market for Ideas* <http://www.themarketforideas.com/a-strategy-of-subversion-a541/>; Andrew C McCarthy, 'In Congressional Testimony, Barr Calls for Unified Response to Violent Assault on U.S. Government', *National Review*, 28 July 2020 <https://www.nationalreview.com/2020/07/in-congressional-testimony-barr-calls-for-unified-response-to-violent-assault-on-u-s-government/>.

[111] See Victoria Taft, '10 Big Fat Lies You're Being Told About the Portland Riots', *PJ Media*, 26 July 2020 <https://pjmedia.com/columns/victoria-taft/2020/07/26/10-big-fat-lies-youre-being-told-about-the-portland-riots-n675861>; Andy Ngo, 'Portland

fear associated with both the pandemic and the faux-politics of the endlessly litigated 2016 election, we see governors using emergency powers to order people to shelter-in-place while also giving free rein to violent protestors, mayors and police chiefs ordering the police to stand down, city councils defunding their police departments, state and local officials defying the president's efforts to protect federal property, and attempts by radicals to set up autonomous zones that put businesses and residents at the mercy of criminals who may never be held legally accountable.[112]

The larger question then is which will prevail: *politics* – the art of persuasion and consensus-building – or *despotism* – the coercion of surrender and acquiescence?[113] Days of Reckoning are upon us.

---

[112] See, for example, Jeff Reynolds, 'Black Portlander Changes His Mind About the Nightly Protests After He Attends One', *PJ Media*, 24 July 2020 <https://pjmedia.com/news-and-politics/jeff-reynolds/2020/07/24/black-portlander-changes-his-mind-about-the-nightly-protests-after-he-attends-one-n697027>.

[113] See Minogue, above n.2, ch 13.

14

Destroying Liberty: Governance by Decree

WILLIAM WAGNER*

ABSTRACT

*Constitutional structures and limits on the exercise of govern-
ment power protect and preserve liberty, even during a pandemic. Many State Governors see Covid-19 as an opportunity to ignore such constraints, autocratically issuing despotic edicts. If
left unaddressed, the rising tyranny threatens to destroy deeply
rooted foundations of good governance under the Rule of Law.*

*The blessings of liberty and prosperity come with responsibility.
Each generation inherits a special trust to ensure the preservation of liberty and the moral administration of justice. As state
governing regimes increasingly use fear to act without constitutional authority, and infringe upon constitutionally protected
liberty, we the people must fearlessly fight to preserve the Rule
of Law. If State Governors go further and tyrannically mandate
vaccines without consent of the governed, the Federal government should exercise its power under the Commerce Clause to
enact pre-emptive Federal legislation.*

I CONSTITUTIONAL REPUBLIC OR TOTALITARIAN REGIME

The founders of the United States government established a representative Republic. Federal in nature, their Constitution promises every
State a republican form of government,

---

* William Wagner currently serves as President and Chairman at Salt & Light Global.
He holds the academic rank of Distinguished Professor Emeritus (Law). Prior to joining
academia, he served with distinction in all three branches of the United States government, including as a federal judge.

Thus, Article IV § 4 of the *United States Constitution* provides that:

> The United States shall guarantee to every state in this union a republican form of government, and shall protect each of them against invasion; and on application of the legislature, or of the executive (when the legislature cannot be convened) against domestic violence.[1]

As used here, a *'republican form of government'* refers to 'a state in which the exercise of the sovereign power is lodged in representatives elected by the people.'[2]

Thus, the people of the various States are citizens of a constitutional Republic, not subjects of a totalitarian regime. The significance of this distinction matters. In totalitarian regimes an autocratic leader exercises power as he wishes without limitation. Governance occurs through coercive 'subordination of the individual to the state and strict control of all aspects of the life and productive capacity'.[3] Elected representatives of the people in a constitutional Republic, on the other hand, legitimately exercise only such power as constitutionally delegated to them by the people. And so, whenever government acts, some constitutional or statutory provision must authorise the action. In exercising power pursuant to such provisions, government authorities must always act within the scope of the power authorized.

The American Constitution expressly enumerates and separates those powers delegated by the people to the national government. By dividing power the Framers sought to protect liberty, despite the sinful and ambitious nature of human beings holding power. James Madison, in Federalist 51 explained:

> In order to lay a due foundation for that separate and distinct exercise of the different powers of government, which

---

[1] *United States Constitution* art IV § 4.

[2] American Dictionary of the English Language (1828) <http://webstersdictionary1828.com/Dictionary/republic>.

[3] *Merriam-Webster Dictionary* <https://www.merriam-webster.com/dictionary/totalitarian>.

to a certain extent is admitted on all hands to be essential to the preservation of liberty, it is evident that each department should have a will of its own;****

But the great security against a gradual concentration of the several powers in the same department, consists in giving to those who administer each department the necessary constitutional means and personal motives to resist encroachments of the others.... Ambition must be made to counteract ambition. The interest of the man must be connected with the constitutional rights of the place. It may be a reflection on human nature, that such devices should be necessary to control the abuses of government. But what is government itself, but the greatest of all reflections on human nature? If men were angels, no government would be necessary. If angels were to govern men, neither external nor internal controls on government would be necessary. In framing a government which is to be administered by men over men, the great difficulty lies in this: you must first enable the government to control the governed; and in the next place oblige it to control itself. A dependence on the people is, no doubt, the primary control on the government; but experience has taught mankind the necessity of auxiliary precautions.[4]

Thus, the American people established a governing structure where the various branches of the national government may act only if an enumerated power authorizes the action. Additionally, the American Constitution reserves all power not expressly given to the national government to the States. Because the American Constitution delegates no police powers to the national government,[5] State governments in

---

[4] James Madison, 'The Federalist No 51', 1788 <https://billofrightsinstitute.org/founding-documents/primary-source-documents/the-federalist-papers/federalist-papers-no-51?>.

[5] To be sure we see national law enforcement action, but such action must find its authority in an enumerated power. Thus, whilst a Federal law makes it a felony to distribute cocaine, the underlying authority authorising the national law is the Power to Regulate Commerce among the States enumerated in Article I of the *United States Constitution* (drugs being commerce). Thus, with proper Congressional authorisation, the Federal government could also exercise significant authority under the Commerce Power.

the USA hold (pursuant to their State Constitutions) the police power to regulate health and safety matters. That is why most of the Covid-19 governing in the USA occurs, not in Washington DC, but in the States.[6] In this regard, the various State Constitutions divide power among legislative, executive, and judicial branches of government. Where state constitutions are silent as to the police actions permitted by the governor, state statutes, enacted by the legislature pursuant to a State Constitution, define the scope of a governor's power.

Even when State constitutional or statutory law authorizes a government action, the action must not infringe upon protected rights and liberty. That is, a State must recognise the constitutional limits placed on the exercise of its power by constitutional liberty interests. The American Declaration affirms the Creator endowed us with the inalienable rights of life, liberty, and the pursuit of happiness.[7] Recognising the significance of this truth, the American Constitution makes clear that one of the key purposes of government is to preserve these unalienable rights:

> We the people of the United States, in order to form a more perfect union, establish justice, insure domestic tranquility, provide for the common defense, promote the general welfare, and secure the Blessings of Liberty to ourselves and our posterity, do ordain and establish this Constitution for the United States of America.[8] (emphasis added)

Some of the liberty interests protected under both the American and State Constitutions include:

- The right to freedom of speech
- The right to petition government
- The right to freedom of association

---

[6] See eg, 'Not One Size Fit All', *Washington Examiner*, 21 April 2020 <https://www.washingtonexaminer.com/opinion/not-one-size-fits-all-different-states-and-cities-varied-in-their-pandemic-responses> (discussing how different states vary in their pandemic response).

[7] United States Declaration of Independence, [3] (1776).

[8] *United States Constitution*, preamble.

- The right to freedom of religious exercise
- The right of a parent to control and direct the upbringing of their child
- The right to be free from State action that Impairs a Contract
- The right to be free from state action that takes Property without Just Compensation

II GOOD GOVERNANCE UNDER THE RULE OF LAW OR TYRANNY THROUGH FEAR

When officials operate within the scope of their legal authority, adhering to constitutional limits placed on the exercise of their power, it is called good governance under the Rule of Law. Conversely, when regimes act outside the scope of their authority, and refuse to adhere to constitutional limits, the people experience the very essence of tyranny. Covid-19 temptingly provided an opportunity for State authorities to sneak a taste this tyranny. Too many State Governors succumbed to the temptation with disquieting consequences. Indeed, if, as Hamilton's observed, '…a sacred respect for the constitutional law is the vital principle, the sustaining energy of a free government' then the Governors' extra-constitutional Covid-19 edicts and decrees place a principal precept protecting liberty in peril.[9]

Constitutional limits on the exercise of governmental power remain especially relevant during a pandemic. Nonetheless, during Covid-19, dictatorial-like executive actions by State governors radically restricted personal autonomy and substantially interfered with constitutionally protected liberty. Many of these decrees generally mandated that healthy citizens *stay at home*.[10] The reasons given for these extraordinary quarantine orders include suppressing the spread of COVID-19, so as to not overwhelm state health care systems. Submit or die, says the govern-

---

[9] Alexander Hamilton, 'Tully No III' (28 August 1794), National Archives (Hamilton Papers), *Founders Online* <https://founders.archives.gov/documents/Hamilton/01-17-02-0130>.

[10] See eg, Whitmer Executive Order No 2020-21 <https://www.michigan.gov/whitmer/0,9309,7-387-90499_90705-522626--,00.html>.

ing regime. Even after hospital capacity concerns failed to materialize, though, Governors continued to despotically wield power. Sometimes the fear of a thing can be more dangerous than the thing itself.

During the early days of the Republic, our founders sought to build a better nation, not on fear, but under the Rule of Law. John Adams contrasted the foundation for such good governance from elsewhere at the time: 'Fear is the foundation of most governments....' because he understood that fear 'is so sordid and brutal a passion, and renders men in whose breasts it predominates so stupid and miserable,' he believed that 'Americans will not be likely to approve of any political institution which is founded on it.' While Adams understood the crippling power of fear, he foresaw not how future generations might so cavalierly assume authorities would continue to respect liberty and the constitutional limits it placed on their actions.[11]

As of this writing numerous Governors continue to rule by edict through fear. Fear not just wrought by a pandemic, but also by the force of law and punishment. To be sure, a virus holds the capacity to make many sick and kill others, especially the elderly. If left unaddressed, though, the government's tyranny in responding to the pandemic holds potential to destroy everyone's liberty. Indeed, our liberty, for which Adams and others so greatly sacrificed, exists on life support with no respirator in sight. Benjamin Franklin warned that 'They who would give up an essential liberty for temporary security, deserve neither liberty or security.'[12] We do well to heed his counsel.

A *Exercising Power Outside the Scope of the Law*

With various degrees of specificity, State constitutions and statutes assign police power to protect health and safety. Too often during Covid-19, Governors exercised power beyond the scope of the authority

---

[11] John Adams, 'Thoughts on Government' (April 1776), *Massachusetts Historical Society* <http://www.masshist.org/publications/adams-papers/index.php/view/PJA04dg2>.

[12] Benjamin Franklin, 'Pennsylvania Assembly: Reply to the Governor' (November 11, 1775), National Archives (Franklin Papers), *Founders Online* <https://founders.archives.gov/documents/Franklin/01-06-02-0107>.

authorized under these State provisions, often encroaching on power belonging to the legislature.

In promoting ratification of the proposed Constitution, James Madison recognized in Federalist 47 that:

> The accumulation of all powers, legislative, executive, and judiciary, in the same hands, whether of one, a few, or many, and whether hereditary, self-appointed, or elective, may justly be pronounced the very definition of tyranny... In order to form correct ideas on this important subject, it will be proper to investigate the sense in which the preservation of liberty requires that the three great departments of power should be separate and distinct.

Citing Montesquieu, Madison then explained:

> ...it may clearly be inferred that, in saying 'There can be no liberty where the legislative and executive powers are united in the same person, ...' [Montesquieu meant] that where the whole power of one department is exercised by the same hands which possess the whole power of another department, the fundamental principles of a free constitution are subverted.
>
> ***
>
> The reasons on which Montesquieu grounds his maxim are a further demonstration of his meaning. 'When the legislative and executive powers are united in the same person or body,' says he, "there can be no liberty, because apprehensions may arise lest the same monarch or senate should enact tyrannical laws to execute them in a tyrannical manner.

The response by the Governor of Michigan, Gretchen Whitmer, to Covid-19 illustrates Madison's point. The most despotically prolific of all the State governors in the USA, Michigan's chief executive issued more edicts than any other State Governor.[13] To put the impact of her

---

[13] 'State Executive Order Tracking', *BallotPedia,* 29 June 2020 <https://ballotpedia. org/Executive_orders_issued_by_governors_and_state_agencies_in_response_to_ the_coronavirus_(COVID19)_pandemic,_2020#State_executive_order_tracking>.

decrees in perspective, Michigan is about the same size population and land mass as Sweden.

What are the implications for a free society when Governors misuse power under the guise of protecting health and safety? As the COVID-19 pandemic commenced, Michigan's Governor enacted numerous lawmaking edicts governing virtually every aspect of life.

Article IV § 1 of Michigan's Constitution states that the legislative power rests in the *legislative* branch of government.[14] Moreover, art IV § 51 expressly provides: '... The *legislature* shall pass suitable laws for the protection and promotion of the public health.'[15]

Recognising the constitution consigns all legislative power in the legislature, the Michigan legislature enacted the 1976 Emergency Management Act. This law expressly includes epidemics, and explicitly limits the maximum duration of a gubernatorial emergency order:

> The state of emergency shall continue until the governor finds that the threat or danger has passed, the emergency has been dealt with to the extent that emergency conditions no longer exist, or until the declared state of emergency has been in effect for 28 days. After 28 days, the governor shall issue an executive order or proclamation declaring the state of emergency terminated, unless a request by the governor for an extension of the state of emergency for a specific number of days is approved by resolution of both houses of the legislature.[16]

Assuming *arguendo* that the legislature properly delegated power to the executive branch during a time of disaster or emergency,[17] no

---

[14] *Michigan Constitution* art IV § 1.

[15] *Michigan Constitution* art IV § 51 (emphasis added). This constitutional provision declares that '[t]he public health and general welfare of the people of the state are ... matters of primary public concern.'

[16] *Emergency Management Act*, MCL § 30.403(3) and (4).

[17] Nothing in the Michigan Constitution authorizes the legislature to delegate its lawmaking power to the Executive Branch. A serious question exists, therefore, as to whether these delegations of lawmaking authority were even proper in the first place, or whether they violate the separation of powers delineated in the State's Constitution.

question exists as to whether the Governor exercised power far outside and beyond the scope of authority authorized by these provisions. For months after the legislature refused a request from the Governor for an extension of an initial authorisation,[18] the Governor defiantly enacted executive edicts legislating where, who, and in what manner individuals may associate, as well as everything from how, when and if businesses, churches, the press, and schools may operate.[19] Both houses of the Legislature, as well as numerous businesses, churches, and individuals, filed lawsuits in court. At issue in all these cases is, *inter alia*, whether the Governor's actions exceed the scope of her constitutional and statutory authority.[20] Refusing to govern within the State's constitutional structures, including structures requiring participation by the people's representatives, affronts the Rule of Law.[21]

B *Exercising Power in Ways that Infringe on Constitutional Rights*

More troubling, Governors throughout the USA ignore constitutional limits placed on the exercise of their power, issuing edicts infringing on constitutionally protected liberty with impunity. A number of

---

[18] Legislative authorisation ceased to exist on 30 April 2020.

19 See 'Executive Orders' <https://www.michigan.gov/whier/0,9309,7-387-90499_90705---,00.html>.

[20] See, eg, Beth LeBlanc, 'Federal Judge asks Michigan's High-Court to Clarify Whitmer's Emergency Powers', *Detroit News*, 18 June 2020 <https://www.detroitnews.com/story/news/local/michigan/2020/06/18/federal-judge-asks-michigans-high-court-clarify-whitmers-emergency-powers/3217956001/>; Bill Chappell, 'Michigan Legislature sues Governor Whitmer', *Detroit News*, 6 May 2020 <https://www.npr.org/sections/coronavirus-live-updates/2020/05/06/851339264/michigan-legislature-sues-gov-whitmer-seeking-to-end-coronavirus-emergency-order>; and Gus Burns, 'Churches sue Whitmer', *Detroit News*, 6 May 2020 <https://www.mlive.com/public-interest/2020/05/churches-sue-whitmer-claim-coronavirus-orders-hinder-religious-gatherings-despite-exceptions.html>.

[21] After the termination of the emergency under the *Emergency Management Act 1976* ('EMA'), the Governor declared new emergencies and contended a World War II era law – *Emergency Powers of Governor Act 1945* MCL 10.31 ('EPGA') – authorizes her actions -- even though the EPGA does not cover epidemics and was enacted in response to the need to control riots. Even if it was applicable here, Michigan law requires it be read together with the EMA. Instead, the Governor incorrectly claims an inapplicable law applicable, and refuses to comply with the law that actually does apply.

the decrees in the Governors' executive decrees substantially infringe upon liberty interests protected under the US and State Constitutions.

The First Amendment to the American Constitution prohibits State authorities from 'abridging the freedom of speech.'[22] 'Government action that stifles speech on account of its message, or that requires the utterance of a particular message favored by the Government, contravenes this essential right....'[23] The First Amendment similarly guarantees the right to 'peaceably to assemble, and to petition the government for a redress of grievances.'[24] '[A]n attribute of national citizenship,'[25] 'the right of peaceable assembly is a right cognate to those of free speech and free press and is equally fundamental.'[26] The First Amendment also prohibits State authorities from abridging an individual's freedom of association.[27] Freedom of speech, petition, assembly, and religion necessarily require association, and is therefore, considered a fundamental constitutional liberty. This First Amendment liberty likewise protects one's right to not associate with others where the exclusion is based upon the expressive message of the group.[28] Additionally, the First Amendment expressly protects the freedom of the press.[29] Finally, under the First Amendment, government also must not prohibit 'the free exercise [of religion]'. These limits on the exercise of government power generally also apply to actions by State entities.[30]

---

[22] *United States Constitution* amend I.

[23] *Turner Broadcasting System v FCC* 512 US 622 (1994).

[24] *United States Constitution* amend I.

[25] *United States v Cruikshank*, 92 US 542 (1876).

[26] *DeJonge v Oregon*, 299 US 353 (1937).

[27] *United States Constitution* amend I; *NAACP v Alabama ex rel Patterson*, 357 US 449 (1958) (holding 'Immunity from state scrutiny of petitioner's membership lists is here so related to the right of petitioner's members to pursue their lawful private interests privately and *to associate freely with others* in doing so as to come within the protection of the Fourteenth Amendment') (*emphasis added*).

[28] See, eg, *Hurley v Irish-American Gay, Lesbian, and Bisexual Group of Boston*, 515 US 557 (1995); *Boy Scouts of America v Dale*, 530 US 640 (2000).

[29] *United States Constitution* amend I.

[30] See, eg, *Cantwell v Connecticut*, 310 US 296 (1940); *DeJonge v Oregon*, 299 US 353 (1937); *Near v Minnesota*, 283 US 697 (1931); *Gitlow v New York*, 268 US 652 (1925).

Notwithstanding the constitutional liberty limiting the exercise of Executive Power, State Governors issued edicts mandating people stay at home and banning any size gathering.[31] Thus, in some places, it became a crime to travel to or gather in front of a State Capitol to petition the government for redress of grievances concerning the draconian regulations. It likewise became a crime for an individual to travel to or gather together at a church to worship, or even to safely live stream a religious message to the homes of congregation members. Other State restrictions include the prohibition of worship songs at church.[32] Michigan's governor prohibited the press from attending her press briefings, or even from verbally asking questions remotely. The governor instead required the press to submit written questions for her approval prior to answering.[33] Other Executive edicts suspended Freedom of Information laws.[34]

One of the oldest fundamental constitutional rights recognized by the US Supreme Court is the right to direct and control the upbringing of one's children, especially with regard to their education.[35] The Michigan Governor's decrees dictated education policy, making it a crime for a parent to personally educate their own child in their own home.[36] Sometimes, in addition to interfering with protected liberty,

---

[31] See, eg, Whitmer Executive Order No 2020-21 <https://www.michigan.gov/whitmer/0,9309,7-387-90499_90705-522626--,00.html>.

[32] Caleb Parke, 'Outrage after California bans Singing in Churches', *Fox News*, 6 July 2020 <https://www.foxnews.com/us/california-singing-ban-church-coronavirus-restriction>.

[33] See, eg, 'Michigan Governor Whitmer Bars the Press', *WBCK-FM*, 7 August 2020 <https://wbckfm.com/governor-whitmer-bars-the-press-from-her-press-conference/>.

[34] Craig Mauger, 'Whitmer Law Easing Transparency Draws Scrutiny', *Detroit News*, 29 April 2020 <https://www.detroitnews.com/story/news/local/michigan/2020/04/29/whitmer-order-easing-transparency-law-draws-suit-senate-scrutiny/3032960001/>.

[35] See, eg, *Pierce v Society of Sisters*, 268 US 510 (1925); *Wisconsin v Yoder*, 406 US 205 (1972).

[36] See, eg, David A Kallman, William Wagner and Stephen Kallman, 'Governor's EO Unconstitutionally Outlaws Home Education and Usurps the State Board of Education Authority Over Public Schools', Great Lakes Justice Center, 9 April 2020 <https://greatlakesjc.org/governors_eo_outlaws_home_education/>.

these decrees lacked any constitutional or statutory authority authorising the executive action. For example, Michigan's Constitution and statutory law assigns power over educational matters to the State Board of Education.[37] While constitutional and statutory authority arguably exists for the governor to close public school buildings during an emergency, her additional actions regulating educational policy improperly usurped power constitutionally assigned to the State Board of Education.

The Fifth Amendment to the *United States Constitution* states: 'nor shall private property be taken for public use, without just compensation.'[38] State Constitutions likewise prohibit the State from taking private property without just compensation. Moreover, under art I, § 10 of the *United States Constitution*, 'No state shall ... pass any ... law impairing the obligation of contracts.'[39] Here the constitution limits exercises of government power where a state law operates as a substantial impairment of a contractual relationship.[40]

Governors, boldly infringing on constitutional liberties, issued numerous edicts shutting down private contracts. For example, lawn care businesses who had entered into contracts to provide lawn care were prohibited from carrying out the terms of the contract when Executive decrees made it a crime for an employee to mow a lawn even where no other person was present.[41] Other businesses faced bankruptcy, directly as a result of executive decrees closing their business or prohibiting them from selling their products, even in manner that posed no increased risk to health or safety. Governors also prohibited, by

---

[37] *Michigan Constitution* art VIII § 3.

[38] *United States Constitution* amend V.

[39] *United States Constitution* art I § 10. State Constitutions likewise prohibit the State from impairing private contracts.

[40] *Energy Reserves Group v Kansas Power & Light*, 459 US 400 (1983).

[41] See, eg, Tony Wittkowski, 'Lawn Care, Landscaping Companies Left Hanging due to Covid_19 Restrictions', *The Herald-Palladium*, 11 April 2020 <https://www.heraldpalladium.com/news/lawn-care-landscaping-companies-left-hanging-due-to-covid-19-restrictions/article_19291184-1f21-5fd2-9d47-d967d52b2ec1.html>; Whitmer 2020 Executive Orders <https://www.michigan.gov/whitmer/0,9309,7-387-90499_90705---,00.html>.

the force of law and punishment, property owners from enforcing the terms of a rental contracts, when a renters refuse to pay contractually agreed to rent.[42]

C Enabling Impact of An Activist Judiciary – Justifying Constitutional Infringements

While no dispute exists as to whether the executive actions by Governors infringe on constitutionally protected liberty, decades of judicial activism diabolically evolve constitutional law, enabling State Governors to justify their infringements and emboldening them to govern despotically.[43]

During the current pandemic, Governors often rely upon a 1905 Supreme Court case, *Jacobson v Massachusetts*, decided in the midst of a small pox epidemic in the United States.[44] The *Jacobson* Court reviewed a challenge to a state law mandating small pox vaccinations for everyone. The Court addressed the scope of the State police power stating, '[t]he Constitution, does not import an absolute right in each person to be, at all times and in all circumstances, wholly freed from restraint.'[45] Thus, citizens may sometimes, 'under the pressure of great dangers, be subjected to such restraint, to be enforced by reasonable regulations, as the safety of the general public may demand.'[46] Here an unelected Court permitted police powers saying that 'a community has the right to protect itself against an epidemic.'[47]

Consequently, it is not surprising today that an activist judiciary enables Executive tyranny by saying it is ok for the State to infringe on

---

[42] See eg, Whitmer Executive Order No 2020-19 <https://www.michigan.gov/whitmer/0,9309,7-387-90499_90705-522509--,00.html>.

[43] For an in-depth discussion of how judges threaten the constitutional order when they engage in politically unaccountable creation of new meaning, see: William Wagner and N Katherine Wagner, 'The Virtue of True Meaning: A Remonstrance Against Politically Unaccountable Judicial Policymaking' (2019) 10 *Western Australian Jurist* 3.

[44] *Jacobson v Massachusetts,* 197 US 11 (1905).

[45] Ibid.

[46] Ibid.

[47] Ibid.

constitutionally protected liberty, as long as it can sufficiently justify the infringement to the Court's satisfaction. The US Supreme Court accomplishes this feat, with virtually no opposition from the politically accountable branches, via relativistic judicial decisions on the value of various liberty interests. In doing so, the Court sets various levels of justification where government authorities may infringe on protected liberty, if the Court-decreed government interest and means used is sufficient.

Even where the Court once historically required a lot of justification, as when government interfered with one's freedom of speech or religion, its evolutionary jurisprudence routinely diminished the value of the liberty interest. For example, when government substantially interfered with one's speech, parental rights, or religious exercise, the Court traditionally required a high level of justification.[48] Here, the Court required the government authority to demonstrate a compelling interest in the interference. If the authority demonstrated a sufficiently compelling government interest, the Court then required that the government show it achieved this interest using the least restrictive means possible.[49] Under this Court-devised approach for valuating liberty, an evolving relativistic jurisprudence thereafter diminished the liberty interests that limit government power.

Preliminarily, if the government's interference in the liberty interest fails to rise to the level of substantial interference, then courts require the authorities to provide virtually no justification for their actions.[50] Moreover, using a relativistic neutrality jurisprudence, courts often decrease the level of justification required. For example, if the government enacts a law restricting speech in a content-neutral way,

---

[48] See, eg, *Turner Broadcasting System v FCC*, 512 US 622, 641 (1994) (stating high level of scrutiny of content-based speech restrictions); *Sherbert v Verner*, 374 US 398 (1963) (denying unemployment benefits to a person who lost her job when she did not work on her Sabbath); *Wisconsin v Yoder*, 406 US 205 (1972) (overturning convictions for violations of state compulsory school attendance laws incompatible with sincerely held religious beliefs).

[49] See, eg, *Republican Party of Minnesota v White* 536 US 765 (2002).

[50] See, eg, *Moore v City of East Cleveland*, 431 US 494 (1977).

the level of justification is much less.[51] Likewise, the Court has permitted state authorities to substantially interfere with a person's free exercise of religious conscience, if it characterizes the statute as a generally applicable neutral law.[52]

The US Supreme Court also diluted the economic liberty interests expressly listed in the Constitution. These economic liberty interests once served an effective means of limiting the exercise of government power.[53] By adjusting the level of justification to a very low level, though, courts now uphold almost any government action infringing on economic liberty interests. For example, even though art I § 10 of the *United States Constitution* expressly prohibits states from impairing the obligation of contracts, the Supreme Court has ruled that States may nonetheless do so if, using their police powers, they have a legitimate reason, 'such as remedying of a broad and general social or economic problem.'[54] And, even though the Fifth Amendment expressly prohibits the government taking property for public use without just compensation, the Court has so broadly defined public use so as to greatly reduce the protection promised in the plain meaning of the provision.[55]

Thus, Governors issuing their Covid-19 edicts and decrees claim their use of "the police power" is justified. Citing court decisions, they contend a government health and safety interest justifies their substantial infringement of constitutionally protected liberty.

D *Enforcement Concerns*

Even assuming *arguendo* governors hold a proper government interest justifying infringement of constitutional liberty, enforcement of Covid-19 orders were executed based on who a governor deemed essen-

---

[51] *Turner Broadcasting System v FCC* 512 US 622, 641 (1994) (comparing content neutral regulation of speech which receives intermediate scrutiny).

[52] See, eg, *Employment Division v Smith*, 494 US 872 (1990).

[53] *United States v Carolene Products Company*, 304 US 144 fn 4 (1938).

[54] *Energy Reserves Group v Kansas Power & Light*, 459 US 400, 411-413 (1983).

[55] See, eg, *Kelo v New London*, 545 US 469 (2005) (holding 'public use' in the Fifth Amendment Takings Clause permits government authorities to exercise the power of eminent domain even for economic development purposes).

tial, rather than on whether some activity could be carried out safely in a way that protects health. Rahm Emanuel infamously stated, 'You never want a serious crisis to go to waste…'.[56] Thus, the Executive edicts almost always favored political constituencies.

For example, when business owners, pastors, parents, and other affected citizens peacefully protested the shut-down, and petitioned the government for redress of their grievances, Governors rebuked and threatened extended closures, blaming it on the protesters.[57] A short while later when leftist-sponsored anti-law enforcement groups rallied, Governors attended and supported, without social distancing.[58] Likewise, the Governor of Illinois, a Democrat, permitted protestors to assemble in large rallies, but banned political gatherings sought by Republicans.[59]

Governors force gun stores and gyms to close, but declared marijuana distributers essential. While barbers were forced to close shop, strip clubs stayed open for business. While you could purchase lottery tickets you could not buy seeds to plant in your garden. Governors closed churches for worship, but allowed casinos to operate. (When a church in the State of Nevada then went to a casino to worship God, the Governor fined the casino).[60] While Executive edicts banned health

---

[56] 'Never let a Crisis go to Waste', *Lexington Chronicle*, 6 March 2020 https://www.lexingtonchronicle.com/business/never-let-crisis-go-waste. Mr Emanuel served as President Barack Obama's Chief of Staff and as Mayor of Chicago.

[57] Rose White, 'We Know that this Rally Endangered People – Whitmer Responds to Lansing Protest', *ABC 13*, 15 April 2020 <https://www.wzzm13.com/article/news/local/michigan/gretchen-whitmer-responds-to-lansing-protest/69-a0006e0c-531d-4d07-8f91-2a14ea629085>.

[58] Craig Mauger and James David Dickson, 'With little Social Distancing, Whitmer Marches with Protesters', *Detroit News*, 4 June 2020 <https://www.detroitnews.com/story/news/local/michigan/2020/06/04/whitmer-appears-break-social-distance-rules-highland-park-march/3146244001/>.

[59] Caitlin McFall, 'Justice Kavanaugh Denies Emergency Request from Illinois GOP Groups Seeking to Hold Large Rallies', *Fox News*, 4 July 2020 <https://www.foxnews.com/politics/kavanaugh-denies-emergency-request-illinois-gop-groups-hold-large-rallies>.

[60] John Nolte, 'Nevada's Democrat Governor Punishes Casino for Holding Worship Service', *Breitbart*, 11 August 2020 <https://www.breitbart.com/politics/2020/08/11/nolte-nevadas-democrat-governor-punishes-casino-for-holding-worship-service/> .

care professionals from conducting elective surgeries, they kept abortion providers in business, allowing elective surgeries that terminate the life of unborn children.[61]

Authorities in Kentucky stopped Christian people from attending an Easter Sunday drive-through service where worshippers stayed in their cars.[62] Authorities throughout the USA turn off water and electricity of those they deem incompliant with their regime's rules.[63] Law enforcement in Colorado handcuffed a father playing outside with his wife and young daughter.[64] Police in Philadelphia physically pulled a man not wearing a mask off a bus.[65] Other law enforcement authorities banned people from sitting on a park bench alone in a public park.[66]

In 1887 Lord Acton observed that "power tends to corrupt and absolute power corrupts absolutely." Unfortunately, the exercise of absolute dictatorial power by State Governors, throughout the COVID ordeal, proves the rule rather than the exception.[67]

III UPCOMING THREAT TO LIBERTY FROM INEVITABLE VACCINE ENFORCEMENT AND A PROPOSED CHECK ON STATE POWER

Given the eagerness of State governors to use Covid-19 as a reason to interfere with constitutionally protected liberty, serious concerns

---

[61] See, eg, Whitmer Executive Order No 2020-17 <https://www.michigan.gov/whitmer/0,9309,7-387-90499_90705-522451--,00.html>.

[62] Editorial Board, 'It's Still America, Virus or Not: Draconian orders and enforcement will undermine public support for social distancing', *The Wall Street Journal*, 13 April 2020 <https://www.wsj.com/articles/its-still-america-virus-or-not-11586718091>.

[63] Brittany De Lea, 'Los Angeles to Cut Off Water, Power to Properties, Hosting Large Gatherings', *Fox News*, 5 August 2020 <https://www.foxnews.com/us/los-angeles-water-power-properties-large-gatherings>.

[64] *The Wall Street Journal*, above n 62.

[65] Ibid.

[66] Ibid.

[67] The only thing more contagious than the virus is abuse of power. Emboldened by the State's draconian decrees, some in Michigan's judiciary unapologetically issue general warrants, broadly authorising police to arrest *anyone* suspected of being sick.

exist as to what will occur when a vaccine finally emerges. Citing Jacobson's small pox precedent, expect governors to mandate vaccinations for everyone, without regard to medical side-effects or religious conscience.

Grave ethical concerns exist regarding the role of abortive fetal cell lines in the development of the potential vaccines.[68] Other concerns exist over potential neurotoxins included in the future vaccines.[69] Additionally, Covid-19 introduces new invasive surveillance techniques for State governments, threating personal privacy.[70] Mandatory vaccines interface with Covid-19 tracking apps, already installed on every smart phone without consent. These apps enable governing authorities to collect and meticulously track detailed private personal data on every citizen.[71] If State Governors mandate vaccines without consent of the governed, Congress should stop them by invoking its power under the Commerce Clause.

A *Amend the Controlled Substances Act – No Vaccine without Consent*

As part of a constitutionally authorised federal regulatory scheme, the US Congress should amend the Controlled Substances Act to express-

---

[68] See, eg, Jonathan Abbamonte, 'Which COVID-19 Vaccines Are Being Developed with Fetal Cell Lines Derived from Abort Babies?' *Population Research Institute*, 4 June 2020 <https://www.pop.org/which-covid-19-vaccines-are-being-developed-with-fetal-cell-lines-derived-from-aborted-babies/>, and Dr Susan Berry, 'Left-wing Media Claim Aborted Baby Parts Needed to Cure Coronavirus', *Breitbart*, 20 March 2020, <https://www.breitbart.com/politics/2020/03/20/fact-check-left-wing-media-claim-aborted-baby-parts-needed-cure-coronavirus/>.

[69] See, eg, 'Vaccines & Immunizations', *Centers for Disease Control and Prevention* <https://www.cdc.gov/vaccines/vac-gen/additives.htm>.

[70] See, eg, Claire Chretien, 'Doctors Lay Out Plan to Punish People Who Refuse Coronavirus Vaccine: "There is no Alternative"', *LifeSiteNews*, 11 August 2020 <https://www.lifesitenews.com/news/doctors-lay-out-plan-to-punish-people-who-refuse-coronavirus-vaccine-there-is-no-alternative; https://www.wsj.com/articles/coronavirus-paves-way-for-new-age-of-digital-surveillance-11586963028>.

[71] See, eg, Lucas Nolan, 'MIT Technology Review Begins Tracking Coronavirus Contact Tracing Apps', *Breitbart*, 19 June 2020 <https://www.breitbart.com/tech/2020/06/19/mit-technology-review-begins-tracking-coronavirus-contact-tracing-apps/>.

ly prohibit mandatory imposition of any federally controlled vaccine drug into a human being without their consent.[72]

Congress may act to regulate the dispensing of vaccine drugs if: 1) empowered to do so under a provision of the *United States Constitution*; and 2) no other part of the *Constitution* limits such regulation.[73] If authority exists under the *U.S. Constitution* for Congress to regulate, and no other part of the *Constitution* limits such regulation, then the Supreme Court should uphold the law when it is rationally related to any legitimate governmental interest. Most importantly, under the Supremacy Clause, such a federal law pre-empts any conflicting State law that cannot consistently stand together with the federal regulation.[74]

1 *The Constitutional Power of Congress to Regulate Controlled Substances*

Article I of the *United States Constitution* vests in Congress the power '[t]o regulate Commerce ... among the several States,'[75] Additionally, the 'Necessary and Proper' Clause empowers Congress to enact laws reasonably necessary to carry out its power under the Commerce Clause.[76] Supreme Court precedent interprets these provisions as empowering Congress to regulate inter alia 'things in interstate commerce' and activities that 'substantially affect' interstate commerce.[77] Article I empowers Congress, therefore, to regulate dispensing of controlled substances like vaccines if either: 1) the drugs are things in interstate commerce or 2) the activity substantially affects interstate commerce.

---

[72] *Controlled Substances Act*, 21 USCA §§ 801-02, 811-14 821-30, 841-44a, 846-56, 858-65, 871-87, 889-90, 901-04, 951-71 (2006).

[73] *United States Constitution* art I.

[74] *United States Constitution* art VI; *see also* 21 USC § 903; *Gonzales v Raich*, 545 US 1, 29 (2005).

[75] *United States Constitution* art I § 8 cl 3.

[76] *United States Constitution* art I § 8 cl 18.

[77] *See United States v Morrison*, 529 US 598, 608-09 (2000); *United States v Lopez*, 514 US 549, 558-59 (1995); *see also United States v Darby*, 312 US 100, 118 (1941).

Drugs dispensed as vaccines have likely traveled in interstate commerce.[78] Such drugs are, therefore, 'things' in interstate commerce. Because the controlled substances are 'things' in interstate commerce, Congress, has the power under the Commerce Clause, to regulate by amending the CSA as proposed.

Congress may also regulate activity concerning controlled substances if the activity substantially affects interstate commerce.[79] In determining whether a substantial effect on interstate commerce exists, a court can aggregate the regulated activity if it is economic activity.[80] '[A]ctivities regulated by the CSA are quintessentially economic' since they involve 'the production, distribution, and consumption of commodities.'[81]

Doctors dispensing federally controlled drugs actively participate in the interstate controlled substances market.[82] Since this economic activity concerning controlled substances substantially affects interstate commerce, Congress may regulate it.[83] When Congress enacts comprehensive legislation to regulate the interstate market in a fungible commodity, it acts 'well within its authority to "make all Laws which shall be necessary and proper" to "regulate Commerce among the several States.'"[84] For example, in *Gonzalez v Raich*, the Court held Congress possessed the power to regulate even the intrastate

---

[78] See, eg, *Gonzales v Oregon*, 546 US 243, 302 n 2 (2006) (Thomas J, dissenting) ('*Oregon*') (drugs dispensed for assisted suicide in interstate commerce).

[79] *Gonzales v Raich*, 545 US 1, 9, 15 (2005) ('*Raich*'). '[A]ctivities regulated by the CSA are quintessentially economic' since they involve 'the production, distribution, and consumption of commodities.' at 25-26.

[80] Ibid (aggregating economic activity); *Morrison*, 529 US 598, 617-18 (holding that court may not aggregate non-economic activity based on its 'aggregated effect on interstate commerce').

[81] *Raich*, 545 US 1, 25-26. Moreover, '[i]n assessing the scope of Congress' authority under the Commerce Clause, … [a court] need not determine whether [the] activities, taken in the aggregate, substantially affect interstate commerce in fact, but only whether a "rational basis" exists for so concluding.' at 22 (citing *United States v Lopez*, 514 US 549, 557).

[82] See *Oregon*, 546 US 243, 302 n 2 (2006) (Thomas J, dissenting).

[83] *Gonzales v Raich*, 545 US 1, 25-26.

[84] Ibid 22 (citing *Unites States Constitution* art I § 8).

manufacture and possession of marijuana for personal use, since such economic activity substantially affected interstate commerce.[85] Justice Stevens, writing for the Court stated, 'When Congress decides the total incidence of a practice poses a threat to the national market, it may regulate the entire class.'[86]

In *Raich* the Court expressly held that 'the CSA is a comprehensive regulatory regime specifically designed to regulate which controlled substances can be utilized for medicinal purposes, and in what manner.'[87] Seven months later, however, the Court in *Gonzales v Oregon* characterized the CSA's comprehensive regulatory regime more restrictively (ie, limiting 'doctors from using their prescription-writing powers as a means to engage in illicit drug dealing and trafficking as conventionally understood').[88] The majority stated Congress should use 'explicit language in the statute' if it desires to prohibit physicians from dispensing drugs to assist suicide.[89] In view of the Court's language, Congress should expressly amend the CSA to prohibit mandatory vaccination without consent of the patient. Since art I of the *United States Constitution* provides an appropriate power source for Congress to enact the proposed amendment – either because the drugs are *things* in interstate commerce or because the *activity* substantially affects interstate commerce – the next issue is whether any other part of the *United States Constitution* limits Congress from exercising its art I powers.

2 Nothing in the Constitution Limits Congress from Using it's Article I Powers to Regulate the Dispensing of Federally Controlled Drugs by Prohibiting Mandatory Vaccination without Consent

No constitutional provision limits Congress from exercising its art I power as proposed here. Some may, however, attempt to misconstrue

---

[85] Congress may regulate even 'purely local activities that are part of an economic "class of activities" that have a substantial effect on interstate commerce.': ibid 17.
[86] Ibid (citations omitted).
[87] Ibid 27; see also 24.
[88] *Oregon*, 546 US 243, 270 (2006) (eg, diversion of drugs into illegal channels).
[89] Ibid 271-72.

the proposed amendment to the CSA by suggesting that it concerns a State's right to regulate the practice of medicine – and that it therefore alters the usual constitutional balance between the states and federal government. The proposed amendment here is not about the regulation of medical practice; it is about the right of the federal government to regulate controlled substances (ie, commerce) in a uniform manner. That is, the proposed amendment, as part of a constitutionally authorized federal regulatory scheme, prohibits mandatory imposition of any federally controlled vaccine drug into a human being without their consent. In any case, no constitutional provision limits Congress from using its powers under art I to regulate commerce in connection with medical matters; no question exists that Congress can establish uniform national standards in the areas of health and safety.[90]

Since no fundamental right limiting Congress' power exists, Congress may regulate federal drugs as long as its legislation is rationally related to a legitimate government purpose.[91] The government has a legitimate interests in preserving human life, preserving privacy and religious liberty interests.[92] A statute prohibiting mandatory imposition of any federally controlled vaccine drug into a human being without their consent is rationally related to these legitimate governmental interests. In amending the CSA, therefore, Congress should clearly articulate that its intent to comprehensively regulate the market of controlled substances includes regulation of such substances used to vaccinate.

---

[90] *Raich*, 545 US 1, 9 (2005); *Oregon*, 546 US 243, 302 n 2 (2006) (Thomas J, dissenting); see also *United States v Darby*, 312 US 100, 115-17 (1941) (renouncing earlier doctrines holding that Congress could not utilise the commerce power to achieve legitimate objectives relating to the health and welfare of the nation).

[91] See, eg, *Hodel v Indiana*, 452 US 314, 323-24 (1981) ('A court may invalidate legislation enacted under the Commerce Clause only if it is clear that there is no rational basis for a congressional finding that the regulated activity affects interstate commerce, or that there is no reasonable connection between the regulatory means selected and the asserted ends.').

92 See, eg, *Washington v Glucksberg*, 521 US 702, 728 (1997) (recognising a number of legitimate state interests including 'preserving life,' 'preventing suicide,' and preventing a moral slide 'toward euthanasia'); *Vacco v Quill*, 521 US 793, 808-09 (same); *see also Planned Parenthood v Casey*, 505 US 833, 846, 878 (1992) (recognising protection of human life as a legitimate state interest).

Moreover, Congress properly can conclude that regulation of drugs, and drug-dispensing vaccination activity, is a reasonably necessary way to achieve its purpose of comprehensively regulating the interstate market in controlled substances in the CSA as amended.[93] As noted, drugs dispensed for vaccination are "things" in interstate commerce Congress may regulate under the Commerce Clause. If a primary purpose of the CSA is to control the controlled substances market,[94] then regulating such a commodity in interstate commerce is rationally related to the government's legitimate purpose. Likewise, since doctors dispensing vaccination drugs actively participate in the interstate controlled substances market, Congress can rationally conclude that, in the aggregate, leaving vaccination drugs outside the regulatory scheme substantially influences price and market conditions. Such is the case even if the manufacture and dispensing of controlled substances for vaccination is purely intrastate, since such economic activity, in the aggregate, substantially affects the larger interstate drug market. Congress should provide clear legislative history establishing this fact.[95]

---

[93] Congress's original purpose in enacting the Controlled Substances Act was to comprehensively regulate the market of such substances. See *Raich*, 545 US 1, 27 (2005). A House Report expressly stated that Congress promulgated the law in order 'to deal in a comprehensive fashion with the growing menace of drug abuse in the United States . . . through providing more effective means for law enforcement aspects of drug abuse prevention and control.' HR Rep No 91-1444, pt 1, 1 (1970), reprinted in 1970 USCCAN 4566, 4567. Moreover, when it enacted the *Federal Controlled Substances Act*, Congress made extensive findings and statements, including that:
(1) Many of the drugs included within this subchapter have a useful and legitimate medical purpose and are necessary to maintain the health and general welfare of the American people.
(2) The illegal . . . distribution, and possession *and improper use* of controlled substances have a substantial and detrimental effect on the health and general welfare of the American people.
(3) A major portion of the traffic in controlled substances flows through interstate and foreign commerce. Incidents of the traffic which are not an integral part of the interstate or foreign flow, such as manufacture, local distribution, and possession, nonetheless have a substantial and direct effect upon interstate commerce . . . . 21 USC § 801(emphasis added).
[94] *Raich*, 545 US 1, 19 (2005).
[95] Although not required, a specific finding to this effect by Congress will be helpful when courts inevitably review the statutory scheme. See *Raich*, 545 US 1, 20-22 (2005).

Congress properly, therefore, can conclude that regulation of drug-dispensing activity is a reasonably necessary way to achieve its purpose of comprehensively regulating the interstate market in controlled substances – especially as amended. Including improper drug-dispensing activity for vaccination purposes within the CSA's coverage furthers its legitimate objective. Indeed, leaving such activity excepted from regulation will undermine a clear legislative intent to regulate the drug market comprehensively in a manner which protects public health and safety.[96]

Under a "rational basis" standard, broad deference is due to congressional judgments concerning whether drug dispensing economic activity by physicians substantially affects interstate commerce.[97] Likewise, such broad deference applies to whether Congress's regulation of drugs is reasonably necessary to carry out its amended legislative purpose under the Commerce Clause.[98]

B *Effects of the Proposed Legislation*

As amended, the *Federal Controlled Substances Act* will preempt State laws mandating vaccinations where doctors involuntarily dispense drugs.

Where federal and state provisions conflict, art VI of the *United States Constitution* controls:

> This Constitution, and *the Laws of the United States* which shall be made in Pursuance thereof .. shall be the supreme Law of the Land; and the Judges in every State shall be bound thereby, any Thing in the . . . laws of any State to the Contrary notwithstanding.[99]

---

[96] This is why, for example, the dispensing of controlled substances is regulated under the CSA by 'provid[ing] for control . . . through registration of manufacturers, wholesalers, retailers, and all others [including physicians] in the legitimate distribution chain . . . .' HR Rep No 91-1444, pt 1, 3, 6 (1970), reprinted in 1970 USCCAN 4566, 4569.

[97] *See Raich*, 545 US 1, 22, 25-26 (2005); *United States v Lopez*, 514 US 549, 557 (1995) (*'Lopez'*).

[98] *Lopez*, 514 US 549, 557-58 (1995).

[99] *United States Constitution* art VI (emphasis added).

In its *Raich* decision, the Supreme Court reiterated:

> The Supremacy Clause unambiguously provides that if there is any conflict between federal and state law, federal law shall prevail. It is beyond peradventure that federal power over commerce is superior to that of the States to provide for the . . . necessities of their inhabitants . . . .. No form of state activity can constitutionally thwart the regulatory power granted by the commerce clause to Congress.[100]

As amended, the CSA will expressly preempt any state laws to the extent 'there is a positive conflict between [a provision of the CSA] and that state law so that the two cannot consistently stand together.'[101] Under conventional conflict preemption principles, therefore, the CSA as amended will clearly preempt State statutes mandating imposition of any federally controlled vaccine drug into a human being without their consent.

Moreover, even if a court could somehow construe the CSA as amended to not expressly preempt a State mandatory vaccination statute, implied preemption exists where 'compliance with both federal and state regulations is a physical impossibility.'[102] The mutually exclusive provisions of an amended CSA and potential State mandatory vaccination laws governing the dispensing of controlled substances make it impossible for a dispensing physician to comply with both. In such situations, the Supreme Court has deemed the state law preempted – even where a distinctive state interest is at stake.[103]

---

[100] *Raich*, 545 US 1, 29 (2005) (internal quotations and citations omitted).

[101] 21 USC § 903. To be sure, nothing in the CSA prevents a state from enacting its own stricter drug legislation, or prosecuting drug offenses at the state level. And nothing in the Federal CSA preempts a state from regulating within the field of physician-assisted suicide (ie, nothing in the CSA preempts a state law authorising physician-assisted suicide *per se*).

[102] *Boggs v Boggs*, 520 US 833, 844 (1997) (internal quotation marks omitted) (citing *Gade v National Solid Wastes Management Ass'n*, 505 US 88, 98 (1992)).

[103] See, eg, *Hisquierdo v Hisquierdo*, 439 US 572, 581, 590 (1979) (finding state community property law preempted by federal military pay law).

IV PRESERVING LIBERTY REQUIRES STEWARDSHIP

The American nation's Great Experiment in government by the consent of the governed requires responsible stewardship and a devoted commitment of the people. Many present at the beginning of this Great Experiment experienced personally the oppressive dictates of a tyrannical regime. Those most responsible for the freedom declared in the Declaration, and guaranteed under the Constitution, understood Acton's admonition that power corrupts with its consequent threat to liberty. They also understood the cost of preserving liberty, lucidly expressed in the words of Patrick Henry at the Second Virginia Convention, in 1775:

> Is life so dear, or peace so sweet, as to be purchased at the price of chains and slavery? Forbid it. Almighty God! I know not what course others may take; but as for me, give men liberty or give me death![104]

For a long while we stood on the shoulders of giants who founded a great nation committed to the preservation of freedom. Today as State regimes infringe on freedoms without to the consent of the governed, we forget the wisdom and warning of President Ronald Reagan:

> Freedom is never more than one generation away from extinction. We didn't pass it to our children in the bloodstream. It must be fought for, protected, and handed on for them to do the same, or one day we will spend our sunset years telling our children and our children's children what it was once like in the United States where men were free.[105]

Today, State regimes infringe on freedoms without the consent of a governed too fearful of a virus to not submit. Instead of living in a fear-induced existence of submit or die, we ought to live the maxim of our founders, *Live Free or Die*, uttered while experienc-

---

[104] Patrick Henry, 'Give Me Liberty or Give Me Death' (March 23, 1775), *The Avalon Project* <https://avalon.law.yale.edu/18th_century/patrick.asp>.

[105] See eg, Ronald Reagan, 'Inaugural Address' (January 5, 1967), Ronald Reagan Presidential Library <https://www.reaganlibrary.gov/research/speeches/01051967a>.

ing far greater life-threatening perils than Covid-19.[106] If Covid-19 is to come my way, let me be in the midst of sharing my faith in an omnipotent and omniscient Creator; let me be preserving liberty so that those who come after me can likewise do so without fear of persecution.

---

[106] During the American Revolution, a major smallpox outbreak existed, in what today is the United States. See eg, <https://www.aier.org/article/the-american-revolution-occurred-in-the-middle-of-a-pandemic/>.

15

The Virus of Governmental Oppression: How the Australian Government is Jeopardising Democracy and our Health

AUGUSTO ZIMMERMANN*

ABSTRACT

This article discusses the legal and moral consequences of draconian measures adopted by our political elites under the pretence that they were necessary to fight the coronavirus. Shutting down the entire country for many months, in a desperate attempt to save everyone and everywhere from a virus whose mortality rate is relatively low, has done far more damage to the people than the virus itself. Although it is important to recognise that the coronavirus appears to pose some health risks to the population, the key word here is proportionality and the arbitrary measures imposed by the ruling elites not only violate the Australian Constitution, but also unleash unprecedented socio-economic consequences, which threaten our very way of life and what it means to live in a free and open society.

I FIRST CONSIDERATIONS

Since March 2020 Australia's governments, both federal and state, are using their powers to excessively coerce, obstruct or otherwise unreasonably interfere with the life, liberty and property of the citi-

---

* LLB, LLM, PhD, Professor and Head of Law, Sheridan Institute of Higher Education; Professor of Law (adj.), The University of Notre Dame Australia (Sydney); President, The Western Australian Legal Theory Association (WALTA); former Law Reform Commissioner, Law Reform Commission of Western Australia (2012-2017).

zen. What these governments are doing is nothing but profoundly arbitrary and unconstitutional. They are using their newly acquired *emergency powers* to oppress the people and undermine basic principles of democratic government – including equality before the law and the right of citizens to be protected from unpredictable and arbitrary interference with their vital interests. In this article I endeavour to demonstrate how, under the pretence of fighting a supposed pandemic, draconian measures have been adopted that not only grossly violate the Australian Constitution but also the fundamental rights of the Australian people.

II GOVERNMENT OVERREACTION

Since the alleged pandemic began, apparently over 500 Australians have died from Covid-19 (25 August 2020). To put this into proper perspective, this is less than half the number of Australians who die every year from skin diseases, and about one-fifth of the number killed in car accidents. Most of these deaths were among people in or above the 80s and living in aged-care homes. We know also that those under 60 without a pre-existing medical condition have an extremely small chance of dying of coronavirus, and little chance of even getting very ill from this virus.

Of course, every life matters. However, according to a seminal study carried out by Justin Silverman and Alex Washburne, the coronavirus mortality rate may well be as low as 0.1 per cent, "similar to that of flu".[1] Based on data coming from New York City (the hotbed of the pandemic in the U.S.), only 1.7 per cent of those in their 70s who contracted the virus have acquired any symptoms which were severe

---

[1] *The Economist*, 'Why a Study Showing that Covid-19 is Everywhere is Good News', 11 April 2020 <https://www.economist.com/graphic-detail/2020/04/11/why-a-study-showing-that-covid-19-is-everywhere-is-good-news>. See also: Edwin Mora, 'Study: Coronavirus Fatality Rate Lower than Expected, Close to Flu's 0.1%', *Breitbart*, 13 April 2020 <https://www.breitbart.com/politics/2020/04/13/study-coronavirus-fatality-rate-lower-than-expected-close-to-flus-0-1/?fbclid=IwAR3_WeIyIPw9ILaFvUnEoyfg60MnUkycuYY7_QEAWckRp5Fwgl7p2WR0CF4>.

enough to require medical care.[2] For those under 18, hospitalisation from the virus was only 0.01.[3]

This is only about hospitalisation and not death caused by the coronavirus. Of course, nothing is said about the many others who never became sick enough to even get tested. The overwhelming majority of people who contract this virus do not have any significant risk of dying, says Dr Scott W. Atlas, a former chief of neurology at Stanford Medical Center.[4] The magazine *Science* reports that 86 per cent of infections are never documented.

In this sense, even if most of us eventually catch the coronavirus, there will be mild or no symptoms for practically everyone. Accordingly, we should be taking special measures only for the most vulnerable – namely the elderly who are already suffering from chronic illnesses – and let the great majority of the population get on with their lives.

Based on fundamental biology and the evidence at hand, the appropriate policy to fight the coronavirus should be focused on protecting only the most vulnerable – those who are very old or suffering from chronic illness. As for the vast majority of us, 'essential socialising' is fundamental to 'generate immunity' and 'limiting the enormous harms compounded by continued total isolation'.[5]

According to Professor Mark Woolhouse, epidemiologist at Edinburgh University and adviser to the UK Government, attempting to control coronavirus through lockdown measures as the Australian government has done is a "monumental mistake".[6] Professor Wool-

---

2 Ibid.

3 E. Bendavid et al., 'COVID-19 Antibody Seroprevalence in Santa Clara country, California', *Stanford University*, 11 April 2020. <https://www.medrxiv.org/content/1 0.1101/2020.04.14.20062463v1.full.pdf>

4 Scott W Atlas, 'The Data is in – Stop the Panic and End the Total Isolation', *The Hill*, 22 April 2020 <https://thehill.com/opinion/healthcare/494034-the-data-are-in-stop-the-panic-and-end-the-total-isolation>.

5 Ibid.

6 Lucy Johnston, 'UK Lockdown Was A "Monumental Mistake" And Must Not Happen Again – Boris Scientist Says', *Sunday Express*, 24 August 2020 <https://www.express.co.uk/life-style/health/1320428/Coronavirus-news-lockdown-mistake-second-wave-Boris-Johnson>.

house believes the harm such lockdowns cause to education, health care access and broader aspects of the economy and society, 'will turn out to be at least as great as the harm done by Covid-19'.[7] Not only do these lockdowns constitute an unnecessary "panic measure", but, according to him, 'history will say trying to control COVID-19 through lockdown was a monumental mistake on a global scale, the cure was worse than the disease'.[8]

In this sense, hundreds of U.S. physicians have composed an important document on May 19th referring precisely to these social problems, and asking governments to immediately end the coronavirus shutdown. The letter reflects the alarm of these medical doctors at what appears to be a disturbing lack of proper consideration for the future health of the population at large.[9] Signed by Dr Simon Gold MD JD and more than 500 hundred other medical physicians, the letter authoritatively states:

> It's impossible to overstate the short, medium, and long-term harm to people's health with a continued shutdown. Losing a job is one of life's most stressful events, and the effect on a person's health is not lessened because it also has happened to 30 million other people. Keeping schools and universities closed is incalculably detrimental for children, teenagers, and young adults for decades to come.

> The millions of casualties of a continued shutdown will be hiding in plain sight, but they will be called alcoholism, homelessness, suicide, heart attack, stroke, or kidney addiction, unplanned pregnancies, poverty, and abuse.[10]

---

[7] Ibid.

[8] Ibid.

[9] Alex Swoyer, '500 Doctors Tell Trump to End the Coronavirus Shutdown, Say it Will Cause More Deaths', *The Washington Times*, 21 May 2020 <https://www.washingtontimes.com/news/2020/may/21/500-doctors-tell-donald-trump-end-coronavirus-shut/>.

[10] Simone Gold MD & >500 physicians, 'A letter signed by hundreds of doctors warning of adverse health consequences stemming from the coronavirus shutdowns', 19 May 2020 <https://www.scribd.com/document/462319362/A-Doctor-a-Day-Letter-Signed>.

As can be seen, all the Australian governments, both federal and state, have created a problem that appears to be much bigger than the coronavirus. More than a million Australians have already sought mental health treatment during the "health crisis". In Victoria, access to health crisis services have jumped more than 30 per cent since September this year. Demand for children's mental health has also skyrocketed. Victoria's own data reveals a 33 per cent spike in 'child and youth contacts in community mental health services for eating disorders'.[11] According to the official data, there were 3,702 calls to the Kids Helpline by Victorians, a 61 per cent increase in just four weeks.[12]

Of all the most pressing problems created by the Australian governments via these lockdowns and other draconian measures, suicide rates are forecast to rise up to 50 per cent due to the socio-economic impact of government measures, particularly among young Australians aged 15-25 years.[13] Carried out by the Sydney University's Brain and Mind Centre and supported by the Australian Medical Association, world-leading researchers predict that the impact of government measures may well result in an extra 1,500 Australian deaths a year over the next five years, which is at least 10 times more deaths than deaths caused by the coronavirus.[14] Of course, as noted by *The Australian*'s columnist Janet Albrechtsen, 'no politician is going to be held responsible for the suicide of an unemployed young man who has lost hope'.[15]

---

[11] Simon Benson, 'Mental Health Crisis: One Million 'Lost' in Coronavirus Lockdown, *The Australian*, 14 October 2020 <https://www.theaustralian.com.au/nation/politics/mental-health-crisis-one-million-lost-in-coronavirus-lockdown/news-story/fc8c1da341ca392166fce6aba9ca4f69>.

[12] Ibid.

[13] Simon Benson, 'Coronavirus Australia: Suicide's Toll Far Higher Than the Virus', *The Australian*, 7 May 2020 <https://www.theaustralian.com.au/nation/suicides-toll-far-higher-than-coronavirus/news-story/25a686904b67bdedbdcd544b1cab7f96>.

[14] Ibid.

[15] Janet Albretchtsen, 'Coronavirus: Charting a Way Out of this Crippling Pollyanna World', *The Australian*, 7 May 2020 <https://www.theaustralian.com.au/inquirer/coronavirus-charting-a-way-out-of-this-crippling-pollyanna-world/news-story/cfd6913dfc2c5c7e082b7e8d398d0075>.

Professor Ian Hickie, former mental health commissioner and Head of the Brain and Mind Centre, has reportedly said the annual rate of suicide caused by the government answer to the pandemic could rise from 3,000 to up to 4,500, with youth suicides making up almost half of the expected deaths. Apparently Professor Hickie has specifically advised the Australian government about the impact of economic measures with the greatest among the young, and those who particularly live in rural and regional Australia. 'What happens in recessions is that suicide rates go up dramatically ... and they hurt the young the most', Professor Hickie says.[16]

Apparently this important advice fell on deaf ears. The Prime Minister and the State and Territory leaders and their so called National Cabinet all have their individual and collective responsibility for this unmitigated disaster. These authorities, both federal and state, accepted the seriousness of the pandemic to be real. They blindly accepted the very alarmist and totally inaccurate World Health Organisation (WHO) prediction of 3.4 per cent mortality, and suddenly brought about all these disruptions of personal freedoms that have cost millions of jobs and the closing down of countless businesses.

The anger and resentment is coming particularly from those who have lost their jobs or had their businesses entirely destroyed. Of course, none of the privileged members of the country's political elite and the two million employees in the public sector are affected. They comprise a superior caste of privileged individuals. For them the present crisis represents no more than an opportunity to increase their power and influence over society as a whole. Government agencies are also acquiring extraordinary powers to monitor people and to detain law-abiding citizens. For example, the Western Australian government has started to use tracking devices on its citizens for monitoring breaches of directions.

Dr John Ionnidis, professor of medicine, epidemiology, population health, and statistics at Stanford University, believes the rate of death for the coronavirus, when adjusted from wide age range, could be as

---

16 Ibid.

low as 0.05 per cent.[17] He explains that no less than 80 per cent of all those who contract the virus have no symptoms or these are very mild. Of those under the 50s age group, at least 99.5 per cent will survive, which is even less problematic than the normal round of the flu. If that is the true rate, Ionnidis concludes, locking down the world with potentially tremendous social and influential consequences may be totally irrational.

A similar opinion is expressed by David L. Katz, founding director of Yale University's Yale-Griffin *Prevention Research Center* and former president of the *American College of Lifestyle Medicine*.[18] Dr Katz has three honorary doctorate degrees and is the recipient of numerous academic awards for his "significant contributions to public health". According to him, the "unique" nature of Covid-19 is that it results in only "mild" symptoms in 99 per cent of cases and that it appears to only pose a high risk to the elderly". Hence his sobering conclusion that "our fight against coronavirus' may end up being worse than the disease".[19]

By taking an "at war" approach to fighting Covid-19 – widespread shutdowns and isolation of the entire population – rather than a "surgical strike" approach focusing on the truly vulnerable, Dr Katz believes that "we have set ourselves on the path of "uncontained viral contagion and monumental collateral damage to our society and economy". "The [normal] flu hits the elderly and chronically ill hard too, but it also kills children. Trying to create herd immunity among those most likely to recover from infection while also isolating the young and the old is dauting to say the least", Dr Katz explains.[20]

---

[17] John P.A. Ionnidis, 'A Fiasco in the Making? As the Coronavirus Pandemic Takes Hold, We Are Making Decisions Without Reliable Data', *Statnews*, 17 March 2020 <https://www.statnews.com/2020/03/17/a-fiasco-in-the-making-as-the-coronavirus-pandemic-takes-hold-we-are-making-decisions-without-reliable-data/>.

[18] See: https://davidkatzmd.com/david-katz-md-biography/

[19] David L. Katz, 'Is Our Fight Against Coronavirus Worse Than the Disease?', *The New York Times*, 20 March 2020 <https://www.nytimes.com/2020/03/20/opinion/coronavirus-pandemic-social-distancing.html>.

[20] Ibid.

These facts make the disease particularly suited for a more strategic containment effort, rather than our current unsustainable, society-wide approach that threatens to undermine the economy. According to Dr Katz, it is deeply concerning that "the social, economic and public health consequences of a near total meltdown of normal life – schools and business closed, gatherings banned – will be long lasting and calamitous, possibly even graver than the direct toll of the virus itself." "The stock market will bounce back in time, but many businesses never will. The unemployment, impoverishment and despair likely to result will be public health scourges of the first order", Dr Katz says.[21]

Unfortunately this sort of advice appears to have been largely ignored by the Australian government. This is so regardless of the Prime Minister always telling us that his government is simply doing what a panel of scientists are telling them to do.

First of all, good leaders do not evade their responsibility by conveniently hiding behind a few medical "experts". Besides, there are a number of leading medical practitioners who strongly oppose any such draconian measures of social distancing and lockdowns solely on health grounds. For instance, a rural GP recently explained:

> The government should open up the economy for people under 65 to get back to socialising and working and those of us who are older to play it safe with continued social distancing and voluntary isolation. It appears our medical system will be able to cope with the much lower rates of hospitalisation and mortality becoming evident from the available data especially if we continue to protect the elderly. What can't be coped with is the social and economic cost of this.

Second, as the term itself conveys, a medical expert is only an expert in one particular field. However, this current crisis is not solely a medical issue and it therefore requires a more holistic approach and the balancing of multiple considerations. These advisers carefully handpicked by the political elites might have no holistic understanding of

---

[21] Ibid.

the matter. They have no expertise in the other and equally relevant fields of psychology, sociology, economics and constitutional law.

During a public health emergency, the Australian State's chief health officers can issue public health directions to assist in containing, or to respond to, the spread of coronavirus within the community. However, some of these health officers have no experience in infectious disease management. Indeed, Queensland's chief health officer, Dr Jeannette Young, reportedly not only has almost no clinical experience but also no expertise in infectious diseases.[22] Still, Premier Annastacia Palaszczuk blames her for the draconian restrictions imposed by her own government, including the State's unconstitutional strict border closure banning citizens who reside in other States (ACT, New South Wales and Victoria) from entering Queensland.

Economist and company director Judith Sloan refers therefore to "the new tyranny" that has emerged during the coronavirus era: "the tyranny of experts". According to her, such a tyranny must be resisted because our political leaders have relied on a few chosen medical experts to conveniently claim that "science" has made them impose these draconian restrictions on the community. These experts may have a role to play but, as she reminds us, 'not in an uncontested way'. Thus she concludes with this important advice:

> When a politician says experts are in charge or the "science" made them do it, be suspicious. These experts don't speak with one voice and many are peddling values they hold dear; as true with COVID-19 as it is with climate change. Politicians are elected to govern us all; this requires judgement about the trade-offs that inevitably exist with all policy decisions.[23]

According to Woodhouse, member of the Scientific Pandemic Influenza Group on Behaviours that advises the U.K. Government, gov-

---

[22] Judith Sloan, 'Once It Was Distance, But A New Tyranny Has Emerged In Coronavirus Era', *The Australian*, 16 September 2020 <https://www.theaustralian.com.au/commentary/once-it-was-distance-but-a-new-tyranny-has-emerged-in-coronavirus-era/news-story/173654a1dfd96ea36e280d0f34b>.

[23] Ibid.

ernment advisory boards dealing with Covid 'need to have members from a wider range of fields'. To avoid more people being harmed by the collateral effects of lockdown and other government measures than by Covid-19, he argues that government advisory boards should be comprised of a broader range of people, 'receiving equal input from economists to assess the damage to incomes, lives and livelihoods; educationalists to assess the damage to children; and mental health specialists to assess levels of depression and anxiety especially among younger adults; as well as psychologists to assess the effects of not being able to go to the theatre or a football match'.[24]

The federal government estimates unemployment to be about 11 per cent. This is rather deceptive and the real numbers will be revealed only when JobKeeper goes and numerous business will be unable to reopen.[25] Out of Australia's 13 million employed in March 2020, there are now 6 million on JobSeeker and JobKeeper.[26] This means that half of those in the private sector are now dependant on government aid and earning at least 30 per cent less than they did. Most of these people will eventually discover they are actually unemployed. They will never be able to resume their jobs simply because the company for which they had been working has been forced to shut down permanently.

The Morrison government has so far spent more than $500 billion allegedly to protect our jobs, although the unemployment rate is now well above 10 per cent (20 per cent in Victoria), with the national debt heading towards a trillion dollars.[27] According to an analysis by the

---

[24] Johnston, above n 6.

[25] Sinclair Davidson, 'The Economic Crisis Is Still to Come', *The Age*, Melbourne/Vic, 6 August 2020. <https://www.theage.com.au/national/victoria/the-economic-crisis-is-still-to-come-20200806-p55j5f.html>

[26] Alan Moran, 'Revealed: The True Cost of Our Stimulus Spending', *The Spectator Australia*, May 7, 2020 <https://www.spectator.com.au/2020/05/revealed-the-true-cost-of-our-stimulus-spending/>

[27] Dennis Shanaham, 'Morrison Keeps Danbursters At Bay Over Second Coronavirus', *The Australian*, 8 August 2020. <https://www.theaustralian.com.au/inquirer/morrison-keeps-danbusters-at-bay-over-second-coronavirus-wave/news-story/f6ab-808ca813beb58856810891a06354>

Institute of Public Affairs ('IPA'), over 230,000 small businesses are expected to close once Covid-19 measures are finally removed. The closure of these small businesses would permanently destroy 470,000 jobs, based on average small business employment.[28]

'The disproportionate destructing destruction of small businesses by the Covid-19 lockdown measures is demonstrated by their heavy reliance on government support, such as JobKeeper, for survival', writes Kurt Wallace, a research fellow at the IPA. He observes also that it is totally unsustainable for small businesses to continue to rely on government support for survival. 'The legacy of the lockdown restrictions will be an economy dominated by large conglomerates with local communities being stripped of the small businesses that are integral to their character', Wallace argues.[29]

However, 'both state and federal governments are in denial', writes economics professor Sinclair Davidson, who then correctly reminds us that

> The economy is about people; their plans, their expectations, their relationships. For all the talk about competition, the economy is about co-operation. The economy is not a machine that can be switched off and on at will. The interrelated web of co-operative relationships that was the February 2020 economy is gone forever. The economy that now exists is a lot smaller than what it was just six months ago. The problem now being that we can't be sure which part of it will revive and which part of it won't.[30]

Here are some tough questions the Australian governments would need to answer: 'How did deaths from Covid-19 compare with an awful flu season that kills young people too? How many people died from other medical conditions that were not treated because of

---

[28] Kurt Wallace, 'Small Business And Jobs Smashed By COVID-19 Lockdowns', *IPA Today*, 10 August 2020 <https://ipa.org.au/publications-ipa/small-business-and-jobs-smashed-by-covid-19-lockdowns>.

[29] Ibid.

[30] Davidson, above n 25.

the lockdown? How many additional suicides were caused by the lockdown?'[31]

Of course, as Janet Albrechtsen correctly points out, 'no politician is going to be held responsible for the future suicide of an unemployed young man who has lost hope. But they imagine they will be held responsible for the immediate death of a 94-year old from, or with, Covid-19'.[32] The level of delusional thinking is truly astonishing, although it certainly reveals the authoritarian mindset of politicians who expect extreme obedience and unquestioning submission from the Australian people.

III THE RISE OF THE PATERNAL LEADER

There was never an emergency that could justify the imposition of these authoritarian measures. Politicians have justified the incredible harm they are causing to the Australian people by getting completely drunk on their own sense of self-righteousness. Full of themselves, they proudly warned that we face a great threat but their policies have saved us from the spread of a deadly virus. The privileged members of our political class are therefore able to block our peaceful protests because they think they know better what needs to be done, and even if we are eventually oppressed, silenced and destitute as a result.

A reasonable concern for our well-being is one thing, but the actions taken by politicians during this pandemic have gone well beyond the extreme. What is happening is simply disgraceful and it gives new meaning to the phrase, 'The cure is worse than the disease'. Of course, some of the worst crimes against humanity have been committed by individuals who believed they were simply doing a 'great good'. Listening to their patronising remarks brings to mind a famous quote by Christian apologist and novelist C.S. Lewis:

---

[31] Janet Albrechtsen, 'Coronavirus: Old or Young – Every Life Has a Different Value and We Accept That', *The Australian*, 6 May 2020. <https://www.theaustralian.com.au/commentary/coronavirus-old-or-young-every-life-has-a-different-value-and-we-accept-that/news-story/ecc95caa9307a7a047aca5847c6bd88d>
[32] Ibid.

Of all tyrannies, a tyranny sincerely exercised for the good of its victims may be the most oppressive… Those who torment us for our own good will torment us without end for hey do so with the approval of their own conscience.[33]

The political philosophy of John Locke is particularly relevant to our understanding of the matter. Locke is known as the 'Founder of Liberalism' due to his immense contributions to political philosophy. In the constitutional struggle of parliamentary forces against the Stuart monarchs in 17th-century England, Locke elaborated a theory in which the primary justification for civil government rests on the preservation of our fundamental rights to life, liberty and property. Locke's main concern in his political writings was the elaboration of a legal-political philosophy to underpin the Glorious Revolution of 1688.

Locke developed a distinctly Western political tradition based on the idea that everyone is endowed by God with inalienable rights, and that no government must ever violate these basic rights of the individual. More importantly, Locke distinguished what is legitimate political power from a situation in which the exercise of power becomes despotic and/or paternalistic. As Locke himself pointed out, 'the great mistakes about government have … arisen from confounding this distinct power [political power] with another [paternal power]'.[34] Hence, as noted by Dr Kalle Grill, 'paternalism is opposed by the liberal tradition' of limited government under the law.[35]

According to emeritus professor of government Geraint Parry, one of the primary purposes in Locke's political theory 'was to separate political power from despotic power and paternal power – in other words, to deny that there is any analogy between the political

---

[33] C. S. Lewis, *God in the Dock: Essays on Theology and Ethics* (William B. Eerdmans, 1948), 74.

[34] John Locke, *The Second Treatise* (Cambridge University Press, 1960), para. 169.

[35] Kate Grill, 'Paternalism', in R. Chadwick (ed.) *Encyclopedia of Applied Ethics* (2nd ed., Elsevier, 2011) <http://kallegrill.se/texts/Paternalism%20preprint.pdf>.

relationship and the relationships which exist between either masters and slaves or father and children.'[36] Accordingly, the paternal leader is the political ruler who does not distinguish the difference between such relationships and limits the liberty of the people with the supposed intent of promoting "their own good" regardless of their personal will. Such an attitude displays a profound disregard for the will of other individuals and it involves behaviour that reveals an attitude of superiority coupled with profound arrogance and self-righteousness.

The Australian Prime Minister is a typical paternal leader. Morrison says he is quite happy that his subjects are behaving well. He is thinking about rewarding us for our "good behaviour". Meanwhile, he says that there will be 'many more [restrictions] in front of us before [the government] can even possibly contemplate the easing of restrictions'.[37] 'There's got to be a reward for all of this great effort that's going in, and there will be, but we've got to make sure that's done at the right time', the Prime Minister told Sky News.[38]

Morrison recently urged his subjects to download a phone app that allows the federal government to trace our every move. His government was initially aiming for a 40 per cent take up of control of 'people's movements and the people they come in contact with'.[39] While the app that the federal government developed apparently is voluntary, its introduction naturally raises concerns of such measures becoming more permanent in the future. It also raises serious privacy issues and concerns that the app will later be used for permanent surveillance. The app presently monitors people's daily interactions using GPS. It

---

[36] Geraint Parry, 'Individuality, Politics and the Critique of Paternalism in John Locke' (1964) 2 *Political Studies* 1, 1.

[37] Malcolm Farr and Daniel Hurst, 'Australian Government Plains to Bringing in Mobile Phone App to Track People With Coronavirus', *The Guardian*, 14 April 2020 <https://www.theguardian.com/australia-news/2020/apr/14/australian-government-plans-to-bring-in-mobile-phone-app-to-track-people-with-coronavirus>.

[38] Ibid.

[39] Ibid.

uses Bluetooth technology to record contact with other people even if they do not know each other.[40]

Although people under 60 have an extremely small chance of dying from coronavirus, the Prime Minister strongly believes that 95 per cent of the population must take the vaccine against such a virus. His first instincts are always inherently authoritarian and he appears to have developed a visceral distrust of the Australian people. That being so, he initially wanted the vaccine to be as mandatory as possible.[41] 'I expect that it would be mandatory as you can possibly make it', he said, adding that he is 'talking about a pandemic which has destroyed the global economy and taking the lives of ... 430 Australians'.[42]

First of all, what has really destroyed our economy is the behaviour of incompetent leaders such as Morrison himself. There were far better and more efficient ways to fight this virus apart from savage bans and gross violations of fundamental rights being inflicted on the people. Second, the Prime Minister appears to ignore that Australia is a country in which the state has been conceived as deriving from the law and not the law from the State.[43] The Morrison government has no more powers than those explicitly granted by the Australian Constitution.[44]

[40] Andrew Probyn, 'Coronavirus Lockdowns Could End In Months If Australians Are Willing To Have Their Movements Monitored'. *ABC News*, 14 April 2020 <https://www.abc.net.au/news/2020-04-14/coronavirus-app-government-wants-australians-to-download/12148210>.

[41] Richard Furgason, 'Future Vaccine Should Be Mandatory, Says PM', *The Australian*, 19 August 2020 <https://www.australian.com.au/nation/coronavirus-australia-live-news-fears-grow-of-sydney-hotel-breach-outbreack/news-story/cf35fb9ae-2901600276fa78ee89a2dc5>.

[42] Jade Gailberger, 'Coronavirus Vaccine Should Be Mandatory: PM', *PerthNow*, 19 August 2020, <https://www.perthnow.com.au/lifestyle/fitness/coronavirus-vaccine-should-be-mandatory-pm-ng-fc7dc9cd495bcc7332487c07731b4c98>.

[43] W A Wynes, *Legislative, Executive and Judicial Powers in Australia* (Sydney: The Law Book Co, 1955), vii.

[44] For instance, whereas Section 51 (xxiiiA) of the Australian Constitution allows for the granting of various services by the federal government, this should not be to the extent of authorising any form of civil conscription. This means that no government in this country, or those acting on its behalf, is constitutionally authorised to make the Australian people take any medicament against their best will, or force children to be vaccinated in order to maintain benefit payments.

Morrison's comments about vaccination follow the signing of Australia's first vaccine deal with drug maker AstraZeneca.[45] This vaccine has been rushed through trials and has never been successfully produced for a coronavirus: it might do more harm than good. Of course, this is the same government that told us that roughly 150,000 Australians would die from Covid-19. It is also the government that unreasonably banned therapeutics such as hydroxychloroquine/zinc, which numerous health experts say "could be our best cure" in the fight against the coronavirus. [46] Furthermore, the Morrison government has miserably failed to protect nursing homes where the highest incidence of victims of Covid-19 has occurred.

We are supposedly living in a free and democratic society. It is therefore quite extraordinary that a supposed democratic leader attempts to coerce citizens to do something they might not really want to do. Instead of using the full power of the State to command his "subjects" to do whatever he might want, the Prime Minister still needs to learn that true democratic leaders do not use their legal authority primarily to coerce, but instead to persuade and convince their fellow citizens to do what is right.

IV "IN GOVERNMENT WE TRUST"

I have never witnessed so much hatred in this country. As stated by The Australian's Chris Kenny, 'some of the worst aspects of our society have come to the fore through panic buying, hysterical reporting dependency and, from some, a masochistic desire to take orders'.[47] The response to Covid-19 is prompting a remarkable number of Australians to effectively treat their fellow citizens as enemies – potential

---

[45] Jade Gailberger, 'Coronavirus Vaccine Should Be Mandatory: PM', *PerthNow*, 19 August 2020 <https://www.perthnow.com.au/lifestyle/fitness/coronavirus-vaccine-should-be-mandatory-pm-ng-fc7dc9cd495bcc7332487c07731b4c98>.

[46] Andrew Bolt; 'I must call Prime Minister Scott Morrison to Account', *Sky News*, 10 August 2020 <https://www.skynews.com.au/details/_6179768424001>.

[47] Chris Kenny, 'If Politicians Know Best, Why So Many Mistakes?', *The Australian*, 15 August 2020 <https://www.theaustralian.com.au/commentary/if-politicians-know-best-why-so-many-mistakes/news-story/61184b5377a4638fbd70b9ef53253f40>.

sources of infection. Daily, citizens are being patronised, spoken down to, as if it is beyond their ability to understand the complexities of the present crisis. As Henry Ergas points out, 'being surrounded by people wearing masks coats daily life with a deep glaze of oddness, casting ourselves and everyone around us as simultaneously risky and at risk, contaminable and contaminable'.[48]

I have also noted how so many people have developed an utterly distorted view of government, or what a government can do for them. Such individuals now expect almost everything to come from government. They blindly worship at the altar of the all-mighty government, expecting their "benevolent" rulers to act as their almighty saviours, believing in government basically as the ultimate provider for all good things. Perhaps this is a result of society's lost faith in the God of Christianity. Be as it may, the undeniable truth is that far too many Australians have acquired a disturbingly unshakable faith in their ruling political masters. Call it a form of idolatry if you wish.

Fortunately, the only discernible benefit of this ongoing pandemic has been to expose the authoritarian behaviour of the ruling elites led by the Australian Prime Minister and State Premiers. It has now become clear that such privileged individuals are developing a real taste for power and unlawful control over the population. The Prime Minister, Premiers, senior advisors and politicians have never had such an energising time as this. They are so full of importance and power that one can only expect them to continue running the country in such a heavy handed manner.

During this supposed pandemic, it almost appears that the political elite is promising to abolish even death itself, and create a new society of people who are happy to exchange their freedoms for "security" and be entirely subordinate to the ultimate control of their absolute masters. This "new politics" has been exercised by political class that has manifested a desires of acquiring absolute control over the population.

---

[48] Henry Ergas, 'Our Face Work Diminished, We Cannot Mask the Cost', *The Australian*, 7 August 2020 <https://www.theaustralian.com.au/commentary/our-face-work-diminished-we-cannot-mask-the-cost/news-story/ed3fed8d5e8bc4f8903bf42915e302ba>.

Perhaps nothing reveals more the mindset of the ruling class than the statement of Finance Minister Mathias Cormann, when he stated in early April that there would be no changes to social-distancing rules over the following six months.[49] Why such measures would need to take six months? On what medical-scientific evidence are such government mouthpieces basing this "six months" timeline?

Of course, a six-month lockdown would cause massive damage to the economy and at the cost of countless Australian lives and livelihoods. As we speak, the state authorities of every Australian jurisdiction have acquired full powers to enforce people to return to their homes if they are supposedly not complying with any directions or regulations regarding Covid-19, under threat of hefty fines and imprisonment.

These measures are in force across every jurisdiction, where there are rumblings of overzealous police officers abusing their power. Meanwhile, the Australian Premiers assure us that the police force will use its powers only in specific circumstances. These circumstances presently include sitting on a park bench, walking too close to another person, meeting with a few friends for a barbecue, or even changing flowers' at a late spouse's grave. This happened in Melbourne last weekend, where a man was told to leave the cemetery shortly after arriving, or he would be receiving a $1,600 fine.[50]

In this Covid-19 crisis we are witnessing a ruling class that claims absolute control over our private associations, our work or business, our schools and churches, our families, and over individuals. The police in Victoria are still interrogating those who are outside without permission. Presumably a couple sitting at a table in a public park ob-

---

[49] Richard Ferguson, 'Coronavirus Australia: NO Early End to Six-Month Lockdwn, says Morrison Government', *The Australian*, 11 April 2020 <https://www.theaustralian.com.au/nation/politics/coronavirus-no-early-end-to-sixmonth-lockdown-says-morrison-government/news-story/5cdf7db1f8a3ce598f8672d58cdc38d1>.

[50] Elizabeth Daoud, 'Melbourne Man Devastated After Turned Away From Wife's Grave Amid Coronavirus Restrictions', *7 News*, April13, 2020 <https://7news.com.au/news/vic/melbourne-man-devastated-after-turned-away-from-wifes-grave-amid-coronavirus-restrictions-c-973169>.

serving the social distance and sipping water will also be found guilty of a crime. Indeed, anyone who deliberately engages in such activity may face arrest and imprisonment. Such politicians view people not as citizens to be engaged with, but as disease carriers to be controlled.[51] In the name of fighting Covid-19, authorities are acquiring new powers to monitor and to detain citizens. This includes powers to use surveillance like drone technology, vehicle license plate recognition and electronic tracking devices.

In New South Wales, and just after another person in his 90s died with coronavirus at Liverpool Hospital, Premier Gladys Berejiklian declared that 'tough social-distancing laws will stay until a vaccine [for Covid-19] is found'.[52] Although acknowledging 'how devastating this is for families', she went on to communicate that such restrictions would not be eased and that social-distancing is now 'the new way of life until a vaccine can be discovered'.[53]

In Western Australia (WA), the police have provided 200 electronic ankle bracelets with GPS tracking to be strapped on any member of the public, for monitoring purposes of non-compliance with police directions. 'We are in a state of emergency ... A non-compliant [person] in quarantine will have one of these devices fitted [to them]', Labor Premier Mark McGowan stated.[54]

Passed by the Western Australian Parliament, the *Iron Ore Processing Agreement Amendment Act* provides the State Premier and his Attorney General exemption from the criminal law and civil liabilities. The Act also bans any matter being taken to court so that, in

---

[51] Brendan O'Neill, 'The Luxury of Apocalypticism', *Spyked*, 17 March 2020 <https://www.spiked-online.com/2020/03/17/the-luxury-of-apocalypticism/>.

[52] Paige Cockburn, 'NSW Coronavirus Social-Distancing to Stay Until Vaccine is found, Premier Gladys Berejiklian says', *ABC News*, 7 April 2020 <https://www.abc.net.au/news/2020-04-07/nsw-coronavirus-social-distancing-to-stay-until-vaccine-found/12126802>.

[53] Ibid.

[54] Aaron Fernandes, 'Electronic Tracking Devices Among New Coronavirus Powers for WA Security Agencies', *SBS News*, 12 April 2020 <https://www.sbs.com.au/news/electronic-tracking-devices-among-new-coronavirus-powers-for-wa-security-agencies>.

theory, it would ban even actions in the High Court of Australia. The Act explicitly terminates legal proceedings in relation to coronavirus measures which were underway in the Supreme Court of Western Australia, the Supreme Court of Queensland, the Supreme Court of New South Wales and the Federal Court of Australia.

Clause 12 of the Act provides that decisions and actions in relation to certain government decisions cannot be appealed. It adds that '[t]he Rules known as the rules of natural justice (including any duty of procedural fairness) do not apply to; or in relation to, any conduct of the State that is, or is connected with, a disputed matter'.[55] In addition, this Act prohibits freedom of information by preventing citizens from obtaining the proper information about what the Western Australian government is doing to hold it accountable. In other words, this legislation 'seeks to make documents connected to a "disputed matter" exempt from freedom of information association laws and grants criminal immunity to the State and its agents'.[56]

Finally, the Act gives the State Premier the power to make laws without reference to Parliament. In essence, this an unconstitutional piece of legislation that completely violates the most basic elements of the rule of law and democratic government, including separation of powers, natural justice and due process of law. This draconian legislation attacks some foundational principles of a free and just society, namely that governments must not apply law retrospectively, that court proceedings are fair, and government decisions subject to review or appeal.[57]

The Western Australian Parliament has also passed the *Emergency Management Amendment (COVID-19 Response) Bill*. Under this Act authorities are allowed to issue directions to a 'class' or group of people, rather than an individual; and to impose penalties of $12,000 fines and 12 months of imprisonment for non-compliance. While these

---

[55] Morgan Begg, 'You Don't Need To Be Like Clive Palmer To Dislike His Arbitrary Treatment', IPA Today, 27 August 2020 <https://ipa.org.au/publications-ipa/you-dont-need-to-like-clive-palmer-to-dislike-his-arbitrary-treatment>.

[56] Ibid.

[57] Ibid.

expanded security powers can only be used during a state of emergency, only one of these several amendments to the Act carries a 'sunset clause', guaranteeing its expiry with the end of such emergency. In sum, the Act does not include a sunset clause but it allows for expanded security powers during an unlimited period of time.

As can be seen, these extraordinary measures may last much longer than that of the duration of the pandemic. This effectively means that the Western Australian government will be using for an indefinite period of time invasive technology to analyse, control and determine everyone's actions according to a plan carefully designed by the political elite. This, of course, is not really about the people's health but about political oppression. For nothing can produce a police state more rapidly than such draconian measures. Not only Western Australians but also Australians in general would be wise to pay attention to the words of Thomas Jefferson, the principal drafter of the American Declaration of Independence: 'A government big enough to give you everything you want, is strong enough to take everything you have'.

V THE NATIONAL CABINET

Established by the federal government, the pompously self-entitled 'National Cabinet' has relied on a discredited modelling based on the misleading assumptions of the Imperial College model, which are notoriously prone to significant exaggeration.[58] Such cabinet has 'unlawfully suspended and destroyed jobs, small business and much of the economic life of the nation, as unconstitutional. These extraordinary controls have no validity because they are not powers intended to be exercised in its present form. They violate both the spirit and letter of the Australian Constitution. There has never been a crisis to justify the use of such extreme measures well as limiting the people's freedom with something approaching house arrest'.[59]

---

[58] David Flint, 'Can Someone Please Change ScoMo's Autocue…?', *The Spectator Australia*, 6 June 2020 <https://www.spectator.com.au/2020/06/can-someone-please-change-scomos-autocue/>.

[59] David Flint, 'Professor Lockdown and the Hypocrisy of the Elites', *The Spectator Australia*, 16 May 2020 <https://www.spectator.com.au/2020/05/professor-lockdown-and-the-hypocrisy-of-the-elites/>.

The Prime Minister is presently using his 'National Cabinet' to ban Australians from leaving their country. He oversees a regime that has shut down international travel, enforcing prohibitions matched only by some of the world's worst totalitarian regimes, notably North Korea and Cuba.[60] As a result, Australians currently need a special certificate even to see their own parents and relatives overseas. They need permission to attend a funeral or seeing a relative who is dying overseas. Now, 57,000 people have so far been allowed to leave Australia, but 16,000 have not. Numerous other Australians did not even bother to try since they know their application would be summarily rejected.

This goes without mentioning thousands of Australians overseas who desire to return but are not being allowed to come back.[61] There is indeed a limit on how many of our fellow citizens can return to Australia. According to the Department of Foreign Affairs and Trade ('DFAT'), there are about 20,000 Australians under such conditions. They are trapped overseas and some are effectively running out of money. They are truly experiencing a desperate situation overseas.[62]

'Essentially you have a humanitarian disaster all around the world that Australian citizens are stranded in terrible conditions', argues Dr Joseph Forgas AM, a renowned social psychologist and one of those prevented from returning to the country. Currently Scientia Professor at the University of New South Wales, Forgas was born in Hungary

---

[60] Paul Collits, 'When We Needed Churchill – We Got ScoMo', Freedoms Project, 16 September 2020 <https://www.thefreedomsproject.com/item/567-when-we-needed-churchill-we-got-scomo>.

[61] Jade Macmillan, 'Travel and Coronavirus Boarder Closures On The Agenda At National Cabinet After Qantas Chief Alan Joyce's Critcism', *ABC News*, 21 August 2020 < https://www.abc.net.au/news/2020-08-21/travel-borders-closed-national-cabinet-agenda-coronavirus/12580580>. See also: Yasmeen Jeffery, 'Stranded On Their Own', ABC News, 23 July 2020. <https://www.abc.net.au/news/2020-07-23/coronavirus-pandemic-why-so-many-australians-still-to-come-home/12464258?nw=0>.

[62] 'Prime Minister Scott Morrison Says National Cabinet Agreed To Keep Current Cap On Overseas Returners' *ABC News*, 21 August 2020. < https://www.abc.net.au/news/2020-08-21/coronavirus-australia-live-news-scott-morrison-national-cabinet/12580216>.

and migrated to Australia at the age of 22 as a political refugee from communism. He is now facing a similar position in which one of his most fundamental rights as a citizen has been grossly violated: the right to return home and be reunited to his wife and children.[63]

Like numerous other Australians overseas, Professor Forgas first obtained a special permission from the foreign affairs department to attend his mother's funeral in Hungary. But he is now facing the serious problem of being prevented from returning home. 'My human rights are being violated. I am deeply disappointed and I believe the Australian government has caused an immense damage to the country's reputation', Forgas says.

The Prime Minister contends that his National Cabinet has agreed 'on the balance of risk' that the number of Australians allowed to return from overseas at present is 4,000 a week. He argues that this must be so because the States may have more people that they can place on quarantine hotels. He does not want to take responsibility and, as a result, Australians overseas are having to suffer enormously. Of course, quarantine should be only for the sick and never for the healthy. And yet, all travellers arriving in Australia, including Australian citizens, not only must quarantine for 14 days at a designated facility, such as a hotel in their port of arrival, but also may be forced to pay for all the costs of their quarantine.[64]

These actions of the 'National Cabinet' are profoundly unconstitutional.[65] Relying on a few experts, politicians are using extraordinary powers to violate fundamental rights and to destroy jobs and much of the productive sector, while leaving the public sector intact.[66] These privileged individuals have chosen a course of action that are destruc-

---

[63] 'Politicians Again Turn Coronavirus Problem Into A Human Disaster', *Sky News*, 15 September 2020 <https://www.skynews.com.au/details/_6190888629001>.

[64] 'Travel Restrictions', *Australian Government – Department of Home Affairs*, 17 September 2020 <https://covid19.homeaffairs.gov.au/travel-restrictions-0>.

[65] Ibid.

[66] David Flint, 'Recover Reparations, Restore Independence', *The Spectator Australia*, 11 April 2020 <https://www.spectator.com.au/2020/04/recover-reparations-restore-independence/>.

tive of the rule of law, although there were far more reasonable alternatives.[67]

Although the meaning of the rule of law is always open to interpretation, there is a general agreement that the rule of law is essentially about protecting citizens from unreasonable interference with their vital interests, and ensuring a legal-institutional 'solution to the problem of abusive, external control over the life, liberty and property of the common citizen'.[68] Forestalling a situation whereby legislation can be oppressive, and fundamental laws become worthless, the rule of law denies political rulers any 'right to destroy, enslave, or designedly to impoverish the subjects'.[69]

It should not be a surprise that we are hearing numerous stories of overreacting government, draconian guidelines, and the countless cases of arbitrary exercise of power. Although most police officers are good people, they are following the orders of an arbitrary government devoid of any commitment to the rule of law. Because there is no deadline for the termination of measures that seriously attempt against the basic rights of the people, what such governments have done in Australia is to effectively undermine the rule of law.

Indeed, the rule of law implies the effective existence of constitutional checks and balances by which 'government can act only through law and law checks the power of government'.[70] Historically, wrote the English constitutional law professor, Owen Hood Phillips, 'the phrase [rule of law] has been used with reference to a belief in the existence of law possessing higher authority — whether divine or natural — than that of the [positive] law promulgated by human rulers which imposed limits on their power'.[71]

---

[67] Ibid.

[68] Suri Ratnapala, *Welfare State or Constitutional State?* (Centre for Independent Studies, 1990), 19.

[69] John Locke, *Second Treatise on Civil Government* [1689], Section 135.

[70] Mighel Schor, 'The Rule of Law' in D Clark (ed), *Encyclopedia of Law and Society: American and Global Perspectives* (Sage, 2005) 231.

[71] O H Phillips and P Johnson, *O Hood Phillips' Constitutional and Administrative Law* (Sweet & Maxwell, 1987) 37.

As can be seen, this ideal of legality presupposes the existence of law serving as an effective check on the executive power. The phrase is designed to minimise government power, so that our fundamental rights and freedoms are adequately preserved by the law. By forcing the executive branch to follow proper rules of law, the rule of law operates to reduce the possibility of government being able to excessively coerce, obstruct or otherwise unreasonably interfere with the life, liberty and property of the citizen. The tradition operates in terms of providing legal and institutional instruments to protect citizens against the arbitrary power by the state. As St Thomas Aquinas pointed out,

> ...once the government is established, this must be so arranged that opportunity to tyrannize be removed. At the same time, the power of government should be so tempered that it cannot easily fall into political tyranny.[72]

The political principle supported by Aquinas – namely, the supremacy of the legislature over the executive – aims ultimately at the protection of fundamental rights and freedoms. As such, his analysis is a prescription for limited government, providing a rational basis on which to affirm that there must be very clear institutional limits to what governments can rightly do. His insistence that the power of the executive be explicitly limited implies a right of the citizen not to be subjected to authoritarian rule by means of executive decree.

On the other hand, modern discussions of the rule of law often start with the views of Albert Venn Dicey (1835–1922). This celebrated 19th-century English constitutional lawyer argued that the rule of law implies three basic elements, namely: (1) supremacy of the law as opposed to the arbitrary exercise of executive power; (2) equality of all before the law to be administered by ordinary courts; and (3) judicial protection of individual rights and freedoms.[73]

The concept of the rule of law therefore stands in frontal opposition to extemporary decisions expressing the arbitrary will of the executive

---

[72] St Thomas Aquinas, *De Regimine Principum*, Book I, Chapter 2.
[73] A.V. Dicey, *Introduction to the Study of the Law of the Constitution* [1885] (Liberty Fund, 1982), 107-122.

branch of government. It is generally observed that the exercise of executive powers invariably necessitates the existence of clear, stable, general rules to regulate such exercise of powers, which must therefore be approved by elected legislature and receive proper public scrutiny. Above all, truly democratic governments are bound to exercise power according to the rule of law.

VI THE LEFTIST PRIVILEGE

While the Australian governments implement draconian measures to allegedly contain Covid-19, thousands of left-wing activists have defied the law to take part in the "Black Lives Matter" and other Leftist protests and marches across Australia. It's one rule for them and another rule for the rest of us. The level of hypocrisy is truly staggering, especially because law-abiding citizens have been forced to withhold wedding ceremonies or been excluded from the funerals of our loved ones.

Until the protests erupted in last April, the order of Australian governments, both federal and state, was that people should not attend gatherings of any kind. Spreading new cases of coronavirus and force more governmental intervention may very well have been the hidden agenda of some protest organisers. They might have hoped that these protests could result in more infections which would then lead to further deaths and government interventions, the greatest burden falling on black communities.

These Leftist rallies were organised in Brisbane, Melbourne, Hobart, Adelaide and elsewhere.[74] They were held throughout the country following the death of an American citizen, George Floyd, by an American police officer, in the U.S. on 25th May. Protesters took to the streets on Saturday, campaigning for, among other things, an end to Aboriginal deaths in custody, for open borders and a new influx of undocumented migrants.

---

[74] Melissa Davey, 'Black Lives Matter: health experts assess risks of Covid-19 transmission at Australia protests', *The Guardian*, 12 June 2020 <https://www.theguardian.com/australia-news/2020/jun/12/black-lives-matter-australia-protest-will-blm-protests-spark-second-covid-19-coronavirus-wave-health-experts>.

Once again these unpopular Leftist groups have achieved their ultimate goal and proven that laws which are supposedly valid for all, and passed to protect us, mean absolutely nothing to them. In Sydney these protests initially defied a court order to take to the city's streets. But organisers took the case to the State Court of Appeal and the ban was astonishingly lifted at the last minute. Although health ministry directions would normally prohibit public gatherings of more than 10 people, the protest in Sydney was legally authorised for 5,000 people. There were violent scenes in the evening at Sydney's Central Station and police used pepper spray to protect themselves, but there were only three arrests in the city overall, police said.[75]

In Victoria it is still illegal to go to work if you can work from home, with fines of $100,000 for employers. However, it is perfectly acceptable to break social distancing rules and gather thousands of people to protest something that happened overseas. A Victorian man who attended the BLM protest in Melbourne was later diagnosed with the virus, with health authorities saying he was likely infected before the rally.

Josh Karpin is an academic with a special interest in democracy and the rule of law. When Premier Andrews, in reference to those who do not wish to be wearing masks, said 'their behaviour is appalling, their views have no basis in science or fact or the law', Karpin notes that the Premier could easily have talked about himself and his government.[76] As Karpin asks rhetorically: 'If there was science to staying apart, with emphasis on social distancing, to keep Victorians together, why was the Black Lives Matter protest in Melbourne not seriously opposed by the government?'

According to Karpin, this lack in consistency in the enforcement of government measures in Victoria have lasting consequences not so

---

[75] 'George Floyd death: Australians defy virus in mass anti-racism rallies', *BBC News*, 6 June 2020 <https://www.bbc.com/news/world-australia-52947115>.

[76] Josh Karpin, 'Government Has Failed Victoria – And Victoria Has Failed Government', *The Spectator Australia*, 6 August 2020 <https://www.spectator.com. au/2020/08/government-has-failed-victoria-and-victoria-has-failed-government/>.

much for the transmission of the disease, 'but the transmission to Victorians of the notion that government policy was insincere and could be conveniently disregarded'. [77] Unfortunately he also reminds us that the Liberal opposition in Victoria has fared no much better, miserably failing to provide any form of 'alternate vision of government in policy or principle'.[78] And this goes without stating also the failure of people in Victoria 'to demand more of those who are trusted to lead the state and to apply adequate scrutiny before ceding liberty'.[79]

In Perth, the turnout for the BLM protests in June was at least double the 8,000 organisers had expected. They completely ignored the pleas of West Australian Premier Mark McGowan and Aboriginal Affairs Minister Ben Wyatt to delay the protest until after the alleged pandemic was over. Instead of punishing the protesters for breaking the law, WA Police Commissioner Chris Dawson had earlier ruled out shutting down the protest amidst concerns that this would further extend the draconian restrictions on businesses, social gatherings, and interstate travel currently imposed by the State government.[80]

Curiously, the Western Australian Premier did not ban the rally but simply urged protesters to maintain some physical distance. He conveniently used the protest to further expand the powers of the State, as an excuse to prolong restrictions and to confirm that the State border will now remain closed for a "considerable period" amid concerns "the protests could add to community transmission of the virus".[81] My thoughts and sympathy go to those in Western Australia who cannot travel interstate or have cancelled their holidays of a lifetime.

---

[77] Ibid.

[78] Ibid.

[79] Ibid.

[80] Michael Ramsey, 'Thousands at WA's Black Lives Matter Rally', *The Australian*, 13 June 2020 <https://www.theaustralian.com.au/news/latest-news/perth-readies-for-black-lives-matter-rally/news-story/dacf3efdf6f9436a34dd50b29d0850f0>.

[81] *Paul Carvey, 'Protests Ensure Borders are Closed', The* Australian, 7 June 2020 <https://www.theaustralian.com.au/nation/coronavirus-australia-live-news-health-officials-fear-second-covid19-spike-after-black-lives-matter-protests/news-story/6ee48b5a626d2391217e59c9ada2c632>.

Incidentally, the constitutionality of board control measures in Western Australia have been thoroughly analysed by law professor Anthony Gray, particularly in light of section 92 of the Australian Constitution. These board control directions have the object of impeding interstate intercourse, or have the predominant purpose of doing so. However, such directions target and attack a fundamental right that every Australian citizen has, namely their freedom of movement guaranteed in Section 92 of the Australian Constitution. As Professor Gray points out, the High Court of Australia has consistently adopted 'an essentially absolutist prohibition on laws which have the object of impending interstate intercourse'.[82]

As explicitly recognised by one of Australia's most celebrated former chief justices, Sir Anthony Mason, the constitutional protection to freedom of movement was deemed by the drafters of the Australian Constitution as one of the most essential goals of constituting the Australian Federation, thus 'bring[ing] into existence one nation and one people' (Mason CJ). Indeed, the Australian founders saw fit to emphatically enshrine this particular freedom in the constitutional text, when they generally eschewed other express rights protections.[83]

However, freedom of movement is precisely the constitutional right being presently violated by the Western Australian government, with the full support of the Morrison government. This important right of every Australian citizen not only has been enshrined in the Constitution, but it is also what gave effect to the very concept of Australia as a free, united and independent nation, thus reflecting in the eyes of our founding fathers one of the primary reasons for the country's very establishment and existence.

The Prime Minister has refused to uphold the Constitution and protect an explicit right of every Australian citizen. In an official letter dated 7 August 2020, Scott Morrison communicates Premier Mark McGowan that the Commonwealth will do nothing to challenge the

---

[82] Anthony Gray, 'COVID-19 Border Restrictions and Section 92 of the Australian Constitution' (2020) 11 *The Western Australian Jurist.*
[83] Ibid.

unconstitutional boarder-control measures imposed in Western Australia, but rather it will 'immediately and completely withdraw from the proceedings, doing exactly what was asked of it by the Western Australian government'.[84] If the court eventually seek a view of his government regarding the submission the Western Australian government is making, Morrison stated that the Commonwealth will 'positively support [the government of] Western Australia in any way it could outside the courtroom, having withdrawn from the proceedings at [the government of] Western Australia's request'.[85]

But going back to those left-wing protests who marched on the streets of our capital cities with absolute impunity, there is the reasonable assumption that such protests may have inadvertently assisted the general population to better understand the radical agenda behind government measures to fight the pandemic, which is essentially justifying an enormous concentration of power on a small minority of privileged people, especially the so called "experts" and a few other bureaucrats and politicians. As noted by Henry Ergas, in a column for *The Australian*, 'with people retreating into isolation of their private sphere, ... society becomes weaker and the state – vastly empowered by the crisis, and always poised to abuse ordinary citizens – becomes even stronger'.[86]

VII DISCRIMINATION AGAINST PLACES OF WORSHIP

Churches services are said to provide hope and comfort in the midst of despair, especially in times of sickness and death. However, the Australian governments are adopting measures which are clearly discriminatory against religious people. In New South Wales, until recently pubs and clubs were allowed to open for 50 people. However,

---

[84] Prime Minister Scott Morrison, 'Letter to The Hon Mark McGowan MLA, Premier of Western Australia' (7 August 2020)

[85] Ibid.

[86] Henry Ergas, 'Our Face Work Diminished, We Cannot Mask the Cost', *The Australian*, 7 August 2020 <https://www.theaustralian.com.au/commentary/our-face-work-diminished-we-cannot-mask-the-cost/news-story/ed3fed8d5e8bc4f8903bf42915e-302ba>.

churches remained restricted to 10 people and only 10 people could attend a funeral at a chapel.

The limit of 10 to attend a place of worship also applied in Queensland, Tasmania, South Australia and the ACT. Up to 20 people could attend a place of worship in Western Australia.[87] 'I guess that's because having a beer and playing pokies is an "essential" service, whereas worshipping God and having a cup of tea or coffee with a small group of people is just too dangerous', wrote Mark Powell ironically to *The Spectator Australia*.[88]

Fortunately there were some religious people with enough courage to speak out on behalf of the people. Catholic Archbishop of Sydney Anthony Fisher openly called on the New South Wales Premier to allow more than 10 people to attend places of worship. As he pointed out, a "double standard" had been applied to people of faith, given that pubs, clubs, cafes, and restaurants could host up to 50 customers from June 1, but religious gatherings and places of worship were only allowed to host up to 10 people. Archbishop Fisher reminded the state government that 'the Church is not asking for special treatment, we are asking for treatment'.[89] He stated also that churches had co-operated at every stage with the government's health directives but religious people were missing gatherings for worship, praying in a sacred space and there were 'spiritual and mental health effects of such isolation'.[90]

Australians of all faiths were denied their fundamental right to come together in worship by their own governments, which used the spurious "safety" argument in order to justify the inconsistent applica-

---

[87] Angelica Snowden, 'Coronavirus: Churches Seek Same Rules as Pubs and Cafes', *The Australian*, 28 May 2020 <https://www.theaustralian.com.au/nation/politics/coronavirus-churches-seek-same-rules-as-pubs-and-cafes/news-story/be9e7ddbd79dd30cb953e3054675563a>.

[88] Mark Powell, 'In a Mental Health Crisis Church Controls Don't Pass the Pub Test', *The Spectator Australia*, 27 May 2020 <https://www.spectator.com.au/2020/05/in-a-mental-health-crisis-church-controls-dont-pass-the-pub-test/>.

[89] Snowden, above n 87.

[90] Ibid.

tion of rules that are in many respects still negatively impacting their daily lives. Although the Prime Minister and State Premiers often argue that such decisions discriminating churches are based on "expert health advice", the truth is that they have shown the arbitrary and discriminatory nature of these draconian restrictions. It was certainly not fair and reasonable that in most of the Australian states pubs and strip clubs were allowed to operate up to a certain number of patrons, and yet places of worship were sometimes prohibited to operate or restricted to no more than 10 people who should then be recorded on a special register, allowing for their control and contact tracing by the government.

VIII DE FACTO MARTIAL LAW IN VICTORIA

On August 2, 2020, Victorians began to live under a "state of disaster" that has seen one of the world's severest restrictions of fundamental freedoms imposed on its citizens and their fundamental freedoms. As state-wide curfew is in place, leaving home after 8.00 pm is strictly banned with hefty fines imposed on those pulled over by the police. There are roadblocks to prevent citizens from moving interstate or, much closer to home, more than the permitted 5 km from their listed addresses.

The Victorian government has effectively become an elected dictatorship. It is August 9 as I write and the latest 19 coronavirus deaths from coronavirus brought the death toll in the state to 247. These 19 deaths were of a man in his 50s, a woman in her 50s, two men in their 70s, one man and six women in their 80s, and one man and seven women in their 90s.[91]

Approximately 99 per cent of all infections for coronavirus have been mild. And yet, Victoria has a public administration crisis. Of the 515 people in hospitals across Australia with coronavirus, 496 are in Victoria. Most of those who have died were in their 80s and

---

[91] Rachel Baxendale, 'Victoria Deaths Include Men in 50s', *The Australian*, 10 August 2020 <https://www.theaustralian.com.au/nation/politics/new-deadliest-day-in-victoria-as-coronavirus-claims-19/news-story/02bbe6b57264d24e37348ca563cc4e14>.

living in aged-care facilities.[92]

Unfortunately, none of these relevant considerations have prevented the Victorian government of imposing what is by far the greatest violation of fundamental rights in Australia's history. Victorians have now been forced into stage 4 lockdown; almost 5 million people have been informed that the police can and will enter their homes for any reason and without a warrant. Police can also stop anyone anywhere at any time and demand to see their papers and determine if they have a valid reason to be away of their homes.

These extraordinary rules imposed on the citizens of Melbourne, Victoria's capital city, will remain in force for at least the next five weeks. They include:

- The police can enter a person's home to carry out spot checks without permission or a warrant.
- Between the hours of 8.00 pm to 5.00 am nobody is allowed to leave their home except for work, medical care or caregiving.
- Daily exercise can only take place within a 5-kilometre distance of a person's home.
- Apart from of maximum 1-hour of daily exercise, never in groups of more than two (even if they are members of the same household), a person is only allowed to leave home for essential supplies and food. Such shopping trips are permitted only once a day.
- In the whole of Victoria nobody is allowed to by more than two of certain essential items, including dairy, meat, vegetables, fish and toilet paper.
- Schools, childcare and kindergarten have been closed until further notice.
- Golf and tennis venues have been closed; fishing is banned.

---

[92] Rachel Baxendale, 'Promising Trend for Victoria's Active Cases', *The Australian*, 10 August 2020 <https://www.theaustralian.com.au/nation/coronavirus-australia-live-news-victorias-deadliest-day-amid-mental-health-crisis/news-story/bbb466e-22a064a01667a6aa59ab66647>.

- Weddings are no longer allowed, and funerals limited to only 10 mourners.

- Facemasks are mandatory for all activities outside the home. A farmer on his tractor, along in the middle of an empty paddock, must be masked. This applies across the entire length and breadth of the state.

- Nobody can receive visitors unless it is for the purpose of giving and receiving care.

The maximum fine for breaching any of these orders currently stands at $4,999. I am unaware of any state/country in the world which levies such enormous on the spot fines for leaving home without a legitimate reason. In just one day, August 6, Victoria Police conducted no less than 4,418 stop checks on homes, businesses and public places, bringing the total to 234,275 since March 21. Also on that very day, more than 50 people were fined for not wearing a facemask as well as 43 penalties were issued for curfew breaches.[93]

Victorians living in Melbourne are forced to remain in their homes for at least 23 hours a day. Police officers have been quick to tackle any locals out on the streets without a 'valid reason', an approach reflected in the 17,682 vehicles whose drivers and occupants have been quizzed at checkpoints. Police have already checked more than 17,682 vehicles in total at vehicle checkpoints. 'We had to smash car windows and pull people out because they wouldn't give us details', declared a senior Victorian policeman. 'They wouldn't tell us where they're going!'[94]

Police issued 276 fines in a single day (August 9). In the midst of these oppressive actions, police have fined a family with little children

---

[93] Remy Varga, 'Arrested Made Over Planned 'Freedom March in Melbourne', *The Australian*, 7 August 2020 < https://www.theaustralian.com.au/nation/coronavirus-australia-arrests-made-over-planned-freedom-march-in-melbourne/news-story/58ff8b5ac2b04f71496990edb0c62757>.

[94] James Delingpole, 'Australian State Goes Full Coronafascist', *Breitbart*, 7 August 2020 <https://www.breitbart.com/europe/2020/08/07/delingpole-australian-state-goes-full-coronafascist/>.

over a trip to playground; five young friends for listening to music in a suburban garage.[95] A 41 year-old man from outer suburban Moorolbark and a 41 year-old man from Chirnside Park have been charged with "incitement" and bailed to appear at Melbourne Magistrate's Court for the alleged crime of attempting to organise a protest against the arbitrary proscriptions detailed above. Images prompting their August 9 rally upset the Victorian regime by inviting concerned citizens to safeguard their traditional liberties and "fight the good fight".[96] The *Spectator Australia* points out that 'curfews are tools of political oppression, of martial law, of military occupation. They are not part of living in a thriving parliamentary democracy'.[97] However, Victorians are living under a nightly curfew. From 8 pm to 5 pm the streets of Melbourne are but deserted, save for police cars.

And the irony as Melbourne is transformed into Tumbleweed Town is that lockdowns don't work. Evidence suggests that the economic destruction they bring is worse than the virus, with large numbers going to die because of the lockdowns and restrictions. Victoria's mental health minister, Martin Foley, has actually confessed that there has been a 9.5 per cent increase in reports of self-harm in the state compared with the same time last year. For young people, there has been a 33 per cent.[98]

Victoria is in this mess because of the staggering incompetence of its government. Business have been closed and jobs are being destroyed. Many shops will never be open again. Many people who lost their jobs will never work again. All this is happening while the gov-

---

[95] Lucy Mae Beers, 'Record Number of State 4 Fines in Victorias Parents Take Children to Playground', *7 News*, 10 August 2020 <https://7news.com.au/news/victoria-police/record-number-of-stage-4-fines-in-victoria-as-parents-take-children-to-wynd­ham-playground-c-1227897>.

[96] Varga, above n 93.

[97] Editorial, 'State of Disastrous Decision-Making', The Spectator Australia, 8 August 2020 <https://www.spectator.com.au/2020/08/state-of-disastrous-decision-making/>.

[98] Jon Lockett, 'Australia Records Highest Coronavirus Daily Death Toll as Victoria Sees 17 Fatalities While Cops Twart Anti Mask Rally', *The Sun*, 9 August 2020 <https://www.thesun.co.uk/news/12353559/australia-records-highest-coronavirus-daily-death-toll-as-victoria-sees-17-fatalities-while-cops-thwart-anti-mask-rally>.

ernment refuses to explain its actions to Parliament, which has been effectively been shut down since March.

We keep hearing that we are all together. But no public servant has lost their job and politicians continue to receive their six figure salaries. They have no understanding of the productive economy are receiving pay rises. Research by the Institute of Public Affairs suggest that stage 4 lockdown will rob mainstream Victorians of almost $3.2 billion dollars a week in lost income, prosperity and living standards. And we can expect as many as 300,000 jobs to be lost. Is this cruel and undemocratic lockdown really proportional to the risk? Will the poverty and mental health crisis be worth it? Of course, being part of the decimated private sector is even more galling when the politicians and bureaucrats who are causing much of the pain have not suffered the loss of a single cent during this whole incident.

One would suspect that, in order to justify these measures, the state of Victoria is experiencing an unprecedented crisis where many people are dying of the virus. In reality, Victoria has seen just 162 deaths attributed to coronavirus (the figure as I write). What is more, 137 of 162 those who died where in aged-care homes. As it turns out, writes Chris Kenny in *The Australian*, without a proper focus on the elderly, we have ended up [as a nation] ended up with the worst of both worlds, society in a coma and our elderly suffering anyway (90 per cent of deaths have been aged over 70, and two thirds have been in aged care homes)'.[99]

There was much made the week before about a person who died in his 30s but the Premier refused to say if he had any other medical conditions. Incredibly, having announced the death, the Premier insisted that releasing any further details would violate privacy considerations. His silence is understandable. With the average age of those who die at standing at 82, the Andrews regime is frantic to both justify its Stasi-like approach to public health and obscure its inept hotel quarantine

---

[99] Chris Kenny, 'If Politicians Know Best, Why So Many Mistakes?', *The Australian*, 15 August 2020 <https://www.theaustralian.com.au/commentary/if-politicians-know-best-why-so-many-mistakes/news-story/61184b5377a4638fbd70b9ef53253f40>.

program by broadcasting the word that anyone can contract coronavirus and die, not just the elderly.

Step back, survey the actual death numbers and the only conclusion is that they are pathetically low. This goes without saying that positive cases are astronomically inflated. The testing process is not designed to test coronavirus. One can be at the age of 90 and die of heart attack. But if they suspect the elderly person had coronavirus, this is how it may be recorded as the cause of death. Despite these inflated numbers, there were actually more deaths in Australia last year from flu with a vaccine, than from coronavirus this year without a vaccine. According to Health Department figures, there were 1,257 deaths from influenza last year and more than 3,010 presented to hospital. Strangely enough, the most recent data reveals no flu-related deaths in Victoria so far this year during the so called coronavirus pandemic.[100] This has prompted a Victorian joke: 'Thank God for coronavirus. No one is dying from cancer, heart disease or anything else.'

Victoria become a police state, but there is no legal basis for what it is being done. Under the so called Disaster Act, any law in Victoria can be suspended with the stroke of a pen. Of course, such legislation is constitutionally invalid as it contradicts basic principles of constitutional government. Indeed, the Victorian government has neither constitutional validity nor democratic mandate to introduce such draconian legal measures. Those responsible for this should be held criminally accountable. It is they, not families in park playgrounds, who should be facing the full force of the law.

The Chief Health Officer Brett Sutton, whose former crusade was to avert the "climate crisis", recommended against parliament sitting because the government did not define it as an essential function. As noted by *The Australian*'s Greg Sheridan, 'his insistence that parlia-

---

[100] 'Coronavirus: Victoria Records Zero Flu-Related Deaths This Year', *The Sydney Morning Herald*, 9 June 2020 <https://www.msn.com/en-au/news/australia/coronavirus-victoria-records-zero-flu-related-deaths-this-year/vi-BB15dvrX>.

ment should not sit is unambiguously a disgrace'.[101] Of course, if you can allow people to shoot up heroin, surely you can allow the state parliament. As reported by the Herald Sun, the government-operated supervised injection room located in North Richmond not only disrespect social distancing rules, but still remains open well past the 8 pm curfew.[102]

Premier Andrews has avoided any reasonable scrutiny and accountability by effectively abolishing democracy in that Australian state.[103] According to Sheridan, 'there has never been a more arrogant episode of disdain for normal democracy than the Victorian Health Minister's decision not to answer any questions on the virus … in the Legislative Council, sitting only because the Coalition and crossbenches insisted'.[104] Furthermore, Health minister Jenny Mikakos has refused to give a verbal answer to questions in the Upper House's question time. She made reference to a retired judge's board of inquiry into the failed hotel quarantine system, although such a person explicitly stated that her inquiry is not a court, so 'there is no general restriction or prohibition which would prevent a person from commenting publicly or answering questions to which they know the answers'.[105]

Naturally, there is no need for a "sham inquiry" to tell us that 'every case of coronavirus in Victoria today stems from this government's utter failure to design and implement an effective quaran-

---

[101] Greg Sheridan, 'Daniel Andrew's Leadership is Superficial and a Failure', *The Australian*, 6 August 2020. <https://www.theaustralian.com.au/commentary/daniel-andrews-cleverly-leads-in-a-vacuum-of-democracy/news-story/075dce1f0b2dda2c6 93077e92e3ac467>.

[102] 'Richard Safe Injecting Room Remains Open', *The Herald Sun*, 8 August 2020 <https://www.heraldsun.com.au%2Fnews%2Fvictoria%2Fnorth-richmond-residents-livid-drug-users-are-breaking-social-distancing-rules-and-curfews%2Fnews-story%2F5037dfc68749f92868e07279f77f6ce>.

[103] Sheridan, above n 101.

[104] Ibid.

[105] Rachel Baxendale, 'Andrews to Give Updated at 11 pm', *The Australian*, 10 August 2020 <https://www.theaustralian.com.au/nation/coronavirus-australia-live-news-victoria-ranks-alongside-african-nations-for-virus-increase/news-story/b5559007e-7b700a3fd18f360b783cd92>.

tine program'.[106] Under Andrews, 'all the mechanisms of democratic accountability have virtually disappeared … [and] Victoria has become a dysfunctional one-party state with a mostly compliant local media', Sheridan wrote.[107] He lists other failures including the catastrophic failure to manage quarantine hotels, and not issuing fines at the Black Lives Matter demonstration, thus 'tacitly endorsing a huge event that broke social distancing restrictions and undermined the message'.[108]

The fact of the matter is that it appears most of Victoria's second wave of the coronavirus apparently came from the breaches of hotel quarantine processes in Melbourne, not least the employment of security guards who were neither properly equipped nor trained.[109] The hotel quarantine program was designed to shield the state from the virus by placing returned travellers in 14-day isolation in hotels manned by private security companies.[110]

Victoria is indeed a state of disaster due to the absolute incompetence of a Premier who behaves far more like a ruthless dictator than the leader of an authentic parliamentary democracy. Alarmingly, the Public Health and Wellbeing Act, the appalling piece of unconstitutional legislation conferring arbitrary powers to the Victorian Premier was passed by the state parliament in 2008 entirely unopposed by the Liberal opposition, 'despite Labor then, as now, not having an upper

---

[106] Sheridan, above n 101.

[107] Ibid.

[108] Ibid.

[109] Dennis Shanahan, 'Morrison Keeps Danbursters At Bay Over Second Coronavirus', *The Australian*, 8 August 2020 <https://www.theaustralian.com.au/inquirer/morrison-keeps-danbusters-at-bay-over-second-coronavirus-wave/news-story/f6ab-808ca813beb58856810891a06354>. See also: Gerard Henderson, 'How Did Victoria Get So Much So Wrong', *The Australian*, 8 August 2020 <https://www.theaustralian.com.au/inquirer/coronavirus-how-did-victoria-get-so-much-so-wrong/news-story/e2c926209c92533971c12f6bba83be7e>

[110] Rachael Dexer and Marissa Calligeros, 'Hotel Quarantine Problems? 'I Found Out In The Media', Says Sutton', *The Age*, Melbourne/Vic, 7 August 2020 <https://www.theage.com.au/national/victoria/hotel-quarantine-problems-i-found-out-in-the-media-says-sutton-20200807-p55jls.html>.

house majority'.[111] It is therefore no virtue for the opposition to complain about these authoritarian measures when the Liberal state MPs allowed for the enactment of legislation that provides for ruling by executive decree without proper democratic accountability.

Perhaps even more disturbing is the Prime Minister's refusal to criticise Premier Andrews, in keeping with his strong belief in "national leadership unity".[112] This is despite Victoria's bungled quarantine system, believed to be responsible for the outbreak of community transmission. As stated by Janet Albrechtsen in *The Australian*, the imposition of stage-four restrictions on Victorians, particularly those living in Melbourne, may lead to far 'more people dying', and also to 'untold economic harm to millions of Victorians and damaging the economy, a dangerous spike in mental health illnesses especially among young Victorians, and negative educational outcomes'.[113]

However, Scott Morrison has publicly backed the Victorian Premier, including his imposing of *de facto* martial law across the State. Indeed, Morrison not only has refused to criticise the Victorian Premier for being unable to stop the spread of the virus, he has further encouraged political arbitrariness and oppression in Victoria by, in his own words, 'encouraging the Victorian government to ensure that there are appropriate penalties for those who do break public health notices'.[114] As Paul Collits points out, 'Morrison and Andrews need one another. While Andrews exists, Morrison escapes even the merest

---

[111] Editorial, 'State of Disastrous Decision-Making', *The Spectator Australia*, 8 August 2020 <https://www.spectator.com.au/2020/08/state-of-disastrous-decision-making/>.

[112] Shanahan, above n 106.

[113] Janet Albrechtsen, 'She Won't Talk, She Tweets – Pericles Would Wince', *The Australian*, 11 August 2020 <https://www.theaustralian.com.au/commentary/she-wont-talk-she-tweets-pericles-would-wince/news-story/44919481b8d7da08c923b96bb8b027e0>.

[114] Heath Parkes-Hupton, 'Scott Morrison Urges Australians to Support Victoria Through Critical New Lockdown Measures, *The Australian*, August 3, 2020. <https://www.theaustralian.com.au/breaking-news/scott-morrison-urges-australians-to-support-victoria-through-critical-new-lockdown-measures/news-story/a7a62eab55e-f290185ed06d72a4d9720>

modicum of scrutiny. While Morrison exists, with his "national cabinet", Andrews get protection'.[115]

Surely we should expect the leader of a Liberal government to be interested in protecting personal freedoms, not suppressing them. Instead, we get this spineless guff: 'Daniel Andrews has my full support ... I will give him every support he needs'. Offering such enthusiastic support to the authoritarian measures of the Victorian government is, according to Morrison, 'the only thing that matters'.[116]

The Prime Minister is also on the record for notoriously stating that he is totally unconcerned about ongoing attacks on freedom of speech, because, according to him, "free speech does not create a single job". Well, he supporting for a premier's oppressive measures that can only destroy the economy is certainly not going to create a single job either, at least not in the productive sector. To the contrary, federal connivance can only lead to more human rights violations as well as inevitable economic disaster and massive unemployment.

Granted, the Liberal governments in New South Wales, South Australia, and Tasmania are also far too willing to rule by decree and impose their own arbitrary measures on their citizens. For example, South Australian Liberal Premier Steven Marshall increased restrictions on home and public gatherings after just two new infections in his state, both from known sources.[117] As noted by Chris Kenny, the draconian measures imposed by the Andrews regime, and supported by the Australian Prime Minister, have been matched, 'scold for scold', by several Liberal state governments across the nation.

The fact that Liberal governments can also completely ignore and

---

[115] Collits, above n 59.

[116] Natalie Oliveri, 'PM Says Victoria's Premier Has His Full Support to Tackle State's Coronavirus Crisis', *Today Channel 9*. <https://9now.nine.com.au/today/coronavirus-australia-scott-morrison-says-daniel-andrews-has-full-support-victoria/fd460c9a-db46-408f-82d2-a6e82ef3b865>

[117] Chris Kenny, 'If Politicians Know Best, Why So Many Mistakes?', *The Australian*, 15 August 2020., <https://www.theaustralian.com.au/commentary/if-politicians-know-best-why-so-many-mistakes/news-story/61184b5377a4638fbd70b9ef5325 3f40>

violate fundamental rights should not come as a surprise for those who have read the most recent *Legal Rights Audit 2019*. The main author of this important report, Morgan Begg, first explains that 'fundamental legal rights are necessary to achieve justice within a legal system and act as a vital constraint on the coercive power of the state'.[118] However, he claims these legal rights have been explicitly breached by 381 separate provisions in Acts of Australia's federal Parliament. As Begg points out, the Morrison government is directly responsible for the substantial in increase in the violation of these fundamental legal rights. 'The Coalition [Liberal/National] government is trashing fundamental legal rights of all Australians, creating unprecedented challenge to individual freedom and human dignity', writes Begg, who is a research fellow with the Institute of Public Affairs.[119]

IX THE USE OF THE STATE OF EMERGENCY IN VICTORIA

Victorians have watched their local government use a broad range of extraordinary powers to remove fundamental freedoms and control almost every single aspect of their personal lives. It did so by both declaring a state of emergency and a state of disaster, thus imposing draconian lockdown measures after a "surge" in coronavirus infections.

Imposed under the pretence of protecting the health of the people, the state of disaster came into effect tin Victoria on August 2. Under the *Emergency Management Act*, a state of disaster can be declared

---

[118] Morgan Begg and Kristen Pereira, 'Legal Rights Audit 2019', *Institute of Public Affairs*, Melbourne/Vic, February 2020, p 1. As Begg points out in his excellent Legal Rights Audit, the federal Liberal governments have been directly responsible for at least 279 fundamental legal rights breaches since 1976, compared with only 102 breaches under Labor. This is the equivalent to 11 breaches for each year of Liberal government compared with 5 breaches each year on average under Labor. – See also: Morgan Begg, 'Coalition Government Trashes Legal Rights', *IPA Today*, 7 February 2020. <https://ipa.org.au/publications-ipa/media-releases/coalition-government-trashes-legal-rights> See also: Nicola Berkovic, 'Coalition Worse than ALP on Human Rights', *The Australian*, 6 February 2020 <https://www.theaustralian.com.au/business/legal-affairs/coalition-worse-than-alp-on-human-rights/news-story/0bc3d71cd4daf8ab425f3bd5d8edba11>.

[119] Begg and Pereira, above n 118, 1.

if the Premier is satisfied an emergency "constitutes or is likely to constitute a significant and widespread danger to life or property in Victoria".[120]

But Victoria is also under a state of emergency, which came into effect on March 16. The declaration was made under the *Public Health and Wellbeing Act 2008*, which allows health officials to detain people, search premises without a warrant, and force people or areas into lockdown if it is deemed necessary to protect public health.

And now the Victorian Premier expresses his desire to extend the state of emergency for an indefinite period. He is effectively repeating history by revealing his intention to extent his emergency powers indefinitely. The Premier is currently working with the State's Solicitor General to enact another provision to extend the state of emergency for an indefinite period of time.[121] He claims this is necessary because of 'the authority and the effectiveness of all the measures that we've put in place'.[122]

This appears to confirm the worst fears of Friedrich Hayek, an Austrian-British economist and philosopher who won the Nobel Prize in Economics in 1974. In his seminal 'Law, Legislation and Liberty' (1981), he contended that "temporary" measures seem to have a way of becoming permanent after the emergency is over. Hayek offered this sobering reflection:

> The conditions under which such emergency powers may
> be granted without creating the danger that they will be re-
> tained when the absolute necessity has passed are among the

---

[120] Rachel Clayton, 'Why Victoria Needs Both State of Emergency and State of Disaster Powers to Fight Coronavirus', *ABC News*, 16 August 2020 <https://www.abc.net.au/news/2020-08-16/victoria-state-of-emergency-disaster-explained-coronavirus/12563680>.

[121] 'Vic Premier Moves to Extend State of Emergency Capabilities Indefinitely', *News.com.au*, 17 August 2020 <https://www.news.com.au/national/vic-premier-moves-to-extend-state-of-emergency-capabilities-indefinitely/video/33c6bc50e2176e504d3e7-38c9309b696?fbclid=IwAR1yWMSDzckVCs0tzs5TPOknhwtEQ9dckJZlgTijFfhb W5RommASpOYyIhA>.

[122] Clayton, above n 118.

most difficult and important points a constitution must decide on. 'Emergencies' have always been the pretext on which the safeguards of individual liberty have been eroded – and once they are suspended it is not difficult for anyone who has assumed such emergency powers to see to it that the emergency will persist.[123]

This is not so dissimilar to what happened to a certain European country in the 1930s. There a certain German Chancellor also turned his own state of emergency into a more permanent one. The correlation between the instrument used by that particular government to continue exercising its emergency and the intention of the Victorian government to turn its emergency power into a permanent one is irrefutable. It can be manifested, among several other things, in the disregard for fundamental rights coupled by the passive behaviour of the population and a considerable silence of the legal profession in upholding the rule of law.

It might be important to remind how dictatorial regimes are brought into existence. There is always a state of emergency used to justify the suspension of constitutional rights and I wish to be absolutely clear about this. However, I do not wish my words to be misconstrued and my opinions mischaracterised. As such, I wish to make myself absolutely clear that I am not comparing the use of emergency powers by the Victorian Premier and the use of similar instruments by a particular German dictator in the 1930s.

This is therefore not about how emergency powers can be used by the respective governments, but the instrument by which such powers can be used to justify arbitrary power and governmental control over the life, liberty and property of the people. After making this proviso I can now explain how emergency powers that appeal to the "health" of the community have served as an instrument of perpetuation of power and oppression of the people.

---

[123] Friedrich A. Hayek, *Law, Legislation and Liberty*, Vol. 3 (University of Chicago Press, 1981), Ch. 17.

The history of Germany in the 1930s provides a good case point. When Adolf Hitler was appointed German Chancellor, on 30 January 1933, the consolidation of the National Socialist regime was in no way assured. To add validity to the new regime, the public needed to be convinced of the necessity, and legality, of the measures justifying the violations of constitutional rights by the government.

Initially, that German government took a strong interest in preserving the impression of legal "normality". When the Enabling Act was passed in March 1933, handing over legislative power to the executive for four years, everything was done under the appearance of absolute legality. That act was passed via an amendment approved by two-thirds of the Reichstag (German Parliament), as strictly required by Article 76 of the Weimar Constitution. According to R C Caenegem, emeritus professor of legal history at Ghent University, the re-enactment of those enabling powers in 1937, 1939 and 1943 provided 'an interesting indication of the regime's schizophrenic combination of legal formalism with ruthless violence and basic contempt for the rule of law'.[124]

The principal characteristic of lawyers who gave the German regime its legal legitimacy was narrow legal positivism, coupled with a blatant disregard for individual rights and freedoms.[125] Those lawyers rationalised that if government had acquired those powers in a strictly legal manner, then the rule of law had also been respected and whatever the government was doing was entirely valid from such a narrow perspective.[126]

By not questioning the renewal of the state of emergency powers in any tangible way, the German legal community failed to protect the rule of law and the fundamental rights of the people. Those lawyers merely acted as "yes-men" to a brutal regime which opposed anything that could jeopardise the "health of the German community",

---

[124] R C Caenegem, *An Historical Introduction to Western Constitutional Law* (Cambridge University Press, 1995), 277.

[125] Paul Johnson, *Modern Times: The World from the Twenties to the Ninetieths* (HarperPerennial, 2001), 111.

[126] Caenegem, above n 124, 283.

as perceived by the regime's leadership.[127] Curiously, the more those lawyers made efforts to legitimise the regime, the greater the contempt displayed towards them by the Nazi leadership. As the German dictator once declared, to the delight of so many people, 'the health of the German nation is more important than the letter of the law'.[128]

Under Article 48 of the Weimar Constitution, the German President was authorised to govern by decree during such times of emergency.[129] In February 1933, President Hindenburg relied on that particular provision to sign an executive decree which suspended constitutional rights and granted the National Cabinet authority to enact any decree to be deemed necessary for the protection of the people.[130]

What followed was a total suspension of individual rights 'until further notice'.[131] Of course, that 'further notice' did not occur until May 8th, 1945, when the decree was finally cancelled by the military government of the Allies. As noted by German jurist Carl Schmitt, in his influential Political Theology (1922),

> Once this state of emergency has been declared... the decision exempts the political authority from any normative restraint and renders it absolute in the true sense of the word. In a state of emergency, the constituted authority suspends the law on the basis of the right to protect its own existence. [132]

Ultimately, the advent of National Socialism cannot be isolated, like some sort of accident, from the prevailing sentiments of the people. In those days Germans were quite willing, even anxious, to receive

---

[127] A. Kolnai, *The War Against the West* (Viking Press, 1938), 300.

[128] M Broszat, *The Hitler State: The Foundation and Development of the Internal Structure of the Third Reich* (New York/NY: Longman, 1981), 293.

[129] These special powers remained in effect for four years, after which they could be renewed if the state of emergency was still in place. Whether or not the fire was really set by the communists, the fact is that that section served the purposes of the declaration of a state of emergency.

[130] R J Evans, *The Third Reich in Power: 1933–1939* (Penguin Books, 2006), 6.

[131] Ingo Müller, *Hitler's Justice: The Courts of the Third Reich* (Harvard University Press, 1991), 37.

[132] Carl Schmitt, *Politische Theologie* (2nd ed, 1934), 20

their ultimate protection from government. They rejected the idea of liberal democracy and preferred instead to be ruled by a government that could "protect" the community from real or imaginary threat.

History tells us that those Germans paid a very heavy price for their trust in government. Such a government led them to a disastrous military conflict that eventually resulted in 75 million causalities. Germany alone sustained 8 million losses, 3 million of them civilians who died because of deliberate massacres, mass-bombings, disease and starvation.[133]

Of course, I am not stating here that Victorians are facing the same challenges. Absolutely not and nobody would be so irresponsible to make such comparison. However, as stated above, history repeats itself in the sense that emergency powers have been used once again to justify the implementation of draconian measures that profoundly violate the most fundamental rights of the individual.

To make things worse, the Victorian government has introduced a bill in Parliament that gives sweeping powers to certain "authorised officers" to arrest and detain people for an indefinite period of time. The proposed legislation will effectively consolidates Victoria as a police state where informers and collaborators will assist the authorities in tracing and incarcerating their fellow citizens without warrants, on the basis of prospective conduct.

Called the *COVID-19 Omnibus (Emergency Measures) Amendment Bill*, this proposed legislation will operate side-by-side with the powers already in operation under the current emergency powers. Its provisions are so broadly construed that any person could be detained for almost anything. These laws will override all other laws and confer extraordinary powers to the Secretary of the Department of Health to appoint public servants as "authorised officers" with the same powers as police. As candidly stated by Jill Hennessy, Victorian Attorney General, in her second reading speech:

---

[133] 'Research Starters: Worldwide Deaths in World War II', *The National WWII Museum of New Orleans* <https://www.nationalww2museum.org/students-teachers/student-resources/research-starters/research-starters-worldwide-deaths-world-war>

The Bill will provide further emergency powers to authorised officers to issue detention notices and detain particular high-risk persons if the authorised officer reasonably believes that a person is likely to refuse or fail to comply with a direction made by the Chief Health Officer... This amendment will enable the authorised officer to detain individuals for the purpose of ensuring compliance with the relevant direction during the COVID-19 state of emergency. [134]

In other words, these laws allow any person the Department of Health and Human Services deems appropriate to become an "authorised officer" to detain people on the belief that they are unlikely to comply with emergency directions. Anyone may be arrested for an indeterminate period of time if such an officer happens to believe the individual is likely to fail to comply with an emergency direction. As such, fundamental legal principles inherited from our common-law tradition, including due process, the presumption of innocence and recourse to the writ of habeas corpus, would be substantially undermined.

This latest development in the consolidation of an oppressive, authoritarian regime, 'seeks to enlist the population as informers and arms of the state in rounding up others who are guilty of no offence'.[135] Under these laws "authorised officers" will be able to detain fellow citizens if 'a direction has been given in the exercise of an emergency power', or if they 'reasonably believe that a person who is required to comply with the direction is a high-risk person and is likely to refuse or fail to comply with the direction'.[136] Citizens will be detained by

---

[134] Hansard, *Parliament of Victoria*, 17 September 2020 <https://www.parliament.vic.gov.au/images/stories/daily-hansard/Assembly_2020/Legislative_Assembly_2020-09-17.pdf>.

[135] Editorial, 'Bill To Create Police State Has No Place In This Nation', *The Australian*, 23 September 2020 <https://www.theaustralian.com.au/commentary/editorials/bill-to-create-police-state-has-no-place-in-this-nation/news-story/0820634e3c835cc8c6733bf6a45bb793>.

[136] *COVID-19 Omnibus (Emergency Measures) and Other Acts Amendment Bill 2020*, Victorian Legislation https://www.legislation.vic.gov.au/bills/covid-19-omnibus-emergency-measures-and-other-acts-amendment-bill-2020.

such officers for an indefinite period and there is no reference to what sort of training is required. As political adviser Ian Hanke points out,

> These extraordinary powers are arbitrary and extreme. They are a draconian attack on civil liberties the like of which Australia has never seen before. Further because all laws are overridden there would appear to be little recourse to any excesses by an authorised officer or their civilians co-opted by them. These laws are so broad and ill-defined that you could be detained for almost anything.[137]

Passed without amendment in the Labor-controlled Lower House on 18 September, the bill is now being debated in the Upper House and will be put to vote soon.[138] Premier Andrews says he is engaged in a "negotiation" process with the Upper House backbench. He argues the provisions are necessary but is unable to specify circumstances where they had previously been required. If this bill is passed, an authoritarian regime will be finally consolidated and there will be an end to the rule of law and legal guarantees that so far have protected the population against all sorts of abuses of power by the State.

It is important to consider that we have already seen police arresting people simply because they have promoted on social media protests against draconian measures. One example of such arbitrariness occurred on September 3, when Victoria police arrested a pregnant mother in front of her little children in their Ballarat home. Zoe Buhler was arrested and charged under section 321 of the *Victorian Crimes Act* 1958, which makes it an offence for a person to 'pursue a course of conduct which will involve the commission of an offence'.[139] Her crime: posting a Facebook message encouraging people to protest against lockdowns in the regional town on 5 September.

Ms Buhler said she was totally unaware that she could be doing

---

[137] Ian Hanke, 'Daniel Andrews' Plan For Indefinite Detention – And More', *The Spectator Australia*, 18 September 2020 <https://www.spectator.com.au/2020/09/daniel-andrews-plan-for-indefinite-detention-and-more/>.

[138] Above n 136.

[139] *Crimes Act* 1958 (Vic), s 321.

anything illegal and police could just have called her, to simply ask to remove the post. She also said she did not believe Covid-19 as a hoax, but just wanted to protest about the impact of lockdown measures on employment and suicide.[140] She had lost her job due to such draconian measures and thought Ballarat's lighter restrictions in comparison to Melbourne's stage 4 lockdown would allow these protests for human rights, 'if people wore masks and socially distanced'.[141]

There are serious questions whether Ms Buhler committed any offence under that specific Act, given the lack of intentionality required by the criminal law. There was no element of intentionality in her behaviour, since she was unaware of any illegality. Besides, her Facebook post did not incite people to protest in a manner that is inconsistent with the city's stage 3 lockdown.

This is leaving the irrefutable violation by Victoria Police not only of the State's *Charter of Human Rights and Responsibilities* but also the constitutional right to freedom of political communication. The Victoria Charter explicitly guarantees to every person their fundamental legal rights to privacy and peaceful assembly as well as freedom of association, movement, thought, conscience, and expression.[142]

As for the constitutional right to freedom of political communication, under the Australian Constitution sovereignty ultimately resides in the people. It is Australian electors who elect representatives to legislative on their behalf. As noted by Justice Brennan of the Australian High Court, in 1992, representative and responsible government 'are constitutional imperatives intended ... to make the legislature and executive branches of [government] ultimately answerable to the Australian people'.[143] It follows that, as sovereign, 'the Australian people

---

[140] Tessa Akerman and Rachel Baxendalle, 'Arrested Anti-Lockdown Mum: Police Admit 'We Stuffed Optics'', *The Australian*, 3 September 2020 <https://www.theaustralian.com.au/nation/absolute-overkill-jacqui-lambie-slams-arrest-of-pregnant-lockdown-protester/news-story/8951edcf08e3cc5e18006cad8b033354>.

[141] Ibid.

[142] *Charter of Human Rights and Responsibilities Act 2006* (Vic), ss 12 to 16.

[143] *Wills* (1992) 177 CLR 1, 47 (Brennan J).

must also be free to communicate about government and political matters fully and freely'.[144]

How does the democratic nature of our Constitution can be reconciled with police going into homes without warrant and arresting a mother in front of her children because of a Facebook message? This does not look like a democratic government but the actions of a deeply authoritarian regime. It certainly should never happen in a true democracy.

However, Victoria's Police Commissioner Luke Cornelius has justified that arrest by saying he was completely "satisfied" that police officers had acted "properly" and "reasonably". He actually said on television that Ms Buhler was engaged in "serious criminal activity", and also warned that hundreds of such officers would be deployed to make other similar arrests,[145] and then attacked people protesting against the State Government as "selfish" and deserving of punishment: 'We are very concerned, and in fact, outraged is probably a fair word, to say there are still people in our community who think it's a good idea ... to leave home and protest on our streets ... Take the selfish option and leave home to protest, we'll be there for you'.[146]

The arrest of citizens for merely speaking out against their government is a mark of every dictatorial regime.[147] However, Premier Andrews has described the appalling arrest of a pregnant woman as an 'operational matter for Victoria Police'.[148] When asked whether the left-wing organisers of the Black Lives Matter protest in Melbourne's CBD, on 6 June 2020, should have also been charged with incitement

---

[144] Joshua Forrester, Lorraine Finlay and Augusto Zimmermann, *No Offence Intended: Why 18C is Wrong* (Connor Court, 2016), 123.

[145] Naaman Zhou, 'Victorian Bar Criticises Arrest of Pregnant Woman for Facebook Lockdown Protests Post as Disproportionate', *The Guardian*, 3 September 2020 <https://www.theguardian.com/australia-news/2020/sep/03/victoria-police-arrested-pregnant-woman-facebook-post-zoe-buhler-australia-warn-lockdown-protesters>.

[146] Ibid.

[147] Tessa Akerman and Rachel Baxendalle, 'Arrested Anti-Lockdown Mum: Police Admit 'We Stuffed Optics'', *The Australian*, September 3, 2020 < https://www.theaustralian.com.au/nation/absolute-overkill-jacqui-lambie-slams-arrest-of-pregnant-lockdown-protester/news-story/8951edcf08e3cc5e18006cad8b033354>.

[148] Ibid.

as the Ballarat woman, he refused to give a proper answer and said he would have to defer the matter to Victoria Police.

Above all, the Victorian Premier exhibits no intention to uphold or defend the Australian Constitution. He has demonstrated an undisputable belief that the executive branch holds all power, and that the other branches of government exist solely for the benefit and enjoyment of the leader. This certainly explains his strong support for the Chinese communist regime, amid growing criticism from the U.S. government. 'Daniel Andrews is standing firm on China', writes political report Richard Willingham for the *ABC News*.[149]

The Victorian government appears to be sending the police into family homes in order to demonstrate the leader's power and strength. In fact, a case could be made that the Andrews Government might be developing a strategy of targeting peaceful protesters so that he can exert more control and fear over the population. With the joblessness and suicide numbers growing every day, this is a leader who appears to demonstrate no empathy for others, being incapable of understanding human pain and suffering at a massive scale.

If the ongoing events taking place in Victoria are not disturbing enough by themselves, the tacit support of the Australian Prime Minister and the passivity of the Victorian Liberal opposition certainly are. In a letter to the Victorian, shadow attorney general Edward O'Donohue contemplates the acceptance of these extraordinary powers being extended. After reminding the Premier that they 'represent a significant erosion of individual freedom and recognising this', he goes on to tacitly accept their continuation by meekly requesting the Premier that 'any further extension must be accompanied by enhanced scrutiny and safe guards enshrined in the legislation'.[150]

---

[149] Richard Willingham, 'Victorian Premier Daniel Andrews is Standing Firm on China Amid Growing Criticism from US, Opposition', *ABC News*, 25 May 2020 <https://www.abc.net.au/news/2020-05-25/daniel-andrews-victoria-standing-firm-on-belt-and-road-deal/12283520>.

[150] Hon Edward O'Donoghe MLC, Shadow Attorney General, 'Letter to the Hon Daniel Andrews MP, Premier of Victoria – Re Proposal to Extend State of Emergency for Indefinite Period', Melbourne, Vic, 17 August 2020.

Due to the impact of these measures on fundamental rights, clearly this is not nearly good enough. And it is really disheartening to see that so many Victorians have accepted this terrible oppression without offering any proper resistance and quite to the contrary. Also deeply disheartening is to witness the tacit consent of the Morrison government to all these authoritarian measures. The Prime Minister has the moral (and legal) duty to inform the Victorian Premier of the unconstitutionality of such oppressive measures, and that this government will intervene in favour of the people of Victoria in order to prevent any further violation of fundamental rights.

Of course, if the Morrison government really valued fundamental legal rights and the principles of constitutional government, there would already be enough grounds for a federal intervention in the State of Victoria. The Prime Minister might begin to show his disapproval by no longer allowing the Australian Defence Forces ('ADF') to back up Victoria Police as they harass people, including pregnant women and old ladies, in Melbourne's parks.

But the sad reality is that Victorians have been miserably betrayed by their federal and state governments in many ways and on many levels. Premier Andrews is a leader of authoritarian inclinations and the Morrison government has tacitly consented to the deplorable oppression of the Victorian population. For all intends and purposes the State of Victoria has now effectively become an elected dictatorship.

X FINAL CONSIDERATIONS

During this coronavirus crisis, our politicians seem to be driven less by a reasoned, evidence-fuelled strategy of limiting the spread of the disease and the disorganisation of economic life, than by an urge to be seen to be taking action.[151] As a result, countless people are losing their jobs, particularly in the entertainment industry. Inevitably, job losses will lead to far more homelessness, with financial pressures leading to more marriage breakdowns and a dramatic growth in crime, which always increases in times of economic crisis.

---

[151] Ibid.

What is happening is nothing short of deeply tragic because, in many ways and on many levels, Australians have been miserably betrayed by their own federal and state politicians. In this present context our political class should be reminded of John Locke, that great 'Founder of Liberalism'. He famously argued that governments have no other end 'but the preservation of these rights, and therefore can never have a right to destroy, enslave, or designedly to impoverish the subjects'. If a government exceeds the limits of its legitimate power, citizens have the fundamental right to resist. As Locke famously put it:

> Whenever the legislators endeavour to take away and destroy the rights of the people, or to reduce them to slavery under arbitrary power, they put themselves into a state of war with the people, who are thereupon absolved from any further obedience, and are left to the common refuge which God hath provided for all men against force and violence.[152]

We should not be too hasty in dismissing Locke's advocacy for fundamental rights and the traditional concept of lawful resistance against political tyranny. This is our classical liberal tradition and it firmly communicates that there cannot be one rule for some and another for the rest of us. Federal, state, and territory leaders in this country have been exposed for their authoritarian behaviour as there was never an emergency that could possibly justify the exercise of such arbitrary powers.[153] The Australian people have a lawful right to resist such acts of tyranny and demand from their ruling political class the lifting of arbitrary restrictions and full restoration of our fundamental rights and freedoms.

---

[152] John Locke, *Second Treatise on Civil Government* [1690] Ch 19, Sec 222.
[153] Ibid.

16

Book Review:

Gabriël Moens, *A Twisted Choice – A Covid-19 Novel*

(Boolarong Press, 2020)

ISBN: 9781925877700 (Paperback)

Gabriël Moens goes to great lengths at the end of his debut novel to emphasise that the story and characters in *A Twisted Choice* are all fictitious. At any other time it would hardly be necessary to make this point. A tale of conspiracy and subterfuge involving a government deliberately creating a global pandemic in order to provide geo-political advantage makes for a great Hollywood blockbuster, but would be considered far removed from reality. It is a sad sign of how much the world has changed, and how much distrust in government and our core institutions has grown, that such a disclaimer is now thought necessary.

There is a risk in any work of fiction that draws inspiration from real-life events. The degree of responsibility that the author of a work of fiction based on fact bears to the truth is a contentious matter. The risk is a further blurring of facts and fiction, which is something of particular concern in a 'post-truth' age shaped by alternative facts, where even the wildest conspiracy theories seem able to find a comfortable home. But the reward for the reader when real-life events are the foundation of a story are that the journey of the characters can truly take centre stage. We can examine their decisions and consider their motivations more clearly.

A Twisted Choice is based around the ongoing COVID-19 global pandemic, with the chain of events commencing in the mid-1980s, taking us up to the present day and then concluding in the near future. The novel, set in Chicago, Wuhan, and Sydney, explores the origins of the Covid-19 pandemic, and weaves a tapestry of intrigue with the threads of many factual events happening around the globe. It follows the exploits of a Chinese virologist, studying at an American university where he meets an American lawyer, who follows him back to Wuhan in China. He deliberately cultivates a friendship with an Australian virologist, resulting in a fetish-driven relationship pursued lifelong.

The novel explores the intentions of the protagonists who undertake actions for different reasons which are incompatible with each other. This incompatibility requires them to make moral judgments and twisted choices. The fact that the characters are relatable and the underlying story is broadly familiar ultimately makes the moral choices they face even more interesting. The central question of whether the ends justify the means resonates because we can recognise ourselves and our world in the story.

A Twisted Choice is a thought-provoking book that raises critical questions about human nature, government power, and individual choice. It explores themes of uncertainty, morality, and honour in a way that leaves the reader thinking about the characters and weighing their actions long after the final page has been read.

But, importantly, the book is absolutely enjoyable to read. Gabriël Moens has a clear love of language, and combines vivid and imaginative prose with a lawyerly attention to detail. A slight hesitation when starting to read *A Twisted Choice* was the question of whether an author best known for his mastery of the technical intricacies of international commercial arbitration could successfully shift his focus from the commercial to the creative. That fear was entirely misplaced. This is an excellent debut novel from an individual who has already had a long and distinguished academic career, and can now add successful novelist to his lengthy list of career accomplishments.

Gabriël Moens is a deeply talented writer whose debut novel asks important questions in an interesting and imaginative way. I am already hoping that a sophomore novel might be in the works.

The Western Australian
Legal Theory Association

President: Professor Augusto Zimmermann
Vice-President: Heath Harley-Bellemore
Secretary: Bianca Cobby

About WALTA

The Western Australian Legal Theory Association ("WALTA") was founded in 2010 by Professor Zimmermann as a learned society of academically interested lawyers, legal scholars and law students. It is presently based out of *Sheridan Institute of Higher Education*, in Perth, Western Australia. Our aim is to promote scholarly discussions on subjects related to legal theory, jurisprudence and contemporary issues in law.

About The Western Australian Jurist

The Western Australian Jurist is the yearly blind peer-reviewed academic publication of the *Western Australian Legal Theory Association* ('WALTA'). Established in 2010, law journal are currently based at *Sheridan Institute*, an Australian Baptist higher education institute based in Perth, Western Australia.

The Editor-in-Chief of *The Western Australian Jurist* is Professor Augusto Zimmermann, Professor and Head of Law at Sheridan. The Academic Editor for the publication is Joshua Forrester, the author of a leading book on freedom of speech and numerous academic articles on the subject of freedom of speech and the implied (constitutional) freedom of political communication.

If you wish to submit an article for *The Western Australian Jurist* please do so via our website located at https://walta.net.au/submit-an-article/. Submissions must be of academic quality in an a .doc or .docx format under 2MB in size, and formatted in compliance with the Australian Guide of Legal Citation. Please note that we reserve the right to reject any article (even those which have been previously accepted) at any time.

www.ingramcontent.com/pod-product-compliance
Lightning Source LLC
Chambersburg PA
CBHW020908210326
41598CB00018B/1812